Changing Valency

This book provides a general perspective on valency-changing mechanisms – passives, antipassives, causatives, applicatives – in the languages of the world. It contains a comprehensive typology of causatives by R.M.W. Dixon, and detailed descriptions of valency-changing mechanisms in ten individual languages by leading scholars, based on original fieldwork. The sample languages span five continents and every kind of structural profile. Each contributor draws out the theoretical status and implications of valency-changing derivations in their language of study, and the relevant parameters are drawn together, and typological possibilities delineated, in the editors' introduction. The volume will interest typologists, those working in the fields of morphosyntactic variation and lexical semantics, and exponents of formal theories engaging with the range of linguistic diversity found in natural language.

R. M. W. DIXON and ALEXANDRA Y. AIKHENVALD are Director and Associate Director of the Research Centre for Linguistic Typology, which was established in 1996 at the Australian National University and relocated in January 2000 to La Trobe University in Melbourne. Professor Dixon's book publications inlcude grammatical studies of the Australian languages Dyirbal and Yidiny, of Fijian and of English, as well as *The Languages of Australia* (1980) and *Ergativity* (1994). One of his current projects is a grammar of Jarawara (Brazil). Professor Aikhenvald has published 6 books and nearly 100 papers in Russian, English, Portuguese and Yiddish, covering a range of subjects including Berber, Hebrew, Indo-European and Native South American languages. Her monograph *Classifiers: A Typology of Noun Categorization Devices* will be published in 1999. She is currently completing a full-length grammar of Tariana. Professor Dixon and Professor Aikhenvald have also edited *The Amazonian Languages* (1999).

Changing valency
Case studies in
transitivity

EDITED BY

R. M. W. DIXON

AND

ALEXANDRA Y. AIKHENVALD

Research Centre for Linguistic Typology
Le Trobe University, Melbourne

CAMBRIDGE
UNIVERSITY PRESS

PUBLISHED BY THE PRESS SYNDICATE OF THE UNIVERSITY OF CAMBRIDGE
The Pitt Building, Trumpington Street, Cambridge, United Kingdom

CAMBRIDGE UNIVERSITY PRESS
The Edinburgh Building, Cambridge CB2 2RU, UK
  http://www.cup.cam.ac.uk
40 West 20th Street, New York NY 10011–4211, USA
  http://www.cup.org
10 Stamford Road, Oakleigh, Melbourne 3166, Australia

First published 2000

Printed in the United Kingdom at the University Press, Cambridge

Typeset in 10/13 Times   [GC]

A catalogue record for this book is available from the British Library

Library of Congress cataloguing in publication data

Changing valency: case studies in transitivity / edited by R. M. W.
Dixon and Alexandra Y. Aikhenvald.
    p.   cm.
Includes bibliographical references and index.
ISBN   0 521 66039 4   (hardback)
1. Grammar, Comparative and general – Verb.   2. Grammar,
Comparative and general – Transitivity.   3. Grammar, Comparative and
general – Voice.   4. Typology (Linguistics).   5. Dependency grammar.
I. Dixon, Robert M.W.   II. Aïkhenval'd, A. ĪŪ. (Aleksandra
ĪŪr'evna)
P281.C48   2000
415 – dc21   99–24413   CIP

ISBN   0 521 66039 4   hardback

Contents

List of contributors

Alexandra Y. Aikhenvald
Research Centre for Linguistic
   Typology
La Trobe University
Bandoora, Vic, 3083
Australia
e-mail:
Sasha.Aikhenvald@anu.edu.au

Mengistu Amberber
School of Modern Language Studies
University of New South Wales
Sydney, NSW, 2052
Australia
e-mail: m.amberber@unsw.edu.au

Lyle Campbell
Department of Linguistics
University of Canterbury
Private Bag 4800
Christchurch
New Zealand
e-mail:
l.campbell@ling.canterbury.ac.nz

Bernard Comrie
Max Planck Insitute for
   Evolutionary Anthropology
Inselstrasse 22–6
D-04103 Leipzig
Germany
e-mail: comrie@eva.mpg.de

R.M.W. Dixon
Research Centre for Linguistic
   Typology
Australian National University
Canberra, ACT, 0200
Australia
no e-mail

Randy J. LaPolla
Department of Chinese, Translation
   and Linguistics
City University of Hong Kong
Tat Chee Avenue
Kowloon
Hong Kong
e-mail: ctrandy@cityu.edu.hk

Jack Martin
Department of English
College of William and Mary
Williamsburg, VA, 23187–8795
USA
e-mail: jbmart@mail.wm.edu

Marianne Mithun
Department of Linguistics
University of California,
Santa Barbara
5607 South Hall
Santa Barbara, CA, 93106
USA
e-mail:
mithun@humanitas.ucsb.edu

Masayuki Onishi
Department of International Cultures
Meio University
1220–1 Okinawa, Japan
e-mail: Masa.Onishi@ics.meio-u.ac.jp

Nicholas Reid
Department of Linguistics
University of New England
Armidale, NSW, 2351, Australia
e-mail: nreid@metz.une.edu.au

Keren Rice
Department of Linguistics
University of Toronto
130 St George Street
Toronto, Ontario, M5S 3H1, Canada
e-mail: rice@chass.utoronto.ca

Preface

This volume includes revised versions of ten of the sixteen presentations at the International Workshop on Valency-changing Derivations, held at the Research Centre for Linguistic Typology of the Australian National University, 18–23 August 1997. The position paper for the workshop was Dixon and Aikhenvald's 'A typology of argument-determined constructions' (pp. 71–113 of *Essays on language function and language type*, edited by J. Bybee, J. Haiman and S. Thompson. Amsterdam: John Benjamins, 1997). Contributors were also sent a short paper by Dixon on the semantics of causatives; this was later revised and greatly expanded, and is chapter 2 below.

All of the authors have pursued intensive investigation of languages, most of them rather little-known in the literature. They were asked to write in terms of basic linguistic theory – the cumulative theoretical framework in terms of which most descriptive grammars are cast – and to avoid formalisms (which come and go with such frequency that any statement in terms of them will soon become dated and inaccessible).

We thank all of the authors included here, for taking part in the Workshop, for getting their chapters in on time, for revising them according to recommendations of the editors and of the publisher's referees, and for completing their revisions on schedule.

We are also grateful to Jennifer Elliott, Administrator of the Research Centre for Linguistic Typology, who organized the Workshop with care and flair, coordinated the gathering of papers, and prepared a collated list of abbreviations. To Suzanne Kite, who prepared the indices. And to Kate Brett, our Cambridge editor – sympathetic and yet firm – who played a critical role in getting this volume into its present shape.

List of abbreviations

1	1st person	BEN	benefactive
2	2nd person	BP	bodypart
3	3rd person	CAUS	causative
I	type I ('agentive') person markers	CL	classifier
		CMPL	completive
II	type II ('non-agentive') person markers	COLL	collective
		COMIT	comitative
A	transitive subject	COMP	complementizer
ABL	ablative	COND	conditional
ABS	absolutive	CONT	continuous
ACC	accusative	CVB	converb
ADV	adverb	DAT	dative
AF	agent focus	DECL	declarative
AFF	affix	DEF	definite
AGT	agentive	DEM	demonstrative
AMG	location in or among	DEP	dependent
ANIM	animate	DETR	detransitivizer
ANT	antipassive	DIM	diminutive
ANTC	anticausative	DIR	directional
APPLIC	applicative	DS	different-subject (switch-reference)
APPR	approximative		
APUD	location near	DTV	derived transitive verb
ART	article	du	dual
ASP	aspect	DUR	durative
AUG	augmentative	DYN	dynamic
AUX	auxiliary	E	extension to core

EMPH	emphasis / emphatic suffix	MAL	malefactive
ERG	ergative	MID	middle / middle voice suffix
ESS	essive (location at)	N-1	non-1st person actor marker
EVID	evidential		
exc	exclusive	N.F	non-feminine
F	feminine/female	N-PAST	non-past affirmative
FGR	falling-tone grade	N-sg	nonsingular
FOC	focus	NEG	negation
FRUST	frustrative	NGR	nasalizing grade
FUT	future	NOM	nominative
GEN	genitive	NOMZR	nominalizer
GENL	general	NP	noun phrase
HAB	habitual	NR	near
HGR	h-grade	NR.PAST	near past
HON	honorific	O	transitive object
IMAG	imaginative	OBJ	object case
IMMED	immediate	OBLQ	oblique (non-subject) case
IMP	imperative		
IMPERF	imperfect	OPT	optative
IMPERS	impersonal	PART	participle
IMPFV	imperfective	PASS	passive
IN	location in	PAST	past tense
inc	inclusive	pauc	paucal
INDEF	indefinite	PERF	perfect
INDEP	independent	PFV	perfective
INDIC	indicative	pl	plural
INDTV	indirect directive	PN	pronoun
INF	infinitive	POSI	positional
INFR	inferred	POSS	possessive
INS, INST	instrumental	POT	potential
INTR	intransitive	PREF	prefix
L	local gender/derivational suffix	PREP	preposition
		PRES	present
LAT	lative (motion towards)	PROG	progressive
LGR	level-pitch grade	PROH	prohibitive
LINK	linker	PRSNTV	presentative
LOC	locative	PURP	purposive
M	masculine/male	Q	interrogative/question

R	co-referential	SUBJ	subjunctive
R/M	reflexive/middle	SUPER	superessive (location on a horizontal surface)
REC	recent		
RECIP	reciprocal	SV	simple verb
REDUP	reduplicated	TAM	tense–aspect–mood
REFL	reflexive	TMdys	past tense marker, 1 day to 1 year ago
REL	relative		
REM	remote	TMhrs	past tense marker, within today
RES	resultative		
REV	reverential	TMyrs	past tense marker, years ago
RTV	root transitive verb		
S	intransitive subject	TOP	topic
S_a	S marked like A	TOP.ADV	topic-advancing voice
sg	singular	TOP.N-A/S	topical non-subject
S_{io}	S marked like indirect object	TR, tr	transitive
		UNW	unwitnessed
S_{irr}	irregular S	VERT	vertical
S_o	S marked like O	vi	intransitive verb
ss	same-subject (switch-reference)	VIS	visual
		VN	verbal noun
STAT	stative	vt	transitive verb
SUB	subordinative	WIT	witnessed

1 Introduction

R.M.W. DIXON AND ALEXANDRA Y. AIKHENVALD

This volume consists of a number of detailed case studies of transitivity across a selection of languages – from North, Central and South America, New Guinea, Australia, the China/Myanmar (Burma) border, North-east Africa and the Caucasus. In the introduction we summarize the theoretical presuppositions and parameters, suggest generalizations that can be made on the basis of comparison of the individual studies, and draw attention to useful directions for further research.

§1 describes varieties of predicate arguments and clause types. §2 deals with classes of verbs, and transitivity-encoding devices. Then §3 presents an overview of derivations which change valency. In §4 we discuss derivations which typically reduce valency – passive, antipassive, reflexive, reciprocal and anticausative (plus the ubiquitous middle). §5 considers derivations which typically increase valency – applicative and causative (there is a full discussion of causatives in chapter 2). In §6 we emphasize the need for a holistic approach; every derivational process is likely to have syntactic, semantic and discourse/pragmatic aspects, each of which interrelates with and helps explain the others. §7 briefly discusses the propensities of different groups of verbs – according to their semantics – for taking part in the various derivations that affect valency. In §8 we look briefly at syntactic alternatives to valency-changing derivations; in some languages there may simply be alternative construction types, with no derivational link. §9 gives a short preview of each of the following chapters. Finally, in §10 we suggest a number of fruitful lines for further research.

1   Predicate arguments and clause types

Most languages have one or more minor clause types which typically involve two NPs, either with or without a copula (e.g. 'My son (is) a doctor'); these are left aside in the following discussion. We here focus on what is the major clause type in every language, consisting of a predicate and a variable number of predicate arguments. The predicate most frequently has a verb as its head (although in some languages a noun, or even a pronoun, may function as head of an intransitive predicate). It is useful to distinguish between core and peripheral arguments. The number and nature of core arguments is determined by the choice of which verb (or other word) is predicate head. The core arguments must be stated – or else be understood – for the clause to be acceptable and to have sense. Peripheral arguments (sometimes called 'adjuncts') are less dependent on the nature of the verb; they may optionally be included to indicate place, time, cause, purpose and the like.

In the following English sentences, peripheral arguments are enclosed in round brackets and core arguments in square ones.

(1)   (On Monday morning,) (in the garden,) [John] danced (around the fountain)

(2)   (On Monday morning,) (in the garden,) [the monkey] bit [John] (on the finger)

(3)   (On Monday morning,) (in the garden,) [John] gave [Mary] [a book] (for her birthday)

The peripheral NPs can be omitted and we still get full sentences – *John danced*, *The monkey bit John* and *John gave Mary a book*. However, core arguments may not be omitted – for example, **The monkey bit* or **John gave Mary* are not acceptable sentences in English. It will be noted that some peripheral NPs – such as *on Monday morning* and *in the garden* – may occur in a wide variety of clauses. Others are more restricted, being determined partly by the verb and partly by the reference of the core argument(s). For instance, *on the finger* is an acceptable peripheral argument only with a verb like *bite* (or *hit* or *sting*) and an O NP with a human referent; one could not say **The monkey saw John on the finger* or **The monkey bit the banana on the finger*.

There are two universal clause types:

intransitive clause, with an intransitive predicate and a single core argument which is in S (intransitive subject) function;

transitive clause, with a transitive predicate and two core arguments which are in A (transitive subject) and O (transitive object) functions.

That argument whose referent does (or potentially could) initiate or control the activity is in A function. That argument whose referent is affected by the activity is in O function (see Dixon 1994: 113–27).

In some languages a further argument has special status. This typically refers to a recipient or a beneficiary or a thing that is seen or an object that is liked or wanted; and is commonly shown by dative case or marked on the predicate by a special set of bound pronominals. It can be represented by E (standing for 'extension to core'). In most languages there is an extended transitive (or ditransitive) construction type, with A, O and E; this typically refers to giving, showing or telling. In a few languages (e.g. Tonga, Trumai, Tibetan, Newari, Motuna) there is also an extended intransitive clause type, with S and E; this is typically used for seeing, hearing, liking and wanting (see Dixon 1994: 122–4). That is:

(a)	intransitive		S	
(b)	extended intransitive		S	E
(c)	transitive	A	O	
(d)	extended transitive	A	O	E

In every language in which they occur, extended intransitive and extended transitive clause types are greatly outnumbered – in dictionary and in texts – by plain intransitive and plain transitive. For instance, in chapter 8 LaPolla reports just two extended transitive and around three extended intransitive verbs in Dulong/Rawang. The types are clearly distinguishable since the S in a plain intransitive and the S in an extended intransitive have the same morphological marking and the same syntactic behaviour; similarly for A and O in plain and extended transitive.

We can usefully distinguish 'transitivity' and 'valency'. There are two main transitivity types – intransitive (with core argument S) and transitive (with A and O) – and plain and extended subtypes of each (depending on whether or not E is also in the core). Valency relates to the number of core arguments. Thus (a) is monovalent and (d) is trivalent while there can be two different kinds of bivalent clauses – (c) with A and O, and (b) with S and E.

In some languages there is distinct marking for A, O, E and peripheral arguments. In others E and peripheral are treated in the same way. In a further group no distinction is made between O and E. In a few languages all of O, E and peripheral arguments are marked in the same way. Thus, using w, x, y and z for marking schemes (where z may indicate a variety of markings for various types of peripheral arguments):

	A	O	E	peripheral	
(i)	w	x	y	z	very many languages, e.g. Latin
(ii)	w	x	y------y		e.g. Jarawara
(iii)	w	x------x	z		e.g. Kinyarwanda
(iv)	w	x------x------x			e.g. Creek

In Jarawara any NP that is not in S, A or O function is marked by the all-purpose preposition *jaa* (Dixon, forthcoming). In Kinyarwanda O and E follow the verb, and can occur in either order (Kimenyi 1980). In Creek there are two case markers, *-t* on a subject and *-n* on a non-subject NP.

Languages vary as to how straightforward it is to distinguish between core and peripheral arguments, and thus to decide on the transitivity of a verb. Tariana (see chapter 5) is like Kinyarwanda in having the same morphological marking for O and E, but these two syntactic functions can be distinguished by the fact that only O can go into derived S function in a passive. The fact that the same marking is used for all non-subject functions in Creek leads Martin to suggest (in chapter 12) that the standard notion of transitivity is not relevant for this language; he has not been able to uncover any syntactic test that sets O apart, in the way that Aikhenvald has for Tariana (see further discussion in §9 below).

2   Verb classes

Verbs can be classified according to the clause types they may occur in. At one extreme we find languages (like Latin and Dyirbal) where each verb is either strictly intransitive (occurring just in intransitive clauses) or strictly transitive (occurring just in transitive clauses).

Most languages show a wider range of transitivity classes of verbs. A typical pattern (found in English and in many other languages) is:

(a)   some verbs are strictly intransitive, occurring only in an intransitive clause (with an S core argument), e.g. *arrive, chat.*

(b)   some verbs are strictly transitive, occurring only in a transitive clause (with A and O core argument), e.g. *recognize, like.*

(c)   some verbs are ambitransitive (or labile) occurring in either an intransitive or a transitive clause. Note that there are two varieties of ambitransitives, according to which of the two core arguments of a transitive construction is identified with the S argument in an intransitive:

(c-1) S = A ambitransitives, e.g. *follow, win* (these are called agentive ambitransitives by Mithun in chapter 3);

(c-2) S = O ambitransitives, e.g. *melt, trip* (called patientive ambitransitives by Mithun).

There can be additional divisions. In Tariana (chapter 5), intransitive verbs divide into two subtypes:

(a-1) S_a verbs, where S is marked in the same way as A in a transitive clause; these verbs typically refer to volitional activity, e.g. *-emhani* 'walk';

(a-2) S_o verbs, where S is marked in the same way as O in a transitive clause; these verbs typically refer to non-volitional activity, e.g. *leka* 'split'.

This is called a split-S system, with every intransitive verb being either of type S_a or of type S_o. Other languages have a fluid-S system, where some verbs can take either S_a or S_o marking, depending on whether or not the referent of the S argument is in control of the activity (e.g. 'slide' versus 'slip' – see Dixon 1994: 70–83).

There are languages with much larger systems of transitivity classes. The classes Onishi lists for Motuna include: (i) S_a intransitive; (ii) S_o intransitive; (iii) S = O ambitransitive (describing a spontaneous process or event in the intransitive); (iv) S = A ambitransitive (where the patient is irrelevant or un-important in the intransitive); (v) a further variety of ambitransitive where the intransitive is reflexive, i.e. S = A = O. There is a full discussion in chapter 4.

A number of languages have affixes to verbs to encode their transitivity. In Fijian for instance, most verbs are ambitransitive; they take a suffix when used in a transitive clause but lack the suffix when used intransitively, e.g. *bale-ta* 'fall on', *bale* 'fall' and *rogo-ca* 'hear', *rogo* 'be audible'. What the suffix does not indicate is the kind of ambitransitivity involved – *bale(-ta)* is of type S = A while *rogo(-ca)* is of type S = O (see Dixon 1988: 45, 200–14).

In chapter 9, Amberber describes derivational prefixes in Amharic; these include intransitivizer *tə-* and causative *as-*. Some verbs may only occur with one of these prefixes, e.g. intransitive *tə-dəssətə* 'be pleased, be happy' and transitive *as-dəssətə* 'please, make happy' (note that *dəssətə* cannot be used alone). In these circumstances *tə-* and *as-* serve as markers of transitivity, similar to Fijian. In chapter 11, Comrie describes similar valency-encoding suffixes in Tsez. In some languages, a causative affix has become lexicalized – so that it now has a semi-idiomatic meaning – and may function as a marker of transitivity (see Rice's account of Athapaskan languages, in chapter 6).

3   Changing valency

Most languages have some verbal derivations that affect predicate arguments. Typically, they may reduce or increase the number of core arguments; alternatively, the number of core arguments may be retained but their semantic roles altered.

Passive and antipassive prototypically apply to transitive verbs and derive intransitives, with the original O becoming S in a passive and A becoming S in an antipassive. Causative and applicative prototypically apply to intransitive verbs and derive transitives, with S becoming O in a causative and A in an applicative. That is (see also Kazenin 1994):

PROTOTYPICALLY APPLYING TO	(a) ARGUMENT REASSIGNMENT	(b) ARGUMENT REASSIGNMENT
(i) TRANSITIVE	O becomes S, passive	A becomes S, antipassive
(ii) INTRANSITIVE	S becomes O, causative	S becomes A, applicative

The two varieties of ambitransitives relate to the two columns – S = O type to (a) and S = A type to (b).

We then need to consider what happens to the other transitive argument in row (i) – A for passive and O for antipassive. And to ask where the other transitive argument comes from in row (ii) – A for causative and O for applicative.

In §4 we examine in detail the derivations from row (i) – various kinds of passive and antipassive and also anticausative, reflexive and reciprocal. Then §5 deals with row (ii) – various kinds of applicative and causative (which is also discussed, at length, in chapter 2).

Each of these derivations has several aspects: syntactic, semantic and discourse-pragmatic. In some instances it may be tempting to suggest that a certain derivation is basically syntactic, and that the syntactic change has certain semantic consequences. In other instances it may seem appropriate to say that a given derivation can best be specified semantically, with the meaning shift having certain syntactic consequences. It may, in fact, be difficult to distinguish between these (and other) alternatives. In §6 we argue in favour of an integrated approach, which will best provide an overall characterization for each derivation, in the languages in which it occurs.

One must also bear in mind that a given derivation may, in addition to its productive use (with constant semantic effect), also be involved in lexicalized forms, in which it has an idiosyncratic meaning. See, for example, Mithun's discussion, in chapter 3, of applicatives in Yup'ik.

4   Valency reduction

There are a number of types of valency-reducing derivation, which will be discussed in turn: (1) passive and anticausative; (2) antipassive; (3) reflexive and reciprocal. Finally, we shall comment on the term 'middle'.

(1) Passive

We work in terms of the following criteria for a prototypical passive (this accords with most, but not all, of the uses of passive in the literature – see below).

(a) Passive applies to an underlying transitive clause and forms a derived intransitive.

(b) The underlying O becomes S of the passive.

(c) The underlying A argument goes into a peripheral function, being marked by a non-core case, adposition, etc.; this argument can be omitted, although there is always the option of including it.

(d) There is some explicit formal marking of a passive construction – generally, by a verbal affix or by a periphrastic verbal construction (or by using a different kind of pronominal suffix, as described by Mithun in chapter 3 for Yup'ik).

Some languages have a derivation which satisfies criteria (a), (b) and (d) but in which the underlying A must be omitted (although it is understood that there was an underlying A argument, i.e. there was some agent who affected the patient). This is an 'agentless passive'.

A number of languages have a valency-reducing derivation where the S of the derived verb corresponds to the underlying O, and there is no marker of (or implication of the existence of) the underlying A. This is, effectively, the inverse of a causative and is often called an 'anticausative'.

These three possibilities can be summarized (where 'S : O' is to be read 'S of the derived intransitive corresponds to O of the underlying transitive'):

			example
(i) prototypical passive	S : O	original A becomes a peripheral argument and may either be included or omitted	'the glass was broken (by John)'
(ii) agentless passive	S : O	original A not stated (but understood to be in underlying structure)	'the glass was broken' (implied: by someone)
(iii) anticausative	S : O	no A stated or implied	'the glass broke'

It will be seen that the two varieties of passive both indicate that the original O (derived S) came into a certain state because of the involvement of an agent (original A). In contrast, the anticausative implies that it came into the state spontaneously. (The anticausative is like an $S = O$ ambitransitive pair, except that here an explicit derivation is involved.) Anticausatives are described for Athapaskan in chapter 6, and for Amharic in chapter 9. In chapter 10 Reid describes a constructional alternation in Ngan'gityemerri which has anticausative effect. And it seems that what LaPolla (in chapter 8) calls (general) intransitivizer and what Martin (in chapter 12) refers to as a 'middle' in Creek could equally be termed anticausatives.

A prototypical passive has three effects:

(I)   to focus attention on the original O (the derived S);

(II) to downgrade the importance of the original A, e.g. when one either does not know or does not want to specify its identity;

(III) to focus on the state the original O (new S) is in, as a result of the activity.

These effects may have varying weighting in different passive derivations. In chapter 7, Campbell describes two passives in K'iche'. The 'simple passive' can only be used if the original A is 3rd person; a 1st or 2nd person A cannot be 'downgraded' in this derivation, in terms of (II) above. The 'completive passive' has no constraints on the types of arguments involved, but just emphasizes the result of the activity, in terms of (III) above.

There are a number of kinds of variation on the prototypical profile of a passive. In a few languages, a peripheral argument of an intransitive clause may become passive subject (e.g. *This bed has been slept in*, in English). And in some languages the passive derivation may be extended to apply to some intransitive verbs, with an impersonal sense – this is described for Tariana by Aikhenvald (chapter 5) and for the Athapaskan language Dogrib by Rice (chapter 6).

Languages with multiple transitivity classes may have further varieties of passive. In Tariana, a language with split-S marking on intransitive verbs, the original O becomes S_a (not S_o) in a passive derivation. In Athapaskan languages there are two passive construction types; in the so-called 'personal passive' the underlying O receives subject marking, while in the 'impersonal passive' it receives object marking.

In some languages active clauses may not allow certain argument combinations. For instance, in K'iche' (chapter 7) an active clause may not have A as 3rd person when O is a 2nd person reverential pronoun; for this combination of A and O a simple passive construction must be employed.

The term 'passive' has been used in a wide variety of senses. Indeed, Siewierska (1984: 255) concluded a survey of the variety of constructions that have been called 'passive' with: 'as a group the whole body of so called passives does not have a single property in common'. In Japanese studies there is a tradition of referring to a derivation marked by suffix -*(ra)re* as an 'adversative passive'. But in fact this appears to increase the valency of the verb to which it is attached, e.g. from the transitive 'Ziroo (NOM) drum (ACC) practise' ('Jiro practises the drums') can be derived the adversative clause 'Taroo (TOPIC) Ziroo (BY) drum (ACC) practise-*(ra)re*' ('Taro was adversely affected by Jiro's practising the drums') (Shibatani 1990: 319). From a cross-linguistic typological perspective, 'passive' is not an appropriate label for this derivation.

(2) Antipassive

Antipassive is syntactically like passive, with O and A interchanged. That is, the criteria for a prototypical antipassive are:

(a) Antipassive applies to an underlying transitive clause and forms a derived intransitive.
(b) The underlying A becomes S of the antipassive.
(c) The underlying O argument goes into a peripheral function, being marked by a non-core case, adposition, etc.; this argument can be omitted, although there is always the option of including it.
(d) There is some explicit formal marking of an antipassive construction (same basic possibilities as for passive).

Corresponding to an agentless passive there can be a patientless antipassive, where the underlying O is not stated (but there is understood to be one). For instance, in the Mayan language Tzotzil, -*maj*- is the verb 'hit'; when the patientless antipassive suffix -*van* is added we get an intransitive verb -*maj-van*- 'have a disposition towards hitting [people]', where the patient 'people' cannot be stated but is implied (Robinson, ms.).

The syntactic iconicity between passive and antipassive may be misleading. In fact they have quite different semantic effects. An antipassive construction downgrades the original O, and focuses on the underlying A argument – on the fact that its referent is taking part in an activity which involves a patient (underlying O argument) while paying little or no attention to the identity of the patient. Thus, while passive generally focuses on the resulting state (that is, on the effect on the patient of what the agent has done), antipassive focuses on the activity itself (that is, on the agent's performing the activity).

We should now examine whether the possibilities (i–iii), outlined above for passives and anticausative, all have correspondents where S : A. Relating to a basic transitive clause 'John [A] ate the mango [O]' these would be:

			example
(i′) prototypical antipassive	S : A	original O becomes a peripheral argument and may either be included or omitted	'John [S] ate (the mango [peripheral])'
(ii′) patientless antipassive	S : A	original O not stated (but understood to be in underlying structure)	'John [S] ate' (implied: something)
(iii′) [correspondent of anticausative]	S : A	no O stated or implied	'John [S] ate'

Now it would seem unlikely that a language would be able to distinguish between (ii′) and (iii′) here. A transitive verb like 'eat' implies the existence of some O argument, even if this is not stated. The rather different semantics of passive and antipassive (relating to the difference between A and O) means that alternative (iii′) is scarcely plausible. That is, whereas one can clearly distinguish between (ii) and (iii), for S : O, it appears unlikely that a language would distinguish between (ii′) and (iii′), for S : A.

Antipassives are most common in languages with ergative characteristics (there is a useful typological survey in Cooreman 1994); they feature in just two of the chapters in this volume. The 'absolutive' antipassive in K'iche' (described by Campbell in chapter 7) has prototypical properties; its major function is to enable the original O argument to be omitted or demoted. Mithun reports (in chapter 3) that in Yup'ik an O argument should be definite. If there is an underlying O which is indefinite then the absolutive antipassive derivation must be applied, and the erstwhile O now takes ablative marking.

We do encounter unusual construction types, which will not easily fit into any of the profiles provided by typological theory. There is a second antipassive-like derivation in K'iche', which Campbell calls an 'agent-focus antipassive'. This focuses on the underlying A, which appears to go into S function in the antipassive; this enables it to function in question, relative and focussing constructions (as in many Mayan languages, these appear to operate in terms of an S/O pivot). Campbell describes the agent-focus antipassive as being morphologically intransitive but, in some respects, syntactically transitive. Verb agreement is usually with the S argument in an intransitive clause (including the absolutive antipassive) but in an agent-focus antipassive the verb may agree with either A or O, according to a person/number hierarchy: non-3rd > 3pl > 3sg (where 2nd person reverential pronouns behave like 3rd person). And there are complex constraints on permitted argument combinations in agent-focus antipassives – see figure 7.2.

(3) Reflexive/reciprocal

Cross-linguistically there are two basic strategies for expressing reflexive and reciprocal with transitive verbs. The first is to retain a transitive structure, placing a reflexive or reciprocal pronoun in the O slot. (The fact that a reflexive/reciprocal pronoun goes in the O slot – not the A slot – appears to be a universal, applying to both accusative and ergative languages.) The other strategy is to employ a verbal derivational suffix which derives an intransitive stem with reflexive and/or reciprocal meaning. The S of this derived verb then indicates the coreferential A and O for a reflexive (S = A = O), and the set of participants involved for a reciprocal. In chapter 5 Aikhenvald describes the reciprocal suffix *-kaka* in Tariana; from transitive *-kolota* 'meet' is derived the reciprocal *-kolota-kaka* 'meet (each other)'. In chapter 8, LaPolla mentions that the general intransitivizing suffix in Dulong/Rawang includes in its range of functions the marking of a reciprocal derivation.

It is often the case that a detransitivizing derivation in a given language will combine several of the functions listed above. In the Australian language Diyari, for example, the verbal derivational suffix *-thadi-* can have passive, antipassive or reflexive sense (details are in Austin 1981: 151–7). For Amharic, Amberber shows (in chapter 9) that the prefix *tə-* can mark passive, anticausative or reflexive. (Haspelmath 1990 is a useful survey of the other senses of passives, across more than twenty languages.)

The term 'middle' is used with a frightening variety of meanings in present-day linguistics. The traditional sense was related to 'middle voice' in Greek – 'that the "action" or "state" affects the subject of the verb or his interests' (Lyons 1968: 373). Commencing with Keyser and Roeper (1984), linguists following various formalist predilections have used 'middle' with a totally different sense, to describe constructions in English and some other languages where a non-subject argument is moved into subject position in the presence of an appropriate adverb, e.g. *Bureaucrats bribe easily.*

Kemmer (1993) takes as her starting point Lyons's explanation of the Greek middle and surveys a number of languages in which she recognizes a 'middle' without, however, providing explicit criteria. She concludes (243): '(1) The middle is a semantic area comprising events in which (a) the Initiator is also an Endpoint, or affected entity and (b) the event is characterized by a low degree of elaboration . . . The first property is a subaspect of the second. (2) Middle marking is in general a morphosyntactic strategy for expressing an alternative conceptualization of an event in which aspects of the internal structure of the event that are less important from the point of view of the speaker are not made reference to in the utterance.' In Kemmer's terms, 'middle' often covers reflexive, reciprocal and passive, as well as constructions like 'I did it myself.'

Contributors to this volume use 'middle' in several different ways. Amberber (following a suggestion from M. Shibatani) puts forward 'middle' as a cover term for passive, anticausative and reflexive, all marked by the prefix *tə-* in Amharic (chapter 9). In chapter 12 Martin uses 'middle' as a label for suffix *-k-* in Creek; this appears to correspond to what other contributors call anticausative. LaPolla (in chapter 8) characterizes the verbal suffix *-shi* in Dulong/Rawang as 'reflexive/middle' – this covers things like 'he is killing a mosquito (on himself)' and 'he is bringing clothing (for himself)', where the parenthesised element conveys the sense of the middle suffix. Discussing Athapaskan languages, Rice follows Kemmer in using 'middle' to cover the many senses of the argument-reducing affix *d* – passive, reflexive, reciprocal, self-benefactive, anticausative, iterative, errative, repetitive/perambulative and several more (see (59) in chapter 6).

Motuna has a wide variety of construction types, for some of which there are no obvious labels in the typological literature. In chapter 4, Onishi uses the term 'middle' for a clause type (marked by special cross-referencing suffixes) which is, essentially, an extended intransitive.

This plethora of different uses for 'middle' scarcely makes for typological clarity. We would recommend that the term be restricted to its original Greek-based sense (or else avoided entirely). Some of the derivations presently characterized as 'middle' could simply be termed '(general) intransitivizer'.

5   Valency increase

We have seen that passive and antipassive show similarities (with A and O interchanged) but also important differences. The tableau at the beginning of §3 suggests that causative and applicative also show similarities (with A and O interchanged). In fact these are outweighed by the considerable differences between these two valency-increasing derivations.

(1) Causative

The characteristics of a prototypical causative are:

(a) Causative applies to an underlying intransitive clause and forms a derived transitive.

(b) The argument in underlying S function (the causee) goes into O function in the causative.

(c) A new argument (the causer) is introduced, in A function.

(d) There is some explicit formal marking of the causative construction.

Chapter 2 provides a full typology of causative constructions, dealing with their form, syntax and meaning. For the purpose of comparison with applicatives we can here note two important characteristics of causatives. The first is that if a language has a causative derivation, it always applies to intransitive verbs, forming transitives. In some – but by no means all – languages a causative derivation will also apply to transitives. The second characteristic is that the new argument (the causer) could generally not be included in the underlying intransitive. (There are exceptions but they are rather rare. Dixon and Aikhenvald (1997: 82) show how in Jarawara the causer may sometimes also be included in the underlying transitive, as a peripheral argument marked by *ehene* 'due to'.)

(2) Applicative

We here need two prototypical schemas, depending on whether an applicative derivation applies to an intransitive or a transitive clause.

EITHER

(a) Applicative applies to an underlying intransitive clause and forms a derived transitive.

(b) The argument in underlying S function goes into A function in the applicative.

(c) A peripheral argument (which could be explicitly stated in the underlying intransitive) is taken into the core, in O function.

(d) There is some explicit formal marking of an applicative construction, generally by an affix or some other morphological process applying to the verb.

OR

(a) Applicative applies to an underlying transitive clause and maintains transitivity, but with an argument in a different semantic role filling O function.

(b)   The underlying A argument stays as is.

(c)   A peripheral argument (which could be explicitly stated in the under-lying intransitive) is taken into the core, in O function.

(d)   The argument which was in O function is moved out of the core into the periphery of the clause (and may be omittable).

(e)   There is some explicit formal marking of an applicative construc-tion, generally by an affix or some other morphological process applying to the verb.

In chapter 12, Martin describes two applicative derivations for Creek. There is what he calls a 'dative applicative', marked by prefix *im-*; the argument which moves into O function can be a benefactive (e.g. X in 'he is singing for X' or 'he is making a doll for X'), or a malefactive (e.g. 'he is cheating on X') or a source (e.g. 'he is running from X'), among other possibilities. There is also an 'instrumental applicative', marked by prefix *is-*, which codes an instrumental argument (e.g. 'Bill is writing a letter with X'); Martin notes that this derivation does not necessarily increase valency.

For Amharic, Amberber (in chapter 9) describes two applicative deriva-tions. That marked by *-bb-* can place an instrumental, malefactive or locative argument in O function, while that marked by *-ll-* places a benefactive in O function.

In a causative derivation a new argument is introduced – this is always in A function and it has constant meaning, that of being a causer. That is, causative derivations all have common semantics, of causation. Applicative derivations all have a common syntactic effect, with a peripheral argument being brought into O function, but the semantic role of this argument varies, and with it the meaning of the applicative construction. We encounter a range of meanings. These include (where X is the new O argument): comitative ('do it in the company of X'), benefactive ('do it for the benefit of X'), malefactive ('do it to X's disadvantage'), instrumental ('do it using X'), locative ('do it at/on X'), presentative ('do it in the presence of X') and others such as 'laugh at X', 'cry over X', 'be frightened of X'. Occasionally, we find a language in which a verb can take two applicative devices, of different types, e.g. in Pajonal Campa (South Arawak) 'give' may take both presentat-ive and benefactive applicatives (see note 14 in chapter 5 below).

As just described for Creek and Amharic, one applicative derivation can cover several of these meanings, with varying combinations showing up in different languages; for example, benefactive and malefactive are coded by the same derivational suffix in Creek but by different affixes in Amharic. In

Yup'ik (chapter 3), Mithun shows that the most productive applicative suffix, *-(u)te*, can have comitative or benefactive sense, or can indicate the addressee for a verb of communication ('talk to X').

In chapter 10, Reid describes the valency-increasing affix *-mi-* (which developed from an incorporated noun meaning 'eye') in Ngan'gityemerri; this can have comitative ('she lives with X') or dative ('she's waving at X') functions. (This is a typologically unusual development, since noun incorp- oration generally either decreases or reassigns valency, but does not increase it – see Mithun 1984.)

The great majority of applicative derivations apply to intransitive verbs, and many of them will also apply to transitives. Both of the applicatives in Creek and both of those in Amharic apply to verbs with any transitivity value. Just occasionally we find an applicative that applies only to transitives, e.g. the instrumental applicative *-b'e-* in K'iche', described by Campbell in §6 of chapter 7.

The transitivity potentiality of an applicative is likely to depend upon its meaning. Specification of an instrument is most common in transitive clauses – the agent uses the instrument to affect the patient (e.g. 'Mary cut the meat with a knife') and instrumental applicatives are thus mostly applied to trans- itives. If any applicative is only used with transitive verbs it is likely to be the instrumental, as just noted for K'iche'.

As with passive, there can be types of applicative which deviate from the prototypical schemas. Aikhenvald describes how in Tariana one function of the derivational suffix *-i(ta)* is to mark that a peripheral argument is now obligatory (however, it remains in peripheral function), e.g. 'show it to X' (see §4.5 of chapter 5). In Dulong/Rawang, LaPolla describes (in §3.2.2 of chapter 8) a benefactive derivation with unusual syntax. When the suffix *-ā* is added to an intransitive verb, a benefactive argument moves into the core, but the original S argument does not receive ergative marking (which is usually included on an argument in A function). When *-ā* is added to a transitive verb, the original A and O stay as is with a new argument, which has benefactive meaning, being marked by a postposition.

Onishi describes the wide range of syntactic effects of the applicative suffix *-jee* in Motuna; this increases the valency of the verb by adding a new argument in O, E or S_0 function, according to the type of verb involved. With 'be angry' we get S becoming A and an NP referring to what the subject was angry over (which was marked by purposive suffix *-ko* in the underlying intransitive) coming into O function. For extended intransitives such as 'know' and 'want', with core arguments in S and E functions, S goes into A and E into O function in a *-jee* applicative. With a transitive verb such as 'make', the A stays as is, underlying O goes into E function, and a benefactive/ malefactive argument comes into O function. There are several other syntactic possibilities, set out in §4.1.2 of chapter 4.

6   An integrated approach

There is a tendency in modern linguistics to compartmentalize things. One asks whether something is a syntactic mechanism; or, alternatively, has semantic effect; or, alternatively, has discourse function. Many of the chapters in this volume show that one must adopt a wider perspective. Each of the types of derivation that is discussed has three aspects:

(1) SEMANTIC. For instance, there may be two causatives, distinguished in terms of whether the causee undertakes the activity willingly or unwillingly.

(2) SYNTACTIC. For instance, an argument will be added to the core in a prototypical causative or applicative derivation; and an argument will be removed from the core in a prototypical passive or antipassive derivation.

(3) DISCOURSE-/PRAGMATIC ROLE. For instance – as discussed by Onishi for Motuna in chapter 4 – an applicative may place what was a peripheral argument into O function, so that it can be identified as topic within a segment of discourse.

These three aspects interrelate. The basic SEMANTIC effect of a causative derivation is to introduce an additional participant, the causer, which naturally has the SYNTACTIC effect of adding an argument. In some languages passive encodes the SEMANTIC information that an activity is completed, and also has the SYNTACTIC effect of placing an underlying O argument into derived S function, to satisfy an S/A pivot constraint, which interrelates with DISCOURSE organisation (a pivot being a grammaticalized topic).

Derivations vary and languages vary. In many languages a passive or antipassive tends to have a predominantly syntactic effect and a causative to be largely semantic. (This, according to Shibatani, forthcoming, explains why a causative mechanism is found in the overwhelming majority of languages, but passive and antipassive have a more restricted distribution.) But a passive or antipassive will always have some semantic component. If a language has more than one passive or antipassive these will be distinguished, at least in part, by their meanings. England (1983) reports a number of distinct passives in the Mayan language Mam – one is used when the underlying A acts purposely; one is used when the A has lost, or does not have, control of the action (done accidentally); one is used when the underlying A 'went to do it'. In Dyirbal there are two antipassives with different semantics, one referring to an actual and the other to a potential or habitual act (Dixon 1972: 91–2).

In languages where there is a pivot (that is, a syntactic constraint involving coreferential arguments in clause linking – Dixon 1994: 152–81) some of the valency-changing derivations will typically feed the pivot. Passive can feed an S/A pivot (including switch-reference) – as described by Aikhenvald in chapter 5 for Tariana – putting an argument that is in non-pivot function (O) into derived pivot function (S). Similarly, antipassive can feed an S/O pivot, putting an argument that is in non-pivot function (A) into derived pivot function (S). Applicative puts a peripheral argument into O function and may thus be used to feed an S/O pivot. For instance, to link together 'I'll take the fish-spear(O)' and 'I'll spear the fish (O) with the fish-spear', the second clause is put into applicative form, with 'fish-spear' becoming O and 'fish' now taking dative case. Now the two clauses share the same O and can be conjoined, with the second occurrence of 'fish-spear' omitted. (This example comes from Wargamay, a language with an S/O pivot – Dixon 1981: 79.)

As noted just above, a causative tends to be largely semantic. But there are languages in which a causative may be used for purely syntactic reasons. Aikhenvald (forthcoming) shows how in Tariana a causative construction can be employed to satisfy the 'same subject and same object' constraint on serial verb constructions. Oswalt (1977) shows how in some Pomo languages, in a clause such as 'I want him to go' or 'I hope that he will go', the verb 'go' will take the causative suffix, so that it should have the same surface subject as the main verb 'want' or 'hope'. (Nichols 1985 describes a similar situation in Chechen-Ingush.) And in chapter 3 Mithun shows how causatives can be used for discourse purposes in Yup'ik. There is a text where the topic is 'grandmother'. One clause is to be 'I stand in the doorway', but this is put into causative form 'grandmother having me stand in the doorway', to integrate it into the text segment with 'grandmother' as topic.

Valency-changing derivations may also feed a constraint that all the verbs in a verb complex should have the same transitivity value; see, for instance, example (18b) from Dulong/Rawang, in chapter 8. (A similar situation applies in many Australian languages.)

We need, in fact, to stand even further back and consider in the most general terms the mechanisms which a language employs. There are examples of a certain suffix, say, which appears to have a range of different functions

– sometimes changing the syntax, sometimes having no syntactic effect but just changing the meaning. What we have here is a single linguistic mechanism, which speakers conceive of and operate with as a unitary idea. However, the implications of the idea, within the language, are wide-ranging, appearing sometimes to be purely syntactic and other times to be simply semantic.

Consider the verbal derivation suffix -:*ji-n* in the Australian language Yidiny. Dixon spent several years collecting examples of the seemingly diverse effects of this form. Eventually, he was able to unify them in a single principle. The prototypical situation in Yidiny is for the syntactic argument which is in A function to be identical with the semantic role of 'controlling agent'. The suffix -:*ji-n* is used to mark any instance of this identity NOT holding. In a purposeful reflexive situation (e.g. 'he cut himself deliberately') we do have a controlling agent (underlying A) but it is identical with the patient (underlying O) and is mapped onto S in a derived intransitive construction; this is marked by -:*ji-n* since the controlling agent is no longer in A function. Yidiny has an antipassive construction, to feed its S/O pivot in relativization and coordination; the underlying A argument goes into S function and the underlying O now takes dative or locative case. Again, the controlling agent is not in A function and -:*ji-n* is used to mark this. In each of these instances -:*ji-n* has syntactic effect, marking the derivation of an intransitive from an underlying transitive clause. But -:*ji-n* is also used when the A argument is something inanimate, which is inherently incapable of control (e.g. 'the fire burnt me'), or when the A argument is human but achieves some result accidentally (e.g. 'by chance I saw the coin on the roadside'). In these two instances the clause remains transitive, with an A argument, but this is not a controlling agent and hence the inclusion of -:*ji-n*. (A fuller discussion is in Dixon 1977: 274–93; a similar example from Kuku-Yalanji, another Australian language, is summarised in Dixon 1994: 151.)

It is often useful to identify what is the primary function of a given derivation. For instance, in her discussion of Yup'ik in chapter 3, Mithun concludes that the primary functions of some derivational affixes are 'not to alter argument structure, but rather to focus on the state resulting from an action'. That is, the effect on argument structure is simply a concomitant property.

In chapter 6, Rice provides an overview of the varied functions of the affix **d* in Athapaskan languages. There is undoubtedly some unitary concept involved (which may differ a little from language to language). When **d* is applied to a transitive verb its effect might tentatively be described as 'lowered differentiation of arguments'. Like -:*ji-n* in Yidiny it appears sometimes to have syntactic effect (passive, reflexive, reciprocal) but in other instances its effect is basically semantic, e.g. to indicate collectivity. We also find *d used on intransitives with meanings such as unintended ('errative'), iterative and perambulative. (See the excellent discussion by Thompson 1996.) What is needed here is an intensive, text-based study of the general meaning of *d – as a unitary concept – in each language in which it occurs. And then an inductive study of common elements of meaning of *d across all Athapaskan languages, leading to a hypothesis about the meaning of *d in proto-Athapaskan (or, at one level higher, proto-Na-déné) and the semantic – and consequential syntactic – changes that have taken place in each individual language.

One thing which is patently clear – from consideration of *d in Athapaskan, -:ji-n in Yidiny, and similar problems – is that one can only make any progress in a deep understanding of how a language works by first looking at the meaning, and then at how some semantic specifications may have syntactic effect while others leave the syntax unchanged and simply constrain the interpretation.

The idea of a 'syntax first' (or 'autonomous syntax') approach to language tends to hold back linguists from obtaining significant insights into how languages are used and understood. What is needed – and has been attempted in most of the chapters in this volume – is an understanding of the underlying semantic and syntactic distinctions that a given language employs, and how these interrelate, and function in discourse context. And then, as a secondary step, how these underlying contrasts are realized.

7   Semantic classes of verbs

Languages vary in their syntactic profiles, and this can motivate the types of valency-changing derivations that they employ. For instance, in some languages a high proportion of underived verbs are transitive; coupled with this there are generally valency-decreasing derivations. In other languages a relatively large number of underived verbs are intransitive; in association with this there are normally some valency-increasing derivations. (Nichols 1982 provides an illuminating discussion of this for Ingush.)

Within a language, the meaning of a verb helps determine its underlying transitivity value. Hopper and Thompson (1980) set forth ten semantic parameters in terms of which transitivity can be measured. Some verbs receive 'high transitivity' values for most parameters and typically belong to the syntactic class transitive (e.g. 'take', 'hit', 'discover'); other verbs score at the 'low transitivity' end of most parameters and are generally intransitive (e.g. 'sit', 'slip', 'yawn'). There are some verbs that fall in the middle section of the transitivity scale (e.g. 'look (at)', 'laugh (at)'); these have the syntactic value of transitive in some languages and intransitive in others. (If there is an extended intransitive class, they are prime candidates to be members of the class.)

One interesting observation is that if a 'middle section of the transitivity hierarchy' verb is syntactically transitive, then it will often be used intransitively, through application of a valency-decreasing derivation. If, on the other hand, it is syntactically intransitive, then it will often be used transitively, through application of a valency-increasing derivation. Compare two languages from the north-east of Australia. Guugu-Yimidhirr has a transitive verb *di:ŋa-* 'laugh at'; from this is derived the intransitive stem *di:ŋa-:dhi-* 'laugh', by application of the detransitivizing derivational suffix *-:dhi-*. Yidiny has an intransitive verb *maŋga-* 'laugh'; this is often used with the valency-increasing derivational suffix *-ŋa-*, used in its applicative sense, giving the transitive stem *maŋga-ŋa-* 'laugh at'.

The meaning of a subclass of verbs will often incline it towards occurring with a certain kind of valency-changing derivation. For instance, if there is a class of verbs which typically have a human O argument (such as *annoy, tire* and *please* in English) these will typically occur in a passive construction, placing the underlying O in derived S function. This relates to the fact that, in many kinds of discourse, if one core argument in a clause is human and the other non-human, there is a preference for the human argument to be coded as surface subject.

It is possible roughly to discern two broad classes of verbs:[1]

(1) Verbs which describe an action that either can happen spontaneously to a patient or can be engineered by an agent, are likely to be $S = O$ ambitransitives. If they are transitive they are particularly likely to take passive and/or anticausative derivation. If they are intransitive they are particularly likely to undergo causative derivation. This class covers meanings such as 'break', 'fall', 'spill', 'bend', 'extend', 'stretch', 'change', 'move', 'turn', 'enter', 'burn' and 'frighten'.

(2) Verbs which relate to an action which may be described just in general terms or, alternatively, with respect to some particular patient, are likely to be $S = A$ ambitransitives. If they are transitive they are particularly likely to take antipassive derivation. If intransitive they

---

[1] The terms 'unaccusative' and 'unergative' are currently used by some writers in investigation of this kind of phenomenon. However, these terms are used with many other senses, without any solid cross-linguistic criteria being involved. In view of this we prefer not to employ them here. See Dixon (1999).

are particularly likely to undergo some variety of applicative derivation. This class covers meanings such as 'eat', 'sweep', 'polish', 'lead', 'win', 'play (at)', 'laugh (at)', 'cry (over)' and 'speak (to)'.

There is only a little literature on this topic. Dixon (1991: 286–93) discusses verb types in English. Austin (1997) surveys verbs which typically enter into valency-increasing derivations in Australian languages; he finds that those intransitive verbs which are most open to a causative derivation are 'fall', 'turn' and 'climb, go up', and those which are most open to an applicative derivation are 'laugh', 'cry', 'play', 'go', 'return' and 'sit'. Kazenin (1994) has a useful discussion of this topic, comparing Fijian (data from Dixon 1988: 204–14), Asiatic Eskimo and Bambara. He notes inter-language similarities and also differences; for instance, 'manipulative verbs with a highly affected O' tend to be in class (1) for Fijian but in class (2) for Asiatic Eskimo. (See also Rice's discussion, in chapter 6, of verbs in Athapaskan languages which take the impersonal passive and the personal passive.)

The transitivity and derivational propensities for verbs of different semantic types is a large topic, which should be a focus for future research. The remarks here are to be regarded as informal and preliminary.

8   Alternative construction types

The syntactic, semantic and discourse effects that are in many languages achieved by valency-decreasing derivations can in other languages be covered by alternative grammatical means. In chapter 10 Reid describes the quite unusual structure of Ngan'gityemerri. In this language a predicate will typically involve two verbal elements, coverb and finite verb, each of which has its own transitivity value. Most often coverb and finite verb agree in transitivity, but they can have different values. For instance, when a monovalent coverb occurs with a transitive finite verb there is a causative effect, and when a high transitive coverb is used with an intransitive finite verb there is an anticausative effect. However, as Reid stresses, there is no derivation involved, merely alternative combinations of coverb and finite verb.

The Jarawara language of southern Amazonia adopts a further scenario. In this language there are simply two transitive constructions. The A-construction has the A argument as pivot (rather like an active clause in a syntactically accusative language) and the O-construction has O as pivot (like an active clause in a syntactically ergative language). It is not sensible to treat one construction type as 'derived' from the other (an active/passive or an antipassive/active pair); each is fully transitive.

The alternation between two construction types in Jarawara fulfils the same sort of discourse role (in pivot feeding) as do valency-changing derivations in other languages. There is no inherent semantic difference between the construction types, but there is a semantic conditioning, which shows similarities to the semantic preferences which motivate the use of passive and antipassive derivations in other languages. The O-construction is restricted to clauses where O is 3rd person (with a historically recent extension to clauses where the A is 3rd person and the O 1st or 2nd person, but only if tense-modal and mood suffixes are included). In a similar way, in other languages a passive derivation is employed most often when A is 3rd and O is 1st or 2nd person, while an antipassive is most often used in complementary circumstances, when A is 1st or 2nd and O is 3rd person. (Full details concerning Jarawara are in Dixon, forthcoming.)

The inverse in Athapaskan (and in some other languages) is another example of alternative construction types (rather than there being one basic type with the other derived from it). Inverses are not treated in this volume but they are discussed in Dixon and Aikhenvald (1997: 98–100; and see references quoted there).

9   The studies in this volume

Chapter 2 provides a cross-linguistic typological study of causatives. This is followed by ten individual case studies.

In chapter 3 Marianne Mithun provides an accessible account of Central Alaskan Yup'ik (Eskimo), discussing the various causative and applicative suffixes, two passive-like derivations (which focus, in different ways, on the resulting state), and several antipassive-like devices. Chapter 4 deals with a language from the other side of the world – Motuna, a Papuan (i.e. non-Austronesian) language spoken on the island of Bougainville in Papua New Guinea. Masayuki Onishi describes the complex array of clause types and transitivity classes of verbs, the causative and applicative valency-increasing derivations, the reciprocal and deagentive valency-decreasing derivations, and finally a stimulative valency-rearranging derivation.

Alexandra Y. Aikhenvald, in chapter 5, discusses Tariana, an Arawak language from northern Amazonia, where all transitive verbs are in fact S = A ambitransitive and there are three subclasses of intransitives – S_a (where S is marked like A in a transitive), S_o (S marked like O) and S_{io} (S marked like an indirect object). She details the passive, the reciprocal derivation, the three strategies for forming causatives (morphological, periphrastic, and by a serial verb construction) and other argument-adding derivations. In chapter 6 Keren Rice provides a comparative study, across the Athapaskan language family, of two derivational affixes, -ł-, which is essentially argument-increasing (typically causative) and *d* which is essentially argument-decreasing, covering a dozen different senses. She provides detailed and insightful information on the parameters of variation – function, meaning, productivity and the like.

Lyle Campbell, in chapter 7, considers K'iche', a Mayan language spoken in highlands Guatemala, also including comparative remarks on other Mayan languages. There are two varieties of passive and two of antipassive (one with non-prototypical syntax), a causative, and an instrumental applicative which only goes on to transitive verbs. In chapter 8, Randy LaPolla discusses a Tibeto-Burman language which is spoken both in China, where it is called Dulong, and in Myanmar (Burma) where it has come to be called Rawang ([rəwaŋ]). There are two valency-reducing affixes, ə- which has a general intransitivizing function (including reciprocal) and -shì, glossed as 'reflexive/middle'. LaPolla discusses two types of causative (morphological and periphrastic) and an applicative benefactive, together with other ways of increasing transitivity. Then, in chapter 9, Mengistu Amberber considers the Ethio-Semitic language Amharic, spoken in Ethiopia. He discusses transitivity classes, the general detransitivizer *tə-* (which covers passive, anticausative and reflexive), two morphological causatives, a periphrastic causative, and two applicatives.

The Australian language Ngan'gityemerri, discussed by Nicholas Reid in chapter 10, has only one actual argument-affecting derivation, a type of applicative marked by -*mi*-, which has developed from an incorporated noun meaning 'eye'. It does, however, have other syntactic devices which are functionally equivalent to the derivational processes reported in other chapters – basically, different combinations (within one predicate) of transitive and intransitive coverbs with transitive and intransitive finite verbs.

In chapter 11 Bernard Comrie discusses Tsez, a Daghestanian language from the North-east Caucasian family. In note 1 he states that 'the trio S, A, P is used in this chapter rather than the S, A, O of most other contributions [in fact, of chapters 1–2 and 4–10], to avoid a terminology that could be misinterpreted as saying that the prototypically patient-like argument of a two-place predicate is necessarily, or even prototypically, a syntactic object; see further Comrie (1978). While this distinction does reflect a significant difference in philosophical standpoint, for the purposes of this chapter the two sets of terms can be taken as notationally equivalent.' Turning to Comrie

(1978: 330–1) we find the statements: 'S refers to the single argument of an intransitive verb . . . A refers to that argument of a transitive verb which would be its subject in a non-ergative language like English . . . and P refers to the argument which would be the direct object.'

Tsez is interesting in that, unlike most other Daghestanian languages, it has no ambitransitive (or labile) verbs, but can use intransitive and transitive suffixes to achieve the same end. The only productive valency-changing derivation involves causative suffix -*r*; this can be added to a verb of any transitivity and may apply iteratively. The balance of Comrie's chapter is devoted to a discussion of which argument is the 'privileged NP', i.e. the 'trigger or target' for a particular aspect of the syntax. This is shown to be S or A with respect to all of (a) constituent order; (b) reflexive constructions; and (c) coreferential NP omission in certain clause combinations. Concerning (b), we noted under (3) in §4 above that in all languages (whether accusative or, like Tsez, ergative) the antecedent in a reflexive is A or S (see Dixon 1994: 138–9). Observation (c) is particularly interesting, indicating that although Tsez has a predominantly ergative morphology, it has accusative syntax, working with an S/A pivot in at least one part of its grammar (in the sense of 'pivot' discussed in Dixon 1994: 152–80). Very little information had previously been published on pivots in languages of the North-east Caucasian family.

In chapter 12 Jack Martin discusses Creek, a Muskogean language spoken in the south-east of the USA. He adopts a different theoretical stance from the other authors in this volume, suggesting that this language lacks obvious diagnostics for transitivity or for distinguishing the core syntactic/semantic functions S, A and O. This could be taken to imply that Creek has a rather different structural profile from the other languages discussed in this volume. We believe that it does not. Martin's difficulties with deciding on the transitivity of such Creek verbs as 'see' and 'go to' are not dissimilar to those faced by a grammarian of English in dealing with, for example, *look (at the beach)* and *sleep (at the beach)*. In fact Martin does refer to transitivity and valency, and to subject and object throughout his chapter. He states: 'describing the Creek middle as valency-reducing fails to explain why it fails to create S = A intransitives'. We would agree; one has to specify which kind of valency-changing derivation it is – passive, agentless passive, anticausative, antipassive, patientless antipassive, reflexive, reciprocal, etc. (In fact it is an anticausative.)

Martin's comments concerning 'the issue of the degree to which grammars have the ability to COUNT' seems to us to be tilting at a straw-man. The types of derivation described in this volume have the effect of adding a core argument, removing a core argument or manipulating arguments. The consequence of forming a causative on an intransitive verb, for instance, is to add a new argument, the causer (in A function). This is what the derivation does; the fact that this serves to increase the valency of the verb by one is simply a concomitant effect.

10   Topics for further investigation

Linguistics is at a rather early stage of development. Our understanding of the kinds of parameters which languages operate with – and why they do – requires considerable refinement. The most basic need is for detailed explanatory grammars of individual languages, primarily based on the study of texts, augmented by judicious elicitation (rather than using elicitation as the main source of data), and cast in terms of basic linguistic theory. These grammars will provide the foundations for future typological work – positing generalizations about the structure of human languages.

The studies in this volume show the value of a holistic approach. A particular valency-changing derivation must be discussed in the context of the overall grammatical organization of the language; this can only be done by someone who has studied the entire grammar and has a finely tuned understanding of how its components interrelate. In particular, for each type of derivation one should simultaneously discuss its meaning, its morphological (or periphrastic) marking, its syntactic effect and its discourse role.

Fruitful lines of enquiry for future research include:

(1)   Study of the types of passive, antipassive, causative and applicative derivations in individual languages and then cross-linguistically. How these differ from the prototypical schemas suggested here. In the case of passive, for example, what sort of different weightings may be given to its three main effects: drawing attention to the original O; downgrading the original A; and focussing on the state the original O is in, as a result of the activity reported by the verb.

For each type of derivation we need to enquire whether one aspect of it is primary – this could be syntactic, semantic or discourse-pragmatic.

(2)   There is need for a typological study of applicatives, parallel to that on causatives provided in chapter 2 here. There are many semantic varieties of applicatives, according to the semantic role of the argument that is brought into O function (and this, in turn, relates to the

meaning of the verb). One particular point for study is the correlation between whether a particular applicative applies to intransitive or to transitive verbs (or to both) and its meaning.

(3) Our preliminary impression is that, across the languages of the world, there tend to be more valency-increasing derivations (comitative and applicative) than valency-reducing derivations (passive, antipassive, reflexive, reciprocal, etc.). This needs to be verified, through study of a large representative sample of languages; if it is true, linguists should seek an explanation.

(4) Diachronic development has only been touched on in a few of the chapters here. We need to ask: (a) how derivational affixes develop (what is their lexical or other source); and (b) how a derivational affix may lose its full productivity, becoming restricted to just a few forms where it is lexicalized (and may have an idiomatic meaning). A further topic for study is how one kind of valency-changing derivation can develop into a different kind (discussed for Yup'ik by Mithun, in chapter 3).

Diachronic development also relates to the patterns of lexicalization of causatives and applicatives (considered, for instance, by Comrie in chapter 12 and by Mithun in chapter 3), of passives (as in Modern Hebrew, see Aikhenvald 1990: 67–8), of antipassives and of reflexives (see Haviland 1979: 126–7 for an account of verbs in the Australian language Guugu-Yimidhirr which inherently include the reflexive/ antipassive suffix -:*dhi*). This topic is also in need of cross-linguistic study.

(5) Syntactic operations such as noun incorporation are likely to have syntactic, semantic and discourse-pragmatic effects. These may extend to argument manipulation and valency change (as described for Ngan'gityemerri by Reid in §4 of chapter 10). This also requires study in individual languages, ahead of attempts at cross-linguistic generalization.

(6) A certain semantic effect can be associated with one type of valency-changing derivation in a given language, but with a quite different type in a further language. For instance, in chapter 3 Mithun describes how adversative effect is associated with one variety of passive in Yup'ik whereas in chapter 8 LaPolla shows how adversative is linked to a valency-increasing derivation in Dulong/Rawang. And, as noted in §4 above, there is an adversative derivation in Japanese (misleadingly called 'adversative passive') which normally

increases valency. Cross-linguistic study of the varied valency-changing associations of a given semantic parameter should be a priority for further research.

(7)   There is real need for study of the possible combinations of derivational processes in individual languages. A few of the contributors below consider this question. In chapter 6 Rice shows that in Athapaskan languages some verbs can take middle (normally marked by *d*) plus causative (normally *ł*), the combination being marked by a fused element *l*. In chapter 8 LaPolla states that Dulong/Rawang allows causative plus reflexive and draws attention to dialect differences. In chapter 12, Martin states that Creek does not permit causative plus middle, but that the dative applicative, the instrumental applicative and the causative are compatible with each other. Dixon (1972: 246–7) shows that in Dyirbal one can have (i) antipassive, reflexive or reciprocal marking; followed by (ii) comitative or instrumental applicative; followed by (iii) reflexive again (but not antipassive or reciprocal); followed by (iv) applicative again.

A language may have a number of applicative derivations, with different meanings; these are particularly likely to co-occur. Study is needed of which combinations are found.

The allowable combinations of derivational processes may be found to depend on the particular meaning and function of these processes in individual languages. Alternatively, some cross-linguistic generalizations may turn out to be possible.

(8)   One important task is to investigate the varying transitivity profiles of languages. As LaPolla mentions (in note 7 to chapter 8), some languages have transitivity as a more prominent category than others; this may relate, in large part, to the number of ambitransitive verbs in the language. Detailed study is needed – of individual languages, and also cross-linguistically.

(9)   A fruitful topic for study would be how the semantics of a verb will determine its transitivity and the type(s) of derivational processes that it takes part in (and the extent to which it takes part in them), following up the preliminary remarks in §7 above.

(10)   There may be a dependency relation between the application of a valency-changing derivation and some category in the grammar. For instance, in chapter 6 Rice mentions that, for Athapaskan languages, perfectivity is not marked in 'middles'. This is another topic worthy of study, across a well-chosen sample of the world's languages.

References

Aikhenvald, A.Y. 1990. *Sovremennyj Ivrit [Modern Hebrew]*. Moscow: Nauka.
   Forthcoming. 'Serial constructions and verb compounding: evidence from Tariana (North Arawak)', to appear in *Studies in Language*.
Austin, P. 1981. *A grammar of Diyari, South Australia*. Cambridge: Cambridge University Press.
   1997. 'Causatives and applicatives in Australian Aboriginal languages', pp. 165–225 of *The dative and related phenomena*, ed. K. Matsumura and T. Hayasi. Tokyo: Hituzi Syobo.
Comrie, B. 1978. 'Ergativity', pp. 329–94 of *Syntactic typology: studies in the phenomenology of language*, ed. W.P. Lehmann. Austin: University of Texas Press.
Cooreman, A. 1994. 'A functional typology of antipassives', pp. 49–88 of *Voice: form and function*, ed. B. Fox and P.J. Hopper. Amsterdam: John Benjamins.
Dixon, R.M.W. 1972. *The Dyirbal language of North Queensland*. Cambridge: Cambridge University Press.
   1977. *A grammar of Yidiɲ*. Cambridge: Cambridge University Press.
   1981. 'Wargamay', pp. 1–144 of *Handbook of Australian languages*, Vol. II, ed. R.M.W. Dixon and B.J. Blake. Canberra: Australian National University Press.
   1988. *A grammar of Boumaa Fijian*. Chicago: University of Chicago Press.
   1991. *A new approach to English grammar, on semantic principles*. Oxford: Clarendon Press.
   1994. *Ergativity*. Cambridge: Cambridge University Press.
   1999. 'Semantic roles and syntactic functions: the semantic basis for a typology', to appear in *CLS* 35.
   Forthcoming. 'A-constructions and O-constructions in Jarawara'.
Dixon, R.M.W. and Aikhenvald, A.Y. 1997. 'A typology of argument-determined constructions', pp. 71–113 of *Essays on language function and language type*, ed. J. Bybee, J. Haiman and S.A. Thompson. Amsterdam: John Benjamins.
England, N.C. 1983. *A grammar of Mam, a Mayan language*. Austin: University of Texas Press.
Haspelmath, M. 1990. 'The grammaticization of passive morphology', *Studies in Language* 14.25–72.
Haviland, J. 1979. 'Guugu Yimidhirr', pp. 27–180 of *Handbook of Australian languages*, Vol. I, ed. R.M.W. Dixon and B.J. Blake. Canberra: Australian National University Press.
Hopper, P.J. and Thompson, S.A. 1980. 'Transitivity in grammar and discourse', *Language* 56.251–99.
Kazenin, K.I. 1994. 'On the lexical alternation of Agent-preserving and Object-preserving transitivity alternations', *Nordic Journal of Linguistics* 17.141–54.
Kemmer, S. 1993. *The middle voice*, Typological studies in language 23. Amsterdam, Philadelphia: John Benjamins.
Keyser, S.J. and Roeper, T. 1984. 'On the middle and ergative constructions in English', *Linguistic Inquiry* 15.381–416.
Kimenyi, A. 1980. *A relational grammar of Kinyarwanda*. Berkeley and Los Angeles: University of California Press.

Lyons, J. 1968. *Introduction to theoretical linguistics.* Cambridge: Cambridge University Press.

Mithun, M. 1984. 'The evolution of noun incorporation', *Language* 64.847–94.

Nichols, J. 1982. 'Ingush transitivization and detransitivization', *BLS* 8.445–62.

1985. 'Switch-reference causatives', *CLS* 21.193–203.

Oswalt, R.L. 1977. 'The causative as a reference switching mechanism in Western Pomo', *BLS* 3.46–54.

Robinson, S. ms. 'Valency changing derivations in Tzotzil (Mayan)'.

Shibatani, M. 1990. *The languages of Japan.* Cambridge: Cambridge University Press.

Forthcoming. *Voice.* Cambridge: Cambridge University Press.

Siewierska, A. 1984. *Passive: a comparative linguistic analysis.* London: Croom Helm.

Thompson, C. 1996. 'The Na-Dene middle voice: an impersonal source of the D-element', *International Journal of American Linguistics* 62.351–78.

2   A typology of causatives: form, syntax and meaning

R.M.W. DIXON

1   Introduction[1]

This chapter will survey causative constructions in terms of three parameters: their formal marking, their syntax and their semantics. It will also investigate dependencies between the parameters.

I work in terms of a basic theoretical framework. In any language verbal clauses can be categorized as (i) intransitive, with one core argument, in S function; (ii) transitive, with at least two core arguments, in A and O functions (there are subtypes: simple transitive and ditransitive); and (iii) copula, involving two core arguments, in copula subject and copula complement functions (in some languages the copula complement may be omittable). Within a transitive clause, that core argument whose referent has the potential to initiate or control the activity is linked to A function, and that core argument whose referent may be saliently affected by the activity is linked to O function.

A causative construction is sometimes described as involving 'two events'. Frawley (1992: 159) talks of 'a precipitating event' and 'a result', and Shibatani (1976a: 1) of 'a causing event' and 'a caused event'. I prefer a quite different characterization – a causative construction involves the specification of an additional argument, a causer, onto a basic clause. A causer refers to someone or something (which can be an event or state) that initiates or controls the activity. This is the defining property of the syntactic–semantic function A (transitive subject).

[1] For their constructive comments on a draft of this chapter I am most grateful to Alexandra Y. Aikhenvald, Mengistu Amberber, Timothy Jowan Curnow, Gerrit Dimmendaal, Geoffrey Haig, Bh. Krishnamurti, Randy LaPolla, Jack Martin, Masayuki Onishi and Nicholas Reid.

That is, if a causative construction is formed by derivation, it will involve the addition of a new argument in A function (the causer). In the causative of an intransitive clause the original S argument (the causee) will almost always go into O function in the new transitive clause (with the causer being A). In the causative of a transitive, the causer always becomes A; then the original A (the causee) and/or O arguments generally have their syntactic functions reassigned. There are several different ways of achieving this, described in §3.2 below.

There are a number of syntactic derivations that change valency. We have valency-reducing derivations such as passive (removing the A argument from the core) and antipassive (removing the O argument). There are two varieties of valency-increasing derivations: causative adds a new A argument (proto-typically to an intransitive clause – the old S becoming O – often also to a transitive) and applicative adds a new O argument (to an intransitive – the old S becoming A – or to a transitive – the old A staying as is and the old O moving to the periphery of the clause).

In some languages a single morphological process may mark more than one syntactic function. In Korean, for example, the suffix -*ita* has causative effect with one set of verbs and passive with another set. The sets do overlap – thus *pota* 'see' has derived form *po-ita*, which can have a passive interpretation 'be seen' or a causative one 'show' (i.e. 'make see') (Sohn 1994: 314.) Presumably, the senses are disambiguated by the syntax of the clause in which they occur and by discourse context. Shopen and Konaré (1970: 238) describe a similar situation in Sonrai (or Songhai, Nilo-Saharan family) where verbal suffix -*ndi* can mark either causative or agentless passive on the same verb (and a verb can take two tokens of -*ndi*, one causative and one agentless passive, so that *ŋa-ndi-ndi* is, literally '[the rice] was made to be eaten [by someone: causee] [by someone: causer]'.

For a morphological process to have both valency-reducing and valency-increasing effect, as in Korean and Sonrai, is quite rare. We more commonly encounter a derivational affix which encodes two valency-reducing functions (e.g. passive and antipassive – see Dixon 1994: 151–2) or the two valency-increasing functions, causative and applicative. In the Australian language Yidiny, for example, the verbal suffix -*ŋa*- has applicative effect with some verbs (e.g. intransitive *maŋga*- 'laugh', applicative *maŋga-ŋa*- 'laugh at') but causative effect with others (e.g. intransitive *warrŋgi*- 'turn around', causative *warrŋgi-ŋa*- 'turn (something) around'). There is again some overlap – from *bila*- 'go in' is derived *bila-ŋa*- which can have either an applicative sense 'go in with' or a causative sense 'put in'; it would be likely to be disambiguated by the discourse context (Dixon 1977: 302–39). See Austin (1997) for similar examples from other Australian languages, and Comrie (1985: 329–30) for examples from Chukchee and Wolof. In this chapter we shall just examine the causative form and meanings of such multi-functional morphological processes.

Other valency-changing derivations typically have discourse-determined roles (among other uses). A passive will put an original O argument into derived S function, which may satisfy an S/A pivot constraint on clause linking. An antipassive will put an original A into derived S function to satisfy an S/O pivot constraint. An applicative will take a peripheral argument and place it in core function O, which may enable it to function as syntactic pivot (in a language with ergative syntax) or as discourse topic.

A causative derivation takes an S argument (which is a pivot function for both syntactically accusative and syntactically ergative languages) and places it in derived O function. This suggests that a causative would be unlikely to be used for discourse effect, and will normally be employed just for semantic reasons. Study of grammars bears out this idea, that a causative construction will seldom be used to satisfy the demands of discourse organization. However, this does happen occasionally. In Tariana a causative construction can be used to satisfy the 'same subject and same object constraint' on serial verb constructions (Aikhenvald, forthcoming); Oswalt (1977), O'Connor (1992) and Nichols (1985) describe a similar function in some Pomo languages and in Chechen-Ingush. And Mithun (in chapter 3 of this volume) exemplifies the discourse-determined use of a causative in a Yup'ik text. The last line of Mithun's example (60) could have been stated as 'I would stand in the doorway and she [grandmother] would bless me.' However, the topic for this stretch of text is 'grandmother' and in order to integrate 'I would stand in the doorway' into the discourse it is stated as a causative: 'She [grandmother] would have me stand in the doorway, blessing me.'

The causer in a causative construction can refer to a person (e.g. 'Mary made me laugh') or an abstract thing (e.g. 'The heat of the sun made me feel dizzy' or 'John's lecture made me feel sleepy') or an event, coded through a complement clause (e.g. 'Walking all day made me tired').

In this chapter I adopt a narrow interpretation of prototypical 'causative construction' – it must involve a morphological process, or a verb which only has an abstract, causative meaning (or a lexical pair whose members are in causative relation). In English, *make* only has causative meaning while *order* also refers to an act of speaking. In view of this, *Mary made John go* is treated as a causative construction, but *Mary ordered John to go* is not. Other investigators permit a wider scope for the label 'causative'. For instance, Song (1996: 36) accepts as a causative construction a sentence which is literally translated as 'I speak and child eats'. The difficulty then is in knowing where to draw the line.

It is not sufficient, when writing the grammar of a language, just to say that it has a causative construction. All causative constructions have in common the addition of an A argument (the causer) to an underlying clause and this provides the basic semantic/syntactic criterion for recognizing a causative construction in a given language. But languages differ a great deal in the syntax of their causatives and in the specific meanings attached to them. There may be a restriction that the causee (the S or A of the underlying clause) must be animate, or that it can only be inanimate. In some languages the causative construction may only be used if the causer acted intentionally (not accidentally). And so on. Some languages have two or more causative mechanisms and these always have different meanings. A study of such constructions reveals nine semantic parameters which relate to causatives; these are discussed and exemplified in §4 below. Note that when dealing with a language that has just one type of causative, a linguist should take care to specify its semantics, in terms of the parameters presented in §4.

§2 describes types of causative constructions in terms of their formal marking. §3 then discusses the syntax of causatives – particularly those based on simple transitive and on ditransitive clauses – in relation to their formal marking. Following the presentation of semantic parameters (in §4), there is in §5 a study of the correlations between meaning and formal marking.

2   Formal mechanisms

I begin by describing causatives marked by a morphological process applied to the verb of the underlying clause, then go on to discuss causatives that involve two verbs making up a single predicate, then biclausal (or periphrastic) causative constructions. §2.4 looks at lexical pairs that are in causative relation, and at ambitransitive verbs of type S = O, which can be regarded as causatives. In §2.5 we look at languages that achieve a causative effect by exchanging the auxiliaries which accompany a lexical verb.

2.1   *Morphological processes*

A causative construction may be marked by a morphological process having applied to the verb of the clause. Such a process can consist in (a) internal

change, e.g. in vowel quality, or consonant mutation; (b) repeating a consonant; (c) lengthening a vowel; (d) tone change; (e) reduplication; or various
processes of affixation, with (f) a prefix, (g) a suffix, or (h) a circumfix
(combination of prefix and suffix). Each of these processes is illustrated, for
one sample language, in table 2.1.

Table 2.1. *Morphological processes for marking causatives*

Process	Basic verb	Causative form	Language (source)
(a) internal change	*tìkti* 'be suitable'	*táikyti* 'make suitable'	Lithuanian (Senn 1966: 283)
(b) consonant repetition	*xarab* 'go bad'	*xarrab* 'make go bad, ruin'	Gulf Arabic (Holes 1990: 185)
(c) vowel lengthening	*mar* 'die'	*ma:r* 'kill'	Kashmiri (Wali and Koul 1997: 211)
(d) tone change	*nɔ̂* (high falling) 'be awake'	*nɔ̄* (low level) 'awaken, rouse'	Lahu (Matisoff 1973: 33)
(e) reduplication	*bengok* 'shout'	*be-bengok* 'make shout'	Javanese (Suhandano 1994: 64–5)
(f) prefix	*gəbba* 'enter'	*a-gəbba* 'insert'	Amharic (Amberber, ch. 9 below)
(g) suffix	*-kam-* 'die'	*-kam-isa-* 'kill'	K'iche' (Campbell, ch. 7 below)
(h) circumfix	*-č'am-* 'eat'	*-a-č'm-ev-* 'feed (make eat)'	Georgian (Aronson 1991: 260)

2.2   Two verbs in one predicate

A number of languages have 'serial verb constructions'. There are two (or
more) verbs in a clause and they have most or all of the properties of a single
predicate; for example, they take a single specification for TAM, evidentiality
and polarity. A serial verb construction may have causative-type meaning,
e.g. 'they-hit pig it-die' meaning 'they killed the pig by hitting it' in the
Austronesian language Paamese (Crowley 1987: 43; Lord 1974 describes a
similar construction in Yoruba). But since this does not involve a strictly
causative verb (one which has no meaning other than as a marker of a causative construction), it falls outside the scope of the present discussion.

In just a few languages the verbs in a serial verb construction must always
share the same subject. Languages of this type do show instances of a strictly
causative verb in a serial construction. Thus, example (40) in Tariana from

chapter 5 below, by Aikhenvald, is translated as 'How will I get my children to eat?' but is, literally, 'my children (O) how 1sg(A)-make 1sg(A)-eat'. The grammatical structure of a serial verb construction in Tariana requires that 'eat' be marked with the same pronominal prefix (indicating the causer) as 'make', although the interpretation of this sentence is that it is the children (shown here by an NP marked for non-subject function) who do the eating; they are the causee in this causative serial verb construction. (Examples (66–7), from Yimas, in §4 below, illustrate a type of serial verb construction in which there is a single set of pronominal prefixes for the two verbs, which are effectively compounded together.)

In some languages with serial verb constructions, the verbs in constructions of this type generally share the same subject, but there may be a special 'causative' type where the object of the first verb is subject of the second; this applies for 'they-hit pig it-die' in Paamese, mentioned in the first paragraph of this sub-section. I have not found any example of a strictly causative verb in such a construction type (although a wider search may well locate one).

There is another type of analytic causative which, in a quite different manner from serial verb constructions, involves a predicate that includes two verbs. For instance, French has a causative verb *faire*, which appears to make up a single predicate with a following verb. As Comrie (1976: 262–3) points out, the causee NP cannot come between *faire* and the following verb (which must be in infinitive form) but must be placed in oblique function (marked by preposition *à*) as normally happens with morphologically marked causatives. For instance:

(1)   je   ferai   manger les gâteaux à   Jean
        1sgA make+FUT+1sg   eat+INF the cakes   PREP Name
        I shall make Jean eat the cakes

Italian, Spanish and Catalan behave in a similar way.

Kiowa (Kiowa-Tanoan family, south-west USA) may constitute a further example of this type; the transitive verb *ɔ́m* 'do, make' can be compounded with another verb to create a causative, e.g. (Watkins 1984: 153):

(2)   bé-kʰɔ́-ày-ɔ̀m
        2sgA-now-start.off-CAUS+IMP
        Go ahead and run it (the tape recorder)! (lit. make it start off)

2.3   Periphrastic causatives

The third type of causative construction involves two verbs in separate clauses. Generally, the causative verb is in the main clause while the lexical verb is in a complement clause or some other kind of subordinate clause. In Macushi (Carib family, Brazil) the causee maintains its original function in the subordinate clause. Thus, in (3), 'Satan' is marked by ergative case since it is in A function in the main clause (with causative verb *emapu'tî*), and 'Jesus' is also marked by ergative since it is in A function in the subordinate clause (Abbott 1991: 40):

(3)   [imakui'pî kupî Jesus-ya] emapu'tî yonpa-'pî makui-ya teuren
       bad   do Name-ERG CAUS   try-PAST Satan-ERG FRUST
       Satan unsuccessfully tried to make Jesus do bad

Persian also has a periphrastic causative in which the causee retains its function in the 'that' subordinate clause (Mahootian 1997: 225).

Canela-Kraho (Jê family, Brazil) employs a subordinate construction for causatives, but with a difference. The causee maintains its normal function in the subordinate clause and is also marked as the O argument of the causative verb, the causer being the A argument. This language has a pronominal prefix to the verb which marks the O argument in a transitive clause and the S argument in an intransitive (an ergative strategy). Thus in (4) the causee ('me') is marked as O for the causative verb *-to* and as S for the lexical verb *-jõt* 'sleep' (Popjes and Popjes 1986: 143):

(4)   Capi te [i-jõt   na]   i-to
       Name PAST 1sgS-sleep SUBORDINATOR 1sgO-CAUS
       Capi made me sleep

English differs from Macushi, Persian and Canela-Kraho in that a causative verb is followed by a *to*-type complement clause, e.g. *I forced him to go*, *I made him go*, *I allowed her to go*. The causee is the original subject of the subordinate clause (with verb *go*) but is coded with accusative case, as the object of the causative verb.

We thus have three different ways of marking the causee within a periphrastic causative construction. In Macushi it is marked for its function in the subordinate clause, as in (3); in English it is marked for its function in the main clause (the clause with the causative verb); and in Canela-Kraho, shown in (4), it is marked for both of these.

A note is in order at this point concerning causative verbs in English. The convention in present-day linguistics is that a grammatical label should be based on a word of Romance origin – hence 'causative'. From this has arisen the misconception that *cause* is the prototypical causative verb in English. It is not; *make* is. *Cause* is a causative verb but it has a more specialized meaning (implying indirect causation) than *make* and it is much less common. *Make* differs from most other causative verbs, and from most other verbs that take *to* complement clauses, in that it omits the *to* in active clauses, although *to* must be included in the passive. (Compare *The nurse made me swallow it* with *I was made to swallow it* (*by the nurse*). For fuller discussion see Dixon 1991: 192–8, 247–8.) This could be the preliminary stage to a diachronic shift which sees *make* become a 'same predicate' causative verb, like *faire* in French, and then perhaps a compounded causative, like *ɔ́m* in Kiowa.

It is interesting to compare Portuguese with the other Western Romance languages. Portuguese is like English in that the causee can come between the causative verb *fazer* and the lexical verb in infinitive form. Thus (cf. Aissen 1974: 354):

(5)   Eu fiz   José comer   os bolos
        1sg make+PAST+1sg Name eat+INFIN the cakes
        I made José eat the cakes

Compare with (1) in French, which has moved towards a more synthetic structure in which nothing can now intervene between the causative verb *faire* and the following infinitive *manger*. But note that French maintains a structure like (5) for other causative-type verbs such as *laisser* 'let, allow'.

Hale (1997) discusses periphrastic causative constructions in languages of the Misumalpan family (Nicaragua and Honduras). These are unusual in that it is the causative verb which is in the subordinate clause, e.g.:

(6)   yang baka kau ât-ing   wauhdi-da
        1sg child ACC CAUS-DS+1sg fall-PAST+3sg
        I made the child fall

Hale notes that causative constructions have different grammatical properties from other kinds of clause sequences with switch-reference marking. For instance, if the verb 'fall' in (6) is negated this has scope over the whole sentence (i.e. we get 'I did not make the child fall' rather than 'I made the child not fall'). If the verb in the subordinate clause were non-causative, a negator applied to the main verb would have scope only over that clause. This suggests that in a Misumalpan causative construction the two clauses are more tightly integrated than in a normal switch-reference construction. This could be the first stage in a process of grammaticalization, which might lead to a 'two verbs in one predicate' construction, and perhaps from that to the development of causative as a verbal affix.

2.4   Lexical causatives

We can now consider a kind of causative that involves neither a morpho-logical process nor separate causative verbs – lexical causatives. These are of two kinds: (a) when a single lexeme can be used in either a causative or a non-causative function; and (b) when there are two unrelated forms, that appear to be in causative relation.

(a) One lexeme

In some languages every verb is either strictly transitive (appearing only in transitive clauses) or strictly intransitive (appearing only in intransitive clauses). Other languages have a number of ambitransitive (or 'labile') verbs that can occur in either clause type. There are two varieties of ambitransitives:

(i)   S = A, e.g. *knit* in English, as in *Mary* (S) *is knitting*, and *Mary* (A) *is knitting a scarf* (O).

(ii)   S = O, e.g. *trip* and *spill* in English, as in *John* (S) *tripped* and *Mary* (A) *tripped John* (O); and in *John* (A) *spilled the milk* (O) and *The milk* (S) *spilled*.

Now for some S = O verbs native speakers' intuitions are that the lexeme is primarily transitive and only secondarily intransitive; this applies to *spill*, *smash* and *extend*, among other verbs. For other S = O verbs the intransitive sense is considered to be primary, e.g. *trip*, *explode*, *melt*, *dissolve*, *walk* and *march* (see Dixon 1991: 291–3). For the latter set it is plausible to suggest that we have a causative relationship.

That is, verbs like *trip*, *dissolve* and *march* are basically intransitive but can be used in a transitive clause and then take on a causative meaning, similar to that marked by a morphological process or by a periphrastic verb in other languages.

Examples similar to those just given for English are provided for Greek by Joseph and Philippaki-Warburton (1987: 170). For the North American language Tunica, Haas (1941: 46) states that any non-causative intransitive stem may become causative through being inflected like a transitive verb. For instance 'we find that *ha'pa* has the function of an intransitive stem meaning "to stop, cease" when it undergoes non-causative inflection but assumes the function of a transitive stem meaning "to cause . . . to stop, cease" when it undergoes causative inflection'. Li and Thompson (1976: 478) list a number of verbs of this type in Classical Chinese.

Fijian (Austronesian family) has a slightly different system. Here about 80 per cent of verb roots can be used either transitively (with a transitive suffix) or intransitively (lacking the suffix). That is, most verbs are ambitransitive, but with the presence or absence of a suffix marking their transitivity value. Just over half are of type S = A (e.g. *laʔo* 'go', *laʔo-va* 'go for') with the remainder being of type S = O (e.g. *loʔi* 'be bent', *loʔi-va* 'bend'). The second set could be regarded as a type of causative patterning. See the discussion under parameter 8 in §4 below (and Dixon 1988: 45, 204–14). Note that other Oceanic languages have similar properties.

(b) Two lexemes
In quite a number of languages one can assemble pairs of lexemes (with quite different forms), one intransitive and the other appearing to be a causative correspondent of it.

Thus, for Yimas (Lower Sepik family, Papuan region), Foley (1991: 289) lists a number of lexical pairs, including the following:

(7)	intransitive		transitive	
	mal-	'die'	tu-	'kill'
	awa-	'burn'	ampu-	'burn'
	aypu-	'lie down'	tɨ-	'lay down'

In Dyirbal (Australian) lexical pairs of this type include:

(8)	intransitive		transitive	
	mayi-	'come out'	bundi-	'take out'
	gaynyja-	'break'	bana-	'break'
	jana-	'stand'	jarra-	'put standing'

And in English we get:

(9)	intransitive/copula	transitive
	be dead	kill
	come out	take out
	lie	lay

It is relevant to enquire what the criteria are for linking distinct lexemes in this way. A major one is semantic, as can be seen by translation between languages. In English we have a single lexeme *burn*, with intransitive and causative senses, e.g. *The grass burned* and *I burned the grass*. Yimas would use *awa-* in translation of the first sentence and *ampu-* in translation of the second.

In Dyirbal there is a further criterion. The verbs given in (8) are from the everyday speech style, called Guwal. There is also a 'mother-in-law' speech style, Dyalnguy, used in the presence of taboo relatives. Dyalnguy has fewer lexemes than Guwal. In the case of two Guwal verbs that have the same meaning but just differ in transitivity, Dyalnguy simply has a transitive verb, which corresponds to the transitive member of the Guwal pair, with an intransitivizing derivational suffix *-rri-* used for the correspondent of the intransitive member. Thus, the verbs in (8) have Dyalnguy correspondents as follows (Dixon 1972: 297; 1982: 83):

(10)		everyday style (Guwal)	mother-in-law style (Dyalnguy)	
(a)	transitive	bundi-	yilwu-	'take out'
	intransitive	mayi-	yilwu-rri-	'come out'
(b)	transitive	bana-	yuwa-	'break'
	intransitive	gaynyja-	yuwa-rri-	'break'
(c)	transitive	jarra-	dinda-	'put standing'
	intransitive	jana-	dinda-rri-	'stand'

The fact that Dyalnguy uses a single verbal form for each pair of verbs in Guwal indicates that they do have the same meaning, and differ just in transitivity.

A further criterion comes from observation of how language is used; we can here quote an example from English. On 12 February 1996, in Australia, there was a televised pre-election debate between the Prime Minister, Paul Keating, and the Leader of the Opposition, John Howard (a few weeks later Howard won the election and became Prime Minister). Keating accused Howard of using his party's numbers in the upper house to kill a bill that would have generated more revenue. Howard denied that he had wanted to kill it. Addressing the chairman and television viewers, Keating responded:

(11)   He didn't want to kill it, he only wanted to make it dead

It is clear that Keating used *make dead* as a paraphrase of *kill*; that is, as having the same meaning.

We saw in §2.3 the mistaken idea that the main causative verb in English is *cause*. In the 1960s it was suggested that, for instance, *kill* can be derived from *cause to die*. Fodor (1970) presented a number of arguments against this analysis, e.g. one can say *John caused Bill to die on Sunday by stabbing him on Saturday* but not **John killed Bill on Sunday by stabbing him on Saturday*. This is because *cause* has a rather special meaning, referring to indirect causation which can involve a time lapse. As demonstrated by Paul Keating, the meaning of *kill* is the same as that of the unmarked causative verb *make* plus *be dead*. All of the difficulties experienced with *cause to die* are eliminated if *make dead* is used instead.

2.5   *Exchanging auxiliaries*

In chapter 10 of this volume, Reid describes how in Ngan'gityemerri (Australian) a predicate generally includes a lexical verb and an auxiliary, each of which has its own transitivity value. An intransitive verb will prototypically be used with an intransitive auxiliary. However, it can be used with a transitive auxiliary, which then has causative effect. Thus the verb 'slip' plus the 'go' auxiliary is used to describe a simple act of slipping. When the verb 'slip' is used with the transitive auxiliary 'move', the predicate has the meaning 'make slip' – see (16) and (21) in chapter 10. This is not a prototypical causative since there is no derivation involved. Rather, Ngan'gityemerri employs a causative strategy, which is functionally and semantically equivalent to causative derivations in other languages.

Other Australian languages with complex predicates – from the same geographical area as Ngan'gityemerri – show a similar mechanism for forming causatives; for instance, Mangarayi (Merlan 1982: 132–4). As a later stage of development, in a further group of Australian languages what was a causative auxiliary has become a causative derivational suffix (Dixon, forthcoming).

3   Syntax

The various varieties of causatives, according to the way in which they are marked, have different syntactic possibilities.

The reported examples of forming causatives by exchanging auxiliaries apply just to intransitive verbs. For lexical causatives involving two forms (such as *be dead / kill* in English or *mal-/tu-* in Yimas) the non-causative member is always intransitive. It appears that this mechanism is also limited to providing causatives of intransitives.

A similar restriction is likely to apply for lexical causatives involving a single form which can be used in two syntactic frames, such as English *trip*, whose basic function is in an intransitive clause, e.g. *John* (S) *tripped*, but which may also be used – with causative function – in a transitive clause, e.g. *Mary* (causer: A) *tripped John*.

The applicability of this kind of causative construction – in a language like English, where syntactic function is shown by place in constituent order – is limited by the surface structure possibilities available. Alongside the intransitive *John tripped* and its causative counterpart *Mary tripped John*, it is not possible to construct a causative counterpart for a transitive clause, e.g. *John ate the apple*. We cannot say **Mary John ate the apple* or **Mary ate John* *the apple*, simply because no verb in English can be preceded by two independent NPs, and *eat* cannot be followed by two NPs.

There is, however, one circumstance where English does allow a causative of a transitive simply by change in constituent order. There is a class of Secondary Verbs (Dixon 1991: 90–1, 172–9) which simply provide semantic modification but add no semantic role to the clause to which they are attached, e.g. *start*, as in *The maid started cleaning the bathroom at ten o'clock*. Here we can form a causative, with the causer (the new A) coming before *start* and the causee (the original A) coming between *start* and the following verb, e.g. *Mother started the maid cleaning the bathroom at ten o'clock*. (There is fuller discussion in Dixon 1991: 296–7.)

Periphrastic causatives generally apply to any intransitive or transitive (including ditransitive) verb. In §2.3 it was mentioned that in some languages the causee is the surface O of the transitive verb, while in others it still maintains its original function with respect to the lexical verb, and in some it may be marked for both functions. The other arguments of the lexical verb are retained, e.g. in English *He gave the bone to the dog*, and *Mary made him give the bone to the dog*.

Periphrastic causatives may sometimes also apply to copula clauses. They do in English, but here the copula verb *be* can be omitted, e.g. *John was jealous* and the causative *Mary made John jealous* (as a preferred alternative to *Mary made John be jealous*).

There is only a little information on languages that have serial causative constructions, with two verbs in one predicate. In Tariana this causative mechanism can apply to verbs of any transitivity (but not to a copula). Consider first the simple ditransitive clause in (12).

(12)   phia kalisi$_o$ Yuse isiu pi-kalite-de
        2sgA story José for 2sgA-tell-FUT
        You will tell a story to José

Here *kalisi* 'story' is in O function (it can become S within a derived passive) and the name *Yuse* is marked by postposition *isiu*. Now consider the serial causative construction in (13).

(13)   nuha pina kalisi Yuse isiu [nu-a-de   nu-kalite-de]
        1sgA 2sgO story José for 1sgA-CAUS-FUT 1sgA-tell-FUT
        I will make you tell a story to José

The causer ('I') is now in A function and is marked by prefix *nu-* on both verbs. Both *pina* 'you' and *kalisi* 'story' have the form of an O argument;

since a serial verb construction in Tariana cannot be passivized there is no criterion for deciding which of *pina* and *kalisi* (if either) is the 'true object' (as there is a criterion of this kind for some morphological causatives – see the discussion of type (iii) in §3.2). Note that constituent order is free in Tariana, and *nu-a-de nu-kalite-de* in (13) make up one constituent; these two words must occur together in this order. (Information on Tariana from Alexandra Aikhenvald, p.c.)

It is possible that causative serial verb constructions have more limited applicability in other languages in which they occur, perhaps not applying to transitive or not to ditransitive verbs. Further information is needed, on other languages that have the construction and employ an abstract causative verb.

Morphological causatives are syntactically varied. In some languages they apply only to intransitives, in others only to intransitives and simple transitives (but not ditransitives), and in others to all verbs. (Examples are given in §4, §3.3 and §3.2 below.)

Hetzron (1976: 383) notes that, in Hungarian, impersonal verbs (of zero valency) such as *fagy* '[it] freezes' and *esik* '[it] rains' 'cannot be causativized for the simple reason that they have no subject that could become a causee'. However, causatives of impersonal verbs are possible in Nivkh (or Gilyak, isolate, north-east Russia; Nedjalkov, Otaina and Xolodovič 1995: 78–9).

It is not usual for a morphological causative to apply to a copula verb, but this does sometimes happen. Example (14) gives a plain copula clause in Petats (Austronesian, Papua New Guinea) and (15) the causative version (information from Evelyn Gitey, via Alexandra Aikhenvald).

(14) u   taul e   ka-nou   taru   lekleki-ta-guan
      ART towel ASP COPULA-3sg+PRES on+ART shoulder-POSS-1sg
      There is a towel on my shoulder (lit. A towel is on my shoulder)

(15) eyaw e   ha-ka-nou   u   taul taru   lekleki-ta-guan
      3sgA ASP CAUS-COPULA-3sg+PRES ART towel on+ART shoulder-POSS-1sg
      He put a towel on my shoulder

Other languages in which a morphological causative can apply to a copula include Hebrew (Alcalay 1974: 519), Turkan (Nilo-Saharan; Gerrit Dimmendaal, p.c.), Qiang (Tibeto-Burman; LaPolla 1996: 114) and Ainu (isolate, Japan/ Russia; Tamura 1988: 69).

Many languages do not allow a transitive verb to be directly causativized. One strategy is to first detransitivize the verb, and then apply the causative derivation. Examples (16–19) are from Paumarí (Arawá family, Brazil; Chapman and Derbyshire 1991: 185–6):

(16)   bi-noki-hi   ida   gora
        3sg-see-THEME ART(F) house(F)
        She saw the house

(17)   noki-a-hi   ida   gora
        see-DETR-THEME ART(F) house(F)
        The house is visible

(18)   bi-na-noki-a-hi   ida   gora
        3sg-CAUS-see-DETR-THEME ART(F) house(F)
        He made the house become visible

(19)   ho-ra   na-noki-a-hi-vini   hi-hi   ida   gora
        1sg-ACC CAUS-see-DETR-BEN-DEP AUX-THEME ART(F) house(F)
        He showed me the house (lit. He made the house become visible to me)

Sentence (16) is a straightforward transitive with root *noki-* 'see'. In (17) the detransitivizing suffix *-a-* has been added, giving *noki-a-* with the O argument of (16) becoming S of (17) and the original A dropping out. In (18), causative prefix *na-* is added, giving *na-noki-a-* with the S of (17) becoming O of (18), and a causer brought in as A. In (19) a further derivational suffix is added, the benefactive applicative *-hi-* (a different suffix from *-hi* 'theme'), producing verb stem *na-noki-a-hi-*. This brings a beneficiary (here 'me') into O function with the original O NP from (18), 'house', becoming second object. In summary:

		she	house	he	me
(16)	transitive	A	O		
(17)	add detransitivizer, becomes intransitive		S		
(18)	add causative, becomes transitive		O	A	
(19)	add benefactive, becomes ditransitive		2nd O	A	O

Other languages in which a transitive verb must be made intransitive before a causative suffix can be added include Bandjalang (Australian; Crowley 1978: 87–8) where an antipassive derivation must first apply, and Southern Tiwa (Kiowan–Tanoan family; B.J. Allen, Gardiner and Frantz 1984) where a noun in O function must be incorporated into the transitive verb, producing an intransitive stem, which then accepts the causative suffix. Further examples are mentioned in Baker (1988: 193–8) and Song (1996: 179–81).

The discussion that follows, in §§3.1 – 3.3, relates to intransitive and transitive clauses whose arguments receive what is the canonical case marking for that language. In some languages there is a small class of verbs (typically describing physiological states) which take non-canonical marking; the subject may receive dative or genitive inflection (instead of the canonical nominative or ergative). In Kannada (Dravidian) a dative-marked subject retains its marking when the clause is made transitive, e.g. 'I-DAT got.a.headache', and 'you-NOM (causer) I-DAT got.a.headache+CAUS' ('you made me get a headache') (Sridhar 1979: 111; 1990: 219). Note that in this language there is difficulty in deciding on the transitivity status of both non-causative and causative clauses with a dative subject.

Other South Asian languages also have a small class of verbs with non-canonically marked subject. In Bengali (Indo-European) there is a genitive-marked subject with verbs like 'have a headache' and 'feel good', but these cannot be causativized (Masayuki Onishi, p.c.). In Marathi (Indo-European) the causee in a causative construction must be in control of the activity; for this reason no causative is possible for dative-subject verbs, such as 'get angry', since these refer to involuntary states (Pandharipande 1997: 406).

3.1   Of intransitives

Virtually every causative mechanism applies to intransitive verbs (quite a few apply only to intransitives). In every language we get the original S becoming O of the causative construction, i.e.:

(20)   CAUSATIVE OF INTRANSITIVE
      underlying clause (intransitive)   S
                                          |
      causative construction (transitive)   causer: A O

While every language has the schema shown in (20), a number also have an alternative marking for the original S, which carries a semantic difference.

(a) Japanese allows the original S either to be in O function, marked by accusative postposition *o*, or to be marked by dative postposition *ni*. The dative alternative indicates that the causee (the original S) does it willingly ('let do'), while the accusative alternative indicates that the causee's intentions were ignored by the causer ('make do'). See (53–5) in §4 below.

(b) In Hungarian the original S can be marked as O, by accusative case, indicating that the causer acts directly, e.g. 'The nurse (causer: A) walked him (original S: accusative) for an hour every day', where the nurse accompanied him on the walk. Or, for some verbs, it can be marked by instrumental case, implying that the causer acted indirectly, e.g. 'The doctor (causer: A) had him (original S: instrumental) walk for an hour each day', where the doctor just told him to do so. (Hetzron 1976: 394, and see the discussion of parameter 6 in §4 below.) Sumbatova (1993: 259–60) describes a similar alternation in Svan (Kartvelian).

Nivkh constitutes a partial exception to schema (20). In this language a causee (whether originally S or A) is marked by a special 'causee case suffix', *-ax*, if it is animate; if inanimate it receives zero marking (like an O argument). See (a) under (i) in §3.2.

There can be another sort of variation on the prototypical schema for causatives of intransitives shown in (20). A number of languages have a split-S system, where some intransitive verbs have their S argument marked like the A of a transitive (S_a) and other intransitive verbs have S marked like O (S_o). For Wayana (Carib family, Brazil), in the causative of an S_o-type intransitive, the original S_o goes into O function. In the causative of a transitive, the original O stays as is and the original A (the causee) is marked by dative suffix *-ya*. In the causative of an S_a-type intransitive, the causer is A and the original S_a is now marked by dative *-ya*, just like the original A in the causative of a transitive (Tavares 1995).

For the great majority of languages each causative construction is syntactically similar to an existing non-causative clause type. Only very occasionally does a causative form a new construction type, not found elsewhere in the grammar. This does occur in Tariana, a split-S language (Aikhenvald, chapter 5 in this volume). Transitive and S_a-type intransitive verbs take a pronominal prefix marking the A or S_a argument while S_o-type intransitives have no prefix. Causatives of S_a-type intransitives are normal transitive clauses with a prefix marking A (the causer).

Just S_o-type intransitives in Tariana have two alternative causative constructions: either (a) with a prefix (for the causer, in A function), indicating that the causer achieved the result intentionally (e.g. 'he frightened them, on purpose'); or (b) with no prefix (the causer being shown just by an NP), indicating that the result was obtained unintentionally (e.g. 'the dog's barking made me frightened' when the dog didn't mean to frighten me). See (22–7) in chapter 5 below. In Tariana a transitive clause with no pronominal prefix is a special construction type, found only with an 'unintentional' causative of an S_o-type intransitive.

3.2 Of transitives

This section provides a general discussion of the syntax of morphological causatives of transitive verbs (including ditransitives as a subclass). §3.3 then looks in more detail at ditransitives.

It is almost always the case that a causative adds an argument; that is, it increases the valency of the verb by one. Mishmi (Bodic branch of Tibeto-Burman, north-east India) is noteworthy in that the causative of a transitive appears to have at most two arguments. There are in fact two causative suffixes: with *-bo* just the causee (not the causer) is stated and with *-syig* just the causer (not the causee) is stated. Thus (Sastry 1984: 155–6):

(21)   hã̃   tapẽ thá-de-bo
        1sg+NOM rice eat-TENSE-CAUS$_1$
        I (causee) was made to eat rice (by someone – unstated but implied causer)

(22)   hã̃   tapẽ thá-syig-a
        1sg+NOM rice eat-CAUS$_2$-TENSE
        I (causer) made (someone – unstated but implied causee) eat rice

If one wishes to specify both causer and causee, then the verb must be stated twice, once with each of the causative suffixes, e.g.:

(23)   hã̃   thá-syig-a,   nyú   thá-de-bo
        1sg+NOM eat-CAUS$_2$-TENSE 2sg+NOM eat-TENSE-CAUS$_1$
        I made you eat

(The source grammar does not say how the original O argument, 'rice', would be specified in (23).)

Mishmi is highly unusual. In virtually every other language all the original arguments may be stated, together with the new argument, the causer. As already described, the causative of an intransitive is a straightforward matter, with the causer coming in as A and, in almost every instance, the original S becoming O. The causative of a transitive is often less straightforward, and shows more variation.

A transitive clause already has two core arguments, in A and O functions. The causer is always placed in A function (I know of no putative causative that could be an exception to this). Now in a periphrastic causative construction, where there are two clauses involved, there is no difficulty in making provision for all the arguments. As shown in §2.3, the causee can be marked as O of the causative verb or still as A of the lexical verb, or both at once; the other arguments of the lexical verb remain unchanged.

A morphological causative of a transitive verb is itself a transitive clause. The question now is: what happens to the A and O arguments of the original clause? There are five main possibilities, shown in (24).

(24)   CAUSATIVE OF TRANSITIVE

type	causer	original A (causee)	original O
(i)	A	special marking	O
(ii)	A	retains A-marking	O
(iii)	A	has O-marking	has O-marking
(iv)	A	O	non-core
(v)	A	non-core	O

In type (i) there is a special marking, used just for the causee in a causative construction. In (ii) both causer and original A receive A-marking. In (iii) the original A and the original O both receive O-marking. In (iv) the original A becomes O, and the original O now takes non-core marking. And in (v) the original O remains as is, while the original A takes peripheral marking.

As already mentioned, a causative generally takes on the form of an already-existing construction type. It may mirror alternations in a corresponding non-causative construction. For instance, in Yup'ik the verb 'give' has two possible syntactic frames – with the gift as O and the recipient in non-core function, or vice versa. In similar fashion, the causative of a transitive has two possible frames – with the original A as new O and the original O as a non-core argument, type (iv), or vice versa, type (v). See chapter 3 below by Mithun.

The five possibilities will now be discussed in turn.

Type (i) – special marking for causee

(a) Nivkh has no case marking for S, A, O or indirect object. However, there is a special case suffix -*ax*, which is used just to mark an animate causee (whether original A or S) in a causative construction. (An inanimate causee takes no marking.) The suffix -*ax* is generally optional but it is obligatory when there are already three unmarked NPs as in (26), the causative counterpart of the ditransitive clause in (25) (Nedjalkov, Otaina and Xolodovič 1995: 78; Comrie 1976: 267, 274):

(25)   ōla   lep   pʰnanak   xim-d'
       child bread his.older.sister give-FINITE
       The child gave the bread to his older sister

(26)   ətək   ōla-ax   lep   pʰnanak   xim-gu-d'
       father child-CAUSEE bread his.older.sister give-CAUS-FINITE
       The father made/let the child give the bread to his older sister

(b) The causative of a transitive in Telugu (Dravidian) has the original O remaining as is with the original A (the causee) being followed by a special marker, *ceeta*. This is in fact the instrumental case form of the noun *ceeyi* 'hand' (lit. 'with the hand') but here functions as a postposition marking the causee argument in the causative of a transitive. Note that for the causative of an intransitive the original S can either be placed in accusative case or can be marked by *ceeta*; there is a semantic difference, the first alternative indicating direct and the second indicating indirect causative – see 6 in §4 below (Krishnamurti and Gwynn 1985: 202, and Bh. Krishnamurti, p.c.).

Type (ii) – causee retains A-marking

(a) In Kabardian (North-west Caucasian), a language with an ergative case system, the causee retains its case marking. Thus the S of an intransitive clause (marked by absolutive case) becomes O in the corresponding causative (still marked by absolutive). In the causative of a transitive the causer takes ergative inflection and the causee (original A) retains its ergative inflection (Abitov *et al.* 1957: 126).

(b) In another ergative language, Trumai (isolate, Upper Xingu region, Brazil) we encounter a similar situation. For example (Guirardello 1999):

(27)   Alaweru-k hai-ts   axos   disi-ka
       Name-ERG 1sg-ERG child+ABS beat-CAUS
       Alaweru made me beat the child

Note that the causer and the causee (original A) are both marked by an ergative enclitic (this has the form *-ts* after the 1sg pronoun and *-(e/a)k* elsewhere); they are distinguished by their order in the clause, causer before causee.

Kabardian and Trumai each have two NPs in ergative case, in the causative of a transitive. Abitov *et al.* (1957: 126) state that in Kabardian the ergative-marked causer is in A function while the ergative-marked causee is now an 'oblique agent' (although the term is not further explained). Further investigation is required to tell whether this also applies for Trumai.

Qiang (Tibeto-Burman family, China) provides a fascinating and unusual example in which causer and causee, in the causative of a transitive, share subject properties. In a plain transitive clause the verb bears a suffix which marks person and number of A. The A NP can take 'agentive marker' *-wu* but this is normally only included when there is marked constituent order (e.g. OAV instead of the normal AOV), or to emphasize the agentivity of the actor. In the causative of an intransitive the causer (A) does not take agentive marker *-wu* unless it is inanimate, e.g. 'The wind (marked by *-wu*) knocked me down.' Consider now the causative of a transitive:

(28)   qa the:-wu pəitsə-e-ze zə-pə̂-ʒa
       1sg 3sg-AG cup-one-CL DIRECTION-buy-CAUS+1sg
       I made him/her buy a cup

Here the pronominal suffix to the verb cross-references the causer; however, the causer NP never, in the material collected, takes agentive marker *-wu*. The causee (the original A) generally takes *-wu*. That is, causer retains one subject property, cross-referencing on the verb, while causee takes over the other subject property, marking by *-wu* (LaPolla 1996: 66, 112–13).[2]

Type (iii) – original A takes on O-marking, original O retains O-marking
There are a number of languages in which the original A (the causee) takes on the marking of an O in a causative construction, while the original O appears to retain its marking. That is, it seems on the surface that we have two Os.

Further investigation shows that, for most of these languages, only one of the arguments has the full properties of an O, e.g. it can be passivized (this could be called the 'full O') while the other NP that is marked like an O lacks these properties (it could be called a 'second object'). It is generally the original A which is the full O while the original O has become the second object (making these ostensively type (iii) languages perhaps a special case of type (iv), where A becomes O and the original O moves out of the core).

In Hebrew there are three syntactic possibilities for the causative of a transitive: type (iv), original A becomes O and original O is marked by locative; type (v), original O stays as is and original A is marked by dative; and type (iii), both original A and original O are marked by the accusative preposition *et*. An example of the third alternative is (Cole 1976: 99):

(29)   hirkadə-ti   [et   ha-talmid-im] [et   ha-rikud   ha-xadaš]
       dance+CAUS+PAST-1sg ACC ART-student-pl ACC ART-dance ART-new
       I made the students dance the new dance

---

[2] It would be interesting to investigate a causative of a transitive where the causer is inanimate (e.g. 'The wind made me drop the cup'), to see whether in this instance *-wu* could go on the causer; and indeed whether *-wu* would then be possible on both causer and causee. Randy LaPolla has promised to check this possibility on his next field trip.

Here the causee NP, 'the students', can passivize and is thus identified as the full O, while 'the new dance' cannot passivize and is identified as second object.

Similar conclusions apply for morphological causatives in Tariana (Aikhenvald, chapter 5 of this volume) and in Imbabura Quechua (Cole 1982: 136–7). The only report we have of the original O staying as full O and the original A taking on O-marking but being a second object is Kozinsky and Polinsky's (1993) account of the *bi*-verbal causative in Dutch, which they consider to constitute a single predicate.

Amharic (Semitic, Ethiopia) has an interesting set of possibilities. In this language an NP in O function can take accusative marking only if it is definite. As Amberber shows in chapter 9 of this volume, there are two basic possibilities for the causative of a transitive clause:

(i) Original A becomes O; it must be definite, and takes accusative marking. The original O can be omitted but it may be retained and is then generally indefinite (it cannot take accusative marking). The original A is plainly a full O, with the original O becoming second object. Thus we can have, in a simple transitive clause, either 'He cut the meat (definite, accusative)' or 'He cut some meat (indefinite, no marking)'. Only the second of these (that in which the O is indefinite) is likely to be causativized.

(ii) If the original O is inherently definite (e.g. a proper noun) it stays as is, in which case the original A (the causee) is generally omitted (but its identity may be inferable from the context).

There are a number of languages where original A takes on O-marking and original O retains O-marking and it is, on the information available, impossible to distinguish between the two objects. In Oromo (Cushitic branch of Afroasiatic family, Ethiopia; Owens 1985: 172–81), passive can apply to the O NP in a plain transitive or in the causative of an intransitive but to neither of the O-marked NPs in the causative of a transitive. In Yagua (Peru; Payne and Payne 1990: 284–7), either or both of the O-marked arguments can be specific and referred to by a clitic; there seems to be no criterial way of deciding between them. In Gamo (Omotic, Ethiopia; Eva 1990: 395) the two O-marked NPs can occur in either order and no criteria are given for distinguishing between them. Martin (chapter 12 of this book) describes how in the causative of a transitive clause in Creek, both original A and original O bear the non-subject marker -*n*. (Comrie 1975: 14–17 and Kozinsky and Polinsky

1993: 181 provide further information on languages that have 'two objects' in the causative of a transitive clause.)

The causative of a transitive is a kind of ditransitive clause. In many languages it has essentially the same syntax as a non-causative ditransitive (involving a verb like 'give' or 'show' or 'tell'). It is relevant to enquire whether languages with 'two objects' in the causative of a transitive also have 'two objects' in a regular ditransitive, that is, with both 'gift' and 're-cipient' marked as object for a verb of giving, etc. It appears that this does apply in the case of Yagua, but not for most of the other languages surveyed here. There is different marking for object and indirect object of an underived ditransitive verb in Hebrew, Imbabura Quechua, Amharic, Oromo and Gamo (information is lacking on the marking in simple ditransitive clauses in Creek). It appears that in these languages 'double object' is a characteristic just of the causative-of-a-transitive construction.

Type (iv) – original A becomes new O, original O moves out of the core
In this variety of morphological causative of a transitive verb each of the arguments shifts its function, the original A (the causee) taking on O function within the causative construction and the original O moving out of the core into a peripheral function.

In Javanese, core syntactic relations are shown by the constituent order AVO, SV (very like English). In a ditransitive clause the indirect object (e.g. the recipient in an activity of giving) is marked by the dative preposition *marang*. Example (30) shows a simple transitive clause and (31) its causative counterpart, which has the structure of a normal ditransitive, with original A becoming O (shown by its positioning immediately after the verb) and ori-ginal O now taking dative preposition *marang* (Suhandano 1994: 67).

(30)   asu-ne   nguyak Bambang
       dog-DEF chase   Name
       The dog chased Bambang

(31)   Sri   nguyak-ake asu-ne   marang Bambang
       name chase-CAUS dog-DEF DAT   Name
       Sri got the dog to chase Bambang

There is a similar causative mechanism, also involving constituent order, in Tolai, another Austronesian language (Papua New Guinea; Mosel 1984: 154–5).

Swahili (Bantu, East Africa) has similar syntax. Here the fact that the original A takes on O function in the causative construction is shown by its being cross-referenced by O pronominals in the verb, while the original O loses its cross-referencing (Vitale 1981: 155–6). Jarawara (Arawá family, Brazil) is like Swahili in having A and O arguments expressed by bound pronominals within the predicate. It has a general postposition *jaa* which marks any non-core argument. In the causative of a transitive the original A is now cross-referenced as O while the original O loses its cross-referencing and is marked by *jaa* (see Dixon and Aikhenvald 1997: 83, and Dixon and Vogel, forthcoming).

Kammu (Austroasiatic, Laos; Svantesson 1983: 103–5) is another language with this kind of causative construction. Here the original O is often omitted but can be included for some verbs, marked by the instrumental preposition. Compare the plain transitive in (32) with its causative counterpart in (33).

(32)   [kɔɔn tɛɛk] màh któŋ
        child Name eat egg
        Tɛɛk's children eat eggs

(33)   tɛɛk pń-màh [kɔɔn tèe] [yʌʌ któŋ]
        Name CAUS-eat child REFL INST egg
        Tɛɛk gave his children eggs to eat (lit. Tɛɛk made his children eat eggs)

Interestingly, 'give' is expressed in Kammu as the causative of 'have', with the recipient being in O function and the gift marked by the instrumental preposition. Compare (32–3) with:

(34)   nàa Ɂàh tráak
        she have buffalo
        She has a buffalo

(35)   kə̀ə pń-Ɂàh   nàa [yʌʌ tráak]
        he CAUSE-have she INST buffalo
        He gave her a buffalo

Babungo (Grassfields Bantu, Cameroon; Schaub 1985: 211) is like Kammu in that the original O is generally omitted but can be included as an optional adverbial, marked by preposition *nə̀* 'with'. Baker (1988: 164–6, quoting Gibson 1980 and Trithart 1977) mentions Chamorro (Austronesian) and some dialects of Chichewa (Bantu) as also being of type (iv). And, as mentioned under type (iii), those languages in which original A becomes full O and the original O, which still retains object-marking, is syntactically a 'second object' are also essentially of this type. See, in addition, the discussion of Awa Pit in §3.3.

Type (v) – original O stays as O, original A moves out of the core
There are two subtypes here: (a) where the original A goes into the first empty slot on a hierarchy of clausal functions; (b) where the original A goes into a fixed function. The first has been made much of in the literature but is in fact rather rare.

(a) Marking of original A is motivated by a hierarchy. In an important and pioneering paper, Comrie (1975) brought into play a hierarchy that had already been suggested to explain the syntax of relative clauses (in work published as Keenan and Comrie 1977):

(36)   Comrie's hierarchy
        subject – direct object – indirect object – oblique – genitive – object of comparison

He suggested that in one group of languages the causee goes into the first available slot in the hierarchy. For example, in French we get causatives of intransitive, transitive and ditransitive clauses as:

(37)   je   ferai   courir   Jean
        1sg+NOM make+FUT+1sg run+INF Name
        I shall make Jean run

(38)   je   ferai   manger les gâteaux à   Jean
        1sg+NOM make+FUT+1sg eat+INF the cakes   PREP Name
        I shall make Jean eat the cakes

(39)   je   ferai   écrire   une lettre au   directeur
        1sg+NOM make+FUT+1sg write+INF a letter   PREP+ART headmaster
        par   Jean
        PREP Name
        I shall make Jean write a letter to the headmaster

The causee, 'Jean', fills the O slot in (37). In (38) the O slot is already filled and it goes into the indirect object slot, marked by preposition *à* 'to'. In (39) both O and indirect object slots are filled so the causee goes into an oblique slot, marked by preposition *par* 'by'.

Comrie refers to this as the 'paradigm case' (1975: 8; 1976: 263–4) or 'the norm' (1989: 174–83) or 'a general tendency' (1985: 342). These labels have been repeated by other writers, e.g. Palmer (1994: 218) uses 'paradigm case'. In fact this pattern is rather rare. It is found in Western Romance languages such as French and Italian. Comrie quotes Turkish as a further example, but the literature on this language gives mixed information. For instance, Kornfilt (1997: 331–2) states that the causee goes into dative case in the causative of both simple transitive and ditransitive clauses (the causative of a ditransitive then having two dative NPs). There may be a few other languages of type (v-a) but they are greatly outnumbered by those of type (v-b). When we also take into account types (i–iv), it will be seen that there is no justification for attaching special importance to the pattern illustrated for French in (37–9).

(b) Original A is assigned a fixed non-core function (irrespective of whether the underlying clause is simple transitive or ditransitive). The possibilities here include:

(i)   DATIVE. This is the mechanism in Sanuma (Yanomami family, Brazil/Venezuela; Borgman 1990: 47–51), Apalai (Carib family, Brazil; Koehn and Koehn 1986: 49–51), Kamaiurá (Tupí-Guaraní branch of Tupí family, Brazil; Seki, forthcoming), Turkish (Kornfilt 1997: 331–2) and Japanese. One of the causative strategies in Hebrew involves original A being marked by dative preposition.

Comrie (1976: 272) mentions this as an alternative strategy in French. That is, most native speakers can say *Je ferai écrire à Jean une lettre au directeur* as an alternative to (39), although he states that the preferred construction type, acceptable to all speakers, is that shown in (39).

We find a variant of this pattern in Sinhalese (Indo-European) where the original A of a simple transitive or ditransitive verb goes into dative case, but this must be followed by the postposition *kiəla* (Gair 1970: 68–70). (We could regard this as a language of type (i), with dative-plus-*kiəla* constituting 'special marking' of original A.)

All of these languages allow a clause to include two dative NPs – the original dative of the ditransitive verb, plus the original O.

(ii) INSTRUMENTAL. Examples here include Hungarian (Kenesei, Vago and Fenyvesi 1998: 186–8), Kannada (Sridhar 1990: 217–19), Punjabi (Bhatia 1993: 238–40) and Marathi (Pandharipande 1997: 401–3).

(iii) LOCATIVE. For example, in Daghestanian languages (Hewitt 1983).

(iv) ALLATIVE. For example, in West Greenlandic Eskimo (Fortescue 1984: 268–9).

(v)   ADESSIVE. For example, the morphological causative in Finnish. Interestingly, the original A of the periphrastic causative in Finnish takes the genitive suffix (Sulkala and Karjalainen 1992: 294–6).

(vi) POSS:ESSIVE. Comrie (chapter 11 in this volume) states that in Tsez (North-east Caucasian) the original A is marked with the poss:essive case suffix, and this applies whether A was originally marked by lative case (with verbs like 'see' and 'find') or by ergative case (with other verbs).

3.3   *Of ditransitives*

The surface syntactic constraints of a language may limit the syntactic – and also semantic – possibilities for causative constructions. It was mentioned in §3.1 that, in the causative of an intransitive, Japanese allows the original S to be marked by either dative or accusative postposition, indicating that the causee performed the action willingly (dative) or that the causer ignored the causee's intentions (accusative). However, Japanese does not allow two accusative-marked arguments in a clause. Thus, in the causative of a transitive (including ditransitive), since there is already an O NP, the original A (the causee) must take dative marking. The syntactic alternation for intransitives is not available for transitives, and with it is lost the possibility of a semantic alternation.

Syntactic constraints are especially evident when we look in detail at causatives of ditransitive clauses, which in underlying form have A, O and indirect object (generally marked by dative case or adposition). As noted under (v-b) in §3.2, there are some languages which allow two dative NPs (rather more, in fact, than allow two accusative NPs), e.g. Japanese, Turkish, Kamaiurá. But other languages do not permit two dative NPs in a single clause. There are a number of different ways of dealing with this situation.

In Evenki (Tungusic, north Russia; Nedjalkov 1997: 231–2), the original A in the causative of a simple transitive has two possible markings: definite accusative or dative (the difference in meaning is not given in the source grammar). In the causative of a ditransitive the original A can only be definite accusative, not dative. (Interestingly, this languages allows two accusative NPs in a clause, but not two dative NPs.)

Causatives of transitives in Georgian are basically of type (v-b) from §3.2, where the original O stays as is, and the original A goes into dative case. But Georgian does not allow two dative NPs in a clause and in the causative of a ditransitive, which already has a dative NP, what we get is the original A becoming the new dative and the old dative moving down to become an oblique constituent, marked by the postposition *-t'* 'for'. Example (40) shows a simple ditransitive clause and (41) its causative correspondent (Sumbatova 1993: 257):

(40)   dena-d kalaxwem   mare-s   diar
        girl-ERG give+AORIST man-DAT bread+NOM
        The girl gave bread to the man

(41)   eže-m kalaxawodnune   dena-s   diar   mare-š-t'
       he-ERG give+CAUS+AORIST girl-DAT bread+NOM man-GEN-FOR
       He made the girl give bread to the man

Other languages have varying ways of responding to the prohibition on two dative NPs in a clause, when attempting to create the causative of a ditransitive. In Hixkaryana (Carib family, Brazil) both causee (original A) and original indirect object should take dative postposition *wya*; but only one *wya* phrase can occur in a clause so that (42a) is ambiguous. In order to disambiguate it one could add a second clause with the same verb 'give', but not in causative form, as in (42b):

(42) (a) kuraha yɨmpoye   Waraka rowya
          bow   3sgA+CAUS+give+3sgO   Name   1sg+DAT
          either (i)   Waraka made me give a bow (to someone)
          or   (ii) Waraka made (someone) give a bow to me

     (b) wɨmye   [Kaywerye wya]
          1sgA+give+3sgO   Name   DAT
          I gave (the bow) to Kaywerye

Taken together, the two clauses of (42) have an unambiguous meaning 'Waraka made me give the bow to Kaywerye' (Derbyshire 1985: 89; cf. 1979: 135). Sonrai behaves in a similar way (Shopen and Konaré 1970).

In Basque the prohibition on a clause including two dative NPs means that one simply cannot form a morphological causative of a ditransitive. In this language the morphological causative applies only to intransitive and to many simple transitive clauses (those with an inanimate O). But there is also a periphrastic causative which applies to all types of clauses, including ditransitives (Saltarelli 1988: 220–1). Similar remarks apply for Dulong/Rawang, as described by LaPolla in chapter 8 below.

In Abaza (North-west Caucasian) a predicate can cross-reference up to four arguments. In the morphological causative of a ditransitive such as 'he couldn't make them give it back to her', all of causer (A, 'he'), causee (original A, 'them'), original O ('it') and original indirect object ('her') can be shown by pronominal prefixes to the verb (W.S. Allen 1956: 139; Dixon 1982: 161). However, Abkhaz (another dialect of the same language) avoids four-argument verbs and as a result causatives of ditransitives can only be achieved by using a periphrastic construction (Hewitt 1979: 171).

A fascinating example of a causative of a ditransitive comes from Awa Pit (Barbacoan family, Colombia and Ecuador; Curnow 1997: 159–64). In the causative of a simple transitive the original A becomes O and the original O becomes an indirect (or 'second') object. But a clause in Awa Pit may not include two Os, or two indirect objects. For the causative of a ditransitive, the original indirect object (the gift, with a verb of giving) remains as is, which leaves the original A and original O competing for the one remaining functional slot, O, in the causative construction. Either can fill it, with the other argument remaining unexpressed. Thus:

(43)

		original A	original O	original indirect object
either	causer (A)	O	unexpressed	indirect object
or	causer (A)	unexpressed	O	indirect object
but not	*causer (A)	*O	*ind. object	*unexpressed

The possibility which is not allowed is that shown in the final row, where the original A becomes new O, and original O becomes new indirect object (as in the causative of a simple transitive) with the original indirect object being left unexpressed.

As a result, the causative of a ditransitive verb in Awa Pit is ambiguous; the sole O argument may refer to the original A or to the original O, as in:

(44)   na=na   Demetrio=ta pala   kwin-nin-ta-w
        1sgA=TOP Name=ACC   plantain give=CAUS=PAST-1st
   either   (i)   I made Demetrio (original A) give [someone, original O]
                    a plantain (original indirect object)
      or   (ii)   I made [someone, original A] give Demetrio (original O)
                    a plantain (original indirect object)

A causative such as (44) could only be disambiguated in terms of the textual context in which it occurs.

There is one syntactic possibility which might be expected but has not yet been encountered. Note that we have a ditransitive version of type (iv) from §3.2, with:

(45)   underlying clause   A   O   dative
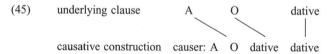
        causative construction causer: A   O   dative   dative

And we have a variety of type (v) found in Georgian (see (40–1)):

(46)   underlying clause   A   O   dative

        causative construction causer: A   O   dative   oblique marking

The one possibility which is not currently attested is a combination of these, an extension of type (iv) whereby in a causative construction each argument shifts one place down on a hierarchy:

(47)   underlying clause   A   O   dative

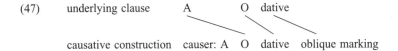

causative construction   causer: A   O   dative   oblique marking

Note that the data on causatives of ditransitives has many gaps; a high proportion of grammars simply do not mention this topic. When more documentation becomes available, I would predict that a language showing schema (47) will be found.

3.4   Double causatives

Some of the varieties of causative mechanisms carry the possibility of being applied twice (although double application may occur only rather occasionally in the daily use of language). This possibility is plainly not available for lexical causatives (§2.4) or for the mechanism which involves exchanging auxiliaries (§2.5) and it is not reported for the 'two verbs in one predicate' construction (§2.2).

One would expect periphrastic causatives to always carry the possibility of being applied iteratively, e.g. English *The king made the general make the captain make the soldiers clean out his goldfish bowl*. I know of no counterexamples to this (although this is not to imply that a detailed search might not uncover some). In fact, whether or not it can be iterated may be one criterion for deciding whether a causative verb enters into a simple predicate or a dual predicate construction type. In Lahu (Tibeto-Burman), for instance, a causative verb such as ci 'make' appears to make up a single predicate with the lexical verb (like *faire* in French, see §2.2). This is confirmed by the fact that a double causative (e.g. 'God made the devil spirit make the boy kick the dog') cannot be achieved by using ci twice within the same surface clause. 'Rather, one must embed the ci clause within a higher causative-purpose clause' (Matisoff 1973: 436).

Turning now to morphological causatives (§2.1), we find that some languages (e.g. Jarawara) only allow the causative process to apply once per verb, whereas others may have it apply twice. Double application sometimes indicates a single causative with a special meaning, e.g. 'force to do' in Swahili, illustrated in (60) below, and intensive meaning in Oromo (Dubinsky, Lloret and Newman 1988). Further examples are quoted in Kulikov (1993: 128–30).

In some languages two morphological causative mechanisms, that have rather different form, can be applied to a single verb. In Nivkh some verbs are causativized by replacing their initial stop or affricate by a corresponding fricative and/or liquid, e.g.

(48)   t'o-   'bend' (intransitive)   zo-   'bend' (transitive)
        pəkz-   'get lost' (intransitive)   vəkz-   'lose' (transitive)
        tʰa-   'fry' (intransitive)   rša-   'fry' (transitive)

The second mechanism involves a suffix -*(g)u*- being added to the verb, e.g. *nok*- 'be narrow', *nok-u*- 'make narrow'. There is also a class of verbs that combines the two changes to form a single causative: they include *t'oz*- 'go out (e.g. fire)', *zoz-u*- 'put (e.g. fire) out'.

    Some verbs in Nivkh can form a causative in either of two ways; we then find that initial consonant mutation (with or without an accompanying suffix) indicates direct causation, e.g. *pol*- 'fall', *vol-u*- 'make fall (e.g. knock down)'; and the use of a suffix (with no mutation) indicates indirect causation, e.g. *pol-gu* 'make fall (e.g. by not supporting)'. Both causatives may apply to a single root. Nedjalkov, Otaina and Xolodovič (1995: 67) present this as a symmetrical array:

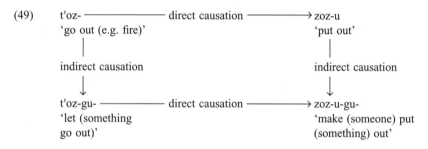

(49)   t'oz- ─────────── direct causation ──────────→ zoz-u
        'go out (e.g. fire)'   'put out'

        indirect causation   indirect causation

        t'oz-gu- ─────────── direct causation ──────────→ zoz-u-gu-
        'let (something   'make (someone) put
        go out)'   (something) out'

    In many languages the same causative process can be applied twice, yielding a causative of a causative. Thus, in Capanawa (Pano family, Peru; Payne 1990: 229) we can get:

(50)   underlying root (intransitive)   -mapet-   'ascend'
        causative (transitive)   -mapet-ma-   'bring [it] up (i.e. make
                                                          ascend)'
        double causative (ditransitive)   -mapet-ma-ma-   'make/allow [someone] to
                                                          bring [it] up'

Similar sequences of two causative affixes added to an intransitive verb are reported for a number of languages. These include two tokens of the same causative suffix in Hungarian and Turkish, and two tokens of the same prefix in Kabardian (Abitov *et al.* 1957: 127) and in Karbi (Tibeto-Burman, Assam; Jeyapaul 1987: 111).

    In Apalai, different suffixes are used for the causative of an intransitive and of a transitive verb. Some intransitive verbs take -*ma*- (e.g. *nyh-ma*- 'make sleep') while others take *-nohpo-* (e.g. *kuma-nohpo-* 'make rise'). A transitive verb is causativized by adding *-po* (e.g. *aro-po-* 'make [someone] take [something]'). An intransitive and a transitive causativizer can be applied in sequence. For example (Koehn and Koehn 1986: 51):

(51)   otuh-   'eat' (intransitive)
        otuh-ma-   'feed [someone], i.e. make [someone] eat' (transitive)
        otuh-ma-po-   'get [someone] to feed [someone]' (ditransitive)

It is also possible to apply the two intransitive causative suffixes in sequence. This produces a single causative but with an indirect meaning, e.g.

(52)   otuh-ma-nohpo-   'oversee [someone] eating' (transitive)

I have not been able to find a reliable textual (as opposed to elicited) example of a causative affix being added twice to a transitive verb. This relates partly to the fact that many languages restrict morphological causative processes to intransitive verbs, and quite a few of the remainder allow these processes to apply only sparingly to transitive verbs. Note that in Hungarian it may be theoretically possible to apply the causative suffix twice to a transitive verb but the result is judged infelicitous by native speakers; they prefer to use a morphological causative plus a periphrastic causative (Edith Moravcsik, p.c.).

4   Semantics

Quite a few languages have two or more causative constructions, involving either different formal mechanisms or different marking of the causee (original S or A). There is always a semantic difference and it may involve one or more of nine semantic parameters, set out below.

If a language has just one causative mechanism, then this generally has a wide semantic range, covering all values of most of the parameters. But it is unlikely to cover *all* values of *all* parameters. Many linguists, when writing the grammar of a language, simply state that there is a causative construction, describing the formal marking and something of the syntax. This is not enough – the meaning must be discussed as well. This is done for Motuna by Onishi (in chapter 4 of this volume) when he specifies 'the Causer acting directly and achieving the result intentionally', and 'the Causee is not in control of the state or activity, and is affected by the result of the whole event'. See also the account of the causative in Dulong/Rawang by LaPolla (chapter 8) and Rice's comparison of the meanings of morphological causatives across various Athapaskan languages (chapter 6).

There can be further semantic specifications that are not known to enter into any of the contrasts between alternative mechanisms – discussed below – but may need to be stated in the semantic characterization of the single causative in some languages. For instance, in Nivkh a causer must be animate. One cannot, as a rule, say something like 'The mist made us stay in the village', using a causative construction. This has to be expressed in another way, e.g. 'We stayed in the village because of the mist' (Nedjalkov, Otaina and Xolodovič 1995: 76).

The nine semantic parameters are:

(a) Relating to the verb

 1. State/action. Does a causative mechanism apply only to a verb describing a **state**, or also to a verb describing an **action**?
 2. Transitivity. Does it apply only to **intransitive** verbs, or to both intransitive and simple **transitive** verbs, or to all types of verbs – intransitive, simple transitive and also **ditransitive**? (Note that there are no causatives that apply only to transitives and not to intransitives. However, the form of a causative mechanism may vary depending on whether it applies to an intransitive or to a transitive verb, as in Carib languages such as Apalai – illustrated in (51) above – and Hixkaryana (Derbyshire 1979: 134–5).)

(b) Relating to the causee (original S or A)

 3. Control. Is the causee **lacking control** of the activity (e.g. if inanimate, or a young child) or normally **having control**?
 4. Volition. Does the causee do it **willingly** ('let') or **unwillingly** ('make')?
 5. Affectedness. Is the causee only **partially affected** by the activity, or **completely affected**?

(c) Relating to causer (in A function in the causative construction)

 6. Directness. Does the causer act **directly** or **indirectly**?
 7. Intention. Does the causer achieve the result **accidentally** or **intentionally**?
 8. Naturalness. Does it happen **fairly naturally** (the causer just initiating a natural process) or is the result achieved only **with effort** (perhaps, with violence)?
 9. Involvement. Is the causer also **involved** in the activity (in addition to the causee) or **not involved**?

For most of the parameters there are many examples available of languages with two causative mechanisms that are distinguished by the parameter; only a selection are given here. Those with the slimmest attestation are 9, Involvement (three instances known) and 5, Affectedness (just one). I quote all known examples for these.

The parameters are not fully independent. If **state** is chosen under 1 then parameter 2 must be **intransitive**. Parameter 4, Volition, can only be applied if **control** is chosen under 3. Parameter 8, Naturalness, is only likely to apply if **directly** is chosen under 6. It can sometimes be difficult to distinguish between 3, Control, and 4, Volition, on the part of the causee, and parameter 8, relating to whether the causer had to act **with effort** or achieved the result **naturally**. In some languages a causative contrast may relate primarily to Control, in another language to Naturalness, but in a third language it may effectively combine these two parameters.

I now discuss and exemplify the nine parameters, in turn.

1. State/action. Whether a causative mechanism applies only to **state** verbs or also to **action** verbs.

In Bahasa Indonesian and Malay (Tampubolon 1983: 45) the causative suffix *-kan* applies only to state and process verbs, e.g. we can get *melebar-kan* 'make wide' and *menggembira-kan* 'make pleased'. For action verbs the only kind of causative is periphrastic, involving a verb like *suruh* 'order', *buat* or *bikin* 'make'.

Amberber (chapter 9 of this volume) reports that in Amharic the shorter causative prefix, *a-*, attaches only to verbs of state and change of state, e.g. 'stand', 'melt' (but not 'dance' or 'laugh'). However, the longer causative prefix, *as-*, occurs with all kinds of verbs. Baker (1996: 348–52) reports a similar restriction on the causative suffix in Mohawk (Iroquoian) – it may only apply to stative verbs.

2. Transitivity. Whether a causative mechanism applies only to **intransitive** verbs, or to both intransitive and simple **transitive** verbs, or to all types of verbs – intransitive, simple transitive and also **ditransitive**.

In many languages a causative mechanism applies only to **intransitive** verbs. This is so for Australian languages such as Kayardild (Evans 1995: 279–80), Uradhi (Crowley 1983: 376) and Yidiny (Dixon 1977: 311–19) and also for Urubu-Kaapor (Tupí-Guaraní branch of Tupí family, Brazil; Kakumasu 1986: 341). In these languages there is no way of forming an abstract causative of a transitive verb (e.g. 'I made John cook the dinner'). One simply has to specify what was done to make the causee act (e.g. 'I told John to cook the dinner').

In other languages the morphological causative applies only to intransitives but there is also a periphrastic causative which may be used with all verbs; it is the only mechanism available for transitives. Languages of this kind include a number from the Austronesian family, including Maori (New Zealand; Bauer 1993: 409–12), Ambae (Vanuatu; Catriona Hyslop, p.c.) and Balinese (Wayan Pastika, p.c.), and a number from the Mayan family such as K'iche' (Campbell, chapter 7 of this volume) and Tzotzil (Stuart Robinson, p.c.). Other languages are mentioned by Nedyalkov and Silnitsky (1973: 7).

Onishi (chapter 4 of this volume) states that in Motuna a morphological causative can be formed on any plain intransitive (whether of type S_a or type S_o) and on an extended intransitive (or 'middle'; that is an intransitive with an obligatory peripheral argument) and on just a couple of transitive verbs. There are a number of ambitransitive verbs in Motuna, and a causative is always based on the intransitive sense. In Fijian almost all verbs are ambitransitive, some of type $S = A$ and others of type $S = O$. For many syntactic purposes it is most appropriate to take the transitive form as basic; however, causatives apply only to the intransitive sense of an ambitransitive verb (Dixon 1988: 45–51, 185–9).

There are a number of languages where a morphological causative applies freely to all intransitive verbs but only rather rarely to transitives and then to just a few verbs. A similar set of verbs is involved, in different languages. For Yimas, Foley (1991: 292) quotes 'weave' and 'eat'. For Tariana (chapter 5 of this volume), Aikhenvald quotes a number of verbs to do with ritual activity, plus 'drink'. In chapter 4 Onishi mentions two transitive verbs that form a morphological causative in Motuna, 'eat (munchable food)' and 'eat (soft food) / drink'. In Jarawara it appears that the only transitive verbs to readily accept the causative prefix *na-* are 'drink' and 'eat'. Nedyalkov and Silnitsky (1973: 16) conclude from their typological survey that if only a few transitive verbs form morphological causatives these are likely to include 'verbs denoting abstract action', such as 'see/show', 'remember/remind' and 'understand/explain', plus 'drink' and 'eat' (their example languages include Chukchee, Arabic, Bats, Hausa, Armenian and Kurdish).

Rice (chapter 6 of this volume) surveys the applicability of the causative affix across languages of the Athapaskan family. In all languages it can be used on an intransitive verb with a 'patientive subject'. In some languages it can be used with all intransitives. Only in Koyukun can it be freely used with transitives. For other languages, just a few transitive verbs take the morphological causative; the examples which Rice quotes for Ahtna, Carrier and Navajo are 'eat' and 'drink'.

There is here a clear generalization – if a morphological causative is used with only a few transitive verbs, these are likely to include 'drink' and 'eat'. It seems that drinking and eating are the transitive activities which people are most likely to make other people do, on every continent.

As mentioned in §3.3, we find languages where a morphological causative can apply to intransitive and simple **transitive** verbs, but not to ditransitives. Sonrai, Basque, Dulong/Rawang and Abkhaz are of this type.

3. Control. Whether the causee **lacks control** or **has control** of the activity.

Creek (Martin 1991 and chapter 12 in this volume) has two morphological mechanisms. Roughly: (i) suffix *-ic* is used if the causee **lacks control** or is **unwilling** (e.g 'feed the baby'); (ii) suffix *-ipa* followed by *-ic* is used if the causee **has control** (e.g. 'make the baby eat'), or if the causee is athematic (e.g. 'make it rain'). (Martin suggests that this difference between causatives basically relates to the separability of events.)

This parameter underlies the meaning of the morphological causative in a number of languages. For example, in Marathi (Pandharipande 1997: 406) and in Japanese and Korean (Shibatani 1976a: 33) the causee must **have control**; as a result, inanimate causees are not permitted.

4. Volition. Whether the causee does it **willingly** ('let') or **unwillingly** ('make').

Japanese has intransitive/transitive verb pairs as lexical causatives (e.g. 'be damaged'/'damage', 'be sold'/'sell', 'become fat'/'fatten' – see Shibatani 1990: 236). These imply that the causee **lacks control**; indeed, with most lexical causatives in Japanese the causee is inanimate. Japanese also has a morphological causative with suffix *-(s)ase*; this implies that the causee **has control**. With intransitives there are two syntactic possibilities, indicating a difference in the causee's volition. If the original S takes accusative postposition *o* in the causative construction it implies that the intentions of the causee are ignored by the causer, as in (54); if the original S takes dative postposition *ni* this implies that the causee is **willing**, as in (55). (See Shibatani 1990: 309; Tonoike 1978; Tsujimura 1996: 247–9.)

(53)   Taroo ga   konsaato e it-ta
        Name NOM concert TO go-PAST
        Taroo went to a concert

(54)   Ryooshin ga   Taroo o   konsaato e ik-ase-ta
        parents   NOM Name ACC concert TO go-CAUSE-PAST
        [His] parents made Taroo go to a concert

(55)   Ryooshin ga   Taroo ni   konsaato e   ik-ase-ta
       parents   NOM Name DAT concert   TO go-CAUSE-PAST
       [His] parents let Taroo go to a concert

We mentioned in §3.2 that Japanese may not have two accusative-marked NPs in a clause; as a result, in the causative of a transitive the original A can only have dative marking (since there is already an accusative NP). Thus, the volitional contrast is only available for the causative of an intransitive.

Bolivian Quechua (Cole 1983: 118) shows a similar contrast, but this time only with transitive verbs. Here the morphological causative is marked by verbal suffix *-či*. In the causative of an intransitive the original S must become O, marked by the accusative postposition *-ta*. However, in the causative of a transitive the original A can be marked with accusative, showing that the causee is **unwilling**, as in (56), or with instrumental, *-wan*, showing that the causee is **willing**, as in (57).

(56)   nuqa Fan-ta   rumi-ta   apa-či-ni
       1sgA Juan-ACC rock-ACC carry-CAUS-1sgA
       I made Juan carry the rock

(57)   nuqa Fan-wan rumi-ta   apa-či-ni
       1sgA Juan-INST rock-ACC carry-CAUS-1sgA
       I had Juan carry the rock (where Juan submits voluntarily to the causer's wishes)

In Swahili (Vitale 1981: 156–7) there is a causative suffix, *-isha/-esha*, to the verb; and also a periphrastic apparatus for causation. Where these contrast, the suffix indicates that the causee acts **willingly** and the periphrastic construction indicates that the causee acts **unwillingly** (is forced to do it). Thus:

(58)   mwalimu hu-wa-som-esha   wanafunzi kurani
       teacher   HAB-3pl-study-CAUSE students   Koran
       The teacher teaches the students the Koran (they want to study it)

(59)   mwalimu hu-wa-lazimisha wanafunzi wa-som-e   kurani
       teacher   HAB-3pl-force   students   3pl-study-SUBJ Koran
       The teacher forces the students to study the Koran (they do not want to study it)

Interestingly, an alternative to the periphrastic construction is doubling the causative suffix on the verb. Sentence (60) has the same meaning as (59):

(60)   mwalimu hu-wa-som-es(h)-esha   wanafunzi kurani
       HAB-3pl-study-CAUSE-CAUSE

Tangkhul Naga (Tibeto-Burman, India; Arokianathan 1987: 65–6) is like Swahili in that there is a morphological causative, with prefix *ci-*, indicating that the causee acted **willingly**, as in:

(61) cannə merili ci-tuntələy
      John Mary CAUS-get down
      John got Mary to get down

A second causative, indicating that the causee acted **unwillingly**, involves causative *-ŋəsək-*, which appears to be compounded to the lexical verb, as in:

(62) i-nə   a-li   conrəm ci   khuy-ŋəsək-sá-y
      1sg-NOM 3sg-ACC luggage THAT take-CAUS-EVID-NON.FUT
      I made him/her take that luggage

5. Affectedness. Whether the causee is only **partially affected** or **completely affected** by the activity.

This parameter is attested just for Tariana. The longer causative suffix *-i+ta* may be used to indicate that the causee was completely affected (e.g. 'you made my house fall down completely'), contrasting with the shorter causative suffix *-i*, which can indicate that the causee was only partially affected (e.g. 'they made some woodchips fall'). Compare (32) and (33) in chapter 5 below, by Aikhenvald.

6. Directness. Whether the causer acts **directly** or **indirectly**.

Hindi (Kachru 1976, Saksena 1982) has two causative suffixes. Both can be used with all kinds of verbs, implying a causee **having control** and the causer acting **intentionally**. They differ in terms of directness – suffix *-a* indicates that the causer acts **directly** and *-va* that they act **indirectly**. The intransitive clause in (63) is the basis for the **direct** causative in (64), where the labourers did the job themselves, and for the **indirect** causative in (65), where the contractor achieved the task indirectly (through 'the labourers', who can be included in the clause, marked by instrumental case).

(63) Məkan bəna
      house was.made
      The house got built

(64) Məzduuro ne məkan bənaya
      labourers ERG house was.made+ CAUS$_1$
      The labourers built the house

(65) Thekedar ne (məzduuro se) məkan bənvaya
      contractor ERG labourers INST house was.made+ CAUS$_2$
      The contractor got the house built (by the labourers)

A similar distinction between **direct** and **indirect** causatives is found in many other languages of the region, for example Gojri (Indo-European; Sharma 1982: 153–4). Masica (1976) surveys **direct** and **indirect** causatives in the South Asian linguistic area.

Jinghpaw (Tibeto-Burman, Burma; Maran and Clifton 1976) has a causative prefix, *sha-*, and a causative suffix, *-shangun*. They are often interchangeable, but contrast with some verbs. If a causative action is **accidental** only the suffix can be used. If it is **intentional** then the prefix will be preferred if the causer acts **directly** while the suffix is preferred if they act **indirectly**. For an event 'X killed Y' imagine the following three scenarios:

(a)   X decapitated Y (**direct**) – prefix preferred.
(b)   X saw Y unconscious in water and didn't rescue them (**indirect**) – suffix preferred.
(c)   X ordered someone to decapitate Y (**indirect**) – suffix preferred.

In §3.4 we mentioned Nivkh, where consonantal mutation (sometimes also accompanied by a suffix) can mark **direct** causation, and a verbal affix (with no mutation) may be used for **indirect** causation. Schema (49) illustrates how these can be combined. Apalai was illustrated in (51–2); here a single causative suffix to an intransitive verb indicates **direct** causation, while a sequence of two suffixes is used for **indirect** causation.

In Telugu (Dravidian) there are two varieties of causative for an intransitive verb: (i) the original S argument is placed in accusative case; or (ii) it is marked by the postposition *ceeta*, which is used to mark the original A in the causative of a transitive, described under type (i) in §3.2. Alternative (i) is used to describe direct causation such as 'the nurse walked the child (e.g. by holding its hands)' while (ii) is used for indirect causation, such as 'the nurse got the child to walk (e.g. by telling it to do so)'. Interestingly, verbs like 'cry' and 'laugh' only accept alternative (i) (Bh. Krishnamurti, p.c.).

Foley (1991: 291) describes causative serial verb constructions in Yimas. There are two verbs which may take on a causative meaning when used in such a construction, *tar- ~ tal-* 'hold' and *tmi-* 'say'. The alternative '*tar- ~ tal-* marks a **direct** causative, the causing of an event by physically manipulating an object, while *tmi-* is used for an **indirect** causative in which the event is brought about through speech, by verbal commands or requests'. Thus:

(66)   na-ŋa-tar-kwalca-t
        3sgA-1sgO-CAUS₁-rise-PFV
        She woke me up (**directly**, e.g. by shaking me)

(67) na-ŋa-tmi-kwalca-t
3sgA-1sgO-CAUS$_2$-rise-PFV
She woke me up (**indirectly**, e.g. by calling me)

The Directness parameter may also be shown by alternation of case mark-ing. In the causative of an intransitive, Hungarian normally puts the original S into accusative case, but some verbs allow either accusative or instru-mental. The accusative alternative marks **direct** causation, where the causer personally directs the activity, while instrumental indicates **indirect** causation (Hetzron 1976: 394). Under (b) in §3.1 we contrasted the direct causative 'The nurse walked him (accusative) for an hour every day' with the indirect causative 'The doctor had him (instrumental) walk for an hour each day (by telling him to do so)'.

In Buru (Austronesian, Indonesia; Grimes 1991: 211) a prefix *pe-* is used to indicate **direct** causation, and a periphrastic verb, *puna*, for **indirect** causa-tion, where the causer 'brought about a situation that caused the resulting action or state'. Compare:

(68) da pe-gosa ringe
3sgA CAUS$_1$-be.good 3sgO
He healed her (**directly**, with spiritual power)

(69) da puna ringe gosa
3sgA CAUS$_2$ 3sgO be.good
He [did something which, **indirectly**] made her well

A similar mechanism–meaning correlation is found in another Austronesian language, Chrau (Vietnam; D.M. Thomas 1969, and D.D. Thomas 1971) where causative prefix *ta-* indicates **direct** action, by physical manipulation (e.g. 'I made the child stand up (by holding him)') while the periphrastic causative verb *ôp* indicates **indirect** causation, e.g. by issuing a command. And in Alamblak (Papuan region; Bruce 1984: 153–9) there are a number of causative prefixes, including *ka-* 'make do by **direct** physical action', while a causative serial verb construction involving the verb *hay* (whose meaning when used alone is 'give') is employed for **indirect** causation, where the causer and causee need not even be at the same place when the event takes place (rather like the verb *cause* in English). Compare:

(70) ka-fkne-më-r-m
CAUS$_1$-enter-REM.PAST-3sg+M+A-3pl+O
He made them enter (by physically taking them)

(71)   yima-r   hay-noh-më-t-a
       person-3sg+M CAUS$_2$-be.unconscious-REM.PAST-3sg+M+A-1sg+O
       A man made me lose consciousness (lit. gave me something, causing me to
       become unconscious)

See also Hinton (1982) on Mixtec (Mixtecan), Austin (1981: 159–60) on
Diyari (Australian) and Haiman (1983: 786) on Korean.

From the examples given it will be seen that **indirect** causation can have
varying significance. In Yimas, Hungarian and Chrau it appears to involve the
causer telling the causee to do something, while in Hindi and Jinghpaw it
can involve acting through an intermediary). There is need for a full study of
the semantics of indirect causation, taking a much larger sample of languages
than those mentioned here, and looking in detail at the meanings and conditions for use of the indirect causative in each language.

7. Intention. Whether the causer achieves the result **accidentally** or
intentionally.

Kammu (Svantesson 1983: 103–11) has two causative mechanisms, a
prefix *p(n)-* and a preverbal particle, *tòk*. If the causer achieves the result
intentionally the prefix is used, and if they achieve the result **accidentally**
the particle is used. Compare the following:

(72)   kə̀ə   p-háan   tráak
       3sg+M CAUS$_1$-die buffalo
       He slaughtered the buffalo

(73)   kə̀ə   tòk   háan múuc
       3sg+M CAUS$_2$ die   ant
       He happened to kill an ant (e.g. by accidentally treading on it)

We mentioned above that in Chrau a causative prefix is used for direct and
a periphrastic verb for indirect causation. These mechanisms can also be used
to mark intention – the causative verb alone for something achieved **intentionally**, with the prefix and verb used together to indicate something that
was brought about **accidentally**. For example (D.M. Thomas 1969: 100):

(74)   ănh ôp   dăq khlâyh
       1sg CAUS$_2$ trap escape
       I made the trap spring (**on purpose**)

(75)   ănh ôp   dăq ta-khlâyh
       1sg CAUS$_2$ trap CAUS$_1$-escape
       I made the trap spring (**accidentally**)

As described in §3.1, there are two syntactic frames available for the causative of an S$_o$ intransitive verb in Tariana (described by Aikhenvald in chapter 5 below). If the causative verb lacks a pronominal prefix this indicates **lack of intention** on the part of the causer, e.g. 'the dog's barking made me frightened' (the dog didn't bark with the intention of scaring me). If it bears a prefix, then this indicates **intentionality**, e.g. 'he frightened them' (he meant to achieve this end). See examples (22–7) in chapter 5.

In other languages one type of causative construction will mark **intentional** causation while another type is neutral as to whether the activity was made to happen intentionally or accidentally. (Note that the reverse situation – where just accidental is marked – is not attested.) In Spanish the verb *hacer* 'make' can be followed either by a 'that' clause, with the verb in subjunctive form, or by a verb in infinitive form. The subjunctive can be used only when the causer acted intentionally, whereas with an infinitive either an intentional or an accidental reading is possible (Curnow 1993). In Javanese there are three morphological mechanisms for marking a causative – suffix *-ake*, suffix *-i* and initial reduplication. Most verbs only take one of these. There are, however, some verbs which can take either *-ake* or *-i* and there is then a difference of both intentionality and number. Suffix *-i* indicates **intentional** activity and plural causee, while *-ake* is neutral with respect to both intentionality and number. Thus *pecah-i* is 'intentionally break many (things)' whereas *pecah-ake* is 'intentionally or accidentally break one or many (things)' (Suhandano 1994: 66).

Motuna, described by Onishi in chapter 4 below, has a number of S = O ambitransitive verbs, e.g. *to-* 'be hit, hit'. The morphological causative suffix, *-wooto*, applies to the intransitive sense of the verb, which then has the same syntax as the verb used transitively. There is, however, a semantic difference. The causative must be used where the referent of the A argument 'initiates a process or activity but does not necessarily act directly or intentionally'.

Kulikov (1993: 134–5) mentions further examples of this parameter.

8. Naturalness. Whether the activity happens **fairly naturally** (the causer just initiating a natural process) or is achieved only **with effort** (perhaps, with violence).

Russian uses a morphological causative describing something that happens **naturally** and a periphrastic causative where **violence or force** (which can include moral force) is employed. Thus (examples from Alexandra Y. Aikhenvald):

(76)   on   na-poi-l   menja   vinom
        3sg+M PREVERB-drink+CAUS$_1$-sg+M+PAST 1sg+ACC wine+INST+sg
        He got me to drink wine (and I didn't resist)

(77)   on   za-stavi-l   menja pitj   vino
        3sg+M PREVERB-CAUS$_2$-sg+M+PAST 1sgACC drink wine+ACC+sg
        He forced me to drink wine (e.g. by threats or blows)

Among the causative suffixes which Mithun (chapter 3 of this volume) lists for Yup'ik is *-cir* which 'indicates causation without direct effort, by waiting and allowing something to happen'.

In English there is a lexical causative (using what is basically an intransitive verb in a transitive construction) and also a periphrastic mechanism with verbs such as *make*. Where these contrast the lexical causative describes something achieved by the causer **naturally** (with the causee being **willing**, if it is animate) while the *make* construction implies definite **effort** (and an **unwilling** causee). Compare the (a) and (b) alternatives in (78) and (79).

(78) (a) He walked the dog in the park (it wanted to walk)
     (b) He made the dog walk in the park (although it didn't want to)

(79) (a) He opened the door/melted the ice (without difficulty)
     (b) He made the door open/ice melt (with difficulty)

Fijian is like Motuna in having many ambitransitive verbs of type S = O (effectively a lexical causative), so that the morphological causative of the intransitive has the same syntax as the plain transitive. There is, however, a semantic difference. The plain transitive will be used for something achieved fairly **naturally**, while the causative must be employed if some special **effort** is required. The intransitive verb *pono* is 'be caught with the hands (of an animal, fish or person)'. If someone catches something or someone easily they would use the plain transitive *pono-ʔa* (where *-ʔa* marks the verb as transitive). If there is difficulty involved, with the catcher running after the prey and making a determined effort to catch it, then the causative of the intransitive would be used, *vaʔa-pono-ʔa* (where *vaʔa-* is the causative prefix) (Dixon 1988: 188).

Aikhenvald (chapter 5 of this volume) describes how in Tariana the use of a periphrastic causative implies a special **effort** on the part of the causer and/ or **unwillingness** of the causee, whereas a morphological causative will be preferred when **no special effort** is needed. (As mentioned above, in some languages alternative causative constructions may link the ideas of control and volition, on the part of the causee, and that of naturalness from the point of view of the causer.)

9. Involvement. Whether the causer is also **involved** in the activity (in addition to the causee) or **not involved**.

In Nomatsiguenga (Arawak family, Peru; Wise 1986: 593) there is a causative prefix *ogi-* and a causative suffix *-hag*. The prefix is used when the causer was **not involved** in the activity, and the suffix when they were **involved**. Compare:

(80)   y-ogi-monti-ë-ri   i-tomi
       3sg+M-CAUS₁-cross.river-NON.FUT-3sg+M 3sg+M-son
       He made his son cross the river (he told him to)

(81)   y-monti-a-hag-ë-ri   i-tomi
       3sg+M-cross.river-EPENTHETIC-CAUS₂-NON.FUT-3sg+M 3sg+M-son
       He made his son cross the river (he helped him across)

A similar distinction is made in Kamaiurá. Here we find two causative prefixes to the verb: *mo-* indicating that the causee is **not involved** in the activity (e.g. 'he stopped the canoe, when he was outside it'), and *(e)ro-* indicating that the causer was **involved** (e.g. 'he stopped the canoe, when he was inside it'). These examples are given in full in Dixon and Aikhenvald (1997: 84).

Alamblak has a number of causative prefixes. One of them is *ha-*, used when the causer is also **involved** in (joins in with) the activity which they make the causer undertake, e.g. 'he made them enter (something) by entering with them' (Bruce 1984: 155).

The list presented here – of nine semantic parameters that characterize causative constructions – is a tentative one. Further work may suggest that it should be re-organized, or that further parameters need to be added. For example, Golovko (1993: 386) describes how Aleut has a distributive causative suffix *-dgu*, indicating that a set of causees is involved (the O NP must take plural marking), distributed in space, e.g. 'the woman is making the hides dry'. Saksena (1982: 827–8) suggests that in Hindi different case markings on the causee in a causative construction can indicate whether the aim is to get the activity done (by anyone), or to get it done specifically by the stated causee. For the causative of an intransitive in Korean, the original S can take accusative marking (indicating 'do fully') or dative ('do to some extent'). Thus 'mother (A) child (DAT) eat-CAUS' signifies that the mother fed the child once, whereas 'mother (A) child (ACC) eat-CAUS' would describe her feeding the child for its whole life. Interestingly, 'die' can only take the accusative alternative, presumably because killing is, by its nature, something that is done fully (Yunseok Lee, p.c.).

We should also note that a certain morphological process may have causative effect with some verbs but a quite different effect with others. Nedyalkov and Silnitsky (1973: 17–20) quote a number of examples of this. For instance, from the Zulu verb *enza* 'work' can be derived *enz-isa* which means 'work persistently' (if there is no direct object) or 'force to work' (if there is a direct object).

5   Meaning–mechanism correlations

We are now in a position to examine the correlation between values of the semantic parameters and types of causative mechanism, for languages that have more than one causative. There is some mention of this in the literature. Comrie (1981: 164–7; 1989: 171–4) recognizes a continuum of causative mechanisms:

(82)   analytic [i.e. periphrastic] – morphological – lexical

He suggests that this correlates with the continuum from less direct to more direct causation, and with that from high control to low control on the part of the causee. Haiman (1983: 783–8; 1985: 108–11) puts forward a 'principle' that if a language has two causatives then 'the conceptual distance between cause and result will correspond to the formal distance between cause and result'. And Givón (1990: 556) makes the following prediction: 'if a language has both a periphrastic – syntactic complementation – causative and a morphological causative, the former is more likely to code causation with a *human-agentive manipulee*, while the latter is more likely to code causation with an *inanimate manipulee*' (his italics).

The present study reveals a correlation between the various semantic parameters and the degree of 'compactness' of a causative mechanism. We can recognize a scale of compactness, set out in (83). (Note that the mechanism of exchanging auxiliaries, discussed in §2.5, does not contrast with any other mechanism, and is not included in (83).)

(83)   Scale of compactness

TYPE OF MECHANISM

more compact   L   Lexical (e.g. *walk*, *melt* in English)

M   Morphological – internal or tone change, lengthening, reduplication, affixation, etc.

CP   Two verbs in one predicate ('Complex Predicate'), including serial verbs; *faire* in French; compounding in Tangkhul Naga, shown in (62); the causative particle in Kammu, shown in (73).

P   Periphrastic constructions with two verbs (a causative verb and a lexical verb) in separate clauses

less compact

We can, in addition, recognize degrees of compactness within M, morphological causatives. Firstly, a shorter affix is more compact than a longer one. Secondly, a causative mechanism which does not lengthen the word – for example, mutation of an initial consonant in Nivkh, illustrated in (48) – is more compact than affixation. When there are two morphological mechanisms that differ in compactness, we use M_1 for the more compact and M_2 for the less compact alternative.

There is a further possibility. One type of causative may be marked by a single mechanism and another by a combination of two mechanisms. Thus in Chrau the intentional causative involves just P (the causative verb *ôp*) whereas something achieved accidentally involves a combination of P plus M (causative prefix *ta-*). The causative involving a single mechanism is plainly more compact than that involving two mechanisms.

We are now in a position to look back over the nine semantic parameters, discussed in §4, and examine how each correlates with the scale of compactness. Note that in some instances the two mechanisms marking different values of a semantic parameter do not differ in compactness, e.g. Yimas has a serial verb construction for both direct and indirect causation, illustrated in (66–67). For parameter 9, Involvement, the **involved** and **not involved** alternatives are marked by an affix of about the same length in the languages for which this parameter is attested (Nomatsiguenga and Kamaiurá). In view of this, Involvement cannot be included in the discussion that follows.

However, for most of the examples of the two causatives with a semantic distinction, given in §4, the mechanisms involved do vary in compactness. We find a significant correlation between the values of each parameter and the compactness scale. This is set out in table 2.2.

The more compact (M_1) and less compact (M_2) morphological mechanisms given in table 2.2 are:

(84)	parameter	language	M_1	M_2
	1	Amharic	short prefix *a-*	longer prefix *as-*
	3	Creek	suffix *-ic*	double suffix *-ipa-ic*
	4	Swahili	suffix *-esha*	repeated suffix *-esh-esha*
	5	Tariana	suffix *-i*	double suffix *-i-ta*
	6	Nivkh	initial mutation	suffix *-(g)u*
		Apalai	one suffix, *-ma*	two suffixes, *-ma-nohpo*
		Hindi	short suffix *-a*	longer suffix *-va*
		Jinghpaw	short prefix *sha-*	long suffix *-shangun*

It will be seen that there is a clear correlation between compactness, as measured by the scale set out in (83), and each of the first eight semantic parameters. For seven of them we have at least two examples, and these

Table 2.2. Meaning–mechanism correlations

Parameter	Meaning		Mechanism		Language
	Causative type 1	Causative type 2	Causative type 1	Causative type 2	
1	state	action	M_1 M	M_2 P	Amharic Bahasa Indonesian and Malay
2	intransitive intransitive and simple transitive	all transitive ditransitive	M M	P P	Austronesian, Mayan, etc. Basque, Abkhaz
3	causee lacking control	causee having control	L M_1	M M_2	Japanese Creek
4	causee willing	causee unwilling	M_1 M M	M_2 CP P	Swahili Tangkhul Naga Swahili
5	causee partially affected	causee fully affected	M_1	M_2	Tariana
6	direct	indirect	M_1 M	M_2 P	Nivkh, Apalai, Hindi, Jinghpaw Buru, Chrau, Alamblak, Mixtec, Korean
7	intentional	accidental	M P	CP M plus P	Kammu Chrau
8	naturally	with effort	L L M	M P P	Fijian English Russian, Tariana

agree. In parameter 6, for instance, the **direct** value of the parameter is always marked by the more compact mechanism, and the **indirect** value by the less compact one. The actual mechanisms are initial mutation versus suffix in Nivkh, one suffix versus two suffixes in Apalai, short affix versus longer affix in Hindi and Jinghpaw, and morphological versus periphrastic mechanism in Buru, Chrau, Alamblak, Mixtec and Korean. Only for parameter 5 is there a single example; in Tariana the suffix *-i* marks causee **partially affected** while double suffix *-i+ta* is used when the causee is **completely affected** by the activity.

These results agree with Comrie's observations regarding the Directness and Control parameters, mentioned at the beginning of this section. Haiman's principle concerning 'formal distance' and 'conceptual distance' is rather vague, but could be interpreted as applying to the correlations established here. Givón's prediction could be taken to relate to parameter 3, Control – the causee can only be in control if human/animate and this does correlate with a less compact mechanism (e.g. periphrastic, as opposed to morphological).

There may be a number of ways of interpreting the correlations shown in table 2.2. One is that each of the meaning columns characterizes some kind of prototype:

Prototype 1 – Causer achieves a result naturally, intentionally and directly, the causee either lacking control or having control and being willing, and being only partially affected. May only apply to intransitive verbs (or just to intransitive and simple transitive), or be more restricted and apply just to state verbs.

Prototype 2 – Causer achieves the result accidentally, or uses effort, or acts indirectly, the causee being in control but acting unwillingly, and being completely affected. It is likely to be used with all types of verbs.

These composite prototypes are artificial – and thus unsatisfying – inasmuch as only two or three of the components are likely to apply together (not all eight) to distinguish the causative mechanisms in a given language.

The interesting point is the correlation between 'more compact' and the parameter values in the Type 1 column – naturally rather than with effort, intentionally rather than accidentally, directly rather than indirectly; causee only partially affected, willing, lacking control; and applying only to some verbs (at the intransitive and/or state ends of the parameters 1 and 2). This is surely a ripe field for investigation of cognitive mechanisms.

Finally, a warning is in order. This is a tentative and preliminary study of the marking, syntax and semantics of causative constructions, and of meaning–

mechanism correlations. A number of parameters of variation have been suggested, but need to be exhaustively tested against a much wider sample of the world's languages. Further work may well reveal that some of the meaning–mechanism correlations are not universally so 'neat' as appears to be the case from table 2.2. The results presented here will certainly need to be revised and extended, when further relevant data on individual languages is consulted.

6   Summary

This chapter has pursued an inductive investigation of causative constructions (interpreted in a fairly narrow sense – that is, by excluding such things as 'I speak and child eats'). We identified five mechanisms for marking a causative – morphological, two verbs in one predicate, periphrastic, lexical and exchanging auxiliaries.

The syntax of causative constructions was covered in some detail, particularly the treatment of the original A and O in the causative of a transitive clause. In (24) I enumerated five strategies that languages employ – (i) having a special marking for the original A (the causee); (ii) allowing both causer and causee to be marked like an A; (iii) allowing both causee and original O to be marked like an O; (iv) making the causee the new O with original O now taking some peripheral marking; (v) original O staying as O, with the causee taking non-core marking. Within (v) there are two sub-types – either the causee gets a fixed marking, or the causee goes into the first empty slot on a hierarchy of syntactic functions. The last alternative – although regarded by Comrie (1975 and following publications) as the 'paradigm case' – is in fact rather rare.

If a language has two (or more) different causative mechanisms these will contrast semantically. We recognized nine parameters of variation: State/ Action, Transitivity (these two relating to the verb); Control, Volition, Affectedness (these three relating to the causee); Directness, Intention, Naturalness and Involvement (these four relating to the causer). If a language has a single causative mechanism it is not sufficient to just say that it is 'causative'. Its semantic profile should be investigated, in terms of the nine parameters given here (and any further ones that may prove to be relevant).

Finally, §5 established a consistent correlation between the values of the semantic parameters and whether the associated causative mechanism is 'more compact' or 'less compact', as set out in table 2.2.

References

Abbott, M. 1991. 'Macushi', pp. 23–160 of Derbyshire and Pullum 1991.

Abitov, M.L., Balkarov, B.X., Desheriev, Y.D., Rogava, G.V., El'berdov, X.U., Kardanov, B.M. and Kuasheva, T.X. 1957. *Grammatika kabardino-cherkesskogo literaturnogo jazyka.* [*A grammar of literary Kabardian-Cherkess.*] Moscow: Akademija Nauk SSSR.

Aikhenvald, A.Y. Forthcoming. 'Serial constructions and verb compounding: evidence from Tariana (North Arawak)', to appear in *Studies in Language.*

Aissen, J. 1974. 'Verb raising', *Linguistic Inquiry* 5.325–66.

Alcalay, R. 1974. *The complete Hebrew–English dictionary.* Bridgeport, Conn.: Prayer Book Press.

Allen, B.J., Gardiner, D.B. and Frantz, D.G. 1984. 'Noun incorporation in Southern Tiwa', *International Journal of American Linguistics* 50.292–311.

Allen, W.S. 1956. 'Structure and system in the Abaza verbal complex', *Transactions of the Philological Society*, pp. 127–76.

Arokianathan, S. 1987. *Tangkhul Naga grammar.* Mysore: Central Institute for Indian Languages.

Aronson, H.I. 1991. 'Modern Georgian', pp. 219–312 of *The indigenous languages of the Caucasus*, Vol. I, *The Kartvelian languages*, ed. A.C. Harris. Delmark, N.Y.: Caravan Books.

Austin, P. 1981. *A grammar of Diyari, South Australia.* Cambridge: Cambridge University Press.

1997. 'Causatives and applicatives in Australian Aboriginal languages', pp. 165–225 of *The dative and related phenomena*, ed. K. Matsumura and T. Hayasi. Tokyo: Hituzi Syobo.

Baker, M.C. 1988. *Incorporation: a theory of grammatical function changing.* Chicago: University of Chicago Press.

1996. *The polysynthesis parameter.* New York: Oxford University Press.

Bauer, W. 1993. *Maori.* London: Routledge.

Bhatia, T.K. 1993. *Punjabi.* London: Routledge.

Borgman, D.M. 1990. 'Sanuma', pp. 15–248 of Derbyshire and Pullum 1990.

Bruce, L. 1984. *The Alamblak language of Papua New Guinea (East Sepik).* Canberra: Pacific Linguistics.

Bybee, J., Haiman, J. and Thompson, S.A. (eds.) 1997. *Essays on language function and language type, dedicated to T. Givón.* Amsterdam: John Benjamins.

Chapman, S. and Derbyshire, D.C. 1991. 'Paumarí', pp. 161–332 of Derbyshire and Pullum 1991.

Cole, P. 1976. 'A causative construction in Modern Hebrew: theoretical implications', pp. 99–128 of *Studies in Modern Hebrew syntax and semantics: the transformational-generative approach.* Amsterdam: North-Holland.

1982. *Imbabura Quechua.* Amsterdam: North-Holland.

1983. 'The grammatical role of the causee in universal grammar', *International Journal of American Linguistics* 49.115–33.

Comrie, B. 1975. 'Causatives and universal grammar', *Transactions of the Philological Society for 1974*, pp. 1–32.

1976. 'The syntax of causative constructions: cross-language similarities and divergencies', pp. 261–312 of Shibatani 1976b.

1981. *Language universals and linguistic typology*. Oxford: Blackwell.

1985. 'Causative verb formation and other verb-deriving morphology', pp. 309–48 of *Language typology and syntactic description*, Vol. III, *Grammatical categories and the lexicon*, ed. T. Shopen. Cambridge: Cambridge University Press.

1989. *Language universals and linguistic typology*, 2nd edn. Oxford: Blackwell.

Comrie, B. and Polinsky, M. (eds.) 1993. *Causatives and transitivity*. Amsterdam: John Benjamins.

Crowley, T.M. 1978. *The Middle Clarence dialects of Bandjalang*. Canberra: Australian Institute of Aboriginal Studies.

1983. 'Uradhi', pp. 306–428 of *Handbook of Australian languages*, Vol. III, ed. R.M.W. Dixon and B.J. Blake. Canberra: Australian National University Press.

1987. 'Serial verbs in Paamese', *Studies in Language* 11.35–84.

Curnow, T.J. 1993. 'Semantics of Spanish causatives involving *hacer*', *Australian Journal of Linguistics* 13.165–84.

1997. 'A grammar of Awa Pit (Cuaiquer): an indigenous language of south-western Colombia'. Ph.D. thesis. Australian National University.

Derbyshire, D.C. 1979. *Hixkaryana*. Amsterdam: North-Holland.

1985. *Hixkaryana and linguistic typology*. Dallas: Summer Institute of Linguistics and University of Texas at Arlington.

Derbyshire, D.C. and Pullum, G.K. (eds.) 1986. *Handbook of Amazonian languages*, Vol. I. Berlin: Mouton de Gruyter.

(eds.) 1990. *Handbook of Amazonian languages*, Vol. II. Berlin: Mouton de Gruyter.

(eds.) 1991. *Handbook of Amazonian languages*, Vol. III. Berlin: Mouton de Gruyter.

Dixon, R.M.W. 1972. *The Dyirbal language of North Queensland*. Cambridge: Cambridge University Press.

1977. *A grammar of Yidiɲ*. Cambridge: Cambridge University Press.

1982. *Where have all the adjectives gone?, and other essays in semantics and syntax*. Berlin: Mouton.

1988. *A grammar of Boumaa Fijian*. Chicago: University of Chicago Press.

1991. *A new approach to English grammar, on semantic principles*. Oxford: Clarendon Press.

1994. *Ergativity*. Cambridge: Cambridge University Press.

Forthcoming. *Australian languages*, Vol. I, *Their nature and development*; Vol. II, *A complete catalogue*. Cambridge: Cambridge University Press.

Dixon, R.M.W. and Aikhenvald, A.Y. 1997. 'A typology of argument-determined constructions', pp. 71–113 of Bybee, Haiman and Thompson 1997.

Dixon, R.M.W. and Vogel, A. Forthcoming. *The Jarawara language of southern Amazonia.*

Dubinsky, S., Lloret, M.-R. and Newman, P. 1988. 'Lexical and syntactic causatives in Oromo', *Language* 64.485–500.

Éva, H. 1990. 'Grammatical relations in Gamo: a pilot sketch', pp. 356–405 of *Omotic language studies*, ed. R.J. Hayward. London: School of Oriental and African Studies.

Evans, N. 1995. *A grammar of Kayardild, with historical-comparative notes on Tangkic.* Berlin: Mouton de Gruyter.

Fodor, J.A. 1970. 'Three reasons for not deriving "kill" from "cause to die"', *Linguistic Inquiry* 1.429–38.

Foley, W.A. 1991. *The Yimas language of New Guinea*. Stanford: Stanford University Press.

Fortescue, M. 1984. *West Greenlandic*. London: Croom Helm.

Frawley, W. 1992. *Linguistic semantics*. Hillsdale, N.J.: Lawrence Erlbaum.

Gair, J.W. 1970. *Colloquial Sinhalese clause structure*. The Hague: Mouton.

Gibson, J. 1980. 'Clause union in Chamorro and universal grammar'. Ph.D. dissertation. University of California at San Diego.

Givón, T. 1990. *Syntax: a functional-typological introduction*, Vol. II. Amsterdam: John Benjamins.

Golovko, E.V. 1993. 'On non-causative effects of causativity in Aleut', pp. 385–90 of Comrie and Polinsky 1993.

Grimes, C.E. 1991. 'The Buru language of eastern Indonesia'. Ph.D. thesis. Australian National University.

Guirardello, R. 1999. 'Trumai', pp. 351–3 of *The Amazonian languages*, ed. R.M.W. Dixon and A.Y. Aikhenvald. Cambridge: Cambridge University Press.

Haas, M. 1941. 'Tunica', pp. 1–143 of *Handbook of American Indian languages*, Vol. IV. New York: J.J. Augustin.

Haiman, J. 1983. 'Iconic and economic motivation', *Language* 59.781–819.

    1985. *Natural syntax*. Cambridge: Cambridge University Press.

Hale, K. 1997. 'The Misumalpan causative construction', pp. 199–216 of Bybee, Haiman and Thompson 1997.

Hetzron, R. 1976. 'On the Hungarian causative verb and its syntax', pp. 371–98 of Shibatani 1976b.

Hewitt, B.G. 1979. *Abkhaz*. Amsterdam: North-Holland.

    1983. 'The causative; Daghestanian variations on a theme', *Papers in Linguistics* 16.171–202.

Hinton, L. 1982. 'How to cause in Mixtec', *Berkeley Linguistics Society Proceedings* 8.354–63.

Holes, C. 1990. *Gulf Arabic*. London: Routledge.

Jeyapaul, V.Y. 1987. *Karbi grammar*. Mysore: Central Institute for Indian Languages.

Joseph, B.D. and Philippaki-Warburton, I. 1987. *Modern Greek*. London: Routledge.

Kachru, Y. 1976. 'On the semantics of the causative construction in Hindi-Urdu', pp. 353–69 of Shibatani 1976b.

Kakumasu, J. 1986. 'Urubu-Kaapor', pp. 326–403 of Derbyshire and Pullum 1986.

Keenan, E.L. and Comrie, B. 1977. 'Noun phrase accessibility and universal grammar', *Linguistic Inquiry* 8.63–99.

Kenesei, I., Vago, R.M. and Fenyvesi, A. 1998. *Hungarian*. London: Routledge.

Koehn, E. and Koehn, S. 1986. 'Apalai', pp. 33–127 of Derbyshire and Pullum 1986.

Kornfilt, J. 1997. *Turkish*. London: Routledge.

Kozinsky, I. and Polinsky, M. 1993. 'Causee and patient in the causative of transitive: coding conflict or doubling of grammatical relations', pp. 177–240 of Comrie and Polinsky 1993.

Krishnamurti, Bh. and Gwynn, J.P.L. 1985. *A grammar of Modern Telugu*. Delhi: Oxford University Press.

Kulikov, L.I. 1993. 'The "second causative": a typological sketch', pp. 121–54 of Comrie and Polinsky 1993.

LaPolla, R.J. 1996. 'Grammatical sketch of the Qiang language with texts and annotated glossary'. Typescript.

Li, C.N. and Thompson, S.A. 1976. 'Development of the causative in Mandarin Chinese: interaction of diachronic processes in syntax', pp. 477–92 of Shibatani 1976b.

Lord, C. 1974. 'Causative constructions in Yoruba', *Studies in African Linguistics*, Supplement 5, pp. 195–204.

Mahootian, S. 1997. *Persian*. London: Routledge.

Maran, L.R. and Clifton, J.R. 1976. 'The causative mechanism in Jinghpaw', pp. 443–58 of Shibatani 1976b.

Martin, J.B. 1991. 'Lexical and syntactic aspects of Creek causatives', *International Journal of American Linguistics* 57.194–229.

Masica, C.P. 1976. *Defining a linguistic area: South Asia*. Chicago: University of Chicago Press.

Matisoff, J.A. 1973. *The grammar of Lahu*. Berkeley and Los Angeles: University of California Press.

Merlan, F. 1982. *Mangarayi*. Amsterdam: North-Holland.

Mosel, U. 1984. *Tolai syntax and its historical development*. Canberra: Pacific Linguistics.

Nedjalkov, I. 1997. *Evenki*. London: Routledge.

Nedjalkov, V.P., Otaina, G.A. and Xolodovič, A.A. 1995. 'Morphological and lexical causatives in Nivkh', pp. 60–81 of *Subject, voice and ergativity: selected essays*, ed. D.C. Bennett, T. Bynon and B.G. Hewitt. London: School of Oriental and African Studies.

Nedyalkov, V.P. and Silnitsky, G.G. 1973. 'The typology of morphological and lexical causatives', pp. 1–32 *of Trends in Soviet theoretical linguistics*, ed. F. Keifer. Dordrecht: Reidel.

Nichols, J. 1985. 'Switch-reference causatives', *CLS* 21, part 2.193–203.

O'Connor, M.C. 1992. *Topics in Northern Pomo grammar*. New York: Garland.

Oswalt, R.L. 1977. 'The causative as a reference switching mechanism in Western Pomo', *BLS* 3.46–54.

Owens, J. 1985. *A grammar of Harar Oromo (Northeastern Ethiopia)*. Hamburg: Helmut Buske.

Palmer, F.R. 1994. *Grammatical roles and relations*. Cambridge: Cambridge University Press.

Pandharipande, R.V. 1997. *Marathi*. London: Routledge.

Payne, D.L. 1990. 'Morphological characteristics of Lowland South American languages', pp. 213–41 of *Amazonian linguistics: studies in Lowland South American languages*, ed. D.L. Payne. Austin: University of Texas Press.

Payne, D.L. and Payne, T.E. 1990. 'Yagua', pp. 249–474 of Derbyshire and Pullum 1990.

Popjes, J. and Popjes, J. 1986. 'Canela-Kraho', pp. 128–99 of Derbyshire and Pullum 1986.

Saksena, A. 1982. 'Contact in causation', *Language* 58.820–31.

Saltarelli, M. 1988. *Basque*. London: Routledge.

Sastry, G.D.P. 1984. *Mishmi grammar*. Mysore: Central Institute of Indian Languages.

Schaub, W. 1985. *Babungo*. London: Croom Helm.

Seki, L. Forthcoming. *Gramática da língua Kamaiurá*. Campinas: Editora da Unicamp.

Senn, A. 1966. *Handbuch der Litauischen Sprache*, Vol. I, *Grammatik*. Heidelberg: Winter.

Sharma, J.C. 1982. *Gojri grammar*. Mysore: Central Institute for Indian Languages.

Shibatani, M. 1976a. 'The grammar of causative constructions: a conspectus', pp. 1–40 of Shibatani 1976b.

(ed.) 1976b. *Syntax and semantics*, Vol. VI, *The grammar of causative constructions*. New York: Academic Press.

1990. *The languages of Japan*. Cambridge: Cambridge University Press.

Shopen, T. and Konaré, M. 1970. 'Sonrai causatives and passives: transformational versus lexical derivations for propositional heads', *Studies in African Linguistics* 1.211–54.

Sohn, H.-M. 1994. *Korean*. London: Routledge.

Song, J.J. 1996. *Causatives and causation*. London: Longman.

Sridhar, S.N. 1979. 'Dative subjects and the notion of subject', *Lingua* 49.99–125.

1990. *Kannada*. London: Routledge.

Suhandano. 1994. 'Grammatical relations in Javanese: a short description'. MA thesis, Australian National University.

Sulkala, H. and Karjalainen, M. 1992. *Finnish*. London: Routledge.

Sumbatova, N.R. 1993. 'Causative constructions in Svan: further evidence for role domination', pp. 253–70 of Comrie and Polinsky 1993.

Svantesson, J.-O. 1983. *Kammu phonology and morphology*, Traveaux de l'institut de linguistique de Lund 18. Lund: University of Lund.

Tampubolon, D.P. 1983. *Verbal affixations in Indonesian: a semantic exploration*. Canberra: Pacific Linguistics.

Tamura, S. 1988. 'Ainugo' ['The Ainu language'], pp. 6–94 of *Gengogaku daijten* [*Encyclopaedia of linguistics*], Vol. I. Toyko: Sanseido.

Tavares, P. 1995. 'Causation in Wayâna (Cariban)'. Handout for paper presented at a meeting of the Society for the Study of the Indigenous Languages of the Americas, held at the University of New Mexico.

Thomas, D.D. 1971. *Chrau grammar* (Oceanic Linguistics Special Publication No. 7). Honolulu: University of Hawaii Press.

Thomas, D.M. 1969. 'Chrau affixes', *Mon-Khmer Studies* 3.90–107.

Tonoike, S. 1978. 'On the causative constructions in Japanese', pp. 3–29 of *Problems in Japanese syntax and semantics*, ed. J. Hinds and I. Howard. Tokyo: Kaitakusha.

Trithart, M. 1977. 'Relational grammar and Chichewa subjectivization'. Ph.D. dissertation. UCLA.

Tsujimura, N. 1996. *An introduction to Japanese linguistics*. Oxford: Blackwell.

Vitale, A.J. 1981. *Swahili syntax*. Dordrecht: Foris.

Wali, K. and Koul, O.N. 1997. *Kashmiri: a cognitive–descriptive grammar*. London: Routledge.

Watkins, L.J. 1984. *A grammar of Kiowa*. Lincoln: University of Nebraska Press.

Wise, M.R. 1986. 'Grammatical characteristics of PreAndine Arawakan languages of Peru', pp. 567–642 of Derbyshire and Pullum 1986.

3   Valency-changing derivation in Central Alaskan Yup'ik

MARIANNE MITHUN

Central Alaskan Yup'ik is a language of the Eskimo-Aleut family, spoken in southwestern Alaska by over 10,000 people. Like other languages in the family, Yup'ik has much to contribute to the study of valency-changing derivation, particularly because of its explicit specification of grammatical relations and its wealth of valency-changing devices. The roles of participants in events and states are distinguished both by case suffixes on nouns and by pronominal suffixes on verbs. The language is highly polysynthetic, with hundreds of derivational suffixes, many of which affect argument structure. The rich inventory of valency-changing devices provides a fruitful basis for cross-linguistic comparison, showing us ways in which such devices can vary in their semantic, syntactic and discourse effects.

The basic grammatical structures of the Eskimoan languages are well understood, thanks to pioneering work on Greenlandic by Egede (1750, 1760), Kleinschmidt (1851), and many others working with Eskimo-Aleut languages since that time. Fine descriptions of Yup'ik are now available, especially Woodbury (1981), Jacobson (1984, 1995), Miyaoka (1984, 1987, 1996 and 1997) and Reed, Miyaoka, Jacobson, Afcan and Krauss (1977). These works have proven invaluable in the investigation of the structures discussed here. Additional studies are in Mithun (1996). Material cited in the present work comes primarily from conversations among members of the Charles family and their friends of Bethel, Alaska, especially Nick Charles (NC), Elena Charles (EC), George Charles (GC) and Elizabeth Charles Ali (EA).

1   Basic morphological structure

Yup'ik words are classified as either uninflected (particles) or inflected (nouns and verbs). Inflected words have a straightforward internal structure: an initial root (traditionally termed a base by Eskimologists), any number of derivational suffixes (termed postbases) and a final inflectional suffix complex (termed an ending).

root	(derivational suffixes)	inflectional suffixes
base	(postbases)	ending

nouns and verbs: internal structure

On nouns, the inflectional ending encodes number, case, and identification of the possessor if there is one. Singular, dual and plural number are distinguished; 1st, 2nd, 3rd and coreferential person for possessors; and seven cases: absolutive (unmarked), ergative (which also serves as the genitive), ablative ('from, about'), allative ('to, towards'), locative ('in, at'), vialis ('through' and instrumental 'with') and aequalis ('like').

(1)   Some sample nouns[1]

qayaq	qayak	qayarmi	qayacetun
qayar	qayar-k	qayar-mi	qayar-cetun
kayak	kayak-du	kayak-LOC	kayak-pl.VIALIS
kayak	two kayaks	in a kayak	with kayaks

Nouns may be derivationally complex.

(2)   Derived noun
kipusviliurtet
kipute-vik-liur-ta-t
buy-LOCATIVE.NOMINALIZER-be.occupied.with-AGENTIVE.NOMINALIZER-pl
storekeepers (lit. those who take care of the store)

Possession is shown by a transitive pronominal suffix referring to the possessor and the possessed.

---

[1] The transcription used here is the practical orthography developed by the Alaska Native Language Center in Fairbanks, Alaska. Stops are plain: *p, t, c* (= [č]), *k, q*. There is a series of voiced fricatives *v, s* = [z], *l, y, g* = [ɣ], *ug* = [ɣʷ]), *r* = [ʁ], *ur* = [ʁʷ], and a series of voiceless fricatives *vv* = [f], *ss* = [s], *ll* = [ɬ], *gg* = [x], *w* = [xʷ], *rr* = [x], *urr* = [xʷ]. Nasals are *m, n, ng* = [ŋ]. There are three prime vowels *i, a, u*, and schwa, spelled *e*. Following consonants the apostrophe (') usually indicates gemination, as in *Yup'ik*. In line one of the examples, the orthographic hyphen (-) separates enclitics. In line two, a hyphen separates suffixes and the equals sign (=) separates enclitics.

Work with speakers of Central Alaskan Yup'ik has been made possible by grants from the Academic Senate, University of California, Santa Barbara. I am especially grateful to Elizabeth Ali and George Charles for their help in transcribing and translating the conversations on which this work was based, and for their discussion of the material. I have also appreciated general discussions about the language with Nancy Caplow, Gary Holton, Jim Reed, Ivo Sanchez, Kathy Sands and Robin Shoaps.

(3)   Possessive suffixes
         qayaqa
         qayar-ka
         kayak-1sg/3sg
         my kayak

         iqvallerminek
         iqvar-ller-minek
         pick.berries-PAST.NOMINALIZER-R/3pl.ABLATIVE
         from her picked berries (lit. [she made it] from the berries she had picked)

On verbs, the inflectional ending contains a mood marker and pronominal suffix. The moods include an indicative, interrogative, optative, participial, subordinative and a set of connectives that link subordinate clauses: past contemporative ('when' in the past), contemporative ('while'), precessive ('before'), concessive ('whenever'), contingent ('whenever'), consequential ('because') and a conditional ('if, when in the future'). For each mood there is a pronominal suffix paradigm that specifies the core arguments of the clause, one for intransitives, two for transitives. Four persons are distinguished (1st, 2nd, 3rd, and co-referential or extended reflexive) and three numbers (singular, dual and plural). There is no gender distinction. The pronominal suffixes are now fused complexes, but within the pronominal paradigms for some moods (indicative, participial), traces of an absolutive category can be perceived, while within the paradigms for others (subordinative, the connectives), traces of a subject category can be discerned. Examples of verb morphology can be seen in (4).

(4)   Sample verbs: GC, EA, EC
(a)   aqumetullruuq
         aqume-tu-llru-u-q
         sit-customarily-PAST-INDICATIVE.INTRANSITIVE-3sg
         He would sit

(b)   tangerrsuumiitamken
         tangerr-yuumiite-a-mken
         see-not.want-INDICATIVE.TRANSITIVE-1sg/2sg
         I do not want to see you

(c)   aguumarlinrilkumeng-llu
         aguumar-li-nrite-ku-meng=llu
         basket-make-not-CONDITIONAL-R.pl=and
         and if they themselves did not make baskets

2   Stem types

The transitivity of every verb is clear from its pronominal suffixes. Verb stems fall into three transitivity classes: intransitive only (inflectable only as intransitives), transitive only (inflectable only as transitives) and ambitransitive (inflectable either way).

(5)   Intransitive only
      amllertuq
      amller-tu-q
      be.much-INDICATIVE.INTRANSITIVE-3sg
      It is a lot

amirlu-	'be cloudy'	malri-	'give birth to twins'
ayarr'ar-	'tell a string story'	naku-	'be cross-eyed'
elrir-	'hold a feast'	uar-	'yelp'
kaig-	'be hungry'	uite-	'open one's eyes, bloom'
kuvviar-	'drink coffee'	qakete-	'resubmerge after coming
mallu-	'find a beached carcass'		to the surface (fish, seal)'
panger-	'paddle with a double-bladed paddle'	qamigar-	'go seal-hunting with small sled and kayak in spring'

(6)   Transitive only
      eguaquraa
      eguaqur-a-a
      persuade-INDICATIVE.TRANSITIVE-3sg/3sg
      She persuaded him

allurte-	'take something from'	kelucar-	'lock'
egte-	'throw (usually away)'	nalug-	'hoist'
equg-	'carry on shoulder'	takar-	'be intimidated by'
kamak-	'suspect someone'	ullag-	'approach'
naive-	'pour from one container to another'	paqrite-	'discover missing (implying taken without permission)'
qacarte-	'hit or slap with the hand, blow against (of wind)'	qamite-	'give something to take along on a journey to'
tapir-	'give something along with'	uskurar-	'harness'

(7)   Ambitransitive: ige- 'to swallow'
      ig'uq   igaa
      ige-u-q   ige-a-a
      swallow-INDIC.INTRANSITIVE-3sg   swallow-INDIC.TRANSITIVE-3sg/3sg
      She swallowed   She swallowed it

The ambitransitives fall into two subclasses, termed 'agentive' and 'patientive' ambivalents or ambitransitives. With agentive ambitransitives, the single argument of the intransitive is agentive; it corresponds to the ergative argument of the transitive.

(8)   Agentive ambitransitives: akqe- 'promise'

akqua   akqaqa
akqe-u-a   akqe-ar-ka
promise-INDIC.INTRANSITIVE-1sg   promise-INDIC.TRANSITIVE-1sg/3sg
I promised   I promised him

amllir-	'step over (something)'	makete-	'get up; set (something)
anger-	'agree (with)'		upright'
callug-	'fight (with)'	naqe-	'ooze (on)'
callur-	'be too big (for)'	pai-	'stay behind; babysit for'
kaaleg-	'rummage (through)'	qakvar-	'win; beat'
kanar-	'emerge from woods	kagi-	'sweep (something)'
	down to body of water;	yuu-	'disembark; remove (net,
	emerge at'		snare), take off (clothing)'

With patientive ambitransitives, the single argument of the intransitive corresponds to the absolutive of the transitive. It thus tends to be a semantic
patient.

(9)   Patientive ambitransitives: cagte- 'scatter, spread out, be in disarray'

cagtuq   cagtaqa
cagte-u-q   cagte-ar-ka
scatter-INDIC.INTRANSITIVE-3sg   scatter-INDIC.TRANSITIVE-1sg/3sg
it is spread out, in disarray   I am spreading it out

akag-	'roll (something)'	mecir-	'be soaked; soak'
akngirte-	'get hurt; hurt'	nalke-	'be found; find'
alleg-	'get torn; tear (something)'	tallegte-	'get scratched; scratch'
amu-	'come out; extract'	tamar-	'be lost; lose, misplace'
egua-	'burn (something)'	palarte-	'not get; not give
kape-	'get stabbed; stab, poke,		enough'
	innoculate'	qacu-	'be loose, wrinkled;
passi-	'get squashed; smash flat'		gather (cloth), wrinkle'

There are never more than two core arguments in a verb. When a beneficiary
is involved in an event, it is often coded as the absolutive, as in *cikir-* 'give'
and *payugte-* 'bring food to':

(10)   *cikir-* 'give': EA

wani-wa,   carrakuinegmek   cikirciqamken
wani=wa ca-rraq-kuineg-mek   cikir-ciqe-a-mken
here=EMPH thing-little.bit-small.amount-ABL give-FUT-INDIC.TR-1sg/2sg
All right, I (ERGATIVE) will give you (ABSOLUTIVE) a little bit (ABLATIVE)

(11)   *payugte-* 'bring food to': EA

taukunek   payugeskii,   apa'urluni
tau-kunek payugte-ke-ii   apa-urluq-ni
that-pl.ABL bring.food-PART.TR-3sg/3sg grandpa-dear-3sg/3sg
She (ERGATIVE) brought those things to her dear grandfather (ABSOLUTIVE)

The semantic patient appears as an ablative (oblique), as can be seen in both (10) and (11). Other verbs with beneficiaries as absolutives include *aruqe-* 'to distribute gifts or shares of a catch' (*aruqai* 'he is distributing (things) to them'), *qamite-* 'to give something to take along on a journey' (*qamitaa* 'he gave <u>her</u> something to take along') and *apete-* 'to inquire, ask a question' (*aptaa* 'he asked <u>her</u>'). But beneficiaries need not always be coded as core arguments. The language offers extensive lexical and derivational alternatives. Other verbs cast the patient (object given/shown) as the absolutive, such as *mani-* 'show, display, put out on view, put on the stove', (*mania* 'she put <u>it</u> out, put <u>it</u> on the stove'), *nasvag-* 'show, display' (*nasvagaa* 'she is showing <u>it</u>'), and *apertur-* 'show, point out' (*aperturaa* 'she pointed <u>it</u> out'), in contrast with the derived *apertuute-* 'show, point out to' (*apertuutaa* 'she pointed something out to <u>him</u>').

3 Valency-reducing derivation

Within its derivational morphology, Yup'ik contains several devices for reducing valency. Some permit the omission of the agent from the set of core arguments, a typical function of passives. Others permit the omission of patients, a typical function of antipassives.

3.1 Agent omission

As seen in the previous section, Yup'ik contains a simple device for eliminating the agent from the set of core arguments. The verbs called patientive ambitransitives, such as *katag-* 'drop', may be inflected as intransitives. The single argument of the intransitive is the semantic patient: 'fall'. A comparison of the transitive and intransitive forms of 'drop/fall' can be seen in (12) and (13).

(12)   Transitive inflection of katag- 'drop': EA
        iggluni   taukut-llu atsat, kataglu<u>ki</u>–   tamalkuita
        igte-lu-ni   tau-kut=llu atsar-t katag-lu-<u>ki</u>   tamalkur-ita
        fall-SUB-3sg that-pl=and fruit-pl fall.off-SUB-<u>R</u>/3pl all-3pl
        <u>He</u> fell (off of his bicycle) and lost <u>all of the fruit</u>

(13)   Intransitive inflection of katag- 'fall': EA
        katalliniuq
        katag-llini-u-<u>q</u>
        fall.out-apparently-INDICATIVE.INTRANSITIVE-3pl
        <u>They</u> must have fallen out

Of course omission of the agent by inflection alone can be accomplished only with patientive ambitransitives. Yup'ik also contains derivational devices that can exclude agents from the core. Two suffixes in particular, *-cir-* and *-ma-*, appear to be passive in function.

(14)   Passive-like suffixes
         -cir-   tegleg-   'to steal'
                  teglegaa   'he stole it'   TRANSITIVE
                  teglegcirtuq   'it got stolen'   INTRANSITIVE

         -ma-   ini-   'to hang out to dry'
                  inia   'she hung it'   TRANSITIVE
                  inimauq   'it's been hung'   INTRANSITIVE

The suffix *-cir-* (with phonologically conditioned alternants *-sciur-*, *-scir-* and *-ciur-*) can be seen in (15). As a boat was being loaded in a rush, it tipped. Water in the bottom got onto the bedding and soaked it. A comparison of this verb with the basic form *mecunguq* 'it is wet', shows that the *-cir-* form does imply that the state of wetness resulted from an earlier event:

(15)   Suffix -cir-: EA
         mecungcirtuq   cf. mecunguq
         mecunge-cir-tu-q   mecunge-u-q
         be.soaked-ADVERSATIVE-   be.soaked-
         INDICATIVE.INTRANSITIVE-3sg   INDICATIVE.INTRANSITIVE-3SG
         It was caused to get wet   It is wet

A survey of the uses of *-cir-* indicates that it consistently carries an adversative meaning. As noted by Shibatani (1996) and others, this is a common though by no means necessary feature of many passives. In fact, it is the valency-changing effect of the suffix seen in (15) that is not a necessary element of its function. The example in (16) was used when someone had allowed the fish to become damp. Both the original verb base and the derived verb are intransitive, with the semantic patient as absolutive. There was thus no change in argument structure.

(16)   Adversative -cir-: EA
         neqerrluk   yukucirtuq
         neqe-rrluk   yuku-cir-tu-q
         fish-departed.from.natural.state be.mouldy-get-INDICATIVE.INTRANSITIVE-3sg
         That beautiful piece of dry fish (ABSOLUTIVE) got mouldy

If an agent is mentioned in such constructions, it is expressed in the allative (oblique) case. (Jacobson 1995 notes that in some areas, the ablative is used for this purpose.)

(17) Oblique agent: EA (elicited)
      neresciurtuq   qimugtemun
      nere-<u>sciur</u>-tu-q   qimugte-<u>mun</u>
      eat-<u>get</u>-INDICATIVE.INTRANSITIVE-3sg dog-<u>ALLATIVE</u>
      It (ABSOLUTIVE) <u>got</u> eaten <u>by</u> a dog (ALLATIVE)

The second suffix with passive-like meaning is *-ma-* (with phonologically conditioned alternants *-uma-*, *-ima-* and *-nga-*). It may be attached to verbs of all transitivity types. On transitive-only stems, it derives an intransitive with just a patient argument, as might be expected of a passive.

(18) -ma- on transitive-only stem
      meleg-   'to close'
      melgaa   'he closed <u>it</u>'
      melg<u>uma</u>uq   '<u>it</u> is closed'

The suffix *-ma-* may also be attached to ambitransitive stems. Here the pattern is slightly more unexpected. On agentive ambitransitives, the derived intransitive may have either an agent argument, as on the left below in (19), or a patient argument, as on the right.

(19) -ma- on agentive ambitransitive stem
      nere-   'to eat'
      ner'uq   '<u>he</u> ate'   neraa   'he ate <u>it</u>'
      ner<u>uma</u>uq '<u>he</u> has eaten'   ner<u>uma</u>uq '<u>it</u> has been eaten'

On patientive ambitransitives, the derived intransitive always has a patient argument.

(20) -ma- on patientive ambitransitive stem
      kitugte-   'to repair'
      kitugtuq   '<u>it</u> is fixed'   kitugtaa   'he fixed <u>it</u>'
      kitug<u>nga</u>uq '<u>it</u> is fixed'   kitug<u>nga</u>uq '<u>it</u> is fixed'

The suffix *-ma-* may also be attached to intransitive-only stems. The argument of the derived intransitive is the same as that of the base stem, semantic agent or patient.

(21) -ma- on intransitive-only stems
      ayag-   'to leave, go'   tuqu-   'to die'
      ayagtuq   '<u>he</u> left'   tuquuq   '<u>it</u> died'
      aya<u>uma</u>uq   '<u>he</u> has left, is gone' tuq<u>uma</u>uq '<u>it</u> is dead'

The pattern is not actually as complex as it first appears. In all derivations, the absolutive argument of the base is the absolutive of the derived intransitive. But what of the agentive ambitransitives, such as 'eat', for which the derived intransitive may be either the eater or the food eaten? As Jacobson points out (1995), the two possibilities result from the ambitransitive status of these stems. They have both agentive intransitive forms (*ner'uq* 'he ate') and transitive forms (*neraa* 'he ate it'). If the base of the derivation is assumed to be the intransitive form, the pattern matches that of 'leave', and the absolutive ('he') of the base remains the absolutive of the derived intransitive ('<u>he</u> ate' → '<u>he</u> has eaten'). If the base of the derivation is assumed to be the transitive form, the pattern matches that of 'close', and again the original absolutive is retained as the absolutive of the derived intransitive ('he ate <u>it</u>' → '<u>it</u> has been eaten').

There has been considerable discussion in the literature on the primary function of passives cross-linguistically, whether it is best viewed as the demotion of an agent, the promotion of a patient, or a focus on the state resulting from an action. An examination of the usage of Yup'ik *-ma-* shows that it has only this third function: it focusses on the lasting resultant state of the most significantly involved participant, the absolutive. It may or may not alter argument structure. It is thus a resultative, in the sense of Nedjalkov (1988). Like the adversative *-cir-*, it denotes the result of an action, rather than an inherent condition. The verb in (22) for example, built on the base *essagte-* 'scatter', was appropriate for beads spilt by someone knocking over a jar, but it would not be used for rocks found here and there on a hillside.

(22)   Resultant state: EA
      essagte-   'to scatter'
      essagtuq   'they are scattered'
      essagc<u>ima</u>ut   'they (beads) are scattered'

In fact, the only semantic contribution of the suffix *-ma-* may be an emphasis on the enduring time of the resultant state. Mrs Ali recounted that, while waiting at the airport, she became so engrossed in her reading that she failed to hear the announcement of her flight. She exclaimed:

(23)   Length of state: EA
      nanikuayartua   uita<u>uma</u>lua
      nanikuqa-yar-tu-a   uita-<u>uma</u>-lu-a
      be.distressed-would-INDICATIVE.INTRANSITIVE-1sg stay-<u>STATIVE</u>-SUB-1sg
      misvigmi
      mit'e-vig-mi
      alight-place-LOC
      I would have been distressed at having to stay <u>a long time</u> at the airport

As she viewed masks that had been collected by early Moravian missionaries and sent to Europe, she mused:

(24) Length of state: EA
      cataicimalliniut   kegginaguat
      cataite-<u>ima</u>-llini-u-t   kegginagur-et
      be.absent-<small><u>STATIVE</u></small>-apparently-<small>INDICATIVE.INTRANSITIVE</small>-3pl   mask-pl
      The masks were apparently out there

    avani   nunani   yaaqvani
    ava-ni   nuna-ni yaaqva-ni
    over.there-<small>LOC</small> land-<small>LOC</small> area.far.away-<small>LOC</small>
    in some indefinite place <u>for a long, long time</u>

As can be seen, though both *-cir-* and *-ma-* might seem at first to function as passives, in many cases converting a transitive stem into an intransitive with just a patient, neither suffix serves the full range of functions expected of prototypical passives. Both imply an event leading up to the resultant state predicated, but neither necessarily produces a change in argument structure. For this reason, neither is heavily utilized for syntactic or discourse functions. The primary function of the suffix *-cir-* is to focus on the adversity of a resultant state, and that of the suffix *-ma-* is to focus on its lasting effect. The fact that their specific functions are distinct is confirmed by their ability to co-occur within a single verb. The sentence in (25) was uttered by a speaker who had been away travelling for some time. She returned home to find that all of her dance wands (drumsticks) had been broken. The suffix *-cir-* emphasizes the adversity, and the suffix *-ma-* emphasizes the time that had elapsed since the breaking.

(25) Combination of adversative and lasting effect: EA
      ayemcirtumaut
      ayem-<u>cir</u>-te-<u>uma</u>-u-t
      snap-<u>get</u>-<small>CAUSATIVE</small>-<small><u>STATIVE</u></small>-<small>INDICATIVE.INTRANSITIVE</small>-3pl
      They're all broken!

It should be noted that the various Eskimo-Aleut languages apparently show different patterns in their uses of passive morphology (Tony Woodbury, p.c.; Fortescue 1984: 265–8 on Greenlandic; and others). Comparison of grammars of the modern languages suggests that they differ both in the forms of the derivational suffixes and in their functions.

3.2   *Patient omission*

Yup'ik also contains several devices for eliminating semantic patients from the set of core arguments of the clause, a function often termed 'antipassive'. A reduction in valency may be accomplished by inflection alone. Agentive ambitransitive verbs like *kitur-* 'to pass (someone/something)' may simply be inflected intransitively, with no mention of the person or object passed.

(26)   Intransitive inflection of agentive ambitransitive
        kitur-   'to pass'
        kituraa   'he passed him/her/it'   TRANSITIVE
        kiturtuq   'he passed by'   INTRANSITIVE

Examples of the use of the transitive and intransitive counterparts can be seen in (27) and (28) respectively.

(27)   Transitive inflection: EA
        ayaginanerani-am   una nasaurluyagaq
        ayag-inaner-ani=am   una nasaurlur-yagar
        leave-PAST.CONTEMPORATIVE-3sg=EMPHATIC this girl-little
        kituk<u>ii</u>
        kitur-ke-<u>ii</u>
        pass-PART.TRANS-<u>3sg/3sg</u>
        As he was going, he passed a little girl

(28)   Intransitive inflection: EA
        una mikelnguq kitulria
        una mikelnguq kitur-lria
        this child   pass-PART.INTRANSITIVE.<u>3sg</u>
        A child passed by

    This pattern of excluding semantic patients from the core by inflection serves an important discourse function in Yup'ik. In Yup'ik, as in a number of ergative languages, there is a grammatical requirement that absolutive arguments of transitives be identifiable (essentially definite; Mithun 1994). Unidentifiable (indefinite) semantic patients must be cast as obliques. In Yup'ik, the oblique category used for this purpose is the ablative. (The Eskimoan languages differ in this area.) An example of a nonspecific indefinite semantic patient can be seen in (29). It is not represented in the pronominal suffix on the verb, since it is not a core argument. The noun carries the ablative plural case suffix *-nek*.

(29)   Oblique indefinite patient: EA
        niitaqluteng   cali yug<u>nek</u>
        niite-aqe-lu-teng   cali yug-<u>nek</u>
        hear-repeatedly-SUB-3pl and person-<u>pl.ABLATIVE</u>
        And they (ABSOLUTIVE) would hear people (ABLATIVE)

The noun 'small bird' in (30) is specific but still indefinite. It carries the ablative singular suffix *-mek* and is also not represented in the pronominal suffix complex *-tek* 'they two'.

(30)   Oblique indefinite patient: GC
         yaqulcuar<u>mek</u>-llu-gguq,   pitellinilu<u>tek</u>   taukuk
         yaqulek-cuar-<u>mek</u>=llu=gguq   pite-llini-lu-<u>tek</u>   tau-kuk
         bird-little-ablative=also=hearsay catch.game-apparently-sub-<u>3du</u> that-du
         And it seems they (absolutive) must have caught a small bird (ablative)

Sentential complements are not sufficiently definite to be cast as core arguments.

(31)   Oblique sentential complement: EA
         Maaten   tangerr<u>tuq</u>,   iliit
         maaten   tangerr-<u>tu-q</u>   ila-it
         suddenly see-<u>indicative.intransitive-3sg</u> one.of-3sg/pl
         issratet   cataunani
         issrate-t cataite-na-ni
         basket-pl absent-sub-3sg
         Suddenly he (absolutive) noticed (intransitive) [that one of the baskets was gone]

Once introduced, participants are immediately eligible for absolutive status. In (32), the pears were indefinite when they were first introduced into the discourse ('this man was picking pears'), so they appeared in the ablative case. As soon as they were introduced, however, they could be considered definite, and so were eligible for absolutive status ('putting them into a basket, arranging them carefully').

(32)   Shift to identifiable and core status: EA
         ciungani-gguq   una angun, napami, atsa<u>nek</u>
         ciu-ngani=gguq   una angute napa-mi atsar-<u>nek</u>
         front-3sg/3sg.loc=hearsay this man   tree-loc fruit-pl.ablative
         In the beginning this man, in a tree,

         iqvalria,   atsarpag<u>nek</u>,   issramun
         iqvar-lria   atsar-rpag-<u>nek</u>   issrate-mun
         pick-part.intransitive.3sg fruit-very.large-pl.ablative basket-allative
         was picking <u>pears (ablative)</u>, <u>large pears (ablative)</u>,

         ellilu<u>ki</u>,   pinqeggcarlu<u>ki</u>
         elli-lu-<u>ki</u>   pinqegg-car-lu-<u>ki</u>
         put-sub-R/<u>3pl</u> neat-try-sub-R/<u>3pl</u>
         putting <u>them (absolutive)</u> into a basket, arranging <u>them (absolutive)</u> carefully

Because of the grammatical restriction against indefinite absolutives, most transitive stems, particularly those that might co-occur with indefinite patients in discourse, have some intransitive counterpart. As we saw above, agentive ambitransitives like 'pass by' may simply be inflected intransitively for this purpose. But transitive-only stems have no intransitive counterparts.

(33)   Transitive only
        ikayur-   'to help'
        ikayuraa   '<u>he</u> is helping <u>her</u>'   TRANSITIVE
        (no *ikayurtuq)

The patientive ambitransitives, such as 'cut fish for drying', do have intransitive counterparts, but their single argument is the semantic patient, the very participant that should be excluded from the core by an antipassive.

(34)   Intransitive inflection of patientive ambitransitive
        ulligte-   'to cut fish for drying in the traditional manner'
        ulligt<u>aa</u>   '<u>she</u> cut <u>it</u> for drying'   TRANSITIVE
        ulligt<u>uq</u>   '<u>it</u> is cut for drying'   INTRANSITIVE

Yet it would seem that speakers would want to use verbs such as these with indefinite semantic patients as well, in order to say such things as 'she's helping out' or 'she cut things'.

Such expressions are made possible by two derivational detransitivizers, *-(u)te-* and *-(g)i-*, originally termed by Kleinschmidt 'half transitives'. They function as derivational antipassives, eliminating the semantic patient from the set of core arguments.

(35)   Derivational detransitivizers -(u)te-, -(g)i-
        ikayur-   'to help'
        ikayuraa   '<u>she</u> helped <u>him</u>'   TRANSITIVE ONLY
        ikayu<u>ut</u>-uq   '<u>she</u> is helping out'   DERIVED INTRANSITIVE

        ulligte-   'to cut fish for drying'   PATIENTIVE TRANSITIVE
        ulligt-aa   '<u>she</u> cut <u>it</u> (the fish)'   TRANSITIVE
        ullig<u>ci</u>-uq   '<u>she</u> cut fish for drying'   DERIVED INTRANSITIVE

Use of the first detransitivizer with another transitive-only base can be seen in (36).

(36)   Detransitivized transitive-only
        tegu-   'to take'
        –   (no basic intransitive *teguuq)
        tegua   'he took it'
        tegu<u>tuq</u>   'he took (something)'

Use of the second detransitivizer with another patientive ambitransitive can be seen in (37).

(37)   Detransitivized patientive ambitransitive: GC
        camiliini   tuai maurluqa
        camiliini   tuai maurluq-ka
        sometimes and grandmother-1sg/3sg
        And sometimes my grandmother

        ulligcinaurtuq
        ulligte-i-naur-tu-q
        cut.fish-<u>DETRANSITIVIZER</u>-HAB-INDICATIVE.INTRANSITIVE-3sg
        luqruuyanek
        luqruuyag-nek [. . .]
        pike-pl.ABL
        would cut up pike [and make Eskimo ice cream]

The diachronic source of these two detransitivizers is interesting. Jacobson (1984: 453) traces *-(u)te-* to a benefactive and *-(g)i-* to a malefactive. In transitive benefactive constructions, the benefactor appears in the ergative case and the beneficiary in the absolutive.

(38)   Benefactive -ute-
        quuyurnitaa
        quuyurni-<u>ute</u>-a-a
        smile-<u>BENEFACTIVE</u>-INDICATIVE.TRANSITIVE-3sg/3sg
        He (ERGATIVE) is smiling at her (ABSOLUTIVE)

In malefactive transitives, the ergative argument acts to the disadvantage of the absolutive.

(39)   Transitive malefactive (Jacobson 1995: 134):
        qimugtem   neria   angun
        qimugte-m   nere-i-a-a   angun
        dog-ERGATIVE eat-<u>MALEFACTIVE</u>-INDICATIVE.TRANSITIVE-3sg/3sg man
        akutamek
        akutar-mek
        mixture-ABLATIVE
        The dog (ERGATIVE) ate some dried fish on the man (ABSOLUTIVE) (ate the man's fish)

It might be wondered how applicative morphemes like the benefactive and malefactive, whose primary function is to increase the valency of a stem, could evolve into detransitivizers. The evolution is explicable in terms of the Yup'ik transitivity classes. The applicatives can derive agentive ambitransitives. When the agentive ambitransitives are inflected intransitively, they leave just an agent absolutive as the only core argument. This result is the essence of antipassivation. Thus for the basic transitive-only root *ikayur-* 'help', there can be no intransitive inflection, but benefactive derivation can yield an agentive ambitransitive: *ikayur-ute-* → *ikayuute-* 'help to the benefit of'. The derived stem can then be inflected intransitively, leaving the helper as the only core argument: *ikayuutuq* 'she is helping out', the desired result. Some semantic motivation can be imagined behind the alternation of the benefactive and malefactive suffixes in this function: helping is usually to the benefit of someone, while cutting up fish is to the detriment of the fish. In general, however, the alternation between the two suffixes in this function is now a lexical matter, not necessarily semantically transparent.

4   Valency-increasing derivation

Yup'ik contains an extensive set of valency-increasing suffixes. Some are common cross-linguistically, such as the causatives, and some are less common, as will be seen. The Yup'ik causative system is somewhat unusual in its elaboration and its pervasive syntactic use.

4.1   Causatives

A number of causatives are built into the lexicon. Many patientive ambitransitives show a causative relationship between their intransitive and transitive forms, such as *akngirte-* 'get hurt', 'hurt someone'. Causation is automatically indicated by the transitive inflection.

(40)   Causative patientive ambitransitive
         akngirte-   'to get hurt (INTR), to hurt someone (TR)'
         akngirt-uq   'he got hurt'   INTRANSITIVE
         akngirt-aa   'he hurt her'   TRANSITIVE

There is also a substantial set of derivational causatives, most with slightly specialized meanings. The nature of the differences among them is not what might be expected, in that they often do not distinguish the degree of compulsion involved.

(41)   Derivational causatives
         -vkar-/-cete-   'let, allow, permit, cause, compel'
         -te-   'let, allow, cause, compel'
         -nar-   'cause'
         -rqe-   'intentionally or deliberately cause'
         -cetaar-   'try to cause'
         -narqe-   'tend to cause'
         -naite-   'tend not to cause'
         -cir-   'let, wait for, make'
         -(r/l)i-   'become or cause to become'

The most general causative has phonologically conditioned variants *-vkar-/ -cete-* (*-vkar-* after vowels, *-cete-* after consonants). It is used for a full range of causation, from allowing to compelling. All of the causatives appear on both intransitive and transitive bases.

(42)   'permit': EC
       alular<u>cec</u>ungramku
       alular-<u>cet</u>-yug-ngrar-mku [. . .]
       operate.motor-<u>permit</u>-want-CONCESSIVE-1sg/3sg
       Even if I wanted to <u>let</u> him to operate the motor [Daddy would not ask him]

(43)   'invite': EA
       nere<u>vkar</u>luki-llu   tamalkuita yuut
       nere-<u>vkar</u>-lu-ki=llu   tamalkuita yug-et
       eat-<u>cause</u>-SUB-R/3pl=too all   person-pl
       and they gave a feast for everyone (lit. And they made everyone eat)

(44)   'let', 'make': EA
       igte<u>vkar</u>aa
       igte-<u>vkar</u>-aa
       fall-<u>cause</u>-INDICATIVE.TRANSITIVE-3sg/3sg
       He <u>made</u> her fall / He dropped it

(45)   'make': EC
       qerali<u>vkar</u>luku-ll'
       qer'aq-li-<u>vkar</u>-lu-ku=llu
       fishrack-make-<u>cause</u>-SUB-R/3sg=too
       and I <u>made</u> him build fish racks

(46)   'force': GC
       tuai-q',   ilateng,   ane<u>vkan</u>gnaqluki . . .
       tuai=wa   ila-teng   ane-<u>vkar</u>-ngnaqe-lu-ki
       and.then=EMPHATIC relative-R/3pl go.out-<u>compel</u>-try-SUB-R/3pl
       They would try to <u>force</u> their relatives out

A second causative *-te-* contributes the same range of meanings: 'let', 'allow', 'cause', 'compel'. Its alternation with *-vkar-/-cete-* appears to be lexically conditioned.

(47)   Causative -te-: EA
       uita<u>se</u>nga
       uita-<u>te</u>-nga
       stay-<u>let</u>-OPT.2sg/1sg
       Leave me alone!

A third causative is no longer productive, but it appears in a number of verbs and nouns:

(48)   Non-productive -nar- 'cause', 'one that causes' (Jacobson 1984: 502):
      kenegnartuq   qatlinaq
      keneg-nar-tu-q   qatli-nar
      love-cause-INDICATIVE.INTRANSITIVE-3sg sting-cause
      She is lovely   nettle

The causatives themselves may be causativized.

(49)   Causative of causative: EA
      igtevkartaanga
      igte-vkar-te-a-anga
      fall-cause-cause-INDICATIVE.TRANSITIVE-3sg/1sg
      He made me drop it

Additional causative suffixes contribute slightly different shades of meaning. The suffix -rqe- includes a component of intention:

(50)   -rqe- 'deliberately cause' (Jacobson 1984: 549):
(a)   qia-   'cry'
        qiarqaa   'he intentionally made her cry'   (qiavkaraa 'he made her cry')

(b)   tupag-   'wake'
        tupagqaa 'he woke her up intentionally'

The causative -cir- indicates causation without direct effort, by waiting and allowing something to happen.

(51)   -cir- 'let, wait for': EC
(a)   anlluki   kinercirluki
        ane-te-lu-ki   kiner-cir-lu-ki
        go.out-with-SUB-R/3pl dry-wait.for-SUB-R/3pl
        . . . they would take them out and wait for them to dry

(b)   tuntuviit,   anerciraqluki
        tuntuvag-et aner-cir-aqe-lu-ki
        moose-pl   exit-wait-would-SUB-R/3pl
        We would wait for the moose to go out

Several causatives with more specific meanings have been formed from the compounding of two suffixes. The suffix -cetaar- 'try to cause' is descended from the causative -cete- followed by a suffix -aar- 'repeatedly' (Jacobson 1984: 439).

(52) -cetaar- 'try to cause': EC
      nau<u>cetaar</u>vigtun
      nau-<u>cetaar</u>-vig-tun
      grow-<u>try.to.cause</u>-place-AEQUALIS
      like a place to <u>try to grow</u> things
      ayuqelartut
      ayuqe-lar-tu-t
      be.alike-habitually-INDICATIVE.INTRANSITIVE-3pl
      they are the same as
      They are like flower pots

Another causative *-narqe-* was formed from a combination of the two causatives *-nar-* and *-rqe-* (Jacobson 1984: 505). It adds the meaning 'tend to cause'.

(53) -narqe- 'tend to cause' on intransitive: EC
      aling   epsalngu<u>narqe</u>llrullini-wall'
      aling   epe-yar-lngu-<u>narqe</u>-llru-llini=wall'
      oh.my suffocate-would-be.indisposed.from-<u>tend.to.cause</u>-PAST-
            apparently=EMPHATIC
      oh my it was apparently very tedious
      It sure was tedious! (epesalngu- 'to feel bad because of lack of fresh air')

(54) -narqe- 'tend to cause' on agentive ambitransitive: EA
      ircinrrat   irr'i<u>narq</u>ut
      ircinrrar-t   ir'i-<u>narqe</u>-u-t
      little.people-pl stare-<u>tend.to.cause</u>-INDICATIVE.INTRANSITIVE-3pl
      The Little People are to be marvelled at

It often occurs with what are termed 'emotional' roots by Jacobson.

(55) -narqe- 'tend to cause' with emotional root: GC
      angla<u>narqe</u>lallruuq,
      angla-<u>narqe</u>-lar-llru-u-q
      be.fun-<u>tend.to.cause</u>-habitually-PAST-INDICATIVE.INTRANSITIVE-3sg
      akakiignek,   qalulleq
      akakiig-nek   qalu-ller
      whitefish-pl.ABL dip-PAST.NOMINALIZER
      It used to be fun dipnetting whitefish

It has a negative counterpart *-naite-* 'tend not to cause', formed from a combination of *-nar-* and the negative *-(ng)ite-* (Jacobson 1984: 502).

(56) -naite- 'tend not to cause': EA
      takumcunaituq
      takumcu-nait-u-q
      pity-tend.not.to.cause-INDICATIVE.INTRANSITIVE-3sg
      He does not engender pity

Finally, causative meaning can be added by a suffix *-(r/l)i-* whose function is primarily inchoative: 'become or cause to become'.

(57)   -(r/l)i- 'cause to become': GC
         uqnariqapiarluku   camiliini-llu   yuut.
         uqnarqe-i-qapiar-lu-ku   camiliini=llu   yug-et
         burning.hot-make-very-SUB-R/3sg sometimes=also person-pl.ERG
         And sometimes the people would make it (the steambath) very hot

4.1.1   The fate of extra arguments

When a causative is added to an intransitive verb, the causer is expressed as an ergative, and the causee or secondary agent, that is the one caused to act, appears as the absolutive.

(58)   Secondary agent of intransitive is absolutive: EA; EA (elicited)
(a)   tutgara'urluq   tauna ayavkaqii
         tutgarar-urluq   tauna ayag-vkar-ke-ii
         grandchild-dear that   go-allow-PART.TR-3sg/3sg
         He (ERGATIVE) allowed the grandchild (ABSOLUTIVE) to leave

(b)   aipama   mingqevkaraanga
         aipar-ma   mingqe-vkar-a-anga
         spouse-1sg/3sg.ERG sew-cause-INDICATIVE.TRANSITIVE-3sg/1sg
         qerrulliigminek
         qerrullii-gminek
         pant-3Rsg/3du.ABL
         My husband (ERGATIVE) had me (ABSOLUTIVE) sew his pants (ABLATIVE)

When the caused action is transitive, the intermediate agent (causee) is not a core argument. The core arguments are the causer (ergative) and the entity ultimately affected (absolutive). The intermediate agent, the causee, may be identified by an allative nominal.

(59)   Secondary agent of transitive is allative: GC; EA (elicited)
(a)   ciin yungcaristamun   kitugtevkarluku   pillrunritececiu
         ciin yugngecarista-mun kitugte-vkar-lu-ku   pi-llru-nrite-ce-ciu
         why doctor-ALLATIVE   repair-cause-SUB-R/3sg do-PAST-NEG-Q-2du/3sg
         Why didn't you (ERGATIVE) get him (ABSOLUTIVE) fixed by the doctor
         (ALLATIVE)?

(b)   angutem paniminun
         angute-m panig-minun
         man-ERG daughter-3R.sg/3sg.ALLATIVE
         mingqevkarak
         mingqe-vkar-a-k
         sew-cause-INDICATIVE.TRANSITIVE-3sg/3du
         The man (ERGATIVE) asked his daughter (ALLATIVE) to sew them (his pants
         (ABSOLUTIVE du))

4.1.2   The syntactic function of causatives

Among the inflectional moods in Yup'ik is one termed the 'subordinative'. The Yup'ik subordinative does much more than mark syntactically subordinate clauses within sentences. It also links sentences over stretches of discourse. It serves to relate sentences, which may be intonationally independent, on a higher level of structure, such as sequences of events in narrative, as in (60). There is a grammatical requirement on such sequences: subordinatives must show the same SUBJECT as the main clause (glossed as the coreferential r).

(60)   Subordinative mood: EC
       kiagmi   uksurpailegan,   ayunek
       kiag-mi   uksur-paileg-an   ayut-nek
       summer-LOC be.winter-PRECESSIVE-3sg Labrador.tea-pl.ABL
       in summer   before winter   Labrador tea

       pit'lallruuq   waten
       pite-lar-llru-u-q   waten
       hunt-habitually-PAST-INDICATIVE.INTRANSITIVE-3sg like.this
       she used to pick (INDICATIVE)   this way

       amllerivkenaki   qillertagluki.
       amller-i-vke-na-ki   qillerte-aqe-lu-ki
       be.many-making-not-SUB-R/3pl   tie-habitually-SUB-R/3pl
       not making many (SUBORDINATIVE) tying them together (SUBORDINATIVE)

       enemun   agartaqluki,   tuai-ll'   tamakut
       ena-mun   agar-te-aqe-lu-ki   tuai=llu tama-kut
       house-ALL   hang-cause-habitually-SUB-R/3pl then=and those-pl
       to the house hanging them (SUBORDINATIVE) and then those

       agiireskata,   atauciin
       agiirte-ku-ata   atauciq-in
       approach.from.distance-COND-3pl one-3sg/3pl.ERG
       when they arrived (CONDITIONAL) one of them

       teguluki,   kumarrlukik   amiigem-llu
       tegu-lu-ki   kumarte-lu-ki   amiig-m=llu
       grasp-SUB-R/3pl   light-SUB-R/3pl   door-ERG=also
       taking them (SUBORDINATIVE) lighting them (SUBORDINATIVE) and the door

       ciuqranun   nangertevkarlua   tarvarlua
       ciuqerr-anun   nangerte-vkar-lu-a   tarvar-lu-a
       front-3sg/3sg.ALL stand-cause-SUB-R/1sg   bless-SUB-R/1sg
       in front of it   having me stand (SUBORD) blessing me (SUBORD).

'In the summertime, before winter, <u>she</u> (my grandmother) used to pick Labrador tea leaves. <u>She</u> would tie them together this way, not very many of them. <u>She</u> would let them hang inside the house. Then when those people were arriving (people invited to a potlatch), <u>she</u> would take one of the bundles, light it, and have me stand in the doorway, blessing me.'

(In spontaneous speech, the controlling sentence is not always overt.) The fact that subject coreference is a grammatical requirement can be seen in the unambiguous interpretation of sentences like that in (61).

(61)   Subject continuity in subordinatives: EA
 wangakii   ayagluni
 tanvag-ke-ii   ayag-lu-ni
 look.at-PARTICIPIAL.TR-3sg/3sg leave-SUBORDINATIVE-3sg
 <u>He</u> watched her as <u>he</u> went

The pattern of linking clauses that share the same subject, or mental point of departure, is not surprising. They are portrayed as elements of a larger discourse unit. On occasion, however, a clause might be considered an integral component of this unit, but involve a different subject. It is here that the causatives are exploited for purely syntactic purposes. In the third line of (60) above, for example, the essential message might have been 'She would tie them together, they were not many'. Instead of making the tea-leaves the subject of the second clause, however, Mrs Charles retained her grandmother as subject by adding the suffix -*i*- 'make, cause': '<u>She</u> tied them together, not making them many'. Causatives can maintain subject continuity by adding a causer that is coreferential with the rest of the sequence. In the last line of (60), rather than '<u>I</u> would stand in the doorway and <u>she</u> would bless me' with different subjects 'I' and 'she', Mrs Charles used a causative: '<u>She</u> would <u>have</u> me stand in the doorway and (<u>she</u>) would bless me'.

These uses of the causative in (60) seem quite natural, a way the events might have been expressed regardless of the syntactic requirement of coreference. In some contexts, however, the purely syntactic function of the causative is clear, as in (62) from Jacobson.

(62)   Causative in purely syntactic function (Jacobson 1995: 333):
 yuurtellruunga   apa'urluqa
 yug-urte-llru-u-nga   apalur-ka
 person-become-PAST-INDICATIVE.INTRANSITIVE-1sg grandfather-1sg/3sg
 I was born   my grandfather

 tuqurraar<u>ce</u>lluku
 tuqu-rraar-<u>cete</u>-lu-ku
 die-first-<u>allow</u>-SUB-R/3sg
 I let him die first
 I was born after my grandfather died

Of course I could not cause or even allow the death of my grandfather before I was born.

A detail adding a final complication to the picture is the fact that purely syntactic causative suffixes are sometimes omitted in natural speech. Their effect is still observable in the argument structures of the pertinent verbs, however, as can be seen in the pronominal suffix 'one/her' on 'go by boat' in (63).

(63)   Omission of purely causative suffixes: EC
        natmun   ayagteciiqaa
        nat-mun   ayag-te-ciiq-a-a
        where-ALL go-cause-FUT-INDICATIVE.TRANSITIVE-3sg/3sg
        angyarluku.
        angyar-(0)-lu-<u>ku</u>
        go.by.boat-<u>(cause)</u>-SUB-<u>R/3sg</u>
        She will be allowed to go somewhere with a boat.

4.2   Other agent addition

In addition to the causatives, Yup'ik contains a more unusual set of valency-increasing derivations that add an agent to the set of core arguments. These are suffixes with meanings something like those of evidentials in certain other languages, but they differ significantly in that they alter argument structure. The suffixes are *-sqe-* 'request that, want', *-ni-* 'claim, say that' *-yuke-* 'think that' and *-nayuke-* 'think that perhaps, expect'.

4.2.1   *-sqe-* 'request that, want'

The suffix *-sqe-* can be added to both intransitive and transitive bases. When added to intransitives, it derives a transitive verb whose ergative argument is the person requesting, and absolutive argument is the person requested to act.

(64)   Derivation from intransitive base: EC; NC
(a)   yungcariste<u>m</u>   tage<u>sqaten</u>
        yungcarista-<u>m</u> tage-<u>sqe</u>-a-<u>ten</u>
        doctor-<u>ERG</u>   go.up/inland-<u>request</u>-INDIC.TR-<u>3sg/2sg</u>
        The doctor (ERGATIVE) has asked you (ABSOLUTIVE) to go (to the hospital)

(b)   uyangterrare<u>sqe</u>luku   pitangqertassiarluku
        uyangte-rrar-<u>sqe</u>-lu-ku   pitar-ngqerr-tassiar-lu-ku
        look.leaning.forward-first-<u>ask</u>-SUB-<u>R/3sg</u>   game-have-determine-SUB-R/3sg
        (You (ERGATIVE)) have him (ABSOLUTIVE) look to see if there is game

When the suffix *-sqe-* is attached to a transitive base, it yields a transitive verb whose ergative participant requests action on the absolutive by the allative participant.

(65)   Derivation from transitive base: EC; EA (elicited)

(a)   tutraragka,   aipak   piyugngakan,
        tutrar-gka   apia-k   pi-yugnga-aqa-an
        grandchild-1sg/3du.ABL   other-du   do-able-CONTINGENT-3sg
        my two grandchildren   one of them   if he is able to do
        When I arrive, I (ERGATIVE) will have one of my grandchildren (ALLATIVE)

        tekiteqataquma,   pairrsaagesqellua
        tekite-qatar-qu-ma   pairte-ssaag-sqe-lu-a
        arrive-going.to-COND-1SG   meet-try-ask-SUB-R/1SG
        when I am going to arrive <u>asking</u> him to come meet <u>me</u>
        try to meet me (ABSOLUTIVE) if he can

(b)   anngama   paniminun
        anngar-ma   panig-minun
        older.brother-1sg/3sg.ERG daughter-3R.sg/3sg.ALL
        atuutesqai
        atur-ute-sqe-a-i
        sing-for-ask-INDICATIVE.TRANSITIVE-3sg/3pl
        My older brother (ERGATIVE) asked his daughter (ALLATIVE) to sing for
        them (ABSOLUTIVE)

4.2.2   *-ni-* 'claim, say that', *-yuke-* 'think that' and *-nayuke-* 'think that perhaps'

The suffixes *-ni-*, *-yuke-* and *-nayuke-* can be added to both intransitive and
transitive bases. Any of the derived verbs can then be inflected either intransitively or transitively. In all of these constructions, the absolutive argument of
the base remains as the absolutive argument of the derived verb. Intransitive
inflection indicates that someone is claiming or thinking something about
himself or herself.

(66)   Intransitive from intransitive: EA (elicited)

(a)   kaigniuq
        kaig-ni-u-q
        hungry-claim-INDICATIVE.INTRANSITIVE-3sg
        She (ABSOLUTIVE) says she's hungry

(b)   kaigyukuq
        kaig-yuke-u-q
        be.hungry-think-INDICATIVE.INTRANSITIVE-3sg
        She (ABSOLUTIVE) thinks she's hungry

If someone else is making the claim or having the thought, the verb is inflected
transitively, with the claimer or thinker in the ergative case.

(67)   Transitive from intransitive: GC (elicited)
(a)   kaig<u>ni</u>a
       kaig-<u>ni</u>-a-a
       hungry-<u>claim</u>-INDICATIVE.TRANSITIVE-3sg/3sg
       She (ERGATIVE) says he (ABSOLUTIVE) is hungry

(b)   kai<u>nayuke</u>luki   ukliuq
       kaig-<u>nayuke</u>-lu-ki   ukli-u-q
       hungry-<u>think.maybe</u>-SUB-R/3pl cut.up-INDICATIVE.INTRANSITIVE-3sg
       She is preparing food, (she (ERGATIVE)) thinking they (ABSOLUTIVE) might
       be hungry

(There is no gender distinction. Different genders are used here in the free
translations simply to keep reference clear.)

If the claim or thought is about a transitive action, the agent of that act can
be identified by a noun in the allative case.

(68)   Intransitive from transitive (Jacobson 1995: 324):
       arnaq   ikayullru<u>ni</u>uq   angut<u>mun</u>
       arnaq   ikayu-llru-<u>ni</u>-u-q   angute-<u>mun</u>
       woman help-PAST-<u>claim</u>-INDICATIVE.INTRANSITIVE-3sg man-<u>ALLATIVE</u>
       The woman (ABSOLUTIVE) says that the man (ALLATIVE) helped her

(69)   Transitive from transitive (Jacobson 1995: 326):
       aatav<u>nun</u>   civtellru<u>yuke</u>kaqa   kuvyaq
       aata-v<u>nun</u>   civte-llru-<u>yuke</u>-ar-ka   kuvyar
       father-2sg/3sg.<u>ALL</u> set-PAST-<u>think</u>-INDICATIVE.TRANSITIVE-1sg/3sg net
       I (ERGATIVE) think your father (ALLATIVE) set the fishnet (ABSOLUTIVE)

4.2.3   Syntactic usage

The derivational suffixes of requesting, claiming and thinking add an agent
argument, much like the causatives do. They are exploited in the same way as
causatives to ensure the maintenance of subject coreference in subordinative
sequences, especially with verbs of requesting, speaking and thinking. Thus
rather than saying 'They$_i$ invited the Yup'ik people (them$_j$) to come to their
house', Mrs Ali used a derived request form: 'They$_i$ invited them$_j$, they$_i$
requesting them to come'.

(70)   Request for intransitive action with -sqe-: EA
       yuut   kelellinikait,   enitnun
       yug-et   keleg-llini-ke-ait   ena-it-nun
       person-pl invite-apparently-PART.TR-<u>3pl</u>/3pl house-3pl/sg-ALL
       aya<u>sqe</u>luki
       ayag-<u>sqe</u>-lu-ki
       go-<u>request</u>-SUB-<u>R</u>/3pl
       It seems they invited the Yup'ik people to come to their house

The same strategy is used with transitives. Rather than saying 'He requested that she sing-for them', Mrs Ali volunteered 'He requested her, he asking (her) to sing-for them'.

(71)   Request for transitive action with -sqe-: EA (elicited)
elliimeraa   atuutesqeluuki
ellimer-a-a   atur-ute-sqe-lu-ki
request-INDICATIVE.TRANSITIVE-3sg/3sg sing-for-ask-SUB-R/3pl
He ordered her to sing for them

The same strategy can be seen with *-ni-* 'claim' in (72). Rather than saying 'When we were about to stop playing tag, the one who was it was the winner', Mrs Charles said, 'When we were about to stop playing tag, we would proclaim the one who was the winner'.

(72)   Claiming with -ni-: EC
taqekugtaqamta   piaqluta   una-llu
taqe-kugte-aqa-mta   pi-aqe-lu-ta   una=llu
stop-about.to-CONTINGENT-1pl do-habitually-SUB-1pl this=and
when we were about to stop   we would say   and this one
taqvailemta   agturcitenritelleq
taqe-vaileg-mta   agtur-cir-te-nrite-ller
quit-PRECESSIVE-1pl touch-get-APPLICATIVE-NOT-PAST.NOMINALIZER
before we stopped   the one who had not been touched
qalliniluku
qalli-ni-lu-ku
one.on.top-claim-SUB-R/3sg
we claimed him/her winner
And when we were about to stop (playing tag), we would say that the one who had not been touched before we stopped was the winner

5   Applicatives

Yup'ik contains several applicative suffixes that function to derive transitives by adding an absolutive argument. The base may be either intransitive or transitive. The most productive applicative is the general *-(u)te-* 'to, for, with, together, reciprocally'. Its precise function depends on the meaning of the verb to which it is attached.

(73)   Verbs of communication: 'to' EA
uumiku   qalaruciiqamken
uumiku   qalarte-ute-ciiqe-ar-mken
next.time talk-to-FUTURE-INDIC.TR-1sg/2sg
I'll talk to you later

(74)   Benefactive 'for': EC
        kalukau<u>ll</u>uta   unuaquani
        kalukar-<u>ute</u>-lu-ta   unuaqu-ani
        hold.feast-<u>for</u>-SUB-R/1pl next.day-3sg/3sg.ABL
        They made us a Kalukaq the next day

(75)   Verbs of motion: comitative 'with' EA
        eliin   aya<u>ull</u>ua
        elliin   ayag-<u>ute</u>-lu-a
        3sg.ERG go-<u>with</u>-SUB-R/1sg
        He took me with him

The applicative is also used with dual or plural intransitive inflection to derive reciprocals.

(76)   Intransitive applicative for reciprocal: EC
        anguya<u>ute</u>llratni, . . .
        anguyag-<u>ute</u>-tu-ller-atni
        fight.in.battle-<u>with.each.other</u>-customarily-PAST.CONTEMPORARIVE-3pl
        When they used to fight <u>each other</u> = when there were wars . . .

If the base is transitive, the semantic patient may be overtly identified by an ablative noun.

(77)   Semantic patient as ablative: EC
        aaniin-wa   qanr<u>ute</u>lallrulliki
        aana-an=wa   qanr-<u>ute</u>-lar-llru-li-ki
        mother-3sg/3sg.ERG=EMPHATIC say-<u>to</u>-habitually-PAST-OPT.TR-3sg/3pl
        her mother   she used to tell her
        I guess her mother used to tell her

        ilallrin   atrit<u>nek</u>
        ila-ller-in   ater-it<u>nek</u>
        relative-PAST-R/3pl.ERG   name-3pl/pl.ABL
        her relatives that used to be their names
        the names (ABLATIVE) of her deceased relatives

As seen earlier, Yup'ik also contains a malefactive suffix -*(g)i*-. The transitive malefactive in (39) is from Jacobson (1995). More usual for the Charles family are intransitive malefactives.

(78)   Intransitive malefactive: EA
        tulukarulkuk   ner<u>i</u>ulkugtur-am
        tulukarug-lkug   nere-<u>i</u>-ur-lkug-tu-r=am
        raven-despicable eat-MALEFACTIVE–purposely-despicably-
                                INDICATIVE.INTRANSITIVE-3sg-EMPHATIC
        That darned raven (ABSOLUTIVE) is deliberately eating food intended for someone else

The victim may be expressed obliquely by a nominal in the ablative case. The sentence in (79) came up in the context of a man digging on the tundra, who uncovered a cache of roots stored by mice.

(79)   Ablative victim of malefactive: EA
        elagiuq   avelnganek
        elag-i-u-q   avelngar-nek
        dig-MALEFACTIVE-INDICATIVE.INTRANSITIVE-3sg mouse-pl.ABLATIVE
        He (ABSOLUTIVE) dug to the disadvantage of the mice (ABLATIVE)

As seen in section 3.2, when this suffix is attached to a transitive-only base like 'help', or a patientive ambitransitive like 'cut up', it functions primarily as an antipassive, usually without malefactive sense. When it is attached to an intransitive-only base such as *ayag-* 'leave' or *ane-* 'go out', it again shows its original malefactive sense, but the absolutive argument of the derived malefactive is the victim.

(80)   Malefactive on intransitive-only: absolutive victim (Jacobson 1984: 452):
        [While he was boating in rough water,]
        aniuq   kevingutnek
        ane-i-u-q   kevirngut-nek
        go.out-MALEFACTIVE-INDICATIVE.INTRANSITIVE-3sg caulk-pl.ABLATIVE
        his caulking came out (of the boat)
        (lit. he (ABSOLUTIVE) was de-caulked by caulking (ABLATIVE))

Two other applicative suffixes have been formed by suffix compounding. One of these is *-(u)teke-* 'on account of, concerning'.

(81)   -(u)teke- 'on account of, concerning': EA
        tuai-w',   naurrlugaan
        tuai=wa   naurrlug-a-an
        because=well ill-CONSEQUENTIAL-3sg
        unegutkaa
        unegte-uteke-a-a
        remain.behind-on.account.of-INDICATIVE.TRANSITIVE-3sg/3sg
        Well, she remained behind because of him, since he was sick

The other is *-(u)cite-* 'in place of, instead of'.

(82)   -(u)cite- 'in place of, instead of' (Jacobson 1984: 446):
(a)   yuracitaa
        yurar-cite-a-a
        dance-in.place.of-INDICATIVE.TRANSITIVE-3sg/3sg
        He danced in her place

(b)   cikir<u>c</u>itaa   avukamek
        cikir-<u>cite</u>-a-a   avukar-mek
        give.to-<u>in.place.of</u>-INDICATIVE.TRANSITIVE-3sg/3sg supplement-ABL
        She is giving bread to eat with tea in his place

Mrs Ali notes that this construction is used often because a child named for a deceased person carries out actions on behalf of that person, in memory of him or her.

6   Summary

The rich inventory of valency-changing devices in Central Alaskan Yup'ik shows us some interesting ways in which such devices may vary cross-linguistically, both in their semantic detail and in their syntactic and discourse functions.

The effects of such devices are particularly clear in Yup'ik, due to the unusually explicit marking of argument structure. The indicative and participial mood suffixes on verbs show distinct transitive and intransitive forms, and all core arguments are specified by pronominal suffixes. The pronominal suffixes, which have now become fused complexes, show traces of an absolutive category in some moods (indicative, participial) but traces of a subject category in others (subordinative, connective). In addition, nouns are inflected for case. Noun case marking follows a clear ergative pattern.

Yup'ik contains both inflectional and derivational valency-decreasing morphology. Several devices can result in the elimination of a semantic agent from the set of core arguments of a clause, a function typically associated with passives. With one class of verbs, the patientive ambitransitives, a passive-like effect may be accomplished by simple intransitive inflection. For other verbs, only derivational suffixes can have such an effect. The uses of the suffixes reveal, however, that their primary function is not to alter argument structure but rather to focus on the state resulting from an action. One suffix, *-cir-*, contributes adversative meaning; the other, *-ma-*, emphasizes the lengthy quality of the resultant state. The two suffixes may affect case relations incidentally, but perhaps because that is not their primary function, they are not generally exploited for syntactic or discourse purposes.

By contrast, several antipassive-like devices play an important syntactic role. Yup'ik has a syntactic requirement that only identifiable (definite) arguments may serve as the absolutives of transitives. Events directed at indefinite patients must be expressed with grammatically intransitive verbs. With one class of verbs, the agentive ambitransitives, intransitive inflection alone is sufficient: the resulting verb has only a single agentive argument. With other transitives, the derivational suffixes -*(u)te-* and -*(g)i-*, descended from a bene-factive and a malefactive respectively, are used as detransitivizers.

Yup'ik also contains a substantial inventory of valency-increasing devices. The language is unusually rich in morphology that adds agents to the set of core arguments, with a rich set of causatives and another set of suffixes with evidential-like meanings. Some causatives are produced inflectionally. Many patientive ambitransitives show a causative relation between their alternate forms, such as *katag-* 'drop/fall'. Transitive inflection alone yields a causative. For other verbs, causatives are formed derivationally. The set of causative suffixes is large, and provides fine semantic distinctions: -*vkar-*, -*te-*, -*nar-* 'let, allow, permit, cause, compel'; -*cir-* 'let, wait for, make'; -*rqe-* 'intention-ally or deliberately cause'; -*cetaar-* 'try to cause'; -*narqe-* 'tend to cause'; -*naite-* 'tend not to cause'; and -*(r/l)i-* 'become or cause to become'. A second set of derivational suffixes add evidential-like meanings: -*sqe-* 're-quest that, want'; -*ni-* 'claim that'; -*yuke-* 'think that'; -*nayuke-* 'think that perhaps'. All of these derivational suffixes may be added to either intransitive or transitive bases. All serve an important syntactic function. Sequences of topically related sentences in Yup'ik are frequently linked in discourse with the subordinative mood. There is a grammatical requirement that all sentences so linked must share the same subject. The causative and evidential agent-adding suffixes are exploited to ensure the maintenance of subject continuity over such sequences. If a linked clause would not otherwise have a coreferent subject, one may be added as the causer, requester, claimer or thinker. (Causatives with a similar function have also been noted in the Pomoan languages of California, in Chechen and Ingush of the Caucasus, and in Coptic (Oswalt 1977, Nichols 1985, O'Connor 1992).)

Finally, Yup'ik contains several applicatives that serve to add an absolutive argument. The general applicative -*(u)te-* 'to, for, with, together, reciprocally' is pervasive. The malefactive -*(g)i-* 'to the detriment of' is rarer. Two more suffixes have come into the language through suffix compounding, -*(u)teke-* 'on account of, concerning' and -*(u)cite-* 'in place of, instead of'. All of these markers function to a certain extent to allow more topical participants, usu-ally humans, to be expressed as part of the core, specified by the pronominal suffixes on the verb.

All of the valency-changing devices may result in the expression of semantic agents or patients outside of the core, with oblique nominals. Passives can result in the exclusion of semantic agents from the core, and antipassives in the exclusion of semantic patients. Valency-increasing processes can result in the exclusion of certain arguments as well. When they are applied to bases that are already transitive, one of the original core arguments is displaced. With causatives and the evidential-like suffixes, the displaced argument is the intermediate agent. With benefactives and malefactives, the excluded argument is the semantic patient. In Yup'ik, the excluded arguments are handled in a systematic way. Semantic agents are expressed obliquely as allatives, and semantic patients as ablatives.

Valency-changing devices in Yup'ik are numerous, pervasive and often highly productive, but they are not simple mechanical operations. All are closely tied to the lexicon in one way or another. Of course some manipulation of argument structure is accomplished by simple lexical choice. The inflectional devices for altering argument structure are dependent on the transitivity class of individual lexical items (intransitive-only, transitive-only, agentive ambitransitive, patientive ambitransitive). The derivational devices are closely tied to the lexicon as well: they create lexical items that are stored and recognized as units by speakers. In many cases, such as with causatives and antipassives, suffix choice is simply a lexical matter, not predictable by general rule. At the same time, the valency-changing morphology serves important syntactic functions, ensuring that indefinite semantic patients are expressed outside of the set of core arguments, and preserving subject-continuity across subordinative sequences. The morphology also serves a discourse function, allowing speakers to cast important participants as core arguments, as with applicatives. The Yup'ik system, like that of most languages, shows the importance of considering the individual devices exploited for the manipulation of argument structure within the context of the language as a whole.

References

Egede, P. 1750. *Dictionarium Grönlandico–Danico–Latinum*. Copenhagen.

1760. *Grammatica Grönlandica–Danico–Latina*. Copenhagen.

Fortescue, M. 1984. *West Greenlandic*. London: Croom Helm.

Fox, B. and Hopper, P.J. (eds.) 1994. *Voice: form and function*, Typological studies in language 27. Amsterdam: John Benjamins.

Jacobson, S.A. 1984. *Yup'ik Eskimo dictionary*. Fairbanks: Alaska Native Language Center, University of Alaska.

1995. *A practical grammar of the Central Alaskan Yup'ik Eskimo language*. Fairbanks: Alaska Native Language Center, University of Alaska.

Kleinschmidt, S. 1851. *Grammatik der grönländischen Sprache*. Berlin. Reprinted 1968 in Hildesheim: Georg Olms Verlagsbuchhandlung.

Mithun, M. 1994. 'The implications of ergativity for a Philippine voice system', pp. 247–77 of Fox and Hopper 1994.

(ed.) 1996. *Prosody, grammar, and discourse in Central Alaskan Yup'ik.* Santa Barbara Papers in Linguistics 7. University of California.

Miyaoka, O. 1984. 'On the so-called half-transitive verbs in Eskimo', *Etudes/inuit/ studies* 8, supplement issue: 'The Central Yup'ik Eskimos' (Département d'anthropologie, Université Laval, Quebec), pp. 193–218.

1987. 'Ergativity in Eskimo (Central Alaskan Yupik)', *Memoirs of the Research Department of the Toyo Bunko* 45 (Tokyo: The Toyo Bunko). 25–51.

1996. 'Sketch of Central Alaskan Yupik, an Eskimoan language', pp. 325–63 of *Handbook of North American Indians*, Vol. XVII: *Languages*, ed. I. Goddard. Washington, D.C.: Smithsonian Institution.

1997. 'A chapter on the Alaskan Central Yupik subordinative mood', *Languages of the North Pacific Rim* 2 (Graduate School of Letters, Kyoto University, Japan). 61–146.

Nedjalkov, V. (ed.) 1988. *Typology of resultative constructions.* Amsterdam: Benjamins.

Nichols, J. 1985. 'Switch-reference causatives', *CLS* 21.193–203.

O'Connor, M.C. 1992. *Topics in Northern Pomo grammar.* New York: Garland.

Oswalt, R.L. 1977. 'The causative as a reference switching mechanism in Western Pomo', *BLS* 3.46–54.

Reed, I., Miyaoka, O., Jacobson, S., Afcan, P. and Krauss, M. 1977. *Yup'ik Eskimo grammar.* Fairbanks: Alaska Native Language Center, University of Alaska.

Shibatani, M. 1996. 'Applicatives and benefactives', pp. 157–94 of Shibatani and Thompson 1996.

Shibatani, M. and Thompson, S. (eds.) 1996. *Grammatical constructions: their form and meaning.* Oxford: Clarendon.

Woodbury, A.C. 1981. *Study of the Chevak dialect of Central Yup'ik Eskimo.* Ph.D. dissertation. University of California, Berkeley.

4 Transitivity and valency-changing derivations in Motuna

MASAYUKI ONISHI

1 Introduction

Motuna is one of eight non-Austronesian, or Papuan, languages from Bougainville, Papua New Guinea.[1] It has several thousand speakers.[2]

Typologically, Motuna is an agglutinative language with considerable morphophonological fusion. It is both head-marking and dependent-marking. NPs are marked by case suffixes. Core case markings are ergative/absolutive (ergative marking is optional in certain environments – see §2(I)). Verbs, kinship terms, classifiers and numerals show extremely complex morphology, with both suffixing and prefixing.

Constituent order tends to be verb-final, with A and O in either order. Any NPs can be left unexpressed if understood from the context.

---

[1] Bougainville is an island on the eastern end of Papua New Guinea, situated next to the border of the Solomon Islands. On the Bougainville main island, there are ten Austronesian languages which concentrate in the north and along the coast, and eight Papuan languages which concentrate in the south and the central part of the island. Siwai, where Motuna is spoken, is situated in the southern part, to the west of Buin.

    Among the eight Papuan languages, Motuna, Buin, Nagovisi and Naasioi constitute a group (named 'East Bougainville Stock' by Allen and Hurd 1965), while the other four languages constitute another group ('West Bougainville Stock', ibid.). The first group is further divided into two subgroups (Buin Family consisting of Motuna and Buin, and Naasioi Family consisting of Naasioi and Nagovisi) based on their lexico-statistical analysis, but the legitimacy of this subgrouping is yet to be examined.

    Motuna has a $C_1V(C_2)$ structure where C_2 is an archiphoneme realized as a glottal stop, a glottal fricative or a nasal homorganic to the following consonant (or a velar nasal word-finally). Other consonants occupy C_1 slot. They are: stops p, t and k; nasals m, n and ng; fricatives s and h; rhotic r; and glides y and w. It has a typical five-vowel system with front high i, front mid e, back high u, back mid o and back low a.

[2] The latest figure is 6,600 based on the 1970 census. The 1980 census doesn't give any specific figure of Motuna speakers. The 1990 census was not carried out due to the political conflict on the island since 1989.

The major characteristics of the grammar of the language which bear on the main discussion of this chapter are summarized below:

(1)　A five-term gender system and classifiers coexist in Motuna. Five genders – masculine, feminine, diminutive, local and manner – are distinguished in singular nouns, but these are neutralized in non-singular number (dual and paucal are marked by diminutive-like agreement, and plural by masculine). The gender of a noun is obligatorily cross-referenced by modifiers within the same NP and/or by the predicate. In addition, most nouns can be classified into one or more of fifty-one semantic types, which can be indicated by classifiers modifying them. Classifiers are combined with numerals, demonstratives, possessive pronouns, etc.

(2)　Nouns distinguish four numbers – singular, dual, paucal and plural. Personal pronouns distinguish singular and nonsingular number. In 1st person nonsingular there is also an inclusive/exclusive distinction. There is no 3rd person free pronoun, and the demonstrative is used instead in deictic/anaphoric function.

(3)　All the verbs mark the person and number of core argument(s), i.e. S, or O and A. Motuna shows both split-S morphology and active/middle voice distinction which will be discussed in §3 in some detail. Verbs also indicate one of fourteen tense/aspect/mood categories. Fully inflected verbs further mark the gender of the topical argument of the sentence by a suffix.

(4)　Like many other Papuan languages, Motuna has medial verbs which usually occupy sentence-medial positions and indicate both tense/aspect **and** switch-reference. Clause coordination is mainly achieved by chaining. Medial verbs, by their tense/aspect and switch-reference suffixes, track the theme(s) of the discourse, often with the help of conjunctions and discourse markers.

In this chapter I will first overview the structure of basic verbal clauses of the language. §3 discusses the morphological structure of the verb, and then verb classes categorized according to the different types of cross-referencing markings they take. §4 deals with valency-changing derivations of the language – two valency-increasing ones (applicative and causative), two valency-reducing ones (reciprocal and deagentive), and one which rearranges valencies without changing transitivity value (stimulative). §5 gives a summary of the foregoing discussion.

2   The structure of basic verbal clauses

As mentioned in §1, Motuna verbs obligatorily cross-reference the person/
number of core arguments – S in the case of intransitive verbs, and O and A
in the case of transitive verbs. NP case marking is ergative–absolutive.[3]

(I) In transitive verbal clauses, verbs obligatorily take suffixes which
indicate the person/number of O and A arguments. O is always realized as an
unmarked (absolutive) NP. The A argument can be marked by the ergative
suffix, but it is usually unmarked if it is the topic of the sentence.[4] See (1a)
and (1b).

(1) (a)   [nii]$_O$ [Aanih-ki]$_A$ tangu-m-u-u-ng
          1sg   Female.Name-ERG slap-1O-3A-NR.PAST-M
          Aanih (F) slapped me (M)   ('me' topic)

(b)   [Aanih]$_A$ [nii]$_O$ tangu-m-u-i-na
          Female.Name 1sg   slap-1O-3A-NR.PAST-F
          Aanih (F) slapped me (M) ('Aanih' topic)

In (1a) the O argument *nii* 'me' is the topic and the A argument *Aanih* is
marked by the ergative suffix -*ki*. In this case, O and A NPs can be placed in
either order, although OA is an unmarked order. Note that the verbal ending -*ng*
indicates the masculine gender of the head of the topic NP, in this case *nii* 'me'.

In (1b), on the other hand, the A argument *Aanih* is the topic. It is usually
unmarked[5] and in such a case word order is rigid, i.e. it must precede the
unmarked O. Note again that the verbal ending -*na* indicates the feminine
gender of the head of the topic NP, in this case *Aanih*.

Four transitive verbs – *o-* 'give to', *nai-* 'show to', *tong-* 'name' and *hohk-*
'throw towards' – require another syntactically obligatory argument in absolutive case which is not cross-referenced by the verb. I call such an argument
'E' (Extension to core) following Dixon (1994: 122–4; see also Introduction of
this volume). E refers to Gift, Thing Shown, Name and Thing Thrown, e.g.:

---

[3] These two criteria coincide well, but in some cases we also need syntactic criteria to determine
the grammatical status of the argument. It is the case with the verbs ('S$_o$' verbs) which take an
O suffix and an invariable 3rd person A suffix. The argument cross-referenced by an O suffix
mostly shows S properties (in terms of imperative formation, verbal derivations such as causative and deagentive, and switch-reference in clause chaining), but O properties in limited
circumstances (e.g. S$_o$ of some applicative verbs, cf. §4.1.2).

[4] I use the term 'topic' roughly in the sense defined by, for example, Li and Thompson (1976).
It is a central argument in a topic-comment structure contrasted with the syntactic category
'subject'.

[5] I found no example in my text corpus where topical A is marked by ergative. According to
my informants, however, topical A can be marked by ergative. In elicitation sessions such
examples show up occasionally.

(2)   [nii]ₒ [ong   miika]ₑ   o-m-i-ng
       1sg   DEM+M leftover.of.betel.mixture give.to-1O-2A-pauc/pl+IMP
       Give that betel mixture (in your mouth) to me

(II) Intransitive verbs obligatorily mark the person/number of the S argument which is manifested as an unmarked (absolutive) NP. Four types of cross-referencing marking are recognized – Sₒ, Sₐ, middle and irregular (the last one marked by the consonant alternation of the stem):

(3)   *toko=tokoh-* 'feel hot' with an Sₒ suffix (reduplication of the stem is obligatory):
       [nii]ₛ toko=toko-mu-u-ng
       1sg   feel.hot-1Sₒ-NR.PAST-M
       I (M) am feeling hot

(4)   *kumar-* 'laugh' with an Sₐ suffix:
       [nii]ₛ kumar-os-i-ng
       1sg   laugh-1Sₐ-NR.PAST-M
       I (M) laughed

(5)   *turu-* 'return' with a middle suffix:
       [Aanih]ₛ   tii   uri   turu-mo-i-na
       Female.Name ART+L village return-MID1S-NR.PAST-F
       Aanih (F) returned to the village

(6)   *pih-* 'go' with an irregular inflection:
       [Aanih]ₛ   tii   uri   pi-i-na
       Female.Name ART+L village go+2/3Sᵢᵣᵣ-NR.PAST-F
       Aanih (F) went to the village

Some intransitive verbs (Sₒ, Sₐ or middle) require an E argument.

(7)   *haa-* 'want' with an Sₒ suffix:
       [nii]ₛ [tuu]ₑ haa-mu-u-ng
       1sg   water want-1Sₒ-NR.PAST-M
       I want water

(8)   *kuuk-* 'know' with an Sₐ suffix:
       hii!   [nii tii]ₛ jaki   [ong-ko   kuna]ₑ   toku
       oh.dear 1sg ART+F as.you.know DEM+M-EMPH traditional.medicine not
       noi kuuk-o-ma-na
       any know-1Sₐ-GENL-F
       Oh dear! As you know, I don't know any of that traditional medicine!

Thus, there are four types of valency structure in Motuna:

  (a)   plain transitive verbs take A and O;
  (b)   extended transitive verbs take A, O and E (or two Es in the case of applicative verbs derived from basic extended transitive verbs, cf. §4.1.2);

(c)   plain intransitive verbs take S; and

(d)   extended intransitive verbs take S and E.

3   Verb structure and verb classes

3.1   *Verb structure*

The verb in Motuna consists of the following morphological elements:

(i)   verb stem;

(ii)   bound pronominal morphemes cross-referencing the person and number of core argument(s);

(iii) tense/aspect/mood (hereafter TAM) suffix; and

(iv)   fully inflected non-medial verbs further cross-reference the gender of the topical argument;

(iv') other non-medial verbs and same-subject (hereafter ss) medial verbs have no additional markings; and

(iv") different-subject (hereafter DS) medial verbs have a portmanteau form indicating both aspect and switch-reference.

Fully inflected verbs are amply exemplified in (1)–(8). Here I will exemplify the forms of verbs which do not take gender marking:

(9) (a)   taapu-r-opi-ti-hee
          help-2O-1A-du-DEF.FUT
          We two will definitely help you (sg) / I will definitely help you two

(b)   kuuto-woo-ro
          wait-MID3S-PERF(+SS)
          After he/she waited, he/she . . .

(c)   kuuto-woro-ku
          wait-MID3S-GENL+DS
          When he/she waited, someone else . . .

Example (9a) is a non-medial verb with a Definite Future suffix which requires no gender marking. Example (9b) is a medial verb, and the suffix *-ro* marks the Perfect aspect without any further marking, indicating that the S of this verb is coreferential with S or A of the controlling clause. Example (9c) is the same verb in another medial form, with the suffix *-ku* marking both General tense/aspect and Different Subject categories.

Note that *taapu-* in (9a) functions as a transitive verb taking active-voice O/A suffixes, while *kuuto-* in (9b) and (9c) functions as an intransitive verb taking a middle S suffix. Both of these verb stems are ambitransitive and can potentially take either type (active or middle) of suffix(es). The voice system of Motuna, thus, is a so-called 'verbal diathesis' (cf. Klaiman 1988, 1991), where distinct sets of person/number markings of core arguments render the active/middle distinction of the verb.[6]

There are five types of cross-referencing marking – three in active voice, one in middle voice and one irregular type.

(I)   In active voice:

    (a)   O and A person/number suffixes, e.g. (1) and (2);

    (b) S_o person/number suffixes consisting of O suffixes and 3rd person singular (dummy) A suffix, e.g. (3) and (7);

    (c) S_a suffixes which are formally identical with A suffixes, e.g. (4) and (8).

(II)   In middle voice:

    middle S person/number suffixes (the first consonant of which is identical with an O person suffix), e.g. (5).

(III)   Irregular intransitive (five verbs):

    consonant alternation of the stem which marks the person of S, and a number suffix. 1st person S is marked by a nasal consonant, and 2nd/3rd persons by a homorganic stop/rhotic/glide or a fricative *h*, e.g. (6).

The underlying forms of person markings (some of which also indicate number and exclusiveness) are given in tables 4.1, 4.2 and 4.3.

4.1 Active voice

	transitive		S_o intransitive (O + 3sgA)	S_a intransitive (A)
	O	A		
1st	*-m* *-mor* (pauc/pl.exc)	*-oC*	*-mu*	*-oC*
2nd	*-r*	*-i*	*-ru*	*-i*
3rd	*-Ø* *-wa* (pauc/pl)	*-u* (sg/du)	*-u* *-wa* (pauc/pl)	*-u* (sg/du)

---

[6] Verbal diathesis of this type is rarely attested in the world's languages. The languages which indicate the voice distinction by different sets of person/number markings include classical Indo-European languages such as Greek and Sanskrit (cf. Klaiman 1988, Haspelmath 1990). At least one other Papuan language from southern Bougainville – Naasioi – indicates the active/middle distinction in the same way as Motuna.

4.2 Middle voice (intransitive)

	(O + sg)	(O + N-sg)
1st	*-moro*	*-mee*
	-mara (pauc/pl.exc)	
2nd	*-roro*	*-ree*
3rd	*-woro*	*-wee*

4.3 Irregular stems (intransitive)

	'be/exist'	'go'	'come'	'die'	'cry'
1st	*n*	*m*	*m*	*m*	*m*
pauc/pl.exc	*u-n*	*u-m*	*u-m*	*m . . . ra*	*m . . . ra*
2nd	*t*	*p*	*h*	*p*	*p*
3rd	*t*	*p*	*h*	*p*	*p*
pauc/pl	*u-r*	*u-w*	*u-h*	*p . . . ra*	*p . . . ra*

These person markings are further followed by a number suffix which is zero in singular and paucal/plural exclusive, *-ti* in dual, and *-ru* in paucal/plural inclusive.

3.2 Verb classes

Verb stems are classified as follows according to which type(s) of cross-referencing marking they take. The majority of verb stems which take O/A suffixes can also take middle S suffixes. They are discussed in §3.2.3. Most intransitive-only verbs take only one type of marking (i.e. S_a, S_o, middle or irregular inflection), but a small number of them are 'fluid' (cf. Onishi 1994: 401ff.).

See Appendix for a list of representative verbs in each class.

3.2.1 Active intransitive (S_o and S_a) verbs

S_o verbs constitute a closed class. Twenty-three S_o-only stems and a few 'fluid' stems have been identified. They all denote inner (both mental and physical) experiences (such as 'want', 'feel shy', 'feel painful', 'be/become ill') or uncontrolled processes/events (such as '(one's blood/tears) drip', 'decay').

S_a verbs constitute a larger, probably open class. They take A-type suffixes. Semantically they are heterogeneous. They may express dynamic activities (e.g. 'walk', 'climb', 'laugh'), inchoative states (e.g. '(get to) know', 'become/be similar'), processes and resultative states (e.g. 'become/be big', 'be/get tired'), bodily functions (e.g. 'hiccup', 'stink'), etc.

3.2.2   Irregular intransitive verbs

Five irregular verbs mark the person of S by the consonant alternation of the stem. They are: *tuh-* 'be, exist', *pih-* 'go', *huh-* 'come', *puuh-* 'die' and *paah-* 'cry'. They represent high-frequency items in the language.[7]

3.2.3   Active-middle verbs

Many verb stems (slightly more than 50 per cent of all the stems) can take both active and middle suffixes. The majority of them function as transitive verbs in active voice, taking O and A suffixes. In middle voice, on the other hand, they function as intransitive verbs, cross-referencing only S.[8] In the case of such active-middle verbs, the S argument in middle voice corresponds to (I) A = O, (II) O, or (III) A in active voice. Accordingly, they show three types of semantic contrast discussed below. Note that the same verb stem may take more than one type of S. For example, *mono-* 'see/look at [active]' can take all the three types, with the meanings 'see/look at oneself', 'appear/ be in the scene' and 'be careful' in middle voice.

(I) A and O (active) correspond to S (middle) – reflexive action   The reflexive action described in middle voice may be a voluntary or involuntary action which directs towards oneself or one's bodypart, e.g.:

(10) (a)   ho-ko   hiuo   mono-ji-'-hee
          ART+M-EMPH clay.pot look.at-3O+2A-pauc/pl-DEF.FUT
          You (all) will definitely look at the clay pot

(b)   pi-hee   impa tii   kannuku-kori mono=mono-roo
          go+2S$_{irr}$-DEF.FUT now ART+L puddle-L   REDUP=look.at.self-MID2S+IMP
          You will definitely go to the puddle now. Look at yourself carefully (in the reflection of the puddle)

   A nominal referring to a bodypart may stand as E:

(11)   [hoo   irihwa n-ajaa]$_E$ u'kisa
          ART+M finger one-CL.wrapped.object.lengthwise long.ago
          haha'-woro-mo   tokis-or-u-ng . . .
          work-MID3S-GENL(+SS) cut.self-MID3S-REM.PAST-M
          . . . a finger (of her own) which she cut long ago while she was working . . .

Verbs of this type often express habitual acts of 'grooming' (cf. Klaiman 1992, Kemmer 1993 and 1994) which still involve one's bodypart but are

---

[7] 'Dying' and 'crying' go together in Siwai culture. Vigorous crying of women over the dead person is one of the most important parts of the funeral. See Oliver (1955: 209ff.).

[8] The only clear exception is the verb *hohk-* 'throw towards'. It requires an ergative NP and an absolutive NP even when it is marked by middle S suffixes; cf. Onishi (1994: 400).

'less agentive activities' at the same time, and are thus semantically close to Type III verbs discussed below. In the following example, the verbs underlined express 'grooming':

(12) ong   Tantanu . . .   <u>uuh-oro-mo</u>   jii
      DEM+M Ancestor's.Name wash-MID3S-GENL(+SS) and
      <u>sii'h-oro-mo</u>   <u>ruhruh-woro-mo</u>
      put.oil.on-MID3S-GENL(+SS) comb.one's.hair-MID3S-GENL(+SS)
      roki=manni nimautu-wo-i   tii   uri
      certainly look.handsome-MID3S-CONT(+SS) ART+L village
      mori'-ki-ng
      return+3S-HAB.PAST-M
      This Tantanu . . . used to <u>have a bath</u>, <u>put oil on his body</u>, <u>comb his hair</u> and
      certainly look handsome and go back to the village

(II) O (active) corresponds to S (middle) – spontaneous process/event The verb in middle voice expresses a spontaneous process or even (a type of) anticausative. The referent of S undergoes the effects of the whole process/event.

The middle verb doesn't imply any external agent. Observe the following examples:

(13) (a) hoo   tuu   ino-o-mo   tu-ku   hoo   o'koo
      ART+M water fill-3O+3A-GENL CONT+3S-GENL+DS ART+M that
      menu   hingng-oro-mo   ti-ko   rokut-u-u-na
      mountain break-MID3S-GENL(+SS) there-PURP bury-3O+3A-REM.PAST-F
      While she was filling the water, that mountain broke and buried her there

(b)   ong   hoo   menu   toku nahah roruki   hingng-or-u-ng
      DEM+M ART+M mountain not possibly however break-MID3S-REM.PAST-M
      This mountain, however, didn't possibly break by itself (there is a reason behind it)

(c)   tii-ngi   mara   ti-ki   tuh-ah   hingng-u-u-ng
      ART+F-ERG evil.woman there-INST be-PART break-3O+3A-REM.PAST-M
      The evil woman who lived there broke the mountain

In (13a), the narrator says that the mountain spontaneously 'broke', using the middle verb. Then, in (13b), she corrects her statement by saying that it can't be a spontaneous event, and then restates the whole event using the active form of the same verb, referring to the external agent 'the evil woman'.

(14) tii poku'-ro   manni ti-ki   po'k-oi-juu . . .
      there hide+3O+3A-PERF(+SS) then there-INST be.hidden-MID3S-CONT+DS
      When she (= the possum) hid her (= the owl) there, and while she (= the owl) was hidden there, (they) . . .

In (14), successive use of the active and the middle forms of the verb *po'k-*
brings the 'owl', which is O of the former and S of the latter, to the centre of
attention in this part of discourse. This combination of active and middle
forms effectively fulfils the pragmatic function of a passive in other languages. Note that in the above example the active verb describes a telic
action while the middle verb describes a state rather than an action.

*(III) A (active) corresponds to S (middle) – less agentive activity in which one
is involved*   The subject of the verb, both in active and middle voices, is the
Agent of the described action or activity. The verb in active voice expresses
a transitive action which the Agent (A) performs towards the Patient (O),
while the verb in middle voice expresses the Agent's (S) activity in which the
Patient is irrelevant or unimportant. As such, the S referent of the middle verb
undergoes the effects of the whole event by him-/herself.

(15) (a) jeewo? ni-ngi   noo   taapu-r-ong-kuu-ng?
          how   1sg-ERG possibly help-2O-1Apauc/pl-IMAG-M
          How? Could I possibly help you all?

(b)   Paanaangah   ehkong taapu-woo-ro
          Ancestor's.Name now   participate-MID3S-PERF(+SS)
          pihk-a-iro-ng
          look.for-3O+3pauc/plA-PRES.PROG-M
          Now Paanaangah participates, and they start (lit. are) looking for it

Again the activity denoted by the middle verb is often associated with
durative or habitual aspect, expressing a state rather than the activity itself.

(16)   Maawo   po-oku   ehkong kuuto-wo-i
          Male.Name his-mother now   wait-MID3S-CONT(+SS)
          okur-u-u-na
          get.tired-3S$_a$-REM.PAST-F
          While waiting, Maawo's mother got tired now

A nominal denoting the activity or event may stand as E:

(17)   [sikuulu]$_E$ komik-oro-ku . . .
          schooling finish-MID3S-GENL+DS
          After he finished schooling, (they) . . .

To sum up the discussion in this section, middle verbs in Motuna tend to
express states, or durative or habitual activities, rather than telic actions. Thus
the clauses with middle verbs are generally low in transitivity not only in
terms of the number of participants but also in terms of aspect (cf. Hopper

and Thompson 1980). In each case, S of the middle verb is characterized semantically as the sole participant who is affected by the event/process denoted by the verb, and pragmatically as the centre of attention in that part of discourse.

3.2.4 Middle-only verbs

Motuna also has many intransitive verb stems which take only middle suffixes (middle-only verbs). They are again of three types:

(I) Those denoting physical actions which crucially involve one's body The denoted action may be voluntary or involuntary.

(18)　　nompa　kuro-roo
　　　　quickly　run-MID2S+IMP
　　　　Run quickly

Other verbs which are included in this subclass are: *ne'w-* 'sit down/be sitting', *turu-* 'return' and *mihw-* 'move/jump vigorously'. Among them, the first two have synonymous S_a verbs *maapu-* 'sit down/be sitting' and *morik-* 'return', respectively.

(II) Those denoting spontaneous processes/events which affect oneself The process or event expressed by the verb of this class is typically somatic. The referent of S is animate, and undergoes the effects of the whole process/event which he/she cannot control.

(19)　　manni turio-woro-mo　　　　　　nok-u-u-na: '. . .'
　　　　then　be.alarmed-MID3S-GENL(+SS)　say-3S-REM.PAST-F
　　　　Then, being alarmed, she said: '. . .'

Other verbs in this class include: *hiiro-* 'become/be hungry', *haring-* 'become/be worried', *kaa-* 'be born' and *kinot-* 'become/be drowned'.

(III) Those denoting complex activities in which one is involved The majority of stems in this subclass are derived from nouns which denote culturally salient complex activities. Original nouns include loan words from English or Tok Pisin such as *sikuulu-* 'school(ing)/be educated' and *kiki-* 'play soccer', and nouns with the derivational suffix *-ai* such as *tupur-ai* 'burning off of the bush' and *siimp-ai* 'sweeping'. The referent of S is the Controller of the described activity. The whole clause, again, is low in transitivity in that it is a habitual event without any specifiable Patient.

(20)   tiko ti-ki   aat-o-mo
         and there-INST stay.overnight-1S-GENL(+SS)
         sikuulu-moro-ki-na
         be.educated-MID1S-HAB.PAST-F
         And I used to stay in the dormitory (lit. stay overnight there) and be
         educated

(21)   nii tii   tupurai-moro-heeta-na
         I   ART+F burn.off.bush-MID1S-FUT-F
         I will (habitually) burn off the bush

3.2.5   Summary

The following is a list of all the verb classes of Motuna which are discussed
in §3.2. See the examples of verbs in each class in the Appendix.

(1)   S$_o$ VERBS
(2)   S$_a$ VERBS
(3)   IRREGULAR VERBS ('be, exist', 'go', 'come', 'die', 'cry')
(4)   AMBITRANSITIVE (ACTIVE-MIDDLE) VERBS:
   (I) 'reflexive action' (S = O = A)
   (II) 'spontaneous process/event' (S = O)
   (III) 'less agentive activity' (S = A)
(5)   MIDDLE-ONLY verbs
   (I) 'bodily action'
   (II) 'spontaneous process/event'
   (III) 'complex activity'

4   Valency-changing derivations

Motuna has five valency-changing processes. They are: (1) causative and
applicative which increase valencies; (2) reciprocal and deagentive which
reduce valencies; and (3) stimulative which rearranges valencies without changing transitivity value. Causative, applicative, reciprocal and stimulative are
morphological, while deagentive is periphrastic.

4.1   Valency-increasing derivations

4.1.1   Causative

As discussed in §3.2.3, Motuna has many active-middle (ambitransitive) verbs
of reflexive (S = O = A) and spontaneous (S = O) types, and in the case of
such verbs the transitive versions often express causative meanings (e.g. 'cut',
'cover', 'hide' and 'awaken'), with the causer acting directly and achieving

the result intentionally. The causee is not in control of the state or activity, and is affected by the result of the whole event.

Motuna also employs medial-verb constructions involving verbs such as 'tell', 'persuade' and 'instruct' to express meanings equivalent to causatives. Transitive verbs, or intransitive verbs with an Agent S, are likely to form medial-verb constructions of this type to express causative meanings where the causee is still a potential Controller of the activity denoted by the original verb, e.g.:

(22)　　ni-ngi　mi'no-ongu　　　　　　tu-u-i-na
　　　　1sg-ERG instruct-3O+1A+GENL+DS hit-3O+3A-NR.PAST-F
　　　　I instructed him and he hit her / I made him hit her

(23)　　kongot-us-uu　　　　　　pi-i-ng
　　　　persuade-3O+1A-CONT+DS go+3S$_{irr}$-NR.PAST-M
　　　　While I persuaded him, he went / I forced him to go

In addition to lexical causatives and medial-verb constructions of the type mentioned above, Motuna has a productive morphological causative derivation where the causative suffix *-wooto* is attached directly to the verb stem. The initial *w* of the suffix is dropped after a consonant-final stem.

The causative suffix can be attached to any type of intransitive verb stems, and many ambitransitive (active-middle) verb stems. In the former case causative derivation introduces a new A argument, and allows the S of the underlying intransitive clause to function as O.

Examples of one-place intransitive verbs:

(24)　　S$_o$ verb *hunok-* 'be/become full in stomach':
(a)　　[hoo　kitoria]$_S$ hoo　pau nee-wa-ro　　　　　　　topo meeng
　　　　ART+M children ART+M food eat-3O+3pauc/plA-PERF(+SS) well very
　　　　hunok-uru-u-ng
　　　　become.full.in.stomach-3pauc/plS$_o$-REM.PAST-M
　　　　After the children had eaten the food, they became very much full in stomach

(b)　　roki=manni topo meeng
　　　　really　　　well very
　　　　hunok-ooto-o-r-u-ng
　　　　become.full.in.stomach-CAUS-3O+3A-pauc/pl-REM.PAST-M
　　　　He made them certainly very much full in stomach (by feasting them)

(25)　　S$_a$ verb *patak-* 'arrive':
(a)　　[hoo　nee　　　muumiaku]$_S$ impa patak-u-ito-ng
　　　　ART+M it.must.be lord　　　　now　arrive-3S$_a$-PRES.PROG-M
　　　　(My) lord must be arriving now

(b)   uko-o-ro   ehkong tii   huhno
         carry-3O+3A-PERF(+SS) now   ART+L mouth.of.river
         patak-ooto-o-ko-ng
         arrive-CAUS-3O+3A-PRES-M
         (The current of the river) carries him and now makes him arrive at the
         mouth of the river

Two-place intransitive verbs become three-place, e.g.:

(26)   S$_a$ verb *rii(h)*- 'become':
(a)   [hoo   Siuai-no-po]$_S$ [nommai tanaku'-ngung]$_E$
         ART+M Place.Name-LINK-CL.people person   industrious-pl
         rii-wa-a-ng
         become-3pauc/plS$_a$-REM.PAST-M
         Siwai people became industrious people

(b)   manni [Kihili]$_O$ inokee [hoo   mision honna]$_E$
         then   Place.Name again   ART+M mission big
         rii-woota-wa-a-no . . .
         become-CAUS-3O+3pauc/plA-REM.PAST-L
         Then they made Kihili a big mission . . .

When the causative suffix is attached to an ambitransitive (active-middle) stem, the causative version tends to be based on the intransitive (middle) sense. This is particularly the case when the original verb stem with a middle suffix has a reflexive (type I) or a spontaneous (type II) reading.

As mentioned at the beginning of this section, reflexive and spontaneous middle verbs have transitive versions which express causative meanings with the causer acting directly on the causee and achieving the result intentionally. The morphological causative of a verb of this type, on the other hand, describes a situation where the causer initiates a process or activity but does not necessarily act directly or intentionally. (Note that in both lexical and morphological causatives the causee has no control over the event.) Observe the following example:

(27) (a) toku-ko   to-wooto-i-heeto-ng
         not-EMPH be.hit-CAUS-3O+2A-FUT-M
         You will never cause [the baby] to be hit (on the ground)

In (27a), the speaker asks the addressee (the causer) to pay enough attention to prevent an undesirable event. In this example the causer is seen as an Initiator but not as an Agent. The verb *to-* 'hit/kill' with active suffixes as in example (22), on the other hand, denotes an intentional transitive action which directly affects the Patient, and thus cannot be used in the context where (27a) is uttered. The morphological causative *to-wooto-* is based on the spontaneous sense of the verb *to-* in middle voice, as in (27b).

(27) (b) kui-kitee to-wor-i-ng
          tree-ABL be.hit-MID3S-NR.PAST-M
          He fell from a tree and was hit (on the ground)

The morphological causative of a type III ambitransitive verb also tends to be based on the intransitive ('less agentive') sense. Observe the following example:

(28) (a) tii   hinra'   tii   kuuto-woota-wa-ro
          ART+F thunder there wait-CAUS-3O+3pauc/plA-PERF(+SS)
          sih-a-a-na
          leave-3O+3pauc/plA-REM.PAST-F
          They left the Thunder, keeping her waiting there [by telling a lie]

The causative verb *kuuto-wooto-* cannot take another argument referring to the person for whom the Thunder is waiting. Thus it is not based on the transitive sense but on the intransitive ('less agentive') sense of the original stem *kuuto-* as in example (16), which is repeated below:

(28) (b) Maawo   po-oku   ehkong kuuto-wo-i
          Male.Name his-mother now   wait-MID3S-CONT(+SS)
          okur-u-u-na
          get.tired-3S$_a$-REM.PAST-F
          While waiting, Maawo's mother got tired now

Causative verbs of some type III verbs, however, are allowed to take two NP arguments.

The verb stem *uko-*, for example, functions as a transitive verb with the meaning 'carry something (O)' when it takes active-voice suffixes, and as an extended intransitive verb with the meaning 'be engaged in carrying something (E)' in middle voice. The former is used to describe a normal transitive action, while the latter is used when the speaker wants to focus on the activity itself, e.g. on how a thing is carried, as in:

(29) (a) [ong]$_E$ ukuna-kori   koto uko-roro-hee
          DEM+M shoulder-LOC up   carry-MID2S-DEF.FUT
          You will definitely carry this up on the shoulder

The causative verb *uko-wooto-* can also take two NP arguments, one with a human referent in O function, and the other with a non-human referent in E function:

(29) (b) tii-ko   peeko-no   uri   turu-wee-m-mo
          ART+L-EMPH 3N-sgPOSS-L village return-MID3S-pauc/pl-GENL
          uru-ku   [hoo   pau ponnaa]$_E$
          CONT3pauc/plS-GENL+DS ART+M food plenty
          uko-wooto-o-r-u-ng
          carry-CAUS-3O+3A-pauc/pl-REM.PAST-M
          As they were returning to their village he made them carry plenty of food
          [he sent plenty of food with them]

Since both the transitive and intransitive versions of the verb *uko-* can take
two NP arguments, it is not clear in this case which version the causative verb
uko-wooto- derives from. Natural interpretation, though, would be that it is
based on the transitive sense, because (29b) tells us the fact that the 'food' was
carried by the people to the village, but it does not describe how it was done.

In Motuna morphological causatives never seem to have an E with a
human referent. Thus a transitive verb with an O referring to a human cannot
be causativized – or if it is ever causativized, the meaning of the causative verb
must be quite different from that of the original verb. For example, the verb
taapu- has the meaning 'help somebody (O)' in active voice and 'participate'
in middle voice (cf. (15a) and (15b), respectively). The causative verb *taapu-*
wooto- can take two argument NPs with non-human referents, with the meaning 'add something (O) to something (E)':

(30)   [ong   tuu]$_O$ [hoo   hiuo-ko   kuu-ngi   tu-ro-ng]$_E$
         DEM+M water ART+M clay.pot-of inside-INST be.3S-PERF-M
         taapu-wooto-i-heeto-ng
         help-CAUS-3O.2A-FUT-M
         You will add this water to what is in the clay pot

Motuna also has a small number of verb stems which are used only as
transitive (active) verbs in normal circumstances. The majority of them cannot be causativized but there are at least two exceptions: *tee-* 'eat (munchable
food)'[9] and *nee-* 'eat (soft food) / drink'.[10] The causatives of these verbs are
used only in the situations where the Causer feeds the Causee who is totally
passive (e.g. a baby). The following example is from an account of a traditional ceremony where a man directly put the meat of a possum into 'our'
mouth (which 'we' are forbidden to eat by ourselves):

---

[9] The verb stem *tee-* may take middle suffixes to express a reflexive meaning ('eat one's own
   body') in unusual circumstances. It is not possible to use the causative form based on this
   reflexive sense.
[10] Dixon (chapter 2 of this volume) notes that if a language uses a morphological causative only
   with a small number of transitive verbs, 'eat' and 'drink' are most likely to be included. This
   appears to be the case with Motuna, too.

(31)   tiko ongingoto [ho-i   no-wori]$_A$ inokee [hoo   napa]$_E$
           then up.there   ART+M-ERG one-CL.animate again   ART+M possum
           tee-wooto-mor-u-kuu-ng
           eat-CAUS-1pauc/pl.inc.O-3A-IMAG-M
           Then up there a man would make us eat (the meat of) a possum

4.1.2   Applicative

The applicative suffix *-jee* is attached to the verb stems of both intransitive and transitive verbs. The initial *j* is dropped after a consonant-final stem. In the case of active-middle stems, it allows only the transitive (active) readings, in contrast with the causative suffix which usually prefers intransitive (middle) readings.

Applicative derivation increases the valency of the original verb by introducing a new O, E or S$_o$, according to the type of the verb. It derives transitive verbs from one- or two-place intransitive verbs, two-place intransitive verbs from one-place intransitive verbs, or three-place transitive verbs from two-place transitive verbs. When it is attached to three-place transitive verbs, it may derive four-place transitive verbs, or the valency may remain as it is. See the discussion and examples below.

The original verb could be S$_a$, S$_o$, irregular intransitive or transitive, but rarely middle.[11] It is presumably because the semantics of applicative derivation centres around a newly introduced O (or S$_o$) whose referent is always seen as a participant affected by the action/process denoted by the verb. The centrality and affectedness of the referent of S are part of the semantics of middle verbs, and if the original S stayed as A of the applicative verb it would compete with the semantics of a newly introduced O.

The applicative suffix can derive transitive verbs from the stems of one-place intransitive verbs which denote motions and feelings. They include many S$_a$ verbs (such as 'laugh', 'get angry', 'feel happy'), three irregular verbs ('go', 'come' and 'cry'), and two S$_o$ verbs ('become/be afraid' and 'feel shy'). It moves the S argument of these verbs to A status, and introduces a new O argument.

Semantically, the new O may be Goal of Action or Source of Feeling / Emotive Action. In general, a purposive NP marked by *-ko* (with an allomorph *-jo*) in the underlying intransitive clause roughly corresponds to the O of the applicative construction.

---

[11] In elicitation sessions my informants sometimes marginally allow middle-only verbs to take an applicative suffix. I found no such examples in my text corpus.

Underlying clause	(NP-*ko*)	S	V
	|	|	|
Applicative construction	O	A	V-APPLIC

There is, however, subtle difference in meaning between the two versions. Observe the following examples:

(32) (a) nii ong-jo   pehkoro iirong-ohna-na
         1sg DEM+M-PURP boy   get.angry-1S$_a$+PRES.PROG-F
         I am angry for the sake of this boy

(b)   nii ong   pehkoro iirong-ee-uhna-na
         1sg DEM+M boy   get.angry-APPLIC-3O+1A+PRES.PROG-F
         I am angry with this boy

Example (32a) simply says that the state of 'this boy' (who was, for example, unduly mistreated by someone else) is the cause of 'my' anger. Example (32b), on the other hand, refers to 'my' anger against 'this boy', often accompanied by an act of scolding. That is, the applicative construction indicates that the referent of the new O may potentially be affected by the anger expressed by the referent of A.

The referent of an O NP in an applicative construction is often restricted to human beings. Non-humans cannot easily be seen as affected participants, and thus do not often occur as O in applicative constructions. Observe the following:

(33) (a) ??Kangku-ko   mi-ino-ng
         Male.Name-PURP go+1S$_{irr}$-PRES.PROG-M

(b)   Kangku   pih-ee-uhno-ng
         Male.Name go-APPLIC-3O+1A+PRES.PROG-M
         I am going to see Kangku (for some purpose)

(34) (a) pau-ko   mi-ino-ng
         food-PURP go+1S$_{irr}$-PRES.PROG-M
         I am going to get food

(b)   *pau mih-ee-uhno-ng

Examples (33a) and (34a) show that the verb *pih-* 'go' can take a Goal NP in purposive case with a non-human referent, but rarely one with a human referent.[12] In (33b) and (34b), on the other hand, the applicative verb *pih-ee-* only allows an NP with a human referent to occur in O function, and not an NP with a non-human referent.

---

[12] This is unless the speaker treats the human referent of the purposive NP (Kangku in (33a)) as if he/she is a dumb object which could be taken away at will.

In the case of some one-place S_o and S_a verbs which describe physical/mental states/processes, a new E denoting a body part is introduced. The applicative verb remains intransitive.

Underlying clause	S		V
Applicative construction	S_o	E (bodypart)	V-APPLIC

(35) (a) [nii]$_S$ siiho-mu-ino-ng
      1sg be.ill-1S_o-PRES.PROG-M
      I am ill

(b) [nii]$_S$ [mu'king]$_E$ siiho-jee-mu-ino-ng
      1sg heart be.ill-APPLIC-1S_o-PRES.PROG-M
      I am ill at heart

In addition, two of those S_o verbs (*siiho-* 'be/become ill' and *musi'ka-* 'feel painful') have an alternative derivation where the original S is demoted to E, and the inalienable Possessor of the original S is introduced as a new S_o of the derived applicative construction.

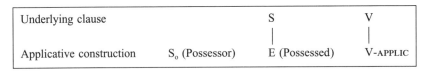

Underlying clause		S	V
Applicative construction	S_o (Possessor)	E (Possessed)	V-APPLIC

(35) (c) nuro [Possessor S, Possessed E] siiho-jee-mu-ina-na
      my.daughter   be.ill-APPLIC-1S_o-PRES.PROG-F
      My daughter is ill (and I am affected by it)

In examples (35b) and (35c), it is the referent of S_o who is affected.

The S_o verb of possession *tuh-ee-* is derived from the copula *tuh-* 'be/exist' in the same way, i.e. the original S is demoted to E and the Possessor of this argument stands as a new S_o:

(36) (a) uri-ngi   [pau ponnaa]$_S$ tu-ro-ng
      village-INST food much   be+3S_{irr}-PERF-M
      There is plenty of food in the village

(b) [tuu noo   no-'ra]$_E$ tuh-ee-nna-na?
      water possibly one-CL.small.amount be-APPLIC-2S_o+PERF-F
      Do you possibly have a little water?

In the case of two-place intransitive verbs such as *kuuk-* 'know' (S_a), *haa-* 'want' (S_o) and *kaah-* 'not want' (S_o), the original S is moved to A and the original E to O.

Underlying clause	S	E	V
	|	|	|
Applicative construction	A	O	V-APPLIC

There are again restrictions with regard to the animacy status of E and O in the case of these verbs. For example, the E of *kuuk-* 'know' always has a non-human referent, but the O of the applicative verb *kuuk-ee-* 'know about' can have a human or non-human referent. The same applies to *haa-* 'want', the E of which must have a non-human referent, while the O referent of the applicative verb *haa-jee-* 'need, want somebody' can be either non-human or human, e.g.:

(37) (a)   [nii]_S [tuu]_E haa-mu-u-ng
      1sg   water   want-1S_o-NR.PAST-M
      I want water

(b)   [ong   tuu]_O [ni-ngi]_A haa-jee-uhno-ng
      DEM+M water 1sg-ERG   want-APPLIC-3O+1A+PRES.PROG-M
      I need this water (for some purpose)

(c)   [oi-ngi   moomoo-nno nuka-nno]_A   [ongi
      DEM+du.pauc.GENDER-ERG my.father-and my.mother-and DEM+L+INST
      tu-i   tuh-arei]_E-ko haa-jee-m-u-ti-ka-na
      be+3S-CONT be-VN-EMPH want-APPLIC-1O-3A-du-PRES-F
      These parents of mine want me to stay here

The example (37b) seems to indicate that the referent of A ('I') is going to do something to this 'water', implying that the water will be affected by this future action. In (37c), *haa-jee* takes a complement clause in addition to a new O with a human referent.

In the case of plain transitive verbs, the original O is demoted to E and a new O is introduced. This new O is an Affected Participant (Beneficiary/ Malefactive) of the whole event, or the (potential) Possessor of the original O who can be seen as an Affected Participant as well.

Underlying clause		O	A	V
		|	|	|
Applicative construction	O	E	A	V-APPLIC

(38) (a) ehkong [hoo   pau]ₒ nga-wa-mo   manni ho-ko
         now   ART+M feast make-3O+3pauc/plA-GENL(+SS) then   ART+M-EMPH
         pa-aromong   hoo   roki=manni no'-ki-ng: '. . .'
         his-younger.brother ART+M really   think+3S-HAB.PAST-M
         Now as they gave a feast, his younger brother certainly thought repeatedly:
         '. . .'

(b)   [Tantanu-ki]_A   [pau honna meeng]_E
         Ancestor's.Name-ERG feast big   very
         ngo-jee-u-r-u-ng
         make-APPLIC-3O+3A-pauc/pl-REM.PAST-M
         Tantanu gave a very big feast for them

(39)(a) [oi   angu]ₒ tokis-i-ro   hoh-roro-hee
         DEM+DIM arm   cut-3O+2A-PERF(+SS) throw.away-MID2S-DEF.FUT
         You will definitely cut this arm and throw it away

(b)   [oi   ngo-ni(O)   angu]_E tokis-ee-m-i-ro
         DEM+DIM 1sgPOSS-DIM arm   cut-APPLIC-1O-2A-PERF(+SS)
         hoh-roro-hee
         throw.away-MID2S-DEF.FUT
         You will definitely cut this arm of mine and throw it away

Other examples include:

(40)   nop- 'take something (O)' → no(e)p-ee- 'take something (E) from/for some-
         body (O)';
         to- 'hit/kill somebody/something (O)' → to(e)-jee- 'hit/ kill somebody/some-
         thing (E) for/against the benefit of somebody (O)', 'hit/ kill somebody's (O)
         somebody/something (E)'
         katuk- 'trim something (O)' → katuk-ee- 'trim somebody's (O) something
         (E)'

As mentioned in §2, Motuna has four extended transitive verbs. When applicative derivation is applied to these verb stems, it demotes the O argument of the underlying clause to E_2 status. It introduces a new O, which occurs as a Possessor NP of the original E_1.

Underlying clause		E_1	O	A	V
Applicative construction	O	E_1	E_2	A	V-APPLIC
	(Possessor)	(Possessed)			

(41) (a)   impa [hoo   ong   koho munu]_E1 manni ehkong no-'ra-no
           then ART+M DEM+M down body   then   now   one-CL.small.amount-L
           toki=tokis-u-mo   o-o-ko-ng
           REDUP=cut-3O+3A-GENL(+SS) give.to-3O+3A-PRES-M
           Then as he cuts the lower part of the body into pieces, he gives them [to the
           Demon]

(b)   ti-ko   ong   koto ku'-kori-ko tokis-u-ro   [hoo
           ART+L-PURP DEM+M up   neck-L-PURP cut-3O+3A-PERF(+SS) ART+M
           ong   koho o-muru]_E1
           DEM+M down DEM-CL.piece.of.long.object
           o-jee-u-u-ng
           give.to-APPLIC-3O+3A-REM.PAST-M
           He cut at the neck and gave that lower part of the body [of his elder brother]
           [to the Demon]

Examples of other three-place verbs:

(42)   nai- 'show something (E$_1$) to somebody (O)' → nai-jee- 'show somebody's
           (O) something (E$_1$) to somebody (E$_2$)'
           hohk- 'throw something (E$_1$) over towards somebody(O)' → hohk-ee- 'throw
           somebody's (O) something (E$_1$) to somebody (E$_2$)'

In the case of *tong-* 'name', the applicative version is chosen when the
speaker wants to focus on the referent of the O argument who will get a new
name. There is no change in valency.

Underlying clause	O	E	A	V
	|	|	|	|
Applicative construction	O	E	A	V-APPLIC

(43)   tiwo-noning-ngori [hoo   pau muukisa muukisa]_O [hoo   mii-ngung]_E
           that.way-towards-L ART+M food different different   ART+M name-pl
           tii-nohno   tonge=tong-ee-wa-r-u-ng
           that.time-length REDUP=name-APPLIC-3O+3pauc/plA-pauc/pl-REM.PAST-M
           That way, they gave those names to many different kinds of food (one by
           one) during that length of time

Note that the O in the above example is the topic of the sentence. Note also
that the paucal/plural number of this argument is marked on the verb, even
though this has inanimate referents. The number of an inanimate noun is not
usually indicated unless the speaker really wants to focus on it.

According to one of my informants, the same kind of choice is available in
the case of the other three-place verbs. If this is the case, then the applicative
suffix can bring the following semantic changes without affecting the valencies:

(44)   o- 'give something (E) to somebody (O)' → o-jee- 'give something (E) to
        somebody (O) for/against O's benefit'
        nai- 'show something (E) to somebody (O)' → nai-jee- 'show something
        (E) for (the benefit of) somebody (O)'
        hohk- 'throw something (E) over towards somebody (O)' → hohk-ee- 'throw
        something (E) to somebody (O) so that O can get E'

The foregoing discussion shows that although applicative derivation increases valencies in general, the movement of core arguments cannot be defined as transparently as in the case of causative derivation. Semantico-pragmatic factors, i.e. affectedness and topicality of the (new) O or S_o argument, often regulate the whole derivational process.

4.2   Valency-reducing derivations

4.2.1   Reciprocal
All the reciprocal verbs are intransitive verbs derived from transitive verbs. Reciprocal verb stems are formed by combining reduplicated forms of original verb stems with the verbal suffix *-tuh*. The suffix *-tuh* derives from, and inflects in the same way as, the copula *tuh-*, marking the person/number of the S argument. The original transitive stems may be underived, or derived by the applicative suffix. There is no reciprocal pronoun in Motuna.

(45)   hoo-jori   ruu ti-ru   manni noo=noo=uru-kuu-ng
        ART+M-LOC day ART-CL.day then   REDUP=gather=RECIP+3pauc/plS-IMAG-M
        On that day, then, they would gather together

(46)   hoo uri-ngi   Mamangota-ki   hoo   nommai tu'ki topo
        so village-INST Village.Name-INST ART+M people   all   well
        taa=taapu=uru-ko-ng
        REDUP=help=RECIP+3pauc/plS-PRES-M
        So in Mamangota village, all the people help one another well

Since reciprocal verbs are intransitive, they can easily be causativized:

(47)   tiwononing to'=to'kai=tuh-oota-wa-ti-kuu-ng
        that.way   REDUP=hold=RECIP-CAUS-3O+3pauc/plA-du-IMAG-M
        They would make two of them hold each other('s hand) that way

4.2.2   Deagentive
Deagentives are formed by combining participles and the auxiliary *rii(h)-* 'become/be'. Participles may be either transitive or intransitive. Those derived from ambitransitive (active-middle) stems are always based on the transitive (active) senses.

The whole deagentive construction describes a spontaneous action/event. One uses this construction to avoid mentioning the central participant (the referent of S or A) of the event, especially when such a participant is a parent-/child-in-law or a brother-/sister-in-law in relation to the addressee, or to the speaker if the referent of the unexpressed S/A is the addressee. Note that unlike passives, O of the transitive verb is not affected by this derivational process.[13]

Compare the following pairs of sentences (sentence (a) in each pair is used in special situations mentioned above, sentence (b) in ordinary contexts). The unexpressed S or A may be Agent as in (48a) and (50a), respectively, or Experiencer as in (49a).

(48) (a) woo-ki   pih-ah   ri-ito-ng
          where-INST go-PART become+3S_a-PRES.PROG-M
          [lit.] Going to which direction is becoming?

(b)   woo-ki   pi-ita-na
          where-INST go+2/3S_{irr}-PRES.PROG-F
          Which direction are you going?

(49) (a) no-'ra   siiho-wah ri-ito-ng
          one-CL.small.amount be.ill-PART become+3S_a-PRES.PROG-M
          [lit.] Being a little ill is becoming

(b)   no-'ra   siiho-o-ito-ng
          one-CL.small.amount be.ill-3S_o-PRES.PROG-M
          He is a little ill

(50) (a) ong   moo   tee-wah   rii-hee
          DEM+M coconut eat-PART become+3S_a-DEF.FUT
          [lit.] The eating of this coconut will definitely become

(b)   ong   moo   te-i-hee
          DEM+M coconut eat-3O+2A-DEF.FUT
          You will definitely eat this coconut

4.3   Valency-rearranging (stimulative)

The stimulative suffix *-sii(h)* is attached to the stems of intransitive (S_o, S_a or middle) verbs which denote subjective feelings or emotive actions. The stimulative suffix demotes the original S which refers to the Experiencer, and introduces a new S which refers to the Stimulus of such experience. The demoted S may be absent, or may be expressed by a locative NP as in (52c). The derived verbs are intransitive with middle-voice suffixes.

---

[13] See Dixon and Aikhenvald (1997) for a definition of prototypical passives.

Participles may be derived from stimulative verb stems as in (52c). Participles are used more frequently than the inflected forms of stimulative verbs themselves.

Morphologically, the final consonant of the original verb stem is dropped before the stimulative suffix *-sii(h)*. Some of the stems are obligatorily reduplicated. The final *h* of *-sii(h)* optionally occurs only before the participle suffix. Examples:

(51)   kamann- 'feel cold' (S$_o$) → kama'sii(h)- 'be cold'
        maajoh- 'become/be ashamed' (S$_o$) → maajo-sii(h)- 'be embarrassing'
        ruutoh- 'be impressed' (S$_o$) → ruuto-sii(h)- 'be impressive'
        toko=tokoh- 'feel hot' (S$_o$) → toko=toko-sii(h)- 'be hot'
        kumar- 'laugh' (S$_a$) → kuma=kuma-sii(h)- 'be funny'
        okur- 'get/be tired' (S$_a$) → oku-sii(h)- 'be tiring'
        haring- 'become/be worried' (middle) → hari=hari-sii(h)- 'be worrying'
        ni'r- 'be surprised' (middle) → ni'-sii(h)- 'be surprising'

(52) (a)   toku-ko   kumar-opeena-na
          not-EMPH laugh-1S+FUT-F
          I will never laugh

(b)   kuma=kuma-sii-wor-i-ng
       REDUP=laugh-STIMULATIVE-MID3S-NR.PAST-M
       He behaved in a funny way / The situation became funny

(c)   nii-jori kuma=kuma-siih-ah
       me-LOC REDUP=laugh-STIMULATIVE-PART
       It is funny to me

Stimulative verbs can be causativized:

(53)   ruuto-sii-wooto-m-i-i-ng
        be.impressed-STIMULATIVE-CAUS-1O-2A-NR.PAST-M
        You made me look impressive

5   Conclusion

Motuna has a typologically rather unusual verb system. It has a verbal diathesis where the active/middle voice distinction is indicated by different sets of person/number suffixes. In addition, verbs in active voice have a split-S system.

Each of the verb classes, categorized according to the types of person/number markings they take, shows certain semantic characteristics. Table 4.4 shows which verb class undergoes which valency-changing derivation(s):

4.4

	valency-increasing		valency-reducing		valency-rearranging
	CAUS	APPLIC	RECIP	DEAGENTIVE	STIMULATIVE
ambitransitive stems					
transitive reading	some	yes	yes	yes	no
middle reading	yes	no	no	no	no
intransitive stems					
S_o	yes	yes	no	yes	yes
S_a	yes	yes	no	yes	yes
middle-only	yes	rare	no	yes	yes
irregular	yes	yes	no	yes	no

Causative derivation is applied to any class of intransitive verb stems if the semantic requirement is satisfied. When it is applied to ambitransitive stems, the causative versions are likely to be based on the intransitive senses of the original verbs, but there are some anomalies.

Applicative derivation is also applied to both intransitive and ambitransitive verb stems. It can, however, rarely be applied to middle verbs. Even when it is applied to an ambitransitive stem, the applicative version is always based on the transitive, and not the intransitive (middle), sense of the original verb. This is explained by the fact that the semantics of applicative derivation centres around a new O argument whose referent is affected by the action/process denoted by the verb. The referent of S of a middle verb is also a central participant affected by the action/process denoted by the verb, and if it stayed as A of the applicative verb it would compete with the semantics of a newly introduced O.

Among valency-reducing derivations, reciprocal derivation can be applied only to transitive verbs, while deagentive can be applied to any class of verbs with an Agent or Experiencer in A or S function. When applied to an ambitransitive (active-middle) stem, the deagentive construction is always based on the transitive sense.

Stimulative derivation is lexically restricted. It applies only to a class of intransitive verbs which express subjective feelings or emotive actions.

In Motuna, a little more than 50 per cent of verbs are ambitransitive, and the rest are mostly intransitive-only verbs. The verbal lexicon is biased towards intransitive verbs, and it is natural that two valency-increasing processes (causative and applicative) are much more productive than the valency-reducing ones.

My study in transitivity and verbal derivations in Motuna suggests that to understand these phenomena both syntactic and semantico-pragmatic parameters need to be carefully examined. It is the interaction of these parameters that determines the classes of verbs that are associated with specific derivational processes.

Appendix: examples of verbs in each class (§3.2)

(1) S_o *verbs:*

haa-	'agree/want'	musi'ka-	'feel painful'
hingh-	'decay'	mutih-	'become/be/feel tasty/sweet'
hunok-	'become/be full in stomach'	naa'h-	'become/be lazy'
		ooruh-	'become/be afraid'
kaah-	'disagree/not want'	piih-	'[one's blood/tears] drip'
kamann-	'feel cold'	riino-	'feel'
maajoh-	'feel shy'	siiho-	'become/be ill'
mongu'ha-	'become/be numb'	urah-	'become/be/feel heavy'

(2) S_a *verbs:*

haann-	'dawn'	kuuk-	'(get to) know'
haarok-	'fall'	maap-	'sit down / be sitting'
honnak-	'become/be big'	mon-	'look / look like'
kiin-	'climb'	morik-	'return'
kipi'tak-	'hiccup'	nok-	'say'
kokopak-	'crawl' (of a baby)	okur-	'get/be tired'
konn-	'walk/move'	rii(h)-	'become/be'
kumar-	'laugh/smile'	rumar-	'stink'
ku't-	'become/be similar'		

(3) *Irregular verbs (exhaustive list):*

huh-	'come'	puuh-	'die'
paah-	'cry'	tuh-	'be, exist'
pih-	'go'		

(4)   *Active-middle verbs:*

Type I ('reflexive action')

	middle (intransitive)	active (transitive)
mono-	'see oneself'	'see [something/somebody]'
ruhruh-	'comb one's hair'	'comb [somebody's] hair'
sii'h-	'put oil on oneself'	'put oil on [somebody's] body'
tokis-	'cut oneself / one's bodypart'	'cut [something/somebody]'
uuh-	'have a bath / wash one's bodypart'	'wash [something/somebody]'

Type II ('spontaneous process/event')

	middle (intransitive)	active (transitive)
komik-	'finish / be finished'	'finish [something]'
mono-	'appear / be seen'	'see [something/somebody]'
po'k-	'hide / be hidden'	'hide [something/somebody]'
tani-	'wake up'	'awaken [somebody]'
tokis-	'cut / be cut'	'cut [something/somebody]'

Type III ('less agentive activity')

	middle (intransitive)	active (transitive)
hunahunai-	'make a visit'	'visit [somebody]'
komik-	'be engaged in finishing [something]'	'finish [something]'
kuuto-	'wait / be waiting'	'wait for [somebody]'
onoh-	'be engaged in thinking'	'think about [something/somebody]'
taapu-	'participate'	'help [somebody]'

(5)   *Middle-only verbs:*

Type I ('bodily action')

kakapi-	'crawl (like a caterpillar)'	turu-	'return'
kuroh-	'run/go fast'	tuuh-	'carry [something] on the shoulder'
mihw-	'move/jump vigorously'		
muhmuhw-	'whisper'	tuu'k-	'slide on the ground like a lizard'
ne'	'sit down / be sitting'		
su'k-	'jump'		

Type II ('spontaneous process/event')

haring-	'become/be upset'	kamanga'w-	'yawn'
hiiro-	'feel/become/be hungry'	nimautu-	'be/become
hurot-	'become/be messy'		handsome (M)'
itikai-	'gain strength'	ni'r-	'be/become startled'
kaa-	'be born'	turio-	'become/be alarmed'

Type III ('complex activity')

haha'w-	'work'	ru'kah-	'do the cooking'
koronong-	'say prayer'	sanaka-	'do the hunting/fishing'
mu'sii-	'have feast at the	siimpai-	'do the sweeping'
	time of mourning;	sikuulu-	'be educated'
	to be in that period'	tupurai-	'burn off the bush'
nihuk-	'plan and organize'		

References

Allen, J. and Hurd, C. 1965. *The languages of the Bougainville district.* Port Moresby: Department of Information and Extension Services.

Dixon, R.M.W. 1994. *Ergativity.* Cambridge: Cambridge University Press.

Dixon, R.M.W. and Aikhenvald, A.Y. 1997. 'A typology of argument-determined constructions', pp. 71–113 of *Essays on language function and language type*, ed. J. Bybee, J. Haiman and S.A. Thompson. Amsterdam, Philadelphia: John Benjamins.

Haspelmath, M. 1990. 'The grammaticization of passive morphology', *Studies in Language* 14.25–72.

Hopper, P.J. and Thompson, S.A. 1980. 'Transitivity in grammar and discourse', *Language* 56.251–99.

Kemmer, S. 1993. *The middle voice*, Typological studies in language 23. Amsterdam and Philadelphia: John Benjamins.

1994. 'Middle voice, transitivity, and the elaboration of events', pp. 179–230 of *Voice form and its function*, ed. B. Fox and P.J. Hopper. Amsterdam: John Benjamins.

Klaiman, M.H. 1988. 'Affectedness and control: a typology of voice systems', pp. 25–83 of *Passive and middle voice*, ed. M. Shibatani. Amsterdam, Philadelphia: John Benjamins.

1991. *Grammatical voice.* Cambridge: Cambridge University Press.

1992. 'Middle verbs, reflexive middle constructions, and middle voice', *Studies in Language* 16.35–61.

Li, C.N. and Thompson, S.A. 1976. 'Subject and topic: a new typology of language', pp. 457–89 of *Subject and topic*, ed. C.N. Li. New York: Academic Press.

Oliver, D. 1955. *A Solomon Island society.* Cambridge, Mass.: Harvard University Press.

Onishi, M. 1994. 'A grammar of Motuna (Bougainville, Papua New Guinea)'. Unpublished Ph.D. dissertation. The Australian National University.

5   Transitivity in Tariana

ALEXANDRA Y. AIKHENVALD

1   Introduction

This chapter considers transitivity alternations in Tariana.[1] There are two valency-reducing operations and four valency-increasing causativizing mechanisms; there is also a valency-increasing mechanism distinct from both causatives and applicatives.[2] Transitivity alternations in Tariana provide evidence as to what grammatical relations must be distinguished in this language.

The chapter is organized as follows. I describe typological properties of Tariana in §2. Then, in §3, I discuss valency-reducing derivations. Valency-increasing mechanisms are analysed in §4. Some conclusions and typological perspectives are given in §5.

2   Typological characteristics of Tariana

Tariana is predominantly head-marking with a few elements of dependent-marking. There are three open word classes – nouns, verbs and adjectives. Relations between word classes and functional slots in a clause are summarized in appendix 5.1. The language has a complicated verb structure, and a large system of classifiers (Aikhenvald 1994a). Constituent order is free, with a strong tendency towards verb-final order. How grammatical relations are

[1] Tariana is a North-Arawak language spoken by around 100 people in the region of the river Vaupés, Upper Rio Negro (Brazil). It is the only Arawak language spoken in the multilingual context of the Vaupés linguistic area (see Aikhenvald 1996), and it has suffered a heavy areal impact from Tucano languages. My corpus consists of several hundred pages of sentences and word lists and about 700 pages of texts. I am extremely grateful to my teachers of Tariana – Cândido, Olívia, Graciliano, Juvino and Jusé Brito. I owe thanks to R.M.W. Dixon for useful discussion and comments.
[2] There is also a mechanism which does not affect the transitivity value of a verb, but rearranges valencies; see Dixon and Aikhenvald (1997).

marked is discussed in §2.1. Verb structure is discussed in §2.2; and in §2.3 we look at transitivity classes of verbs.

2.1   Grammatical relations

Grammatical relations in Tariana are marked in two ways.

2.1.1   Cross-referencing on the verb

Verbs in Tariana divide into two classes: those which take prefixes (cross-referencing, relativizing and negative) and those which do not. Active transitive and intransitive verbs obligatorily take cross-referencing prefixes to mark the A/S_a constituent (following the terminology in Dixon 1994). Stative verbs (S_o) and verbs of physical states (S_{io}) do not take any cross-referencing markers. This division roughly corresponds to the morphological distinction between active and stative intransitive verbs inherited from Proto-Arawak.

Active intransitive and transitive verbs have one obligatory prefixal position, so that when prefixed negation *ma-* is used, personal cross-referencing prefixes are omitted, and person/gender/number distinctions are neutralized.

2.1.2   Case marking

Tariana also uses case marking of an accusative type[3] (see Aikhenvald 1994b). In a straightforward transitive clause, a pronominal NP with an animate referent in non-subject function is marked by suffix *-na*. Any NP, nominal or pronominal, which is not in A, S_a or S_o function, may optionally take topicalizing clitic *-nuku*. (Thus, a free pronoun in non-subject function with an animate referent can take both *-na* and *-nuku*.) If a subject NP (A, S_a or S_o), whether nominal or pronominal, is in contrastive focus, it is marked with a suffix *-ne* 'agentive'.[4] An S_{io} pronominal constituent takes *-na* case; if it is topical it can take *-nuku*. Verb types and the marking of grammatical relations are shown in figure 5.1.

Figure 5.1. Verb types in Tariana

	prefixed		prefixless		
	A	S_a	S_o	S_{io}	other arguments
Non-focussed subject		Ø		*-na*/Ø	*-na*/Ø
Focussed subject	*-ne*		–	–	–
Topical non-subject	–			*-nuku*	*-nuku*

---

[3] In this, Tariana is almost unique among Arawak languages. I have shown elsewhere (Aikhenvald 1996) that case marking in Tariana is most probably the result of areal diffusion from East Tucano languages.

[4] For nouns it is homophonous with the instrumental marker; see further discussion in Aikhenvald (1994b).

2.2   Verb structure

There are three main types of predicates – simple predicates, serial verb constructions and complex predicates.

Each verb is either transitive (with a pronominal prefix cross-referencing A) or active intransitive (with a prefix for S_a) or stative intransitive, with an S_o argument (but no prefix), or intransitive of physical state, with an S_{io} argument (and again no prefix).[5] Simple predicates have one prefix position and up to eight suffix positions. In the scheme below, positions marked with * do not appear with prefixless verbs.

1   *Cross-referencing prefixes or Negative *ma-* or Relative *ka-*
2   ROOT
3   *Thematic syllable
4   Causative *-i(-ta)*
5   Negative *-(ka)de*
6   *Resultative *-karu* and/or one of the following: Topic-advancing *-ni*, or *Passive *-kana* or Purposive *-hyu*;
7   Verbal classifiers
8   Benefactive *-pena*
9   *Reciprocal *-kaka*
10   Relativizers or nominalizers (relative and converb *-li*, past relative *-kali*, nominalizers *-mi*, *-nipe*).

Suffixes may be followed by enclitics. Unlike suffixes, enclitics may be omitted; they preferably go onto the verb, but may appear on any constituent provided it is in focus; all enclitics (except mood and evidentiality) allow variable ordering. Enclitics longer than one syllable can acquire a secondary stress. The most frequent order of enclitics[6] is:

I   Mood (imperative, frustrative, conditional);
II   Tense and evidentiality;
III Aktionsart (manner or extent of action, associated action);
IV   Aspect (completive, durative, repetitive, etc.);
V   Degree (augmentative, diminutive, approximative ('a little bit'));
VI   Switch-reference.

Serial verb constructions (SVCs) are known to include up to seven simple verbs. They are strictly contiguous (i.e. no other constituent can intervene

---

[5] A verbal root can shift classes if a transitivity-increasing suffix is added to it (see §4). There is just one verb which can be used as prefixless and as prefixed without any additional marker: *ira* 'need', *-ira* 'order'.
[6] Some of the enclitics are given in appendix 5.2.

between their components). Each component of a SVC is an independent phonological word, and they all receive the same inflection for person, number and gender of subject (A/S$_a$). All the components of a SVC have the same tense, aspect, mood, evidentiality and polarity value. The order of the components may be fixed or not depending on the construction type. A SVC cannot consist of stative (S$_o$) verbs only. SVC are widely used to express aspectual, directional and modal meanings.[7]

Complex predicates consist of two verbs; they differ from serial verbs only in that they do not have to share the same subject marking. One example is the passive – see §3.1.

2.3   Verb types
Verbs in Tariana fall into further classes according to their transitivity.

2.3.1   Transitive and ambitransitive verbs
In some languages every, or almost every, verb is strictly transitive or intransitive; in other languages at least some verbs can have either transitivity value. These verbs are called ambitransitive, or labile (Dixon 1994: 18, 54). All transitive verbs in Tariana are A = S ambitransitive (e.g. *-hna* 'eat', *-inu* 'kill, fight, hunt', *-ɲa* 'hit', *-ka* 'see', *-hima* 'hear', *-sata* 'greet', etc.). This means the object NP can always be optionally omitted, as in English *eat* (*he has eaten dinner* or *he has eaten*). Example (1) illustrates an ambitransitive verb.

(1)   (a:si)   nu-hyã-ka
       (pepper)   1sgA-eat-DECL
       I eat / am eating (pepper)

Ditransitive verbs form a subclass of A = S ambitransitives. Their second argument can be either gift or recipient, e.g., *-a* 'give', *-phya* 'sell', *-waɹita* 'offer' (ritual offering), *-wãya* 'buy'.

All transitive verbs are prefixed, with four exceptions. There are the following ambitransitive prefixless verbs: two verbs of liking – *hui* 'like (food)', *nhesiɾi* 'like (not food)' – and two verbs of fearing – *kaɾu* 'be afraid' and *haɾame* 'get frightened'. A transitive prefixless verb is shown in (2).

---

[7] I can give an example of a serial verb construction which has a directional meaning (the construction is underlined):

    na-musu   na-nu   nema   diha-pua-nuku
    3pl-go out 3pl-come 3pl+stand he-CL:RIVER-TOP.NON.A/S
    They (the ancestors of the Tarianas) were coming out towards (lit. go out-come-stand) this (river)

For a further analysis of serial verb constructions in Tariana, see Aikhenvald (forthcoming-c).

(2)   duhua inaɾu-ne   nhesiɾi-kade-pidana   diha ʧiãli-nuku
         she   woman-AGT   like-NEG-REM.PAST.INFR   he   man-TOP.NON.A/S
         This woman did not like the man

S = O ambitransitives constitute a smallish, closed class. Most verbs of breaking can be used as S = O ambitransitives, e.g. *-makha*, *-thuka* 'break' (split), *-sawa* 'tear' (clothes), and a few more verbs, e.g. *-hwaweta* 'breathe, make breathe', *-kuseta* 'swing', *-dukunia* 'switch on, light', *-hipa* 'take, succeed'. S = O ambitransitives are more frequent in narratives told by younger people. In (3) *-thuka* 'break' is used transitively, and then intransitively; both instances are underlined.

(3)   duhua-ne heku-kena   <u>du-thuka,</u>   duka
         she-AGT   tree-BRANCH <u>3sgN.F-break+TR</u> 3sgF+arrive
         du-pe-pidana   du-kolota du-ɲa   diha-na-nuku
         3sgF-let-REM.PAST.INFR   3sgF-meet 3sgF-hit he-CL:VERT-TOP.NON.A/S
         dhi-ni-na-nuku,   kayu duhua
         3sgN.F+copulate-TOP.ADV-CL:VERT-TOP.NON.A/S, so   she
         du-ɲa-ka-pidana,   <u>di-thuka-kha</u>   di-ruku
         3sgF-hit-DEP-REM.PAST.INFR   <u>3sgN.F-break+INTR-AWAY</u> 3sgN.F-fall
         di-a   diha-na-ne
         3sgN.F-go   he-CL:VERT-AGT
         She (the widow) <u>broke</u> a branch, she managed to hit (the evil spirit) on his penis, after she did so, it (the penis) was <u>breaking</u> and falling off

2.3.2   Intransitive verbs

Intransitive verbs may be prefixed – S_a (active) – or prefixless – stative (S_o) and verbs of physical states (S_{io}).
(a) Active (S_a) verbs include verbs of motion, stance, verbs of beginning and finishing and a few others, e.g., *-musu* 'go out', *-emhani* 'walk', *-kana* 'go', *-nu* 'come', *-ma* 'sleep, close one's eyes', *-keɲa* 'start', *-sisa* 'be finished'. See (4).

(4)   nu-ɾuku   nu-a
         1sgS_a-go down 1sgS_a-go
         I am going downstream

(b) Stative (S_o) verbs denote physical states, mostly involuntary results of processes, e.g., *lama* 'burn, get burnt', *leka* 'split', *ke:ka* 'split open', *hala* 'be open'. Any adjective or noun can be used as an S_o verb in the predicate slot (see appendix 5.1), cf. (5).

(5)   nuha keɾu-mha
       I   angry-PRES.NON.VIS
       I am angry

(c) Verbs of physical state (S_{io}) form a small class; they denote physical states, e.g., *dai* 'be sleepy', *unina* 'be thirsty', *mhaisiki* 'be hungry', *mhaisiki kai* 'be very hungry' (lit. 'ache of hunger'). They do not take cross-referencing prefixes, and the S_{io} is marked by the *-na* case (see §2.1 and figure 5.1), if expressed with a pronominal constituent, as in (6).

(6)   dai-mha   nu-na
       be sleepy-PRES.NON.VIS 1sg-OBJ
       I am sleepy

These verb types differ as to their morphological properties, i.e. application of transitivity-reducing and transitivity-increasing derivations.

3   Decreasing transitivity

Transitivity-decreasing operations in Tariana are the passive and the reciprocal. Reflexive is very limited in its application. These operations are applicable only to prefixed verbs (transitive and active intransitive).

3.1   Passive

Passive is marked with prefix *ka-* and suffix *-kana* (see §2.2). It can be followed by an auxiliary verb *-a* 'go, do, give' which takes the subject prefix. When a passive form is negated, *ka-* is replaced by *ma-* 'negative'.

Passive derivation of transitive verbs has the following properties:

(a)   a passive clause is active intransitive;
(b)   the underlying O argument goes into S_a function and is cross-referenced on the auxiliary verb;
(c)   the underlying A of the transitive verb is demoted to the periphery and may optionally be omitted, as in (7b) and (8); it takes non-subject case-marking (i.e. if it is a pronoun it is marked by *-na*; and if it is topical, it may also take *-nuku*, as in (12)).

If the verb is ditransitive, only 'gift' (not 'recipient') can acquire the S_a function. (7b) is the passive of (7a).

(7) (a)   wali-da   episi-da-nuku   nu-phya-ka   di-na
           new-CL:ROUND iron-CL:ROUND-TOP.NON.A/S 1sg-buy-REC.PAST.VIS 3sgN.F-OBJ
           I bought him a new motor

(b)   wali-da   episi-da   <u>ka-phya-kana-ka</u>   di-a
      new-CL:ROUND iron-CL:ROUND REL-buy-PASS-REC.PAST.VIS 3sgN.F-AUX
      A new motor <u>was bought</u>

Passive derivation of an intransitive verb has impersonal reference. If there is an auxiliary it takes 3rd person plural cross-referencing marker *na-*.

Passive is used when the underlying O argument is the topic of a stretch of discourse. (8) comes from a narrative about what objects cannot be touched and what one should not do before going hunting.

(8)   ne inaɾu-ne   mhaĩda-mha   pa-kwa ne syawa
      NEG woman-INS PROH-PRES.NON.VIS IMP-hang NEG fire
      <u>ma-kuka-kana-de-mha</u>
      <u>NEG-light-PASS-NEG-PRES.NON.VIS</u>
      One should not sleep (lit. hang in hammock) with a woman. The fire is not lit.

(9) is an example of a passive with the A overtly marked. The Moon is talking to a man who did what the Moon told him not to; the 2nd person pronoun is the topic.

(9)   phia pi-ni-ka   nu-na   <u>ka-ɲa-kana-mhade</u> phia
      you 2sg-do-DEP 1sg-OBLQ <u>REL-eat-PASS-FUT</u>   you
      You having done (what I told you not to), you will be eaten by me

Impersonal passive formed on intransitive verbs is widely used in general statements, e.g. (10) and (11):

(10) <u>ma-whawheta-kana-de</u> wha ita-whya-misini-nuku
      <u>NEG-rest-PASS-NEG</u>   our canoe-CL:CANOE-too-TOP.NON.A/S
      <u>mema-kana-de</u>   na
      <u>NEG+sleep-PASS-NEG</u> 3pl+AUX
      One does not rest on our canoe, too, one does not sleep

(11) kiaku   <u>ma-kama-kana-de-na</u>
      strong <u>NEG-get.drunk-PASS-NEG-REM.PAST.VIS</u>
      One did not get really drunk (on a certain type of manioc beer)

Another function of the passive can be called 'switch-reference' feeding. In complex sentences, passive may be used in the main clause if the subordinate clause contains a sequencing enclitic which requires the same subject in the two clauses. Passive is used to bring a non-subject argument into subject function so that a sequencing enclitic which requires same subject can be used. (12) illustrates the use of passive in the main clause, when the subordinate clause contains the sequencing enclitic *-hyume* 'after, because' which requires the same subject. In this case, passive can be considered a 'switch-reference' feeding operation. In (12), the underlying A is marked with *-nuku* 'topical non-subject', since it belongs to the topic of the narrative. The passive form is underlined.

(12)   di-pumi   dihya salu   peme   di-ka-hyume   di-na
        3sgN.F-after he   armadillo one+SIDE 3sgN.F-see-AFTER:SS 3sgN.F-OBJ
        yawi-nuku   ka-na-kana-pu-pidana   di-a
        jaguar-TOP.NON.A/S REL-hit-PASS-AUG-REM.PAST.INFR 3sgN.F-AUX
        Because after that (after the jaguar tore away his eye) the armadillo could
        only see on one side, he was badly beaten by the jaguar

3.2   Reciprocal *-kaka*

Reciprocal marked with a suffix *-kaka* is used under the following syntactic conditions.

(a) When added to transitive verbs with plural A, it makes the verb intransitive, and indicates that A is identical to O and the action is symmetrical. This is a straightforward reciprocal; it has one core argument, in S function. If one of the participants (in the S function) is in focus, it can be overtly expressed and is then marked with suffix *-ne* 'instrumental; comitative', as an oblique. Compare the transitive verb in (13) and its reciprocal version in (14) (underlined). (14) means that the elder brother and the younger brother encountered each other; the younger brother is in contrastive focus as a recently introduced participant.

(13)   ne-pidana   yawaru di-kolota   dhipa   dina
        then-REM.PAST.INFR Yawaru 3sgN.F-meet 3sgN.F+take 3sgN.F-OBJ
        e:ta-nuku
        eagle-TOP.NON.A/S
        Then Yawaru grabbed (lit. met-took) the eagle

(14)   di-we-ri-ne   na-kolota-kaka-sina
        3sgN.F-younger sibling-M-INS 3pl-meet-RECIP-REM.PAST.NON.VIS
        They met each other, with his younger brother (i.e. older brother and younger
        brother met each other; the older brother met the younger brother, and not
        somebody else)

(b) When added to a transitive verb with a singular subject, the *-kaka* derivation also makes the verb intransitive; the action implies multiple participants. The verb *-inu* means 'kill, fight'; in (15) it is used with *-kaka* in the meaning of 'fighting in a war' (lit. 'kill / fight with lots of people').

(15) nuhua pi-sa-niɾi   nu-a-ka   <u>nu-inu-kaka</u>
I   2sg-spouse-M 1sg-go-REC.PAST.VIS 1sg-kill-RECIP
kasina-wya-nuku
now-just-TOP.NON.A/S
I, your husband, have gone to fight war just now

(c) When *-kaka* is added to an intransitive verb, the verb remains intransitive; it then implies the participation of multiple participants and also the presence of oblique argument(s). (16) illustrates an intransitive use of *-nalita* 'be quarrelsome, quarrel'. In (17), the same verb appears with the reciprocal marker *-kaka* and means 'quarrel with each other'. The oblique argument is in focus and is marked with *-ne* 'instrumental, comitative', like in (14).

(16) <u>di-nalita</u>   kiaku
<u>3sgN.F-quarrel</u> strong
He was very quarrelsome

(17) di-ne-pidana   na <u>na-nalita-kaka</u>
3sgN.F-INS-REM.PAST.INFR 3pl+go <u>3pl-quarrel-RECIP</u>
They (Tariana tribes) quarrelled with him (the first-born son)

Unlike passive, reciprocal does not make an intransitive verb impersonal (i.e. it does not reduce valency of the intransitive verb).

The suffix *-kaka* is occasionally used with a transitive verb to mark reflexive. The usual way of expressing a reflexive meaning consists in simply using a transitive verb intransitively. A transitive use of *-pisa* 'cut' is shown in (18); its intransitive use with a reflexive reading in (19).

(18) diwhida   <u>na-pisa</u> na-pala-pidana
3sgN.F+head <u>3pl-cut</u> 3pl-put-REM.PAST.INFR
They cut its (the snake's) head and put it (down)

(19) maliye-ne <u>nu-pisa-makha-niki</u>
knife-INS <u>1sg-cut-REC.PAST.NON.VIS-COMPLETIVE</u>
I cut myself with a knife

A *-kaka* reflexive with a transitive verb *-pisa* is shown in (20).

(20) <u>nu-pisa-kaka-mha</u>
1sg-cut-REFL/RECIP-PRES.NON.VIS
I have just cut myself

There are reasons to believe that the reflexive use of *-kaka* is on its way out in Tariana, due to areal diffusional patterns from East Tucano languages. All other neighbouring North-Arawak languages have one intransitivizing derivation used for marking reflexives and reciprocals (Aikhenvald forthcoming-a).

In contrast, East Tucano languages have a reflexive pronoun, and use serial verb constructions, or verb compounding, for marking reciprocals (Aikhenvald forthcoming-b). Tariana is gradually becoming more similar to East Tucano by differentiating reciprocals from reflexives.

3.3   Summary

Table 5.1 summarizes correlations between valency-reducing mechanisms and verb types.

Table 5.1. Valency-reducing mechanisms and verb types

Verb types	Passives	Reciprocals	Reflexives
transitive	yes	yes	(yes)
intransitive S_a	yes	yes	no
intransitive S_o	no	no	no
intransitive S_{io}	no	no	no

Transitivity-decreasing derivations apply only to prefixed verbs (they cannot apply to transitive prefixless verbs). These derivations provide an important clue for distinguishing core constituents from oblique – they affect only core arguments: A/S_a and O. Arguments other than these (e.g. 'recipient' for ditransitive verbs, or oblique constituents) cannot be passivized or 'reciprocalized'.

4   Increasing transitivity

Typically for an Amazonian language, Tariana has more valency-increasing mechanisms than valency-decreasing ones. There is a morphological causative typically used with intransitive verbs, a serial causative construction and two types of periphrastic causative. All these causative constructions are functionally and formally distinct, and show intricate interrelations as to the role of the causer, that of the causee, and the properties of predicate classes. These are discussed in §4.1–4.3 and contrasted in §4.4.

The use of the morphological causative with transitive verbs correlates with the promotion of an oblique argument into the core; it also makes ambitransitive verbs strictly transitive. Thus, the causative morpheme, when added to a transitive verb, marks a kind of argument-adding derivation – see §4.5.

4.1   Morphological causatives

4.1.1   Morphological causatives and active intransitive verbs

Morphological causatives are regularly formed on active intransitive verbs
(S_a type). They are marked with a suffix *-i-ta* which follows the thematic
suffix. Their semantics is usually quite straightforward, e.g. *-eku* 'run', *-eku-
ita* 'make run'; *-yena* 'pass', *-yeneta* (from *-yena-i-ta*) 'make pass'; *-musu*
'go out', *-musu-i-ta* 'make go out, drive out'; *-thaka* 'cross', *-thaketa* 'make
cross'; *-kukume* 'tremble', *-kukumeta* 'make tremble'. Occasionally, a morphological causative can acquire an idiosyncratic meaning, e.g. *-pusuka* 'be
muddled, confused', *-pusuketa* 'muddle, confuse, gossip'; *-ɲami* 'die', *-ɲameta*
'abort a baby'. A morphological causative of the verb *-pita* 'have a bath' is
illustrated in (21). See §4.1.4 for the explanation of a 'double' causative.

(21)   di-pumi   nha-ma-pe-nuku   maini-ne na-ɲapa
       3sgN.F-after they-CL:F-pl-TOP.NON.A/S tar-INS   3pl-bless
       na-pite-ta-mha   na-yũ   naka
       3pl-have.a.bath+CAUS1-CAUS2-PRES.NON.VIS 3pl-go.up 3pl+arrive
       After they (old people) bless them (menstruating girls) with tar, they <u>make</u>
       <u>them</u> <u>bathe</u> upstream

4.1.2   Morphological causatives, stative verbs and verbs of physical state

Morphological causatives can be formed on stative (S_o) verbs if the meaning
of the verb presupposes a state changeable through the intervention of a
causer. Verbs denoting physical state and emotions belong to this class, e.g.
sakamu 'be luke-warm', causative *-sakamu-ita* 'warm up'; *hiwiri* 'be cool',
causative *-hiwiriketa* 'cool down (e.g. by stirring)'; *makara* 'be dry', causative
-makareta 'to dry'; *-pusa* 'be wet', causative *-pusita* 'wetten, moisten'; *inasua*
'be lazy or weak', *inasueta* 'make lazy, weaken'. So also do S_o verbs which
imply change of state, e.g. *kawhi* 'be awake, wake up', causative *-kawheta* 'to
wake (somebody) up'; *hiku* 'appear', causative *hikweta* 'create, make come
into being'.

Verbs which refer to an inherently unchangeable state cannot form a
morphological causative. Thus, no morphological causative can be formed
on verbs describing physical states such as colour: *hale* 'be white', *kada* 'be
black', *iri* 'be red'; physical properties: *hamu* 'be hot', *hape* 'be cold'; size:
hanu 'be big', *tsu* 'be small'; taste: *hipisi* 'be bitter'; value: *maʃa* 'be good';
other physical states, e.g. *kasitana* 'be annoyed'. Note that in Tariana stative
verbs which denote such concepts as 'cool' and 'luke-warm' belong to a
different system from 'cold' and 'hot'.

S$_{io}$ verbs also cannot form a morphological causative (e.g. *unyana* 'be thirsty', *mhaisiki* 'be hungry', *inuna* 'be lazy'). Serial causative constructions are then used.

Morphological causatives of S$_o$ verbs can be prefixed or prefixless, depending on whether the the result is achieved intentionally, or not. For instance, the action of warming something up, or toasting food is perceived as intentional; corresponding causative verbs are prefixed. (22) shows an S$_o$ verb *meri* 'be toasted, dry'; its causative counterpart is prefixed (23).

(22)   ke:ri-ne-mha   pana-phe   meri
        SUN-INS-PRES.NON.VIS leaf-CL:LEAF.LIKE be.toasted
        The leaf is dry (lit. toasted) because of the sun

(23)   pa-ita   kuphe di-merita-ka
        one-CL:ANIM fish   3sgN.F-be.toasted+CAUS-REC.PAST.VIS
        He has toasted one fish

In contrast to this, 'weakening' is achieved unintentionally, and the resulting causative verb is prefixless, e.g. (24).

(24)   adaki nu-na   inasueta-mahka
        fever 1sg-OBJ be.weak/lazy+CAUS-REC.PAST.NON.VIS
        Fever weakened me

Some morphological causatives can be assigned to both S$_a$ and S$_o$ classes. If they are prefixless, the result is achieved unintentionally. In (25), a dog barks, and this frightens the speaker; the dog did not mean to frighten him.

(25)   tʃinu nu-na   harameta di-kwisa-ka
        dog 1sg-OBJ fear+CAUS 3sgN.F-bark-REC.PAST.VIS
        The dog scared me, it barked

In contrast, in (26), a mythical character used to go out every afternoon to frighten people intentionally. The morphological causative is prefixed.

(26)   daikina-pe   hɨda-pada-pidana   na-na   di-rahmeta
        afternoon-pl every-AFF-REM.PAST.INFR 3pl-OBJ 3sgN.F-fear+CAUS
        di-na-nhi
        3sgN.F-stay-IMPERF
        He used to frighten them (villagers) every afternoon (with his cries)

Activities typical for mythical creatures are usually unintentional. It is believed that a new moon makes women menstruate (then they become dangerous); this typical activity is illustrated in (27a). A further explanation is provided by the speaker in (27b): that a woman menstruates is a natural result of her having sexual intercourse with the Moon.

(27) (a) hĩ   depite   keɾi hiku-ka   wali-pi
      this:ANIM night+CL:ANIM moon appear-DEP young-CL:LONG
      keɾi-nuku   ina-nuku   puimeta-mha
      moon-TOP.NON.A/S woman:pl-TOP.NON.A/S menstruate+CAUS-PRES.NON.VIS
      When this moon appears, during young moon, it makes women menstruate

(b) hĩ   keɾi di-thi-kayami   hĩ
     this:ANIM moon 3sgN.F-have.intercourse-after:DS this:ANIM
     ina   puima-mha
     woman:PL be menstruating-PRES.NON.VIS
     After the moon has intercourse (with woman), these women menstruate

The correlation between prefixed and prefixless morphological causatives and intentionality of the causer is reminiscent of fluid-S languages. It is noteworthy that Baniwa, a North-Arawak language very closely related to Tariana, and spoken in the adjacent linguistic area, also displays some elements of fluid-S marking (see Aikhenvald 1995).

4.1.3   Morphological causatives and transitive verbs

Morphological causatives can be formed on very few transitive verbs.[8] Almost all of these refer to traditional actions performed during rituals. The only exception is *-iɾa* 'drink' with the corresponding causative *-iɾeta* 'make drink, make drunk'.[9] These are shown in (28) and (29).

(28) kasina-nuku   na:-sina   naha na-iɾa-kaɾu
      now-TOP.NON.A/S 3pl+go-REM.PAST.NON.VIS they 3pl-drink-RES
      kapi   na-kuliɾa-kaɾu
      ritual.whisky 3pl-be.painted-RES
      Now they all went to drink ritual whisky and to paint themselves

(29) ne-pidana   di-na   iɾa-kasi   diɾe-ta-daka
      then-REM.PAST.INFR 3sgN.F-OBJ drink-NOM 3sgN.F+drink+CAUS1-CAUS2-YET
      And yet he gave him a drink

Other transitive verbs which have a morphological causative are: *-sita* 'smoke a traditional cigar', causative *-siteta* 'get one's partner to smoke in the cigar-smoking ritual'; *-eme* 'sniff snuff', causative *-emeta* 'get someone

---

[8] The causer becomes A, while both underlying A and O of the causativized verb get marked with the non-subject case. Since a morphological causative of a transitive verb cannot be passivized, there is no way of determining whether these two arguments are direct or indirect object(s).

[9] In closely related languages the morphological causative is usually formed on intransitive verbs only. The only exception is 'drink' (Baniwa *-iʒa*, Bare *-dia*, Warekena *-kulua*). Cross-linguistically, verbs describing digestive processes often display abnormal behaviour with regard to their transitivity (Ken Hale, p.c.).

to sniff snuff'; *-ɲapa* 'bless', causative *-ɲapeta* 'get a shaman, or an older man, to bless someone'; *-peru* 'lick tobacco from partner's tongue in the cigar-smoking ritual', causative *-perita* 'get someone to lick tobacco from partner's tongue'. (30) shows the verb *-sita* 'smoke'; (31) is an example of the causative *-siteta*, from a narrative about the tobacco-smoking ritual.

(30)   yema   di-sita-naka
       tobacco 3sgN.F-smoke-PRES.VIS
       He is smoking tobacco

(31)   nuri   nuhua yema   nu-de-ka   nuhua pi-na   yema
       1sg+son I   tobacco 1sg-have-DEP I   2sg-OBJ tobacco
       nu-site-ta-de
       1sg-smoke+CAUS1-CAUS2-FUT
       My son, when I have tobacco, I will get you to smoke (this) tobacco

That morphological causatives of transitive verbs are mostly used with verbs which describe highly ritualized traditional activities suggests that they are archaic.

The same suffix, *-i-ta*, is used as a marker of argument-adding derivation with transitive verbs. Some verbs can form both a morphological causative and an argument-adding derivation – see §4.5.

4.1.4   'Double causative' marking and further functions of *-i-ta*
Causativizing *-i-ta* in Tariana can be further analysed into *-i* and *-ta*. While *-i* is a straightforward marker of causative, addition of *-ta* has two functions with prefixed verbs (with prefixless verbs, only *-ita* is used). Firstly, *-ta* may imply complete affectedness of O. In (32) devils fell some woodchips; *-ta* is not used.

(32)   na-ɾuku-i-pidana   naha itʃida-pe-ne
       3pl-fall-CAUS-REM.PAST.INFR they turtle-pl-INS
       They (devils) made (some woodchips) fall down with the help of turtles (axes)

In contrast, in (33) the house was completely destroyed; *-ta* is used on the causativized verb *-ɾuku* 'go down':

(33)   phia nuha panisi-nuku   pi-ɲa-bala
       you I   house-TOP.NON.A/S 2sg-hit-EVERYWHERE
       pi-ɾuku-i-ta-ka
       2sg-go.down-CAUS1-CAUS2-DECL
       You destroyed my house completely (lit. hit everywhere – make come down) (said the evil spirit to a man in his dream)

Secondly, *-ta* is used on a causativized verb if the action is completed and its spatial extent is large. In (34) the magic spell is cast a little bit, and so *-ta* is not used; in (35) it is done a lot.

(34)   ne-pidana   na-whya   <u>na-sue-nha</u>   nha tu:me-ne
            then-REM.PAST.INFR 3pl-breathe <u>3pl-stay+CAUS-PAUSAL</u> they breath-INS
            Then they breathed (over the village) with their (magic) breath (i.e. cast a
            spell)

(35)   na: tsome na-whyã-ka   <u>na-sue-ta-pidana</u>
            3pl+go much 3pl-breathe-DEP <u>3pl-stay+CAUS1-CAUS2-REM.PAST.INFR</u>
            na-na   adaki-kuma-pidana   <u>na-sue-ta</u>
            3pl-OBJ fever-CL:RITE-REM.PAST.INFR <u>3pl-stay+CAUS1-CAUS2</u>
            They cast a big spell, they cast a fever spell all over them

In (36) action is not completed; in (37) it is. Both come from the same text.

(36)   kwana ha-na   hyapa-na   kheta   <u>ka-thake</u>
            who   this-CL:VERT hill-CL:VERT REL+take <u>REL-cross+CAUS</u>
            peme-kema-se   nu-itu-nuku   ka-sa-do-mhade
            one side-CL:SIDE-LOC 1sg-daughter-TOP.NON.A/S REL-spouse-F-FUT
            Who takes the hill across to the other side will marry my daughter

(37)   nuhua-ka nhuta   <u>nu-thake-ta</u>
            I-DECL   1sg+take <u>1sg-cross+CAUS1-CAUS2</u>
            I am the one who took (the hill) across (said the soldier)

Suffix *-i-ta* is also used to derive transitive verbs from nouns and adjectives, e.g. *sie* 'firewood', *-sieta* 'put on fire'; *kepitana* 'name', *-pitaneta* 'give a name, name'; *kape* 'ritual stick', *-kapeta* 'hit with a ritual stick'. In other Arawak languages of the region, e.g. Warekena and Bare, *-(i)ta* is the only causative marker.

4.2   *Causative serial verb constructions*

Causative constructions in serializing languages require 'that the object of one verb and the subject of another be coreferential' (Foley and Olson 1985: 25; Crowley 1987: 38–9). Most often, the components of a serial verb construction have independent inflection; they cross-reference the two different semantic subjects. Such a construction in Paamese (called 'switch-subject' serial constructions: Crowley 1987) is shown in (38) (Crowley 1987: 48, ex. 27).

(38)   kaiko <u>ko-muasi-nau</u>   <u>nau-vaa</u>   <u>netano</u>
            2sg   <u>2sg-real.hit-1sg</u>   <u>1sg-real.go</u> <u>down</u>
            You hit me down (lit. you hit – I fall)

The other technique, labelled 'concordant dependent inflection' (Durie 1997) involves putting the same subject marking on all the components of a serial verb construction.[10] This is the way causative serial constructions are marked in Tariana. The components of a serial syntactic causative construction have different underlying subjects, realized as the same subject in the surface form. The subject of the verb of causation is cross-referenced on the two verbs which form a causative serial verb construction.

The underlying subject of the causativized verb, if expressed with a personal pronoun, is marked with the object case, e.g. *di-na* (3sgN.F-OBJ) 'him' in (39); if it is expressed with a noun which is topical, it can be marked with -*nuku* 'topical non A/S', as in (40).

The serial causative construction can be used with transitive and active intransitive verbs; it is never used with a stative verb (S$_o$) or a verb of physical state (S$_{io}$). The most frequent verbs of causation used in serial causative constructions are -*ira* 'order', as in (39), -*wana* 'call' and -*matara* 'allow, give permission', or the abstract verb of causation -*a*, as in (40).

(39)   di-na   taliwa nara-ka   na-phya   diha nawiki
       3sgN.F-OBJ flute   3pl+order-DEP 3pl-whistle he   man
       dira-pidana
       3sgN.F+drink-REM.PAST.INFR
       After they ordered the man to play a flute (lit. whistle a flute), the man drank

(40)   nu-inipe-nuku   kwaka-mhade nu-a   nu-hɲa
       1sg-children-TOP.NON.A/S how-FUT   1sg-make 1sg-eat
       How will I get my children to eat (if I can't hunt anything)?

Serial causative constructions have the following properties of a single predicate, as do all serial verb constructions in Tariana:

(i)   They have the intonational properties of a monoverbal clause, and not of a sequence of clauses.

(ii) They can be distinguished from subordination or coordination, or complex predicates, since they contain no markers of syntactic dependency.

(iii) They share tense/aspect, modality, evidentiality and polarity value, i.e. verbs which form a serial construction cannot receive independ-

---

[10] This technique is rather rare in the languages of the world; such a construction was reported for Akan by Schachter (1974: 258–9), e.g.:

       mede aburow migu msum
       I-take corn I-flow water-in
       I pour corn into water (lit. I take corn I flow in water)

ent marking for these categories. In (41) there is just one negative marker in a causative serial construction. It is ambiguous: it could mean either 'he did not order to kill many fish', or 'he ordered not to kill many fish (to kill just a few)'. It is clear from the context of the narrative that the latter translation is the right one.

(41)   hanupe-se   maɾa-kade-ka   dinu   diha-yawa
            many-CONTRAST NEG+order-NEG-REC.PAST.VIS 3sgN.F+kill he-CL:HOLE
            i-minali   du-a-tha-pidana
            INDEF-master 3sgF-say-FRUST-REM.PAST.INFR
            The master of the (water)hole ordered not to kill many (fish)', said she (the widow) in vain

Serial causative constructions are the only productive mechanism used to causativize transitive verbs, alongside periphrastic causatives.

They are also used to causativize active intransitive verbs which have a morphological causative. Then, a serial causative construction implies indirect involvement of the causer, and a morphological causative implies that the causer acts directly on the causee. Example (21) contains a morphological causative of the verb *-pita* 'bathe'; there the old people physically make pubescent girls bathe as a part of the ritual of female initiation. In contrast, in (42) the evil mother ordered her children to bathe without physical interference.

(42)   na:-na duɾa   du-pita   du-yã-nhi
            3pl-OBJ 3sgF+order 3sgF-bathe 3sgF-stay-IMPERF
            She ordered them to bathe

Serial constructions of a different kind are used to causativize S_{io} verbs. In these constructions, the verb *-eme-ta* 'put' (a morphological causative of *-ema* 'stand') is used as the verb of causation. In (43), a serial construction consists of an S_{io} verb *mhaisiki* 'be hungry' and *-eme-ta*. Unlike serial causative constructions with transitive and active intransitive verbs, the verb of causation follows the S_{io} verb. (Note that plural marking on nouns is optional if the referent is not human.)

(43)   diha kewiɾi-mha   nu-na mhaisiki neme-ta
            he   ant-PRES.NON.VIS 1sg-OBJ be.hungry 3pl+stand+CAUS1-CAUS2
            The (edible) ants make me (feel) hungry

4.3   Periphrastic causatives

There are two kinds of periphrastic causatives – those with an optional dependency marker (§4.3.1), and those with an obligatory dependency marker

(§4.3.2). The reasons why periphrastic causatives are not serial verb constructions are given in §4.3.2. Periphrastic causatives are used with intransitive
verbs of S_a and S_o types.

4.3.1   Periphrastic causatives with an optional dependency marker

I mentioned above that S_o verbs which refer to an inherently unchangeable
state (colour, physical properties such as size or taste, etc.; see §4.1) cannot
form a morphological causative. Periphrastic causatives which contain the
verb of causation *-ni* 'do, make' are used to causativize these stative verbs.
The dependency marker *-ka* can optionally be used on the causativized stative
verb, with no semantic difference. (44) is an example of a periphrastic causative used without a dependency marker; (45) is an example with one.[11] In each
case periphrastic causatives are underlined.

(44)   phia pi-ka   kaya wa-na   <u>pedalia-ma-pe</u> <u>di-ni</u>
         you 2sg-see so   1pl-OBJ <u>be.old-CL:F-pl</u> <u>3sgN.F-make</u>
         In front of you (lit. so that you saw) he made us into old women

(45)   nawiki <u>ka:da-ka-naka</u>   <u>pi-ni</u>   phia
         person <u>be.black-DEP-VIS.PRES</u> <u>2sg-make</u> you
         You make people black (said the Moon to the Sun)

4.3.2   Periphrastic causatives with an obligatory dependency marker

Periphrastic causatives with the verb of causation *-ni* 'do, make' formed
on intransitive active verbs, and on stative ones which refer to changeable
properties, require a dependency marker. They imply a special effort by the
causer and/or unwillingness of the causee to bring about the activity. This is
illustrated with (46). The subject (a female evil spirit) had to make a special
effort to achieve the result. The dependency marker *-ka* on the causativized
verb is obligatory. Its omission results in an ungrammatical sentence.

(46)   hĩ   ma:ʧite-thasika   nu-na   ikasu depita
         DEM:ANIM bad+CL:ANIM-FRUST:MAL 1sg-OBJ now   night+ADV
         <u>mema-kade-ka</u>   <u>du-ni-paɾa</u>
         <u>NEG+sleep-NEG-DEP</u> <u>3sgF-make-IN.VAIN</u>
         This bad one (female evil spirit disguised as a bird) kept me awake (lit.
         made me sleep in vain) this night

In contrast, (47) involves no dependency marker; here the result is achieved
with the help of the magic power of the cigar, without any special effort. The

---

[11] Periphrastic causatives are quite regular; for instance the name for 'freezer' in Tariana is a
nominalized periphrastic causative with a dependency marker: *uni hape-ka ka-ni-ni-pasole*
'water cold-DEP REL-make-TOP.ADV-CL:BAG'.

corresponding morphological causative of the verb *-ima* 'close eyes / sleep' is used here.

(47)   di-na   maʧia yema-ne <u>neme-ta</u>
        3sgN.F-OBJ well   cigar-INS <u>3pl+close eyes / sleep+CAUS1-CAUS2</u>
        They made him really asleep with a cigar (i.e. through a cigar-smoking ritual)

Similarly, a morphological causative of a stative verb which refers to change-able properties describes effortless causation: in (48) a dog makes someone angry without doing anything special, just by barking.

(48)   ʧinu nu-na   ke:ru-neta-mahka
        dog 1sg-OBJ   be.angry-AFF+CAUS-REC.PAST.NON.VIS
        The dog made me angry

In contrast, a periphrastic causative implies special efforts undertaken to make the evil spirit angry, as in (49).

(49)   nuhua keweri-peri nu-ni-ka   ɲamu-nuku   keru-ka
        I   fried-COLL 1sg-make-DEP evil spirit-TOP.NON.A/S angry-DEP
        nu-ni-mahka
        1sg-make-REC.PAST.NON.VIS
        After I prepared a fried dish, I made an evil spirit angry

Periphrastic causatives do not qualify as serial verb constructions for the following reasons.

(i) Every verb in a periphrastic causative construction is marked for its surface and underlying subject independently, as in (50). In a causative serial verb construction the subject of the verb of causation is cross-referenced on both verbs.

(ii) The two components of a periphrastic causative may have an independent tense/aspect/aktionsart value, and get independent marking for these categories. Each component can be negated separately, as in (46). In (50), *-mha* 'non-visual present' goes on *-rena* 'feel', and *-yha* 'approximative' characterizes the verb of causation *-ni* 'do, make':

(50)   nu-na   ma:ʧi <u>nu-rena-ka-mha</u>   <u>i-ni-yha</u>
        1sg-OBJ bad   <u>1sg-feel-DEP-PRES.NON.VIS</u> <u>2pl-do-APPR</u>
        'You made me feel miserable a little bit', i.e. 'you did a little bit for me to feel miserable' (said the mother to the young man who had gone to live with snakes)

(iii) Periphrastic causatives do not have the intonational properties of a monoverbal clause; a pausal marker can be inserted after every verb.

(iv) Unlike serial causative constructions, periphrastic causatives with a dependency marker cannot be considered one predicate, because there is a subordinating marker on one of the components.[12]

4.4   *Causative mechanisms in Tariana: a comparison*

Tariana has four causativizing mechanisms: morphological causatives, serial causative constructions and two types of periphrastic causatives. They have different semantics and are in a partial complementary distribution as to the verb types. Figure 5.2 summarizes the distribution of causatives among classes of verbs, and their semantics.

Of all verb types, S_o and S_{io} verbs have the most restrictions on causativization.

• MORPHOLOGICAL CAUSATIVES are productively formed on intransitive active (S_a) and stative (S_o) verbs which refer to changeable qualities. There are just a few instances of morphological causatives on transitive verbs which describe traditional activities. Morphological causatives of stative verbs can change a verb from prefixless to prefixed, if the causer is acting intentionally. This semantic parameter is cross-linguistically well attested (see Dixon's typological survey in chapter 2).

All prefixed verbs can have double causative marking which implies complete involvement of O, and completeness of action.

• SERIAL CAUSATIVE CONSTRUCTIONS are used to form causatives of transitive and intransitive active verbs using a number of verbs of causation; they are also used to causativize S_{io} verbs. Only with intransitive active verbs do serial causative constructions imply indirect causation (in contrast to morphological and periphrastic causatives). Serial verb constructions are the only productive mechanism available for causativizing transitive verbs and the verbs of S_{io} type.

• PERIPHRASTIC CAUSATIVES formed with the verb of causation -*ni* 'do, make' WITH AN OPTIONAL DEPENDENCY MARKER on the causativized verb are used to causativize stative verbs which refer to unchangeable properties.

• PERIPHRASTIC CAUSATIVES WITH AN OBLIGATORY DEPENDENCY MARKER are used to form causatives of intransitive active verbs and stative verbs referring to changeable properties, and imply a forceful causer, unwillingness on the part of the causee, and direct causation (see chapter 2).

---

[12] Periphrastic causatives are found more frequently in texts and other data from younger speakers, so some sort of influence from Portuguese cannot be excluded.

Figure 5.2. Causativizing mechanisms, verb types and their semantics

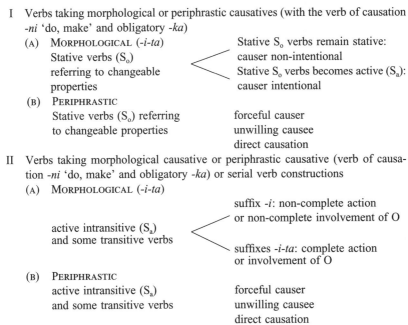

I Verbs taking morphological or periphrastic causatives (with the verb of causation -*ni* 'do, make' and obligatory -*ka*)

   (A) MORPHOLOGICAL (-*i-ta*)   Stative S_o verbs remain stative:
        Stative verbs (S_o)   causer non-intentional
        referring to changeable   Stative S_o verbs becomes active (S_a):
        properties   causer intentional

   (B) PERIPHRASTIC
        Stative verbs (S_o) referring   forceful causer
        to changeable properties   unwilling causee
                                           direct causation

II Verbs taking morphological causative or periphrastic causative (verb of causation -*ni* 'do, make' and obligatory -*ka*) or serial verb constructions

   (A) MORPHOLOGICAL (-*i-ta*)

                                         suffix -*i*: non-complete action
                                         or non-complete involvement of O
        active intransitive (S_a)
        and some transitive verbs
                                         suffixes -*i-ta*: complete action
                                         or involvement of O

   (B) PERIPHRASTIC
        active intransitive (S_a)   forceful causer
        and some transitive verbs   unwilling causee
                                          direct causation

   (C) CAUSATIVE SERIAL VERB CONSTRUCTIONS
        active intransitive (S_a)   indirect causation
        and some transitive verbs

III Verbs taking no morphological causative, only periphrastic causative (verb of causation -*ni* 'do, make' and optional -*ka*)

   (A) PERIPHRASTIC
        Stative verbs (S_o) referring to unchangeable properties

IV Verbs taking no morphological causative, only causative serial verb constructions

   (A) CAUSATIVE SERIAL VERB CONSTRUCTIONS
        Most transitive verbs

V Verbs taking no morphological causative, only serial verb constructions with -*eme-ta* 'put'

   (A) CAUSATIVE SERIAL VERB CONSTRUCTIONS
        Verbs of physical state (S_{io})

There is a cross-linguistic tendency among languages of the world for periphrastic causatives to express causation which involves a special effort on the part of a causer and, possibly, unwillingness on the part of the causee (see §5 of chapter 2 above; and also Haiman 1983). Morphological causatives tend to express direct causation. Tariana conforms to this tendency. In languages which distinguish morphological and periphrastic causatives, the latter also tend to express indirect causation (§5 in chapter 2). In the case when there are three causativizing mechanisms available – i.e., for S_a type and for some transitive verbs – Tariana uses serial verb constructions for this purpose.

4.5   *Argument-adding derivation*

When *-i-ta* is added to intransitive verbs and a limited number of transitive verbs, it has causativizing effect. When added to the majority of transitive verbs, it has two, quite different, effects.

4.5.1   Ambitransitive verbs become obligatory transitives when they receive the transitivizer *-i-ta*

It was mentioned in §2 that all transitive verbs in Tariana are $A = S$ ambitransitives. Strictly transitive verbs are the ones which contain the transitivizer *-i-ta*.

4.5.2   When *-i-ta* is added onto a transitive verb, it also indicates that a peripheral constituent has to be obligatorily stated in the clause

This constituent may be (a) addressee, (b) location, (c) purpose and/or instrument. Its choice depends on the semantics of a verb.

The following examples illustrate this.

(a) ADDRESSEE. The transitive verb *-hɲa* means 'point at' – see (51).

(51)   diha ɾapao-ne   di-hɲa   di-a-pidana
        he   harpoon-INS 3sgN.F-show 3sgN.F-go-REM.PAST.INFR
        He (the liar) pointed with his harpoon (at an otter which he wanted others to
        believe to be a fish)

Its counterpart with *-i-ta* means 'show something to somebody':

(52)   nuhua-de pi-na   nu-a   nu-hẽ-ta
        1sg-FUT 2sg-OBJ 1sg-go 1sg-show+CAUS1-CAUS2
        I will show you (the way out of the jungle)

(b) LOCATION. The transitive verb *-pala* means 'get, put' (53); when *-i-ta* is added, *-paleta* means 'put in a particular location', as in (54).

(53)   diwhida   na-pisa na-pala-pidana
        3sgN.F+head 3pl-cut 3pl-put-REM.PAST.INFR
        They cut his head and put (it) somewhere

(54)   ita-whya   hi-nuku   pi-pale-ta
        canoe-CL:CANOE DEM:ANIM-TOP.NON.A/S 2sg-put+CAUS1-CAUS2
        Put the canoe here

(c) PURPOSE AND/OR INSTRUMENT. The addition of *-i-ta* marks the obliga-
toriness of a purpose with other verbs. The transitive verb *-wana*, used without *-i-ta*, means 'call', 'emit sound', as in (55), or 'call (for no particular
purpose)', as in (56), or 'call a name', as in (57).

(55) di-wana   di-nu-pidana   iɨi! di-a-pidana
      3sgN.F-call 3sgN.F-come-REM.PAST.INFR iɨi! 3sgN.F-say-REM.PAST.INFR
      The spirit called as he came, 'iɨi', he said

(56) ne   di-sa-do-nuku   di-wana-tha-pidana   hãwa
      then 3sgN.F-spouse-F-TOP.NON.A/S 3sgN.F-call-FRUST-REM.PAST.INFR eagle
      Then the eagle called his wife('s name) (in vain)

(57) naha hĩ   wa-kesi-pe   taɾia   wa-na   ine-ne   na
      they DEM:ANIM 1pl-relative-pl Tariana 1pl-OBJ 'devil'-pl 3pl-say
      na-wana-naka
      3pl-call-PRES.VIS
      Our relatives, [also] Tariana, call us 'devils'

When *-wana* is used with *-i-ta*, giving *-wane(-ta)*, it means 'call for something', as shown in (58).

(58) na-wane-ta-pidana   diha yakale-peni   diha
      3pl-call+CAUS1-CAUS2-REM.PAST.INFR he   village-pl:ANIM he
      katu-nuku   na-hɲa-kasu
      piraiba.fish-TOP.NON.A/S 3pl-eat-INTENTIONAL
      The villagers called him to eat piraiba fish

Or it may mean 'call with the help of something'. Example (59) is a
description of evil habits of a feared tribe, Makiritare, who are reported to
excel in magical practice; they call rain this way.

(59) wheɾu neme   iya-nuku   na-wane
      snuff 3pl+sniff rain-TOP.NON.A/S 3pl-call+CAUS
      They sniff snuff, (this is how) they call rain

The verb *-wapa* means 'attend to, serve or wait', as in (60); *-wape(-ta)*
means 'wait with something, or for a particular purpose'. This is shown in
(61) and (62).

(60) wasã dapa wa-wapa di-a-pidana
      let's paca 1pl-wait 3sgN.F-say-REM.PAST.INFR
      Let's wait for a paca (a large rodent) (to come along)', he said

(61) i-na   pa-hɲa-nipe-ne-ka   nu-wape-ta   nuhua
      2pl-OBJ IMP-eat-NOMZR-INS-DECL 1sg-wait+CAUS1-CAUS2 I
      I am waiting for you with food

(62)   mawali-nuku   na:-ka   na-wape-ta
       snake-TOP.NON.A/S 3pl+go-DECL 3pl-wait+CAUS1-CAUS2
       na-walita-kaɾu-pena-nuku
       3pl-offer-RES-BEN-TOP.NON.A/S
       They were going to wait for another snake for a ritual offering

The meaning of -*i-ta* derivation may be rather idiosyncratic. With a number of verbs, it implies the presence of a speech complement; for instance, -*mayã* means 'act in a false, treacherous way', while *mayẽ(-ta)* means 'tell a lie'; -*ira* means 'order', and -*ireta* means 'order by saying something'.

Thus, the morpheme which marks the causative of intransitive and just a few transitive verbs is used to mark a kind of argument-adding derivation when used with transitive verbs.

In §4.1 we saw four transitive verbs which refer to traditional activities and form a morphological causative with -*i-ta*. In just one case, the argument-adding or causative reading of -*i-ta* derivation depends on which constituent is present in the surface structure.[13] The transitive verb -*ɲapa* 'bless', without -*i-ta*, is illustrated in (63). The O is omitted.

(63)   diha-kuma khema-kali   na-ɲapa-sina
       he-CL:RITE REL+hear-PAST.PART 3pl-bless-REM.PAST.NON.VIS
       Those who understand the ritual, used to bless (do the blessing)

If just an O constituent is present, the -*i-ta* derivation has a causative reading, as in (64).

(64)   waha haniɾi-nuku   Kose
       we   father-TOP.NON.A/S Concessão
       du-ɲape-ta-sina   duri-nuku
       3sgF-bless+CAUS1-CAUS2-REM.PAST.NON.VIS 3sgF+son-TOP.NON.A/S
       Concessão made our father bless her son (to cure him)

It has an argument-adding reading if there is an overt instrumental constituent (65).

(65)   maini-ne na-ɲape-ta
       tar-INS 3pl-bless+CAUS1-CAUS2
       They blessed (the game) with tar

---

[13] Different readings are impossible for -*sita/-siteta*, -*eme/emeta*, and -*peru/-perita* because these verbs are restricted to traditional stories.

The choice between argument-adding and causative reading is often achieved by context. In (66), the *-i-ta* derivation has a causative reading, because it is 'common knowledge' that Yunuli is a shaman. In contrast, (67) has an argument-adding reading, because this is what the Moon is supposed to do.

(66) nu-whida kai-kayami   yunuli-nuku   nu-ɲape-ta
      1sg-head ache-AFTER:DS Yunuli-TOP.NON.A/S 1sg-bless+CAUS1-CAUS2
      Because my head ached, I made Yunuli bless [me]

(67) keːɾi di-ɲape-ta-ka   wa-na
      moon 3sgN.F-bless+CAUS1-CAUS2-REC.PAST.VIS 1pl-OBJ
      Moon has blessed us [with its power, for a trip] (said before people go on a trip, to make sure it is safe)

There are cases in which, if the context is unknown, both readings are possible. For instance, *di-ɲapeta* could be understood both as 'he made someone bless someone else', or 'he blessed someone with the help of something, or for some purpose'; note that this homonymy can be solved in a number of ways. (68) can only be understood as 'he$_i$ got someone else to bless him$_i$ but he$_i$ died anyway' because the subordinating enclitic *-nikhe* can only be used if both clauses have the same subject.

(68) di-ɲape-ta-nikhe   di-ɲami   di-a
      3sgN.F-bless+CAUS1-CAUS2-IN SPITE:SS 3sgN.F-die 3sgN.F-go
      Though he$_i$ had made (someone) bless him$_i$, he$_i$ died

Argument-adding *-i-ta* cannot appear on verbs from a number of semantic groups (e.g. 'want, look for', 'eat', 'dig'). With verbs of perception *-i-ta* derivation yields unpredictable semantics: *-ka* 'see' vs *-keta* 'meet, encounter'; *-hima* 'hear' vs *-himeta* 'think, feel'.

5   Transitivity and grammatical relations in Tariana

Tariana has two valency-reducing derivations, passive and reciprocal. A typologically unusual property of Tariana is that there are four mechanisms for marking causatives: one morphological, two periphrastic and a causative serial verb construction. It is not unusual for a language to have more than one mechanism for forming causatives, or to use different techniques of causative marking techniques depending on the transitivity value of a verb (see chapter 2 above).

A very unusual property of Tariana is that the same morpheme (*-i-ta*) is used to mark causatives with intransitive and a few transitive verbs, and also to specify that an ambitransitive verb is obligatorily transitive and that a peripheral constituent must be stated. This argument-adding derivation is extremely rare cross-linguistically. It is a special subtype of valency-increasing mechanisms distinct from both causatives and applicatives.[14]

The problem with the status of this derivation in Tariana involves distinguishing core and oblique constituents. The most easily distinguishable core constituent is A/S_a which is obligatorily cross-referenced on prefixed verbs; since there is one marker used with all types of $A/S_a/S_o$ (agentive *-ne*) one can say that they are morphologically one class. This may account for the fact that all underived transitive verbs are ambitransitive. In contrast, all topical non-$A/S_a/S_o$ are marked in the same way (there is optional locative and instrumental–comitative marking).

There are a number of techniques Tariana uses to distinguish core from oblique. One is valency-decreasing derivations – passive and, to a certain extent, reciprocal affect only core arguments: A/S_a and O. The only arguments of stative verbs (S_o) and verbs of states (S_{io}) behave differently; they are obligatory and thus belong to the core.

The argument-adding derivation also helps to distinguish between core and non-core arguments – when it is applied to transitive verbs, they become obligatorily transitive. It also signals that one more oblique constituent has to be present in the surface structure. In a way, transitive verbs become extended transitive (Dixon 1994: 123). Note that one cannot say that this oblique constituent is 'promoted' into the core – it cannot be passivized.

Transitivity-changing mechanisms in Tariana provide evidence in favour of the grammatical relations: A, S_a, O, S_o, S_{io} which behave in different ways, and obliques which can become obligatory by means of the argument-adding derivation.

---

[14] There is one typological analogy to it. A few Campa languages, from the South-Arawak subgroup, have a number of applicative derivations (see Dixon and Aikhenvald 1997) which affect the argument structure of the predicate by putting a benefactive, or an instrumental, or a 'presential' (meaning 'in the presence of') constituent into the O slot. One verb can have more than one derivational suffix of this sort. In this case one of the derivational suffixes just shows that a peripheral constituent is obligatory. The Pajonal Campa sentence *no-p-ako-ts-imo-tsi-ro-ri Irena Irocarto paŋo* '1sg-give-REFERENCE.TO-EPENTHETIC-IN.PRESENCE.OF-ASPECT-3sgF-3sgM Irene Richard scarf' ('I gave Richard the head scarf in Irene's presence'; Shaler 1971: 45) contains an applicative derivation, *-ako* 'benefactive; with reference to'; there is another suffix *-imo* 'in the presence of' which just indicates that a peripheral constituent (in this case, Irene) has to be overtly expressed.

Appendix 5.1: word classes and functional slots in Tariana

	verb	adjective	noun
head of intransitive predicate	yes	yes	yes
head of transitive predicate	yes	no*	no*
head of NP	no*	yes	yes
modifier in NP	no*	yes	no*

* means that certain morphological processes have to be applied for a member of a given word class to appear in this function.

Appendix 5.2: Tariana verbal categories

Table 5.2. Evidentials and tense in affirmative clauses in Tariana

	present	recent past	remote past
Visual	*-naka*	*-ka*	*-na*
Nonvisual	*-mha*	*-mahka*	*-sina*
Inferred	*-sika*	*-nihka*	*-pidana*
Secondhand	–	*-pidaka*	*-nhina*

Table 5.3. Evidentials and tense in interrogative clauses in Tariana

	present	past
Visual	*-tha*	*-nihka*
Nonvisual	–	*-hna*
Inferred	–	*-sõ*

Table 5.4. Aspect enclitics in Tariana

	semantics	form	gloss
completion	non-completed, on-going	*-daka*	'still, yet'
	completed, complete involvement of S/O	*-niki*	'completive'
	completed, finished (perfective-like)	*-sita*	'perfective'
	not quite completed	*-maɲa*	'almost'
duration	durative, prolonged	*-nhi*	'prolonged'
	repetitive	*-pita, -ta*	'repeated'
	short duration, little by little	*-ina*	'little by little'
	habitual	*-hyuna*	'habitual'

Table 5.5. Switch-reference-sensitive enclitics in Tariana

SS	DS
-hyume/-yuhme 'after, because' *-nikhe* 'during, in spite of'	*-kayami* 'after' *-nisawa, -kanada* 'during'

References

Aikhenvald, A.Y. 1994a. 'Classifiers in Tariana', *Anthropological Linguistics* 36.405–65.
  1994b. 'Grammatical relations in Tariana', *Nordic Journal of Linguistics* 17.201–18.
  1995 'Person-marking and discourse in North-Arawak languages', *Studia Linguistica* 49.152–95.
  1996. 'Areal diffusion in North-West Amazonia: the case of Tariana', *Anthropological Linguistics* 38.73–116.
  forthcoming-a. 'Reciprocals and reflexives in North Arawak languages of the Upper Rio Negro (Warekena, Bare, Baniwa of Içana)', in *Typology of reciprocals*, ed. V.P. Nedialkov. Munich: Lincom Europa.
  forthcoming-b. 'Reciprocals and sociative in Tariana: their genetic and areal properties', in *Typology of reciprocals*, ed. V.P. Nedialkov. Munich: Lincom Europa.
  forthcoming-c. 'Serial constructions and verb compounding: evidence from Tariana (North Arawak)', *Studies in Language*.
Crowley, T.M. 1987. 'Serial verbs in Paamese', *Studies in Language* 11.35–84.
Dixon, R.M.W. 1994. *Ergativity*. Cambridge: Cambridge University Press.
Dixon, R.M.W. and Aikhenvald, A.Y. 1997. 'A typology of argument-determined constructions', pp. 71–113 of *Essays on language function and language type*, ed. J. Bybee, J. Haiman and S.A. Thompson. Amsterdam, Philadelphia: John Benjamins.
Durie, M. 1997. 'Grammatical structures in verb serialization', pp. 289–354 of *Complex predicates*, ed. A. Alsina, J. Bresnan and P. Sells. Stanford: CSLI Press.
Foley, W. and Olson, M. 1985. 'Clausehood and verb serialization', pp. 17–60 of *Grammar inside and outside the clause*, ed. J. Nichols and A.C. Woodbury. Cambridge: Cambridge University Press.
Haiman, J. 1983. 'Iconic and economic motivation', *Language* 59.781–819.
Schachter, P. 1974. 'A non-transformational account of serial verbs', *Studies in African Linguistics*, Supplement, 5.153–271.
Shaler, D. 1971. *Identification of clause types and participant roles in Pajonal Campa*. Peru: Summer Institute of Linguistics.

6 Voice and valency in the Athapaskan family

KEREN RICE

Every language or language family has its sets of problems that anyone working on that language/family must have their say about. One of these problems for the Athapaskan family involves the so-called classifier system, a poorly named system of the first type of voice/valency-affecting derivation outlined in Dixon and Aikenvald (1997) – there is overt marking of suppression and addition of arguments. In this chapter, I focus on the commonalities and differences in use of this system across the Athapaskan family.

1   Background

I begin with some background on the languages and language family. Athapaskan languages are geographically widespread in western North America, falling into three major discontinuous geographic regions. The northern group is spoken in parts of Alaska and in the Canadian provinces and territories of Manitoba, Saskatchewan, Alberta, British Columbia, the Yukon and the Northwest Territories. Three of the languages that I examine here come from the northern group: Ahtna and Koyukon, which are spoken in Alaska, and Slave [slevi], which is spoken in the Northwest Territories, one community in the Yukon, a small area of northern British Columbia, and northern Alberta. The Pacific Coast languages are/were spoken in northern California and Oregon. I draw data from Hupa here. Hupa is the most divergent of the Athapaskan languages covered in this survey. Finally, the Apachean

Thank you to Leslie Saxon, Chad Thompson and the participants in the International Workshop on Valency-changing Derivations, Canberra, 1997, especially Sasha Aikhenvald, Bob Dixon, Marianne Mithun and Matt Shibatani. This work was partially funded by a Killam Fellowship.

group is found in New Mexico, Arizona, Utah and Colorado in the south-western United States. I use Navajo as an exemplar of this group. I occasionally bring in other languages as well to illustrate particular points.

Why focus on a family, rather than on a particular language, as other people have done in their chapters? First, there is a tradition of comparative typological work in Athapaskan linguistics. Moreover, the languages of the family differ in interesting ways. With respect to voice and valency, a range of different characteristics exists across the family.

2   Background on the argument system

2.1   *Grammatical roles*

The verb in Athapaskan languages has a complex structure, and allows within it for the marking of three basic grammatical roles. An overall, and over-simplified, schema of the verb is shown in (1). This outline is basically applicable to the family as a whole; see Rice forthcoming-b for comparative discussion of morpheme order.

(1)   Athapaskan verb structure (simplified)
       Preverb – Quantifiers – (Argument Incorporates) – Direct Object – 3 Subject
       – Qualifier – Aspect – 1/2 Subject – Voice/Valency – Verb Stem

First consider subjects. As can be seen in (1) 'subject' is not a unitary category as far as position is concerned. 1st and 2nd person discourse-participant subjects and 3rd person subjects are in different locations within the verb. The terms '1st person' and '3rd person' must be approached with care. 1st/2nd person subjects include, in all languages, 1st person singular, 2nd person singular and 2nd person plural. 3rd person subjects include a human subject, often called unspecified, indefinite, or 4th person, and a plural human subject. The human subject, often compared with the French pronoun *on*, is used to indicate a 1st person plural subject as well; in some languages (e.g. Ahtna, Koyukon) this is the only way of marking 1st person nonsingulars; in others this is used for 1st person plurals and a prefix in the 1/2 subject position for 1st person duals (e.g. Dogrib, Sekani).[1] See Story (1989) for discussion.

All subjects, be they subjects of transitive or intransitive verbs, have the same morphological form and appear in the positions in (1). Some typical paradigms are given in (2); the verb is transitive, but intransitives pattern identically. Stems are separated by hyphens from the remainder of the verb

---

[1] Hupa differs in many ways that are not relevant here. For instance, the general human subject developed into a 3rd person topical human subject in Hupa. For discussion, see Golla 1970, 1997; Rice forthcoming-b; and Thompson 1989a.

and the subject markers are bolded. The abbreviation 'YM' stands for the Navajo reference dictionary by Young and Morgan (1987).

(2)   subject marking

	Ahtna	Slave	Navajo	Hupa
1sg	*'es-yaan*	*heh-'á*	*yish-dlá̧*	*'iwh-tsit*
2sg	*'i-yaan*	*ne-'á*	*ni-dlá̧*	*'in-tsit*
3	*yaan*	*he-'á*	*yi-dlá̧*	*ch'i-tsit*
1pl	*ts'e-yaan*	*hít-'á*	*yii-dlá̧*	*'i di-tsit*
human	*ts'e-yaan*	*ts'e-'á*	*ji-dlá̧*	
2pl	*'oh-yaan*	*hah-'á*	*woh-dlá̧*	*'oh-tsit*
3pl	*ke-yaan*	*ke-'á*		
	'eat'	'eat'	'drink'	'pound'
	imperfective	imperfective	imperfective	imperfective
	(Kari 1990: 680)	(Rice 1989)	(YM 145)	(Golla 1985: 89)

There is a caveat to the claim about marking of subjects – subjects of low topicality (see, e.g., Rice forthcoming-b; Saxon and Rice 1993; Thompson 1989a, 1996b; Willie and Jelinek 1996) may show object rather than subject morphology, as evidenced by the position and form of the pronominal.

Direct and oblique objects have the same form, although the 3rd persons differ somewhat in distribution. These forms for the different languages are shown in (3).

(3)   direct and oblique object marking

	Ahtna	Slave	Navajo	Hupa
1sg	*s*	*se*	*shi*	*whi*
2sg	*ne*	*ne*	*ni*	*ni*
3 (1/2 S)	*Ø, b*	*Ø, be*	*Ø, bi*	*Ø, xwi* (human)
3 (3 S)	*y*	*ye*	*yi*	*Ø, xwi* (human)
AREAL	*ko*	*go*	*hwi*	*xwi* (rare)
INDEF	*c'*	*'e*	*'i*	*ky'i*
1pl	*ne*	*naxe*	*nihi*	*noh*
2pl	*nhw*	*naxe*	*nihi*	*noh*
3pl (1/2 S)	*ku*	*ku*		
3pl (3 S)	*hw*	*go*		
RECIP	*nił*	*'ełe*	*'ahi*	*n-łi*
REFL	*d*	*'ede*	*di*	*di*

In terms of the grammatical relations of S, A and O, then, two of these are distinguished morphologically in the Athapaskan family – subjects of transitives and intransitives are identical in form and position (S = A) and objects of transitives (O) differ in position and sometimes in form.[2]

---

[2] The so-called classificatory verbs (intransitive – verbs of location; transitive – verbs of hand-ling) are determined by the subject in intransitives and the object in transitives, yielding S = 0. I do not deal with this problem.

2.2   *Lexical verb classes*

Verbs divide into three major lexical classes in terms of argument structure.
First are lexical intransitives. Such verbs either have an actor or an undergoer
subject. All examples are from Ahtna (Kari 1990). The lexical entries should
be interpreted as follows. 'G' abbreviates gender; these elements are actually
more like classifiers (Aikhenvald forthcoming, Corbett 1991), and verbs with
G in their lexical entry enter into the classifier system. The stem is the final
element of the verb. The symbols #, +, – are phonological boundary types;
these are not important to this chapter. Directly preceding the stem is a
marking for lexically specified voice/valency; see §8.

(4)   lexically intransitive verbs (Ahtna)
(a)   G +l   -t'uuts
      CL+VOICE/VALENCY-STEM
      be black, dark in colour (352)

(b)   G +d   -ghotl'
      CL+VOICE-STEM
      break, become broken, shatter (222)

      s-ghu'   s-d   -ghoł
      1sg-tooth ASP-VOICE -break
      My tooth broke

(c)   l   -let
      VOICE/VALENCY-STEM
      sg person, animal moves quickly, walks quickly, runs, leaps, jumps (355)

      t-i-l   -tlaat
      INCEPTIVE-2sgS-VOICE-move quickly.IMPERF
      run, move quickly!

(d)   ta # d + ł -t'en
      swim (348)

      men yii ta-s-de-ł-t'en
      lake in water-1plS-water-VALENCY -swim.PERF
      We swam in the lake

Verbs can be lexically transitive, with a subject and direct object (or actor
and undergoer). In these examples, the symbol 'O' indicates the transitivity
of the verb.

(5)   lexically transitive verbs (Ahtna)
(a)   O Ø -t'ogh
      paddle, row O (349)

      c'e-t'ogh
      UNSPECIFIED paddle
      He is paddling (unspecified object)

(b)   O ł -dzak'
       divine, foretell, prophesy O (168)

       ye-ł-dzak
       DISJOINT.ANAPHOR-VALENCY-divine.customary form
       He divines it (customarily)

Third, there are verbs that require two arguments, an actor and undergoer, where the undergoer has oblique rather than direct status.

(6)   lexically intransitive verbs with oblique object (Ahtna)
       P-e # da # d + Ø-niic
       hear (309)

       k-e-da-'s-de-nes
       AREAL.O-postposition-mouth-1plS-CL-STEM.repetitive form
       We hear a noise
       (da#d – verbally, oral noise, speech (131))

With this basic survey of the marking of grammatical roles and of verb types, I turn to the main topic, namely the marking of voice/valency.

3   On argument-transferring constructions in Athapaskan languages: background

Two basic argument-transferring morphemes are found across the family. These are traditionally known as classifiers (Goddard 1905) although it has long been recognized that this term is a misnomer (see Krauss 1969: 81, and many others). Nevertheless, Athapaskanists have not been able to agree on other terminology. I discuss below why this is the case; I use the terms voice and valency for these elements. After a brief introduction, I examine the morphological, syntactic and semantic characteristics of each of these elements in their productive uses and then look at how they combine. Finally, as has long been recognized, these elements are often lexically frozen with a particular verb stem, and I shall discuss this.

The Athapaskan voice/valency elements are well studied. Any description of an Athapaskan language includes a summary of their form and function. Both are necessary – they are often obscure in form (I do not discuss this; see a grammar of any Athapaskan language and the examples in this chapter) and long lists of functions are generally enumerated. In recent years, work has been done to try to unify the productive functions of the voice/valency elements. See Thompson (1989a, 1996a) and Kibrik (1993, 1996) in particular for detailed discussion.

The voice/valency elements have long been recognized to play two roles. First, every lexical entry of a verb has associated with it a voice/valency marker (it can be unmarked for one), as can be seen in the examples above. These are lexicalized with the verb stem, and are listed as part of the basic lexical entry. I return to discussion of lexicalization of voice/valency markers following discussion of productive uses, in §8. The second role that voice/valency markers play is a truly functional one. The valency marker *ł* basically creates causatives; the voice marker *d* basically creates middles, and the marker *l* is complex in nature, marking a middle built on a causative.

There is disagreement in the Athapaskan literature about how to characterize the roles of the voice/valency markers, and this is the reason, I believe, that the term 'classifier', although recognized by all as a misnomer, persists. Some linguists argue that voice/valency markers directly affect the argument system: they are argument-increasing (*ł*) – adding an argument – or argument-decreasing (*d*) – eliminating an argument. See, for instance, McDonough (1989) for this position. A second stance is that the classifiers are transitivity indicators. They can be transitivity-increasing (*ł*) or transitivity-decreasing (*d*), or combine these two functions (*l*); see Kibrik (1993, 1996) for this position. Kibrik argues that the transitivity indicators 'do not designate high or low transitivity by themselves. They cannot be ascribed any invariant and definite **meaning**. They are precisely **indicators** signalling **shifts** in transitivity – either increase or decrease' (1993: 50, highlighting from Kibrik).

The position that I take in this chapter combines features of the other approaches. I argue, after Thompson (1996a), that *d* is a marker of middle voice, to be defined below. It has no effect on argument structure but reduces transitivity, as Kibrik (1996) argues. On the other hand, *ł*, which I call a causativizer, in its most productive cross-family roles is argument-increasing. However, as Kibrik (1993) argues, it is sometimes transitivity-increasing without being argument-increasing. Finally, *l* combines voice and valency functions, marking a middle formed on a causative.

4   On marking middle voice: *d*

I begin with discussion of the voice element *d*. This marker is much discussed in the Athapaskan literature; see Arce-Aranales, Axelrod and Fox (1994), Kibrik (1996) and Thompson (1996a) for recent discussion.

Before turning to exemplification and analysis of middle voice, two warnings are in order. First, it is often difficult to identify this element (or other voice/valency elements) from the phonetics of the verb, but there is consider-able evidence for its presence in all languages from morphosyntactic patterning. Second, when *d* combines with *ł*, a portmanteau of the form *l* results, as has long been recognized by Athapaskan linguists (e.g. Hargus 1988, Kari 1990, Rice 1989, Stanley 1969).

Let me begin with a definition of middle voice. Middle voice includes a range of constructions – reflexives, reciprocals, passives, etc. Kemmer (1993), whose definition I follow, argues that middle voice has to do with the relative elaboration of events (including states). She defines the property of relative elaboration of events as 'the degree to which the facets in a particular situ-ation, i.e. participants and conceivable component subevents in the situation, are distinguished' (1993: 208). Kemmer further notes that the 'speaker has a choice of either marking reference to events as undifferentiated wholes, or making reference to their substructure or component parts' (208). Middles fall somewhere between prototypical two-participant events, or events in which 'a human entity (an Agent) acts volitionally, exerting physical force on an inanimate definite entity (a Patient) which is directly and completely affected by that event' (50) and prototypical one-participant events where 'the conceptual differentiation of Initiating and Endpoint facets is utterly non-existent: there is no Endpoint, but simply one participant of which a state or action is predicated' (73). Thus active two-participant events include an initiator and an endpoint which are distinct from one another while single-participant events involve one participant. Middles typically involve two participants which are not differentiated. While Kemmer concentrates on their aspectual func-tion, middles also interact in the argument system (Thompson 1996a) – in the middle voice, one finds both suppression of differentiation of arguments and suppression of differentiated events.

Kemmer identifies a large number of domains as potential middles. These include, amongst others, reflexives, reciprocals, middle passives, nontransitional motion, change in body posture, facilitative structures, grooming, other body actions, translational motion, positionals, cognition middle, perception middle and spontaneous events. Athapaskan languages mark some of these as middles, through the use of *d*, and, as Thompson (1996a) discusses, also mark certain other events with low elaboration.

I now survey the range of constructions in which *d* middle voice is used productively. See Thompson (1996a) for a cross-family survey of the func-tions of middle-voice marking in both the Athapaskan language family and the larger Na-Dene, a grouping which includes not only the Athapaskan languages, but also Eyak and Tlingit.

4.1   *Middle construction types*

4.1.1   Reflexive: initiator and endpoint not differentiated

A reflexive shares with a prototypical two-participant event that one entity affects or acts on another; it is distinguished from the prototypical two-participant event in that the two entities are referentially identical, yielding an instance of low elaboration because the participants are not differentiated. Examples are given in (7–12). In the left-hand column, the structure in question and the lexical voice/valency marker are shown. Forms for comparison are given on the right, with glosses below. The voice marker is highlighted when the phonology allows for its appearance, as are any other elements in the verb that enter into the voice system.

(7)   Ahtna (Kari 1990)
      transitive Ø   tl'ogh t'aas
                     grass cut.IMPFV
                     He is cutting grass
      reflexive d   **de** -s -t -'as
                     REFL-ASP-MID-cut.PERF
                     He cut himself (reflexive)

(8)   Koyukon (Jones and Jetté forthcoming)
      transitive Ø   yeghee-ghonh
                     DISJOINT.ANAPHOR+ASP-make/kill.pl.O
                     He made them, killed them, beat them up
      reflexive d   **ho**he**do-de**-ghonh
                     REFL+3plS+REFL+ASP-MID-make/kill.pl.O
                     They killed, overexerted themselves

(9)   Slave (Rice 1989)
      transitive Ø   dahyedį-lu
                     up+DISJOINT.ANAPHOR+CL+ASP-handle.rope
                     S/he hung it
      reflexive d   dah'**ede**dí-**d**lu
                     up+REFL+CL+ASP-MID+handle.rope
                     S/he hung him/herself

(10) Navajo (Young and Morgan 1987: 69)
      transitive Ø   yi-ch'id
                     He's scratching it
      reflexive d   '**ádí**-ch'id
                     He's scratching himself

(11) Hupa: no change to d (Golla 1970: 108)

(12)   Carrier (Morice 1932: 353)
        transitive Ø   ûs-t'ah
                       I beat it (with stick, rod, etc.)
        reflexive d   udedez-t'ah
                       I beat myself

4.1.2   Reciprocal: initiator and endpoint not differentiated

Reciprocals too occur with the middle-voice marker. Reciprocals involve low elaboration in that the subject is both the origin and target of the action.

(13)   Ahtna (Kari 1990: 204)
        transitive Ø   ggax kubii-ghaan
                       Rabbits are killing them
        reciprocal d   dzuuggi na-**niɬ**-gha-**d**-ghaan
                       The princesses killed each other

(14)   Koyukon (Thompson 1996a: 355)
        transitive Ø   yeto-ts'eyh
                       S/he will pinch him/her once
        reciprocal d   **neeɬ**-heeto-**de**-ts'eyh
                       They will pinch each other once

(15)   Hupa (Golla 1970: 81)
        transitive Ø   O ni-Ø-yod
                       chase O
        reciprocal d   ya-**n**-ɬi-ni-**di**-yod-i
                       chase one another

(16)   Navajo (Young and Morgan 1987: 69)
        transitive Ø   yi-ghá̧
                       He's killing them
        reciprocal d   **'ah**i-gá̧
                       They're killing each other

(17)   Slave (Rice 1989: 634)
        transitive Ø   náyenii̧-ta
                       S/he kicked him/her
        reciprocal d   ná'eɬena-ta
                       They kicked each other

4.1.3   Indirect reflexive: initiator and location not differentiated

Indirect reflexives are related to two or three participant events; they differ from direct reflexives in that the actor and an oblique argument are identical, thus lowering the elaboration of the event.

(18)   Koyukon (Jones and Jetté forthcoming)
         indirect reflexive d   **ed**e-nodo-**de**-tson'
                                 REFL-splash.on+lexicalized-MID-defecate
                                 He defecated on himself

(19)   Navajo (Young and Morgan 1987: 69)
         transitive Ø   béé-ghaz
                                 I scraped it off it
         indirect reflexive d   **'ád**-éés-gaz
                                 I scraped it off myself

(20)   Slave (Rice 1989)
         transitive ł   yek'ená'eneyi̧-h-tse
                                 S/he washed it (handled unspecified object (water)
                                 on it)
         indirect reflexive l   **'ede**-k'ená'ena-tse
                                 S/he bathed him/herself (handled unspecified O
                                 (water) on self)

In Slave, indirect reflexives (and indirect reciprocals) are found with only a
limited number of postpositions; indirect reflexives and indirect reciprocals
(§4.1.4) do not occur in the middle voice in some languages.

4.1.4   Indirect reciprocal: initiator and location not differentiated
Indirect reciprocals, like indirect reflexives, indicate that the origin of the
event and an oblique target are identical to each other.

(21)   Slave (Rice 1989)
         transitive ł   bek'ená'enii-h-tse
                                 I washed him/her
         indirect reciprocal l **'ełe**-k'ená'ekena-tse
                                 They washed each other

Indirect reciprocals, like indirect reflexives, are less likely to require middle
voice.

4.1.5   Self-benefactive: initiator and recipient not differentiated
Self-benefactives are a type of indirect reflexive in which the agent performs
an action for his or her own benefit (Thompson 1996a: 356).

(22)   Ahtna (Kari 1990)
         transitive ł   ize-ł-ghaen
                                 He killed it (213)
         self-benefactive l   i-**d**-ze-**l**-ghaen
                                 He killed it for his own benefit (131)

(23)   Koyukon (Thompson 1996a: 356)
         transitive ł   le-tl-baats
                               I boiled it
         self-benefactive d   d-aalge-baats
                               I boiled it for myself

(24)   Slave (Rice 1989)
         transitive Ø   nį-lu
                              You (sg) sew
         self-benefactive d   **d**e-nį-**d**-lu
                              You (sg) sew for yourself

(25)   Carrier (Morice's 'appropriative'; Morice 1932: 334)
         transitive Ø   tenes-'aih
                              I take something out of the house
         self-benefactive d   te-**d**-is-**t**-'aih
                              I take something out of the house for myself
         transitive Ø   nenes-kaih
                              I put the contents in an open pan
         self-benefactive Ø   ne-**d**-is-kaih
                              I put the contents in an open pan for myself, for my
                              own use

4.1.6   Incorporated body parts: endpoint part of initiator

Many northern Athapaskan languages allow incorporation of body parts into
the verb. Middle voice accompanies bodypart incorporation when, as Axelrod
(1990) argues, the verb marks the movement of the body part in a typical
manner. This, as Thompson (1996a: 357) points out, is not surprising since
something that affects one part of the body affects the entire self.

(26)   Ahtna (Kari 1990: 74)
         other incorporate Ø   c'edzigha-'ał
                                    It (*c'edzi* – four legged animal) is running along
         bodypart incorporate d   its'e **laa-t**-'aas
                                    He's waving his hand (*laa* – hand) at him

(27)   Koyukon (Thompson 1996a)
         non-incorporate Ø   de-lo' neenee-'onh
                                    REFL.hand
                                    S/he put her/his own hand (*de-lo'*) there
         bodypart incorporate d   nee-**lo'**-ee-**t**-'onh
                                    S/he put her/his own hand (*-lo'*) there, at rest

(28)   Tsuut'ina (Cook 1984: 136)
       no incorporate Ø   sítsì dìnìsís-'ó
                              I turned my head (*tsì*)
       bodypart incorporate d   dígá **tsì**-dìnìsí-**t**-'ó
                              I turned my head (*tsì*)

4.1.7   Mediopassive: initiator and endpoint not differentiated

The term 'mediopassive' is used in two senses in the Athapaskan literature. First, Young and Morgan (1987) use it to refer to situations where the object is part of the subject. These verbs include classifiers – *d* with sticklike objects (arms and legs) or *n* with small round objects (head). The noun class markers are highlighted here as well.

(29)   Ahtna (Kari 1990)
       transitive Ø   nayghi-'aan
                          He brought it down (71)
       mediopassive d   na-**n**-da-**t**-'aan
                          He put it (his hat) on himself (72)

(30)   Navajo (Young and Morgan 1987: 122)
       transitive Ø   yiih yiyíí-'ą́
                          He put a 3-dimensional object into it
       mediopassive d   yiih **n**-oo-**t**-'ą́
                          He put his head into it

(31)   Slave (Rice 1989)
       transitive Ø   O tenį-'ǫ
                          S/he put 3-dimensional O in water
       mediopassive d   te-**d**-ę́-se
                          S/he$_i$ put her/his$_i$ hand in water

The term 'mediopassive' is also used to refer to cases where a reflexive is understood, but not overt. The following examples show verbs of grooming.

(32)   Koyukon (Jones and Jetté forthcoming)
       transitive Ø   noyele-tl'oonh
                          S/he dressed him/her (e.g. a child)
       mediopassive d   nolse-tl'oonh
                          I dressed

(33)   Ahtna (Kari 1990: 365)
       transitive Ø   nayiz-tl'uun
                          He gave him clothes
       mediopassive d   nas-tl'uun
                          He got dressed

(34)   Slave (Rice 1989)
         transitive Ø   ráyereh-tl'ǫ
                          S/he dresses him/her
         mediopassive d   ráre-tl'ǫ
                          S/he dresses her/himself

4.1.8   Spontaneous middle (anticausative): initiator suppressed

Thompson (1996a) shows that many verbs in Athapaskan languages can have
either a passive or a spontaneous middle translation; spontaneous middles
have inanimate patients and no implied agent; passives, on the other hand,
have implied agents. Thompson (1996a: 359) speculates that the Athapaskan
passives (§4.1.9) developed out of spontaneous middles.

(35)   Koyukon (Thompson 1996a: 359)
         transitive Ø   dekenh denaal-yes
                        stick
                        S/he broke the stick
         middle l   dekenh denaałe-yes
                        The stick broke / The stick was broken

4.1.9   Passive: initiator suppressed but implied

Athapaskan languages form agentless passives through middle-voice marking
and, generally, suppression of the agent. It is often pointed out (e.g. Kibrik 1996,
Thompson 1996a) that passives have an implied agent. See also §4.3.

(36)   Ahtna (Kari 1990)
         transitive Ø   ighi-ghaan
                        He made them (130)
         passive d   a-**d**-ghaan
                        They were made
         transitive Ø   ighi-yaan'
                        He ate it (429)
         passive d   **d**-aan
                        It is being eaten (130)

(37)   Hupa (Golla 1970)
         transitive Ø   O adverb-Ø-liW/la
                        move O (several, rope) somewhere (79)
         passive d   adverb-wi-**di**-la
                        several, rope have been moved somewhere
         transitive Ø   O adv-Ø-mił/metł'
                        throw O (several in bunch) (79)
         passive d   adverb-**di**-mił
                        (several in bunch) move precipitously, fly, throw themselves

(38)   Navajo (Young and Morgan 1987)
        transitive Ø   yiz-taɫ
                       He gave him a kick (121)
        passive d   yis-taɫ
                       He was given a kick
        transitive Ø   yizh-t'éézh
                       He blackened it/him (121)
        passive d   yish-t'éézh
                       It was blackened

(39)   Koyukon (Thompson 1996a: 360)
        transitive ɫ   neeto-ɫ-dzes
                       S/he will hit you once
        passive l   eeteghee-l-dzes
                       You will be hit once

(40)   Slave (Rice 1989)
        transitive Ø   yú k'e'edé-'o̧
                       S/he ironed the clothes (lit. handled unspecified object on the clothes)
        passive d   yú k'e'edéh-t-'o̧
                       The clothes are ironed (unspecified O was handled on the clothes)
        transitive Ø   léyi-ghe
                       I cut it
        passive d   léye-ge
                       It was cut

(41)   Carrier (Morice 1932)
        transitive ɫ   es-'a
                       I hire O (283)
        passive d   ez-'a
                       I am hired
        transitive ɫ   des-ghel
                       I plane it (286)
        passive d   de-gel
                       It is planed / It can be planed
        transitive Ø   nes-'a
                       I deceive O (286)
        passive d   nes-t-'ah
                       I get deceived

4.1.10   1st person plural subject: low elaboration of subject

Some Athapaskan languages have a morpheme that marks a 1st person dual or duo-plural subject (depending on the language). This element occurs with *d* middle voice marker, and is lexically listed as such.

(42)   Navajo (Young and Morgan 1987)
        3rd plural subject Ø   t'óó 'aha-yói
                                 They are many (114)
        1st person plural d (') t'óó 'ahonii-'-yói
                                 We are many
        1st person singular Ø   yah 'íí-'ą́
                                 I carried it inside (114)
        1st person plural d   yah '**ii-t**-'ą́
                                 We carried it inside

(43)   Slave (Rice 1989)
        1st person singular Ø   heh-'á
                                 I eat
        1st person plural d   hí-**t**-'á
                                 We eat
        1st person singular Ø   leh-xe
                                 I cut it
        1st person plural d   lehí-ge
                                 We cut it

(44)   Hupa (Golla 1970)
        3rd person Ø   ch'e'i-ya'n
                                 He eats it (303)
        1st person plural   k'i-**di**-yan
                                 We eat (71)

In Galice (Hoijer 1966), both the 1st and 2nd person plural forms require middle voice when the verb has a lexical ɬ.

(45)   Galice (Hoijer 1966: 325)
        1st person singular ɬ   dash-**ɬ**-bad
                                 I boil it
        2nd person singular ɬ   nį-**ɬ**-bad
                                 You sg boil it
        1st person plural l   di-**l**-bad
                                 We boil it
        2nd person plural l   do'o-**l**-bad
                                 You pl boil it

4.1.11   Extension of argument

In some languages, middle voice is used in a construction that indicates that an entity is situated in an extended way rather than in a single location. Such an extended object is conceived of as unidimensional rather than having two or three dimensions. This can be thought of as lowly elaborated since individual pieces are not differentiated.

(46)   Navajo (Young, Morgan and Midgette 1992: 41)
      state Ø   dahdzil-ba
                  There is a grey patch or spot
      extension d   dzi-bá
                  A grey stripe or streak extends away into distance

(47)   Ahtna (Kari 1990)
      state Ø   z-'aan
                  It (compact O) is in position (70)
      extension d   testa   'utgge u-kaen'
                  hill.among up   3-den
                  kades-**t**-'aan
                  series.of.3-dimensional.objects.is.in.position
                  Its dens extend up into the hills (73)

4.1.12   Iterative: initiator and endpoint not differentiated

Most Athapaskan languages have a construction known as the iterative. The iterative has the form *na-* or cognate and has more than one reading – it indicates a return to a previous state (often translated 'back') and repetition of an event (generally translated 'again' or 'another'). It may also co-occur with a customary aspect verb stem in most languages. When combined with intransitives, middle-voice marking is found; it is unusual to find this with transitives. The iterative construction with intransitives is parallel to reflexives and reciprocals, indicating a common source and goal.

(48)   Ahtna (Kari 1990)
      non-iterative Ø ni-yaa
                      He arrived (422)
      iterative d   **na**-'i-**d**-yaa
                      He returned (291)

(49)   Koyukon (Jones and Jetté forthcoming)
      non-iterative Ø ne-yo
                      S/he arrived
      iterative d   **no**-'ee-**de**-yo
                      S/he came back

(50)   Navajo (Young and Morgan 1987: 122)
      non-iterative Ø sé-líí'
                      I became
      iterative d   nísís-**d**-líí'
                      I reverted, turned back (into)
      iterative d   **náá**-sís-**d**-líí'
                      I again became
      non-iterative Ø baa ní-yá
                      I went to him

iterative d   baa **ná**-nís-**d**-zá
                             I returned to him
iterative d   baa **náá**-nís-**d**-zá
                             I again went to him

(51)   Hupa (Golla 1970: 80)
        non-iterative Ø   adverb-xo-Ø-'aW/'an
                         pl subject run somewhere
        iterative d   adverb-**na**-xo-**di**-'aW/'an
                         pl subject run back somewhere

(52)   Slave (Rice 1989)
        non-iterative Ø   dé-'é
                         S/he starts off by boat
        iterative d   **ra**-de-**t**-'é
                         S/he starts off again, starts back by boat
        iterative d   **ra**-**t**-'ó
                         S/he goes customarily by boat
        non-iterative Ø   'ane-le
                         You sg do it
        iterative d   '**a**-**ra**-ne-**d**-le
                         You sg do it again

4.1.13   Errative: initiator control suppressed

A construction known as the errative is found in many Athapaskan languages.[3] It is used to indicate unintentional action. Axelrod (1993: 108) provides the following definition: 'doing the activity referred to by the verb excessively or incorrectly and being unable to stop or escape from the consequences'. Morice (1932: 327), who seems to be the first to use the word 'errative', points out that the errative in Carrier 'quite often connotes a reflex idea not only of impropriety, but of unwished for consequences for the subject of the verb'. The errative occurs with a qualifier *n* as well as with the *d* middle element.

(53)   Ahtna (Kari 1990)
        non-errative Ø   kahghi-yaa
                         S/he spoke out (285)
        errative d   kah-**n**-es-daa
                         S/he accidentally spoke it
        non-errative ɬ   ite-ɬ-na'
                         He swallowed it (286)
        errative l   it-**n**-e-**l**-na'
                         He choked on it (285–6)

---

[3] The errative is found in at least a few verbs in Slave – '*enéhdǫ* 's/he overate, got drunk'.

(54)   Koyukon
        non-errative Ø   k'eghee-hon'
                          S/he ate (Axelrod 1993: 108–9)
        errative d   k'e-**n**-aał-**d**-on'
                          S/he overate
        non-errative Ø   ghee-do'
                          S/he was sitting, staying (Axelrod 1993: 109)
        errative d   **n**-aałee-do'
                          S/he started staying and couldn't make her/himself leave

(55)   Carrier (Morice 1932)
        non-errative Ø   es-t'en
                          I work (327)
        errative d   e-**n**-es-t'en
                          I work uselessly, wrongly, make a mistake, err
        non-errative Ø   tas-'aih
                          I put something in the water (328)
        errative d   ta-**n**-es-**t**-'aih
                          I put the wrong piece in the water

The Navajo aspect that Young and Morgan call the prolongative has the
same semantics as the northern errative, and requires the middle-voice marker
and the qualifier *n*.

(56)   Navajo 'prolongative' (Young, Morgan and Midgette 1992)
        non-errative Ø   'i'nish-'aał
                          I start to chew (28)
        errative d   ná-**n**-ésh-**t**-'aal
                          I ate too much, got stuffed (29)
        non-errative Ø   haash-chééh
                          I start to cry (70)
        errative d   nadí-**n**-ísh-chééh
                          I cry and cry, prolongedly
        non-errative Ø   niníł-chozh
                          I finished eating (90)
        errative d   ná-**n**-ésh-chozh
                          I ate too much of O, overate on O

4.1.14   Repetitive/perambulative: endpoint of event suppressed
Intransitive verbs in what is called the perambulative aspect in Koyukon and
the repetitive aspect in Slave take middle voice.

(57)   Koyukon (Jones and Jetté forthcoming)
        motion Ø   ts'enee-datl
                          We arrived
        perambulative d   **kk'o**-ts'ee-**de**-daał
                          We are travelling around

(58)   Slave (Rice 1989)
        continuative Ø   náwhe-ya
                          S/he made a return trip
        repetitive d   **k'ína-ye-da**
                          S/he walked around

In this aspect, the event is not a distinct, discrete one, and thus middle voice is not inappropriate. It is interesting that in the distributive aspect, where a series of discrete arguments are involved rather than a collective, middle voice is not found.

4.2   Summary

Middle voice is marked by an affix, *d*. I use the term middle voice as the affix has a variety of uses which are unified by the fact that all of them indicate low elaboration, as defined in Kemmer (1993).[4] The different uses are constructionally differentiated through the presence of additional material in all but the passive, as summarized in (59).

(59)   construction of middles

CONSTRUCTION	ADDITIONAL MARKING (*d* middle voice in all)
passive	no additional marking
reflexive	reflexive direct object prefix
reciprocal	reciprocal direct object prefix
indirect reflexive	reflexive oblique object prefix
indirect reciprocal	reciprocal oblique object prefix
self-benefactive	*d* prefix
incorporated bodypart	incorporate
plural subject	subject marking
iterative	*na* iterative
customary	customary stem, (*na* iterative prefix)
errative	*n* prefix
repetitive/perambulative	preverb (e.g. *kk'o* Koyukon, *k'ína/k'e* Slave)

The particular meaning is constructionally based; the middle voice marker designates low elaboration, but not the specific reading; this must be derived from context. Not too surprisingly, some ambiguities are found. Some examples are given in (60):

(60)   Koyukon ambiguities (Jones and Jetté forthcoming)
(a)   neeł'ek'ehe-l-onh
        They are feeding each other / One is feeding the other

---

[4] See Thompson (1996a) for arguments about the historical source of middle voice in Athapaskan languages.

(b)   edek'e-l-zes
        He is drinking by himself, giving himself something to drink

4.3   Passive revisited

4.3.1   Personal and impersonal passives

I now return to passives. The passive construction in Athapaskan languages has been studied extensively by Thompson (1989a, b, focussing on Koyukon) and Kibrik (1996, focussing on Navajo). Two basic passive constructions can be identified across the family and a third one in Navajo. The first two types are alike in that they are non-agentive. They differ by the grammatical marking of the argument: it may have the form of an object – these are known as non-promotional/impersonal/mediopassive – or it may have the form of a subject – this construction is called promotional/personal/passive; I use the terms impersonal and personal. In some languages, both personal and impersonal passives appear.

In order to distinguish personal and impersonal passives, it is necessary to examine forms with 1st or 2nd person arguments or with 3rd person human plural and unspecified arguments. The morphology is such that it is impossible to discern the nature of a passive with an unmarked 3rd person argument – morphological marking of subject for this type is null and object marking is only present when two arguments occur. Passive subjects are highlighted in the following forms, as is voice marking. In personal passives, the passive argument is a morphological subject; in impersonal passives, the passive argument is a morphological object.

(61)   Dogrib (Saxon 1990)
        personal passive
        transitive Ø   etenets'eè-'i̧
                       We pity you sg
        passive d   eteè-**h-t-**'i̧
                       I am to be pitied (h = 1sgS)
        impersonal passive
        transitive Ø   'o̧nayee-nde ha
                       S/he is going to divorce him/her
        passive d   'o̧na-**s**-eè-h-do
                       I've been divorced (s = 1sgO)
        transitive ɬ   eɬàeh-who
                       I kill it
        passive l   k'àhjone eɬà-**s**-i̧-wo
                       I was almost killed (s = 1sgO)

Saxon (1990) comments that the personal passive is quite uncommon in Dogrib. In the closely related Slave, on the other hand, it appears that passives are personal with personal subjects:

(62)   Slave (Rice 1989)
         personal passive
         transitive Ø   rásereyi̧-'a
                        S/he fooled me
         passived   ráreye-**h-t**-'a
                        I was fooled (h = 1sgS)

Koyukon has both personal and impersonal passives:

(63)   Koyukon
         personal
         transitive ɬ   yinee-ɬ-'aanh
                        S/he is looking at him/her (Thompson 1989a: 10)
         passive l   n-**een-la**-'aanh
                        You are being watched (een = 2sgS)
         transitive ɬ   neeto-ɬ-dzes
                        S/he will hit you once with fist (Thompson 1996a: 360)
         passive l   eetegh-**ee-l**-dzes
                        You will be hit once (ee = 2sgS)
         impersonal
         transitive Ø   ghes-on'
                        I ate it
         passive d   **s-o-d**-on'
                        I was eaten (s = 1sgO)
         transitive ɬ   yeghee-ɬ-zook
                        He took them
         passive l   **hebo-l**-zook
                        They were taken (hebo = 3pl human O)

Tsuut'ina has both types:

(64)   Tsuut'ina (Cook 1984)
         personal
         transitive Ø   s-à-'í là
                              really
                        He saw me (really) (169)
         passive d   yì-**s-t**-'í
                        I was seen (s = 1sgS)
         impersonal
         transitive Ø   nàmíst-li
                        I am expecting him (170)
         passive d   nà-**s-í-d**-li
                        I am expected (there is an expectation for me) (s = 1sgO)

In the personal passive example, the single argument has subject morphology, while in the impersonal passive the single overt argument has the object form. This 'subject' is non-topical, indicated by the gloss that Cook provides – 'there is an expectation . . .'

A similar set of constructions is found in Mattole (Li 1930: 70):

(65)   Mattole (Li 1930)
        personal
        transitive Ø   djiɣaːsiː-tl'íː'd
                       I smashed it to pieces (70)
        passive d   djiɣaːsi-**s-di**-tl'íː'd
                       I am smashed to pieces (s = 1sgS)
        impersonal
        transitive Ø   ło'cgai gwonist'é' 'o-yíː
                       You call mice people (70)
        passive l   **c**-óː-l-yiː
                       I am called (c = 1sgO)
        passive l   **n**-óː-l-yiː
                       You sg are called (n = 2sgO)

Here it appears that verbs with affected objects require the personal passive, and verbs with non-affected objects require the impersonal passive. However, it is not clear if this will be confirmed by further data.

Navajo has personal passives based on examples with subject personal pronouns:

(66)   Navajo
        personal
        transitive Ø   yish-'į̨
                       I see it
        passive d   yi-**sh-t**-'į̨
                       I am seen (sh = 1sgS)
        transitive ł   nei-ł-'a'
                       S/he sends her/him on errands
        passive l   naa-**sh**-'a'
                       I am sent on errands (sh = 1sgS)
        passive l   nasí-**ní-l**-'a'
                       You sg were sent on errands (n = 2sgS)

Kibrik (1996) argues that these forms are not passives, but form a construction that he terms 'potential'. To a large degree, his argument is based on his conclusion that passives are impersonal in Navajo. However, the evidence is sparse – when the argument of a passive verb is 3rd person, verb morphology offers no clues to the position of that argument. This type of passive with a personal subject appears to be rare in Navajo; see below for further discussion.

Dena'ina has, by the form of the argument, impersonal passives: object pronouns are used, as in the Tsuut'ina and Mattole impersonal passives.

(67)　Dena'ina (Tenenbaum 1978)
　　　impersonal passives
　　　transitive ł　yi-ł-jeh
　　　　　　　　　　He punched him (122)
　　　passive 1　　**shi**-**l**-jeh
　　　　　　　　　　I got punched (sh = 1sgO) (127)
　　　transitive ł　chiqevda'e-ł-yuq
　　　　　　　　　　I killed them (122)
　　　passive 1　　chi-**sh**-da-**l**-yuq
　　　　　　　　　　I got killed (sh = 1sgO) (127)

In Hupa too, passives are impersonal, with object pronouns:

(68)　Hupa (Golla 1970)
　　　impersonal
　　　transitive ł　ł-ten
　　　　　　　　　　move (one person) somewhere (181)
　　　passive 1　　no-**n**-iwi-**l**-teːn
　　　　　　　　　　You have been put down (n = 2sgO) (182)

Carrier has personal passives, as can be seen by the presence of 1st person subject- rather than object-marking.

(69)　Carrier (Morice 1932: 286)
　　　personal
　　　transitive Ø　nes-'a
　　　　　　　　　　I deceive O
　　　passive d　　ne-**s**-**t**-'ah
　　　　　　　　　　I was deceived (s = 1sgS)
　　　transitive Ø　es-'ał
　　　　　　　　　　I eat
　　　passive d　　e-**s**-**t**-'aal
　　　　　　　　　　I was eaten, eatable (s = 1sgS)

Thompson (1989a, b, c) studies the semantics of the passive construction (personal or impersonal) in Koyukon and Navajo through text analysis. He argues that the function of the passive is an unusual one. First, and part of a standard definition of passive, the passive demotes the logical subject, making it either of low topicality or non-topical. Second, and unusually, he argues that functionally the patient is non-topical. Thompson found this in both Koyukon, where structurally both personal and impersonal passives are found, and in Navajo. If his conclusion is correct, then the formal grammatical role of the patient does not affect its topicality; it is likely that in languages that have both personal and impersonal passives, some other semantic factor, not topicality, differentiates the two. More careful study is required.

4.3.2   Verbs subject to passivization (1): thematic roles

Many kinds of verbs are subject to passivization. Transitive verbs such as 'eat' or 'pinch' or 'kill' have agentive subjects, while those such as 'look at' or 'know' or 'pity' have experiencer subjects, and both types are subject to passivization. Affected objects can be passivized (eat, kill), as can non-affected objects (look at, pity, call). I am sure that there are conditions within these classes on possibilities of passivization, but overall, there are few constraints of which I am aware on the types of transitive verb that are subject to passivization.

4.3.3   Verbs subject to passivization (2): passives of intransitives

The examples given so far show that transitive verbs are subject to passivization, as expected. Intransitive verbs can be passivized in at least some languages. The following Dogrib examples are given by Saxon (1990). The objects of these verbs are structurally oblique rather than direct. The second example of each set is passive; the single grammatical role remains oblique.

(70)   Dogrib
        intransitive Ø   wek'èe-zhǫ
                          I know her/him/it
        passive d   sǫ̀ǫmba k'èe-jǫ le
                          money   negative
                          There isn't knowledge of money (no subject)
        intransitive Ø   chekoa k'è-ndi ha
                          child
                          S/he will look after the child
        passive d   'ekàani ts'inàkè wek'èho-dì
                          that way orphan
                          Orphans were treated that way (expletive subject *ho*)
        intransitive Ø   ts'e-ghǫ
                          We make war
        passive d   gik'e e-gǫ
                          3pl.on war-is
                          There was war going on upon them (no subject)
        intransitive Ø   sekègeè-zhǫ
                          They know me
        passive d   sek'èè-jǫ
                          I am known (no subject)

Navajo too has passives of intransitives, although I did not find many clear examples.

(71)   Navajo (Young, Morgan and Midgette 1992)
         intransitive Ø   yisé-nah
                          I forget (407)
         passive d   hoyoos-'-neh
                          It is forgotten

The conditions on passives of intransitives require further study.

4.3.4   Navajo 'semipassives' (agentive passives)

The passives discussed so far are grammatically agentless. Navajo has a type of passive that has been called an agentive passive (Young and Morgan 1987) or a semipassive (Kibrik 1996), illustrated in (76). These examples have middle voice, an object pronoun and an unspecified subject (*'*); these elements are bolded in the examples.

(72)   Navajo semipassives (Kibrik 1996)
         transitive Ø   'asdzą́ą́ 'ashkii tánéíz-giz
                         woman boy   washed
                         The woman washed the boy (275–6)
         semipassive d   'ashkii táá**bí'**dís-giz
                         boy
                         The boy was washed
         transitive ł   nish-hash
                         It bit you (280)
         semipassive l   **ni'**dish-ghash
                         You have been bitten

Kibrik (1996: 276) outlines four characteristic features of semipassives:

(73)   characteristics of semipassive
         • the unspecified pronoun *'* is present, and represents the actor
         • the object is animate and has the form *b* in the third person
         • middle-voice marking is present
         • a morpheme *d* occurs, marking transitivity decrease

Kibrik contrasts the semantics of passive and semipassive constructions. Recall that for Kibrik, passives are impersonal; the personal examples in (66) are of a category he calls 'potential'. He argues that the actor is animate, usually human, in both his passive and semipassive types. He further argues that his passive occurs with inanimate undergoers, while the semipassive construction is found with animate undergoers; non-human animate undergoers are found in both constructions.

If, based on the patterning of the overt 1st and 2nd person arguments, passives are personal, then Kibrik's claim is not completely true, as (74) shows.

(74)   Navajo passives with human undergoer (Kibrik's 'potential') (Young and
         Morgan 1987)
         transitive ł   yiní-ł-'á
                         He sends him on errands (123)
         passive 1   naa-l-'a'
                         He's sent on errands
         semipassive 1   na**bi'd**i-l-'a'
                         He's sent on errands, ordered around

In this example passive (Kibrik's 'potential') and semipassive constructions
are shown, where there is a human undergoer in both. However, generally,
if the undergoer is animate, the semipassive construction is found. The examples in (75, 76) contrast passives with inanimate or non-human animate
undergoers and semipassives with animate undergoers, in the same verb.

(75)   Navajo passive with inanimate undergoer; semipassive with human undergoer
         transitive 1   niiní-l-tlah
                         He stopped him (YM: 123)
         passive 1   nii-l-tlah
                         It was stopped
         semipassive 1   ni**bi'd**ee-l-tlah
                         He was stopped

(76)   transitive ł   né-sá̧ / biné-sá̧
                         I raised, reared, brought up (child, lamb) (Young, Morgan
                         and Midgette 1992 (YMM): 681)
         passive 1   nees-yá̧
                         It (calf) is reared, raised
         semipassive 1   **bidi'**nees-yá̧
                         person is raised, reared, brought up

Kibrik (1996: 288) suggests that in cases where both constructions are available, in the passive the undergoer is interpreted as an object while in the
semipassive it is interpreted as a rational human-like being. He contrasts the
following examples:

(77)   Navajo (Kibrik 1996)
         transitive 1   dibé yoo-l-ghal
                         He/it ate the sheep (288)
         passive 1   dibé doo-l-ghał
                         The sheep will be eaten
         semipassive 1   dibé **bi'd**oo-l-ghal
                         The sheep was eaten

In the passive form the sheep will be eaten up, and be dead, while in the
semipassive form, the sheep is still alive. Kibrik suggests too that the patient

in the semipassive is more topical than the patient of the passive. The passive and semipassive appear to differ in terms of the involvement of the patient – in the passive, the patient is affected; in the semipassive the patient is, in some sense, involved in the event in some voluntary way.

Structurally the semipassive has two arguments, an unspecified subject (') and a direct object. The 3rd person direct object is *b* regardless of subject. While Kibrik proposes functional reasons for this, there are also formal reasons as well: the subject ', being non-topical, is contained within the verb phrase; see Rice (forthcoming-a) for discussion.

4.4   Summary

This completes my discussion of middle voice. I have argued that *d* is a marker of middle voice. It appears on its own in passive constructions, and in combination with another item in other middle-type constructions, where the *d* indicates the low elaboration and the additional morpheme indicates how the low elaboration is to be interpreted. Different kinds of passives are possible in different languages and sometimes in the same language. The semantics of passives is not well understood.

5   Causatives

While the middle-voice element has been well studied in the Athapaskan literature, somewhat less attention has been paid to the causativizer; see Hale and Platero (1996), Kibrik (1993), Rice (1991, forthcoming-a) for some discussion. The *ł* element marks valency generally, adding an argument. Cross-family variation exists in terms of the kind of verb that the causativizer can combine with. Patientive intransitives are subject to causativization in all languages, agentive intransitives in some languages, and transitives in fewer languages. The split in intransitives, where patientive intransitives and agentive intransitives differ in how susceptible they are to causativization, suggests that the relevant classes for causativization are better thought of in terms of thematic roles rather than strictly grammatical roles. The languages also differ in terms of the kinds of possible causers that can be introduced (only human controllers, any potential controller).

In examining the causativizer, I start with intransitive verbs with patientive subjects, and then move through various constructions working up to transitive verbs.

As with the middle-voice marker, the basic form of the causativizer is often obscured by morphophonological operations. I highlight it when possible.

5.1   Intransitive verbs with patientive subjects

5.1.1   Causatives of events

In all Athapaskan languages that I know of, the causativizer can causativize an intransitive verb with a patientive subject. Many verbs that are subject to the causativity alternation inherently involve a change of state, or a process and an inherent goal. The verbs below are, by and large, event verbs of the change-of-state type.

(78)   Koyukon (Jones and Jetté forthcoming)
        intransitive Ø   too daadle-tsʉhtl
                          Water made a splashing sound
        causative ł   too de-ł-tsʉhtl
                          He is causing the water to make a splashing sound / He
                          made the water make a splashing sound

(79)   Ahtna (Kari 1990)
        intransitive Ø   z-ggan
                          It is dry (191–2)
        causative ł   c'etsen' ł-ggan
                          meat
                          He is drying the meat (192)
        intransitive d   s-t-caats
                          It was liquefied (110–11)
        causative ł   yi-ł-caats
                          He rendered it (111)
        intransitive d   c'ezes gha-dloz
                          skin
                          The skin got crumpled (164)
        causative ł   ighi-ł-dloz
                          He softened it by crumpling (164)
        intransitive Ø   nen' ghighi-na'
                          The earth was shaking (288)
        causative ł   łts'ii ts'abaeli dghe-ł-naa
                          wind tree
                          Wind is moving the trees (288)
        intransitive l   na-l-ghex
                          It is melting (214)
        causative ł   hwngi-ł-ghaen
                          It (sleeping moose) melted an area

(80)   Slave (Rice 1989)
        intransitive Ø   we-gǫ
                          It is dry
        causative ł   yé-**h**-gǫ
                          DISJOINT.ANAPHOR+ASP-CAUS-dry
                          S/he dried it

intransitive Ø   zhátthíį-zí
The heads are roasted
causative ł   zhátthíį-**h**-sí
S/he roasted heads
intransitive Ø   ré-zhǫ
It grew
causative ł   re-**h**-shǫ
I raised it, grew it
intransitive d   satsóné behchiné k'ína-tłah
metal   sled
The car goes around
causative ł   satsónébehchiné k'ína-**h**-tłah
S/he drove the car around

(81)   Navajo (Young and Morgan 1987)
intransitive Ø   yi-bézh
It is boiling (119)
causative ł   yi-**ł**-béézh
He's boiling it
intransitive l   yi-l-zhoł
It's sailing along (as a cloud)
causative ł   yoo-shoł
He's dragging it along (as a trunk)
intransitive Ø   na'ni-yęęsh
Something flows about in a meandering fashion (119)
causative ł   na'ni-**ł**-hęęsh
He is making something flow about in a meandering fashion
intransitive Ø   tin yí-yíį'
ice
The ice melted
causative ł   yas yí-**ł**-híį'
snow
I melted the snow

(82)   Hupa (Golla 1970)
intransitive Ø   daw
melt
causative ł   **ł**-daw
melt (transitive)
intransitive ł   gyas
break, snap
causative ł   **ł**-gyas
cause to break, snap
intransitive Ø   xIs
drop, fall
causative ł   **ł**-xIs
send dropping, falling

5.1.2   Causatives of states

The examples above involve events (activities, achievements and accomplishments). Verbs indicating states are also subject to causativization when the subject is patientive, as are transitions. Two types of verbs are included in the examples below. First are verbs of location or position. When such a verb is causativized, the reading assigned is a type of resultative, usually translated 'keep, maintain in a position'. Second are descriptive verbs; when these are causativized, a transition is involved, and this is signalled by an aspectual change – these verbs become events through causativization.

(83)   Koyukon (Jones and Jetté forthcoming)
　　　　intransitive Ø   hedaadle-tl'ee
　　　　　　　　　　　　They are staying, sitting
　　　　causative ł   yeh hʉdaa-tl-tl'ee
　　　　　　　　　　　She keeps them in the house
　　　　intransitive Ø   nelaan le-kkonh
　　　　　　　　　　　　The meat (in dish) is there
　　　　causative ł   yeh yee-tl-kkonh
　　　　　　　　　　　She has it (dish of food) in the house
　　　　intransitive Ø   ne-dlogge
　　　　　　　　　　　　It is light in weight / He is nimble, agile, light
　　　　causative ł   yee-ł-dlogge
　　　　　　　　　　　He keeps it light

(84)   Hupa (Golla 1970)
　　　　intransitive Ø   sa-'aːn
　　　　　　　　　　　　It (compact object) is lying
　　　　causative ł   seh-ł-'aː
　　　　　　　　　　　I have it lying there
　　　　causative ł   ch'iwi-ł-'a'
　　　　　　　　　　　S/he kept it
　　　　intransitive Ø   ni-Ø-Won
　　　　　　　　　　　　be good (76)
　　　　causative ł   O ni-ł-Won'
　　　　　　　　　　　cause O to be good
　　　　intransitive Ø   ti-Ø-ch'e'
　　　　　　　　　　　　wind starts to blow (201)
　　　　causative ł   O ti-ł-ch'e'
　　　　　　　　　　　cause (wind) to blow, cause O to blow like the wind (202)
　　　　intransitive ł   ni-ł-cay
　　　　　　　　　　　　be dry
　　　　causative ł   O ł-cay'
　　　　　　　　　　　cause to be dry

(85)   Slave (Rice 1989)
      intransitive Ø   bet'ádé-'a
                      post extends, sticks up
      causative ł   yet'ádé-**h**-'a
                      S/he has post stuck up
      intransitive Ø   the-da
                      S/he sits
      causative ł   yé-**h**-da
                      S/he has him/her sit

(86)   Navajo (YMM)
      intransitive Ø   'íí'á
                      pole/tree extends away out of sight, sticks up into air (1)
      causative ł   'íí-**ł**-'á
                      I held slender rigid object so it extends away into space (2)
      intransitive Ø   di-bááh
                      It is turning grey (41)
      causative ł   yiish-bááh
                      I am turning it grey

(87)   Ahtna (Kari 1990)
      intransitive d   di-t-baets
                      It turned tan/brown/blond (103)
      causative ł   detse' tatni-**ł**-baets
                      She dyed her hair blond

(88)   Carrier (Morice 1932)
      intransitive Ø   ezte-tsen
                      We are dirty (282)
      causative ł   ezte-**ł**-tsen
                      We dirty someone
      intransitive l   hani-l-t'uz
                      He is bald (282)
      causative ł   hanuhezni-**ł**-t'uz
                      We make you (pl) bald

Kibrik (1993: 56) suggests that the primary meaning of causatives of statives is 'causing an existential/locative state to be maintained, controlling a Goal in a position' – these are resultatives. Secondary to the major point here, when a stative is causativized, it remains a state; when a descriptive is causativized, it becomes a transitional aspectually.

It is worth pointing out that there are intransitive verbs with patientive subjects that do not participate in the causativity alternation.

(89)   Ahtna
         gige' ndlet
         The berries get ripe (161)

No causative form is given by Kari (1990) for this verb, while in general causatives are listed. I take this, with hesitation, to indicate that the verb is not subject to causativization. There may be a semantic account of this – here the subject of the verb must undergo the change autonomously, and thus is not compatible with an added initiator of the event.

5.1.3   Summary

The examples in this section include both events and states. Based on these verbs, the following generalizations can be drawn.

(90)   When the causativizer is added to an event, it adds an initiator of the event. When the causativizer is added to a state it:
         (a)   creates a resultative of a locative verb
         (b)   adds an initiator of a transition to a descriptive verb (it makes the state into an event, thus adding an initiator)

When the causativizer is added to an event, it adds an initiator, independent of the argument structure of the verb (whether the event is intransitive or transitive) and independent of the aspectual class of the verb (whether the event is punctual, durative, telic or semelfactive).

5.2   *Intransitive verbs with agentive subjects*

When intransitive verbs with agentive subjects are examined, we see a split in the family – some of the languages allow the simple causative construction seen so far, some allow causativization of these intransitives but require what Hale and Platero (1996) term a 'complex causative' construction (e.g. Navajo), and some of the languages do not freely allow the verbal causative construction with agentive transitives (e.g. Slave).

5.2.1   Ahtna, Koyukon, Carrier

Consider first Ahtna, Koyukon and Carrier. The examples in (91–3) illustrate that the complement in a causative construction can be an intransitive with an agentive subject.

(91)   Koyukon (Jones and Jetté forthcoming)

        intransitive Ø   e-tsah
                        S/he cries
        causative ł   deketl'e e-ł-tsah
                        He makes his younger brother cry
        intransitive Ø   nee-yo
                        He arrived
        causative ł   yeenee-ł-yo
                        He arrived walking him, he made him walk
        intransitive Ø   tleenee-baatl
                        He walked out energetically, in a huff
        causative ł   tleeyeenee-ł-baatl
                        She jerked him out
        intransitive Ø   hedo'eel-zoot
                        He slid into/inside the house
        causative ł   hedoyeenee-ł-zoot
                        He slid it into the house

(92)   Ahtna (Kari 1990)

        intransitive d   gha-t-na'
                        He was working (288)
        causative ł   ighe-ł-na
                        He is making him work (288)
        intransitive Ø   ni-yaa
                        He arrived (422)
        causative ł   gaa sni-ł-yaa
                        He made me walk here (423)
        intransitive Ø   nc'e-dlo'
                        He is laughing (163)
        causative ł   nsc'e-ł-dlo'
                        He makes me laugh
        intransitive Ø   tez-kaen
                        He started off in a boat (239)
        causative ł   c'etsen' nini-ł-kaen
                        He transported the meat (by boat)

(93)   Carrier (Morice 1932)

        intransitive Ø   ne-be
                        He swims (282)
        causative ł   neye-ł-be
                        He makes him swim
        intransitive Ø   e-yał
                        He is going on (282)
        causative ł   yi-ł-yał
                        He causes him to go on

5.2.2   Navajo

Navajo too allows causatives of verbs with agentive subjects.

(94)   Navajo
          intransitive Ø   'awéé' naa-ghá
                            baby
                            The baby is walking around
          causative ł   'awéé' nabiish-ł-á
                            baby
                            I am walking the baby around
          intransitive Ø   'awéé' yi-dloh
                            baby
                            The baby is laughing
          causative ł   'awéé' biyeesh-dloh
                            I am making the baby laugh
          intransitive Ø   heesh-ááł
                            I step along, shuffle along (YMM: 674)
          causative ł   biyee-ł-sháál
                            I walk (baby) along (by holding its hand); move O along by
                            'walking it' (e.g. heavy refrigerator) (675)
          intransitive Ø   yí-yóół
                            The wind blows (YMM: 724)
          causative ł   binii-sóół
                            I make O bloat up, fill up O with gas (e.g. beans)
          intransitive Ø   'íí-zhil
                            I drew in breath sharply, inhaled, gasped (YMM: 773)
          causative ł   'ashíí-shil
                            It made me gasp for breath

The causative construction in these Navajo forms is distinct from that used
when the subject is patientive. The two classes of verbs differ in that in one
case no overt direct object pronoun is required in the causative construction
when the subject is non-third person and the object third person (examples in
(86)), while in the other case (examples in (94)), a direct object pronoun is
required when the object is non-third person. Hale and Platero (1996) argue
that the difference between whether the object pronoun is absent or present
rests in the structural configuration of the verb – if the verb is unaccusative,
or has a verb-phrase-internal subject, then the object is not found, while if
the verb is unergative, or has a verb-phrase-external subject, then the object
pronoun is required. However, this generalization does not seem to be completely correct, as is shown by the forms discussed below. First consider the
verbs in (95), where verbs that seem to be unergative, or have agentive subjects,
occur in the simple causative construction, without an object pronoun.

(95)   Navajo unergatives? (YMM)
        intransitive Ø   náá-baɫ
                          S/he is whirling around (48)
        causative ɫ   náásh-baɫ
                          I am twirling, whirling O around
        intransitive Ø   'aníí-cháá̧'
                          I fled away out of sight (77)
        causative ɫ   'aníí-ɫ-cháá̧'
                          I chased O away out of sight (78)
        intransitive Ø   nisé-teel
                          I skated (501)
        causative ɫ   nisé-ɫ-teel
                          I rode/drove O around (e.g. snowmobile)
        intransitive Ø   'ee-t'a'
                          It (bird, insect, plane) flies away out of sight (522)
        causative ɫ   'íí-ɫ-t'a'
                          I flew O away out of sight (527)

Second, consider the verbs in (96), where verbs that appear to be unaccusative, or to have patientive subjects, occur in the complex causative
construction.

(96)   Navajo unaccusatives? (Young and Morgan 1987)
        intransitive Ø   'aneez-dá
                          Something sat down (116)
        causative ɫ   binish-daah
                          I sit O down, seat O, give O a seat, make O sit down
        intransitive Ø   shii-jéé'
                          We are lying (263)
        causative ɫ   bishéé-ɫ-jéé'
                          I keep pl. O'
                          naa'ahóóhai tádiingo bishééɫjéé'
                          I keep 30 chickens
        intransitive Ø   nétį
                          I lay down, recline (YMM: 510)
        causative ɫ   biné-ɫ-tį
                          I lay O down, made O lie down, put O to bed (baby)
        intransitive Ø   né-yá̧
                          I grew up, reached maturity (YMM: 681)
        causative ɫ   biné-sá̧/né-sá̧
                          I raised, reared, brought up (child, lamb)

A causativized verb with an experiencer subject also occurs with the object
pronoun.

(97)   Navajo (YMM)
        intransitive 1 tsídees-yiz
                        I was astonished, startled, amazed (708)
        causative ł   tsíbidíí-ł-hiz
                        It startled, frightened, shocked me

While Hale and Platero propose a structural difference between these constructions, there are counterexamples in two ways – verbs that appear to be
unergative (95) need not take the object in the causative and verbs that appear
to be unaccusative (96) can take it. What is the appropriate generalization? It
appears that the appropriate generalization is a semantic one: when the causee
is animate or human, the pronoun occurs. However, it is not required, as the
examples in (98) show.

(98)   Navajo
        intransitive Ø né-yą́
                        I grew up, reached maturity (YMM: 681)
        causative ł   né-są́
                        I raised, reared, brought up (child, lamb)
        causative ł   biné-są́
                        I raised, reared, brought up (child, lamb)

The direct object pronoun can also occur when the object is inanimate, but is
functioning in some kind of animate way, as in (94) above, with walking the
refrigerator. The example in (99) is similar, where the object involved appears
to be inanimate. However, cars and their parts often have animate properties
in Navajo.

(99)   Navajo (YMM)
        intransitive Ø haash-chééh
                        I start to cry (70)
        intransitive Ø béésh haa-chxééh
                        A whistle, siren starts to blow or wail
        causative ł   habiish-chxééh
                        I honk it (horn) one time after another

I show below that in the Navajo causative construction, the causee is not in
control. Perhaps the presence of the direct object pronoun in the causative
construction has something to do with whether the causee is human or
animate, or capable of being regarded as such. When the causee of the verb
cannot be or is not perceived as a potential controller, then the pronoun is not
found; when it is a potential controller, or is perceived as such, although not
controlling, then the object is found. This is reminiscent of the discussion of

semipassives in Navajo, where animate nouns could occur in the semipassive when they are imbued with some kind of human quality.

5.2.3   Slave
Causatives of intransitives with agentive subjects are not possible in all languages. This type of construction is not usual in Slave, for instance.

(100)   Slave (Rice 1989)
        intransitive Ø   yį-tse
                          S/he cries
        causative ł   *seyį-h-tse
                          S/he made me cry

A periphrastic construction is found instead.

(101)   Slave periphrastic causatives (Rice 1989)
        bebí déh-w'a 'ah-lá
        baby 3S-burp 1sgS-cause
        I burped the baby

        hehtse   'asene-lá
        1sgS+cry 2sgS+make-1sgO
        You made me cry

        nadéhtla   'ayį-lá
        3S+go.back 3S+make-DISJOINT.ANAPHOR
        He made him go away

5.3   *Transitive verbs*
I now consider causativization of transitive verbs. Koyukon allows transitive verbs to be the complement in the causative construction.

(102)   Koyukon (Jones and Jetté forthcoming)
        transitive l   ts'eh nedaa-l'onh
                     He is wearing a hat
        causative ł   ts'eh yendaa-ł-'onh
                     She let him wear a hat
        transitive l   eet needaal-tset
                     He (quickly) put his hand there
        causative ł   yaayedaanee-ł-tset
                     S/he made him touch it, s/he put his/her hand on it
        transitive Ø   k'eghee-zes
                     He was drinking something (alcohol), sipping something (hot)
        causative ł   yek'e-ł-zes
                     He is giving him something to drink

In Ahtna, I found only a few transitive verbs that enter into the causative construction. All of these are given in (103):

(103)   Ahtna (Kari 1990)
         transitive Ø   O-G-Ø-(y)aan
                         eat O (429)
         causative ł   ic'e-ł-yaan
                         He is feeding something to him
         transitive d   O-d-naan
                         drink O (290)
         causative ł   iy'ghi-ł-naan'
                         He gave him something to drink
         causative ł   tuu ughe-ł-naan'
                         I made him drink water

Morice (1932) lists a few transitive verbs that can be causativized as well:

(104)   Carrier (Morice 1932)
         transitive Ø   in-'ał
                         You sg. eat (it) (283)
         causative ł   be'i-ł-'ał
                         You sg. make him eat it, feed him
         transitive d   'eh-tnai
                         You pl. drink (it)
         causative ł   be'e-ł-tnai
                         You pl. make him drink it

In Navajo too, the same transitives, 'eat' and 'drink', enter into the causative construction:

(105)   Navajo (YMM)
         transitive Ø   yish-dlą́
                         I drink O, eat O (soup) (153)
         causative ł   O biish-dlą́
                         I make P drink O
         causative ł   bi'yíí-ł-dlą́ą́'
                         I gave P a drink, fed P (baby, lamb), watered P
         transitive Ø   yí-yą́ą́'
                         I ate (692)
         causative ł   biyíí-są́ą́'
                         I fed O (food) to P (baby)

In the causatives of transitives, the original direct object, or the direct object of the embedded clause, remains a direct object and the original subject, or the subject of the non-causative verb, is expressed as an oblique object.

Navajo also allows causatives to be formed from verbs that are transitive, with the unspecified object as the direct object. In this case, the added argument is oblique.

(106)   Navajo (Young and Morgan 1987)
        transitive ł   'al-zhish
                        He's dancing (119)
        causative ł   yi'ii-shish
                        She's dancing it (as a puppy or baby)

Koyukon is the only language in this survey with a productive morphological means of forming causatives of transitives; in other languages, causatives of transitives are formed periphrastically.

The causativizer is used under another condition – it can add an 'extra'
argument to a transitive verb.

(107)   Koyukon (Axelrod 1996)
        transitive Ø   yeel-dzaakk
                        S/he caulked it with pitch; S/he buttered it; S/he spread
                        jam on it
        extra argument ł   heyee-**tl**-dze
                        S/he glued, stuck it onto a place

(108)   Ahtna (Kari 1990)
        transitive Ø   ukey'nini-tsaes
                        Put something (pole) against it! (392)
        extra argument ł   itse c'a-**ł**-tses
                        He is leading him on ahead (with baited pole)
        transitive Ø   tsiitez-tsaet
                        He threw it (rock, compact O) (376)
        extra argument ł   u'statsi'nen-**ł**-tsaet
                        I chased it off by throwing a rock

(109)   Navajo (YMM)
        transitive Ø   'ashé-lizh
                        I urinated (374)
        extra argument ł   bíshé-łizh
                        I urinated it (e.g. blood)

In Ahtna, the causativizer can also add an oblique argument to an intransitive
verb.

(110)   Ahtna (Kari 1990)
        intransitive Ø   ghi-lets
                        He urinated repeatedly (278)
        extra argument ł   P#ł-lets
                        Urinate P, pass P in the urine
                        del łets
                        blood
                        He is urinating blood

5.4   Summary

I have argued that the causativizer can take the following types of verb bases:

(111)   Bases for causativization
    1   intransitive verb with patientive argument (all languages)
    2   intransitive verb with agentive argument (Ahtna, Koyukon, Carrier, Navajo)
    3   both intransitive verb and transitive verb (productive) (Koyukon)

There is a hierarchy, with intransitive verbs with patientive arguments the most likely to be causativized, and transitive verbs the least likely. This hierarchy is not a surprising one. Intransitive verbs with patientive arguments are the most likely to undergo causativization because these contain no lexically specified initiation of the event that they depict. The eventive dyadic verbs include an initiation of the event in their lexical representation, and thus are the least likely to allow the addition of an argument that specifies an initiation.

5.5   On the semantics of the causer

The languages also differ in what kind of causer is possible. To begin with the most narrow definition, in all languages the causer can be human. I do not repeat examples here; this is shown in many of the examples.

In some languages, a non-human that is capable of control can be a causer. This is true of Ahtna and Koyukon.

(112)   Ahtna (Kari 1990)
    intransitive l   naagha-l-'uuts
                I am relaxed (93)
    causative ł   tuu nilaeni nasghi-ł-'uuts'
                beer
                The beer limbered me, relaxed me
    intransitive l   na-l-ghaex
                It is melting (214)
    causative ł   naghaay kaghi-ł-ghaen
                frog
                It (nature) thawed out the frogs

(113)   Koyukon (Jones and Jetté forthcoming)
    intransitive Ø   k'edeghee-lee'
                He sang
    causative ł   sotseeyh ek'ede-ł-lee
                happiness
                Happiness is making him sing

causative ɬ	gheeno' yedenaa-tl-dlut
	maggot
	It became full of maggots (maggots brought it to a boil)
intransitive Ø	daaneel-lenh
	There is a stream, current is flowing in stream
causative ɬ	too kk'ʉtl ets'aadaanee-ɬ-leenh
	water
	Cold water runs out of there (current is causing cold water to flow out)

In other languages, it appears that the causer is limited to humans. Thus, in all languages the causer, or initiator of the event, can be human, while in some languages, the initiator can be non-human, but must be something with volitional force.

Dixon (this volume) lists several ways in which one causer might differ from another. It might act directly or indirectly. To my knowledge, causers act directly in Athapaskan languages. Another causer-related parameter that Dixon proposes is that the causer may achieve the result intentionally or unintentionally. This type of intentionality on the part of the causer is not expressed directly in the causative construction in these languages; an event is indicated as unintentional or not by other means. For instance, consider the following examples from Ahtna.

(114) Ahtna intentionality/non-intentionality of causer (Kari 1990)
(a)   tuu nilaeni nasghi-ɬ-'uuts'
       beer
       The beer limbered me, relaxed me (93)

(b)   hwngi-ɬ-ghaen
       It (sleeping moose) melted an area (214)

(c)   ciiɬ 'uygge ya-ɬ-ghax
       boy 3 OBLQ.on
       The boy melts it by lying down on it (214)

It is impossible for beer to intentionally cause the achieved state of relaxation; it is possible but not necessary that the moose melted the area intentionally; it is likely (but not necessary) that the boy melted the ice intentionally. This must be stated elsewhere in the discourse.

A third parameter involving causers concerns whether the causer initiates a natural process or one requiring effort. Again to my knowledge the causer may carry the action out with or without difficulty; this must be expressed elsewhere in the discourse.

It appears that, across the languages that I have examined, the most typical causer is one that represents the sole initiator or cause of the event.

5.6   On the semantics of the causee

The semantics of the causee remains to be examined. Causees can differ in that they may or may not be in control; if the causee is in control, then the action may be carried out willingly or not (see chapter 2). In general, in Athapaskan languages the causee does not act volitionally, and is not in control; thus the action is not carried out willingly.

I begin with the most limited case, a language like Slave where causees are generally non-human since only patientive intransitives are normally subject to causativization. In this case, the question of willingness or control does not arise, as typical patients are not volitional beings. It is thus in languages where the causee is potentially capable of control that the question of control becomes interesting.

Consider next Navajo. Recall that Navajo allows patientive and agentive subjects to function as causees in causative constructions. The semantics of the agentive causees is interesting. Examples are given in (94) above. The translations are revealing – they involve babies and refrigerators in the examples in (94), and also drunks and puppies. In all cases, the causees are animate or functioning as animate-like (refrigerator). The causees are not in control and are not volitional, but are controlled by the causer. It is not necessarily the case that the causee is unwilling to carry out the activity or achieve the state specified by the verb, but the causee is not volitional. The English translation is 'make, have'; it can, but need not, be 'force'.

Koyukon exhibits a different range of possibilities, as can be seen in the following examples. First, the causee may be controlling.

(115)   Koyukon willing causees (Jones and Jetté forthcoming)
         intransitive l   ts'eh nedaa-l-'onh
                           hat
                           He is wearing a hat
         causative ł   ts'eh yendaa-ł-'onh
                           She let him wear a hat

Second, the causee may be non-controlling. This seems to be the general case.

(116)   Koyukon non-controlling or non-volitional causees (Jones and Jetté
         forthcoming)
         intransitive Ø   nee-yo
                           S/he arrived

causative ł	yeenee-ł-yo
	He arrived walking him, made him walk
intransitive l	hedenaadle-tl'ee
	They sat down
causative ł	hʉdenaa-tl-tl'ee
	He sat them down, made them sit down
intransitive l	eet needaa-l-tset
	there
	He (quickly) put his hand there
causative ł	yaayedaanee-ł-tset
	She made him touch it, put his hand on it
intransitive Ø	ghee-zeeł
	S/he was shouting
causative ł	ye-ł-zeł
	S/he is making him cry out

In these examples, the causer controls the causee. In Koyukon, then, there may be ambiguity as to whether the causee is in control, or willing, or is unwillingly involved in an event.

It appears that, in general, causees are not volitional, and do not exercise control in the morphological causative construction. It is interesting to consider the glosses of causatives of transitive verbs. Recall that in languages other than Koyukon where transitives can be causativized, the verbs that are subject to causativization are restricted to 'eat' and 'drink.' The causative of 'eat' is usually translated 'feed,' implying that the causer puts the food in the mouth of the causee; the causative of 'drink' could also involve such direct control. The best causee across the family then is one that is not autonomous, but is controlled.

Athapaskan languages have a syntactic periphrastic causative construction as well as a morphological one. It is possible to express permission as well as force through the use of this periphrastic construction. Interestingly, at least in Slave, the causative verbs that take complements are ambiguous, allowing either a causative or a permission reading.

(117)   Slave periphrastic causatives (Rice 1989)

(a)   Mary yek'ago-li   gú   'ayi̱-lá
        3S   taste-DISJOINT.ANAPHOR COMP 3S+let/make/allow-DISJOINT.ANAPHOR
        S/he let Mary taste it (1304)

(b)   nadéh-tlah 'ayi̱-lá
        3S-taste   3S+let/make/allow-DISJOINT.ANAPHOR
        He made him go away

5.7   Summary

To summarize, we find the following situations:

(118)   semantics of the causee
    1   When the causee is incapable of control, only a 'make' reading is poss-
       ible (all languages).
    2   If the causee is capable of control, either a 'make' reading or a 'let'
       reading is possible (Koyukon).

The table in (119) summarizes the findings about causatives.

(119)   Causatives

language	Ahtna	Koyukon	Slave	Navajo	Carrier	Hupa
aspectual characteristics	state, event	state, event	state, event	state, event	state, event	state, event
conditions on causee	agent or patient	agent or patient	patient (normally)	agent or patient	agent or patient	patient
causee control	no	possible	no	no	no	no
causee willingness	make	make, let	make	make	make	make
causer direct or indirect	direct	direct	direct	direct	direct	direct

6   On the interaction of middles and causatives

So far, we have seen evidence for morphological marking of middles and
causatives. In this section, I consider situations which involve both a middle
and a causative. I begin with the less common case, situations where two overt
voice/valency markers are present on the surface, and then turn to the more
common case, that in which a single voice/valency marker is present on the
surface, but both a middle and a causative meaning are contained within
the verb.

6.1   Overt double voice/valency in Navajo

Young and Morgan list a few cases with two voice/valency markers in Navajo.

(120)   Navajo double voice/valency
    l middle
    yi-**l**-woł
    He is going along flexing, he is running along (YMM: 885)

ł causative
'ahání-ł-hod
I broke it in two by flexing it
ł + l causative of middle
yiyoo-ł-wol
He is causing it to run along, he is running it along

In the middle form, only *l* is present; in the causative only *ł* is. In the causative of the middle, there is an overt causativizer (*ł*) but *l* is also present. This can be seen from the presence of voicing on the stem-initial consonant; it would be voiceless, as in the causative form, if *l* were not present.

Another Navajo example is given in (121):

(121)   Navajo
         d
         ndish-'-na'
         I got up (YMM: 885)
         ł + d
         nábidii-ł-'-na'
         I stood it back up (e.g. fallen corn plant)

In the first example, *d* is present, as can be seen by the presence of the glottal preceding the stem-initial *n*. In the second example, *d* is still present, but the causativizer is as well. Thus, in these two examples of causatives of middles, both a lexical middle marker (*d*, *l*) and a causative marker (*ł*) surface.

This is not the norm in Navajo; see, for example, YMM: 885 for discussion. In general, when a verb is a causative of a middle, just the causativizer is present on the surface. This can be seen in the examples in (122).

(122)   Navajo: single voice/valency phonologically; double voice/valency
         semantically
         lexical l   hani-l-gháásh
                        It bubbles, boils, comes to a boil (YMM: 234)
         causative ł   'anii-ł-haazh
                        I brought it to a boil
         lexical l   'ii-zhood
                        It slides away out of sight (YMM: 787)
         causative ł   'iish-shood
                        I drag it away out of sight (heavy, long trunk, sled)
         lexical d   hodii-'-nááh
                        area starts to move or shake (YMM: 420)
         causative ł   hodiish-nááh
                        I cause area to shake

    lexical d   yish-jį́įh
                 It turns black, becomes tarnished, gets sunburned (YMM: 782)
    causative ɫ   yish-shį́įh
                 I dye O black (wool), colour O black, oxidize O, turn O black

In these causatives, the *l* or *d* is missing. This can be seen in the verbs with lexical *l* in that the stem-initial fricative is voiceless; it can be seen in the verbs with lexical *d* in that the D-effect (glottal before /n/; stop counterpart of fricative) is absent. Thus, in Navajo, the surface double voice/valency forms may represent a historical state, but synchronically the forms with double voice/valency must be regarded as frozen.

6.2   Overt double voice/valency in Hupa

Hupa is different from Navajo in providing two overt markings of voice/valency in a way that seems to be at least somewhat productive.

    Consider first iteratives. These take *d* middle voice, as in (123).

(123)   Hupa double voice/valency (Golla 1970)
        intransitive Ø   adverb-xo-Ø-'aW/'an
                       pl. subject run somewhere (80)
        middle d   adverb-na-xo-di-'aW/'an
                       pl. subject run back somewhere

If the verb has a lexical voice/valency marker with phonetic content, two voice/valency markers surface.

(124)   Hupa double voice/valency (Golla 1970)
        transitive ɫ   O wi-ɫ-teɫ
                       move (one person) along (87, 119)
        middle ɫ-d   O na-wi-ɫ-di-te:l
                       move (one person) along back
        intransitive l   wi-l-daɫ
                       (one) runs along (87)
        middle l-d   na-wi-l-di-daɫ
                       (one) runs along back

Double marking of voice/valency is found in other cases also. The examples in (125) and (126) are causatives of stative verbs; these yield possessives, where the resultant state implies a prior event. These causatives contain not just the causativizer, but an optional middle-voice marker as well.

(125)   Hupa double voice/valency (Golla 1970)
        intransitive l   si-l-q'as
                       (stones) lie thrown (158, 191)

causative ł-d   O si-ł-di-q'as
                    have O (stones) lying thrown

(126)   Hupa double voice/valency – analogy (Golla 1970)
         intransitive Ø   si-da
                           sg. animate sit, dwell
         causative ł(d)   O si-ł-da / O si-ł-di-da
                           have O sitting, own a pet (192)

Golla suggests that in the first type, as in (125), the stative verb is historically
a middle derived from a transitive; hence the presence of a middle-voice
element. The second class, as in (126), he proposes was derived analogically
from the first.

A complex derivation is shown in (127).

(127)   Hupa causative of passive (Golla 1970)
         transitive ł   O ł-tiW
                         move (one person) somewhere (181)
         passive l   l-ten
                         (one person) has been moved somewhere
         causative ł   ł-di-ten
                         have (one person) moved somewhere (182)

Here a passive is formed through the addition of *d*, yielding *l*, and a further
causative is formed on the passive, yielding the compound voice/valency
marker.

6.3   *Covert double voice/valency*

One might expect that middles of causatives and causatives of middles should
be possible, even if markings for both do not surface because of, for instance,
constraints on possible consonant clusters in a language. This is indeed the
case. In this section I look at forms with both voice and valency. The trees in
(128) show the general situation – basically, a middle formed on a causative
has *l* voice/valency while a causative formed on a middle has the *ł* valency
marker.

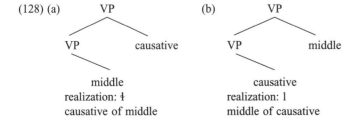

(128) (a)   VP   (b)   VP

         VP   causative   VP   middle

              middle   causative
         realization: ł   realization: l
         causative of middle   middle of causative

6.3.1 Middles built on causatives

Having sketched the general situation, I turn to specific examples, beginning with middles built on causatives. In the expression 'causative + middle', I mean that the middle is built on a causative as in (128b).

(129)   Koyukon middles built on causatives (Jones and Jetté forthcoming)
        intransitive Ø   tsaanee-let
                                    He woke up (Ø)
        causative ł   ts'aayeenee-ł-let
                                    He woke her up
        causative + middle l   ts'aahodee-let
                                    He woke himself up
        intransitive Ø   e-tsah
                                    He cries
        causative ł   deketl'e e-ł-tsah
                                    He makes his younger brother cry
        causative + middle l   yede-l-tseh
                                    He makes him cry for his own satisfaction, by his
                                    own selfishness
        intransitive Ø   ne-dlogge
                                    It is light
        causative ł   yee-ł-dogge
                                    He keeps it light
        causative + middle l   beł de-l-dlogge
                                    He keeps his sleep light (is a light sleeper)

(130)   Ahtna middles built on causatives (Kari 1990)
        intransitive Ø   di-k'aan
                                    It ignited (248)
        causative ł   idi-ł-k'aan
                                    He lit it, he built a fire
        causative + middle l   i'di-l-k'aan
                                    He built a fire for himself

(131)   Navajo middles built on causatives (Kibrik 1996)
        intransitive Ø   yi-tin
                                        It is freezing
        causative ł   yi-ł-tin
                                        S/he is freezing it
        causative + middle (passive) l yi-l-tin
                                        It is being frozen

Another Navajo example is more complex. In (120) above, repeated below, a causative of a middle was shown.

(132)   Navajo
        l middle
        yi-l-woł
        He is going along flexing, he is running along (YMM: 885)
        ł causative
        'ahání-ł-hod
        I broke it in two by flexing it
        ł + l causative of middle
        yiyoo-ł-wol
        He is causing it to run along, he is running it along

This can be further passivized. (The stem form is in a different aspect here.)

(133)   Navajo passive of (132)
        passive of causative
        habii-l-yeed
        It is being run up out (Young and Morgan 1987: 373)

This is a middle-causative-middle derivation. In this form, a direct object pronoun, *b*, occurs. We have already seen two cases in which an unexpected direct object pronoun surfaces, in semipassives with 3rd person subjects and in causatives with causees that are capable of being volitional. Here a semipassive is found. It appears that something that is capable of running has animate-like qualities, suggesting the use of *b*. Clearly, the function of this pronoun requires further study.

(134)   Carrier middles built on causatives (Morice 1932)
        intransitive Ø   i-tsagh
                                                I weep (285)
        causative ł   i-ł-tsagh
                                                I cause O to weep
        causative + middle (passive) l   i-l-tsagh
                                                I am made to weep
        intransitive Ø –   nes-yeh
                                                I grow
        causative ł   nes-yeh
                                                I raise/rear O
        causative + middle (passive) l   nez-l-yeh
                                                I get raised/reared

(135)   Hupa middles built on causatives (Golla 1970)
        intransitive ł   ł-cay'
                                                get dry (177)

causative ɫ	O ɫ-cay'
	dry O
causative + middle (passive) l	O l-cay'
	O has been dried

These are basic intransitives, with causatives built on them, and then a middle. The combination of a middle built on a causative is marked by *l*. Hupa allows a recausativization, where we see the dual voice/valency marking, with *d* marking the middle voice and *ɫ* the further causativization.

6.3.2   Causatives built on middles

There are also causatives built on middles. These are most obvious in Hupa.

(136)   Hupa causatives built on middles (Golla 1970)

transitive ɫ	O ɫ-taq'
	count O (170)
middle (passive) l	O l-taq'
	O is counted
middle + causative ɫ-d	O **ɫ-di**-taq'
	cause O to be counted

In this example, a causative is built on a passive, which in turn derives from a transitive. In the following example, two causative derivations can be seen, with a middle (passive) sandwiched in-between.

(137)   Hupa: a complex derivation (Golla 1970)

intransitive ɫ	ɫ-cay'
	get dry (177)
causative ɫ	O ɫ-cay'
	dry O
causative + middle (passive) l	O l-cay'
	O has been dried
causative + middle + causative ɫ-d	O **ɫ-di**-cay'
	have O dried

I have not found many examples of causatives of derived middles (only of lexical middles) in the Ahtna, Carrier, Koyukon or Navajo material that I have worked through. There could, perhaps, be a phonological reason for this. Notice that in Hupa, the plain causative and the causative of the middle differ in that the plain causative has just the *ɫ* valency marker while the causative of the middle has marking for both middle voice and causativity. In the other languages, overt double marking is not found. Thus, the causative and the causative of the middle would look the same. It is worthwhile to examine causatives to see if they can be ambiguous in meaning between a reading where the complement is a transitive or a middle.

7   Summary: the productive use of the voice/valency elements

I have reviewed the major functions of the voice/valency elements, following others in assuming that *d* indicates middle voice and *ł* is a causativizer. Both are functional predicates; the specific meaning is derived through constructional analysis. While in all Athapaskan languages that have been studied the voice/valency markers have productive functions, it has also long been recognized that lexicalization of these elements is rampant, and I turn to this topic now.

8   Lexicalization

In previous sections, I have generally used verbs with a null marking for voice/valency in their basic lexical entry. However, this is quite artificial – all the voice/valency elements (Ø, *ł*, *d* and the compound *l*) can be part of the basic lexical entry. It is thus generally assumed in the Athapaskan literature that the voice/valency elements are used idiosyncratically as well as productively; see, for instance, Kibrik (1993, 1996), Thompson (1996a) and Axelrod (1996) for recent discussion. Basically, what we see is that many different classes of verbs are compatible with the full range of voice/valency markers. All data here is from Ahtna, although similar facts are reported across the family.

   First, basic transitives can appear with any of the four voice/valency elements.

(138)   transitives
         Ø   O-G-Ø-taatl'
              kick, step on, shove O with sole of foot (323)
         Ø   O-G-Ø-ghaan
              make pl. O, kill pl. O (204)
         ł   O-G-ł-tsii
              make sg. O (204)
         d   O-d-naan
              drink O (290)
         l   O-G-l-daetl'
              eat pl. O (261)

While the middle voice hypothesis might account for the presence of *l* in 'eat pl. O' – there is low elaboration of the object – the verb 'make pl. O, kill pl. O' does not have a marking for middle voice. The verb 'make sg. O' has the causativizer; this is not surprising for a basic transitive verb, but all of these verbs are transitives.

Similar patterning is found with intransitives. The full range of voice/ valency markers is possible. The examples in (139) show intransitive verbs with agentive subjects.

(139)   Ø   Ø-bae
             sg. swim on surface (101)
         ł   ł-yaał
             jump, move, run quickly, vigorously; bird lands (423)
         d   d-tsaak'
             pl. run, leap, jump
         l   l-tlet
             sg. run, leap, jump (368)

The singular and plural of 'run, leap, jump' differ by the presence of the causativizer only. While it is possible to explain some of these forms by the middle-voice hypothesis, just which verbs are marked for middle voice and which are not, and which of those that are have *d* and which have *l* can perhaps be explained historically (see Axelrod 1996; Kibrik 1993, 1996; Thompson 1996a) but is idiosyncratic synchronically.

Intransitives with patientive subjects likewise appear with the full range of elements.

(140)   Ø   G-Ø-t'aes
             roast, fry, bake (347)
         ł   G-ł-kaets'
             enclosed object moves independently, falls
         d   G-d-caats
             be rendered, liquefied (111)
         l   G-l-ts'et
             animate or compact object moves independently, falls

Similar properties are found in other classes of verbs. The choice of voice/ valency does not appear to correlate with semantic properties in descriptive or locative verbs.

(141)   descriptive
         Ø   G-Ø-k'ats'
             weather, inanimate is cold (253)
         ł   G-ł-caax
             be big, large, tall, high, great in quantity or volume (109)
         d   G-d-gak'
             be dirty (179)
         l   G-l-ggaak
             be stout, fat, thick, big in girth (189)

(142) locative
Ø Ø-tae
    sg. animate lie, recline
ł ł-taets
    pl. animate lie, recline (331)
d d-l-ts'ii
    pl. sit, stay

In verbs relating to eating, all four voice/valency markers are possible.

(143) Ø O-G-Ø-(y)aan
          eat O
      Ø O-G-Ø-tsaet
          eat, gulp whole O
      ł O-ł-k'on
          gnaw, eat O (bone) with crunching noise
      d O-d-naek
          devour O, eat O greedily
      l O-G-l-ghel
          eat pl. O

The presence of *d /l* in the verbs 'devour O' and 'eat pl. O' might be considered to be middle voice, but one might expect 'eat, gulp whole O' to be middle voice as well. Some of these have overt marking for causativity, but not all of them do. While some of the marking for voice/valency is predictable, overall it is idiosyncratic.

Some verbs allow more than one voice/valency marker.

(144) Ø/ł G-n-Ø/ł-yaa
          grow, grow up, mature (420)
      l/d G-l/d-baats'
          be round, circular (with *n* noun class marker), be cylindrical (with *d*
          noun class marker) (99)
      l/ł G-l/ł-bets
          be wide, broad (106)
          ł uk'e'sdeyaani de-ł-bets
             table
             The table is wide
          l tsaani uk'e hwne-l-bets
             bear 3 POSS.track
             The bear's track is wide

Kari remarks in several cases that the variation in voice/valency marking is baffling.

Kibrik (1993, 1996) and Axelrod (1996) argue that much of what is called lexicalized follows from the basic functions of the voice/valency elements. Axelrod defines these basic functions as follows for Koyukon:

(145)   definitions of *d* and *ł* (Axelrod 1996)
        d   affectedness of object or subject; overlap of subjects and objects in space; indeterminacy of subject
        ł   coordinate/complex subject or object; addition of extra argument or instrument; purposeful, deliberate or habitual/attributive activity

Note that the first definition of *d*, affectedness of object or subject, differs from the middle-voice definition. Lack of individuation is more important under the middle hypothesis; under Axelrod's description, there is no reason to deny individuation, although other pieces of the definition (overlap, indeterminacy) are consistent with the middle-voice hypothesis.

Axelrod argues that *d* is used when the object is completely affected by the activity, and provides the following Koyukon pairs.

(146)   affectedness of object (Axelrod 1996)
        Ø   O-Ø-zes
            sip O (hot liquid), drink O (alcoholic beverage)
        d   O-de-noon
            drink O, absorb O (liquid)
        Ø   O-G-Ø-'oyl
            chew O (meat), bite O
        l   O-G-l-daatl
            eat pl O (pieces of meat, bits of food, scraps), snack on O

Axelrod points out that in the first of each pair, the object is not wholly affected, while in the second example of the pair, it is.

Axelrod argues that *ł* can be used when the object is coordinate or complex.

(147)   Koyukon coordinate or complex object (Axelrod 1996)
        Ø   O-de-G-Ø-tl'oo
            weave, knit O
        ł   O-ne-ł-tl'ool
            braid O, splice O by braiding

It can also be found when the subject is complex or coordinate.

(148)   Koyukon coordinate or complex subject (Axelrod 1996)
        ł   G-ł-ton
            bag or enclosed object is there
        ł   G-ł-kooł
            flat, flexible or clothlike object is there

The marker *l*, on the other hand, is used if the subject is a group or collective entity.

(149)   Koyukon group or collective subject with *l* (Axelrod 1996)
       l l-'aatl
           pl. animals, flock of waterfowl swim in group, fish spawn
       l l-'ots
           (herd, flock) mill around, move slowly; (insects) swarm

The lexical *ł* can be used with verbs with an instrument.

(150)   Koyukon instrumental verbs with *ł* (Axelrod 1996)
       ł   O-G-ł-tlaatl
           split O (wood), strike O with axe
       ł   O-G-ł-dzets
           strike, hit O with fist, punch O, box O

However, as Axelrod notes, there are verbs of this class that do not occur with *ł*.

(151)   Koyukon instrumental verbs without *ł* (Axelrod 1996)
       Ø   O-G-Ø-t'ekk
           bat, strike, beat O with sticklike object
       Ø   O-G-Ø-tletl
           chop O, strike O with axe

This is simply a sampling of the patternings noted by Axelrod. She argues that these are not completely regular, but illustrate language change – the voice/valency prefixes are obligatory, representing 'the ghost of what was once a productive grammatical and lexical system, which is now losing grammatical function, and merging its lexical, semantic character with the semantics of the stem' (21).

The uses of the causativizer described so far all involve adding an argument. Kibrik (1993) discusses a number of additional uses where argument structure is not affected. One is what he calls agentivization. A few examples are found in Navajo where a verb with an experiencer argument can have an agentive argument in the presence of the *ł* causativizer.

(152)   Navajo derived agentive subjects (Kibrik 1993, citing first edition of Young and Morgan (YM) 1987)
       Ø   yoo-'į̇
           S/he sees him/her
       ł   yini-ł-'į̇
           S/he looks at, examines him/her (YM 1980[dictionary]: 420)

> Ø disíní-ts'ą́ą́'
> You heard it
> ł yíní-ł-ts'ą́ą́'
> You listened to it (YM 1980[grammar]: 344, 767)

A second function that Kibrik assigns the ł is action perfectivization / patient affection.

(153)   Action perfectivization / patient affection (Kibrik 1993)
         Hupa
         Ø k'iwing-ya'n
         S/he ate it
         ł ch'ineh-ł-ya:n
         S/he ate it up

The causativizer is also used in action intensification in some languages.

(154)   Navajo action intensification (Kibrik 1993)
         Ø yii-nod
         S/he licks it
         ł yi-ł-naad
         S/he is licking it

Finally, the causativizer appears in comparative constructions in some languages.

(155)   Hupa comparative construction (Kibrik 1993)
         Ø ne:s
         It is long, tall
         ł 'a-ł-ne:s
         It is so long, quite tall

(156)   Navajo comparative construction (Kibrik 1993)
         Ø yi-tsoh
         It (e.g. snowfall) is big
         ł biláá 'ání-ł-tsoh
         It is bigger than that (YM 1980[dictionary]: 794, 117)

Many subpatterns exist to suggest that the ł element was once more than a causativizer. Historical accounts are often available for single lexical items or for small groups of lexical items. However, other items with what appears to be similar synchronic semantics pattern differently, making a synchronic explanation for all voice/valency marking *post hoc*. The two functions that really seem to be of productive status synchronically are those of middle voice (e.g. reflexive, reciprocal, passive, iterative, self-benefactive, errative) and causativity (with different conditions in different languages).

9   Summary and conclusions

I have argued for the following points in this chapter:

(157)   1   two major voice/valency elements
        2   middle voice
            (i)   productive in construction with some elements (e.g. passive, reflexive, reciprocal, iterative)
           (ii)   lexicalized in other cases, with many productive subpatterns
        3   causative
            (i)   productive as causativizer
           (ii)   conditions differ from language to language on whether agentive verbs can be causativized
          (iii)   causatives generally involve unwilling ('make') or non-controlling rather than willing ('let') causees
          (iv)   may be lexicalized with other subpatterns

As is obvious from this discussion of voice/valency, this system is part of the overall transitivity system of the language. Hopper and Thompson (1980) provide a number of correlates of high- and low-transitivity situations. These correlates are involved in both the argument system and the aspect system of the verb. The following table shows properties of prototypical transitivity.

(158)   Properties of prototypical transitivity (Hopper and Thompson 1980)

	high	low
participants	2 or more participants	1 participant
kinesis	action	non-action
aspect	telic	atelic
punctuality	punctual	non-punctual
volitionality	volitional	non-volitional
affirmation	affirmative	negative
mode	realis	irrealis
agency	A high in potency	A low in potency
affectedness of O	O totally affected	O not affected
individuation of O	O highly individuated	O non-individuated

The Athapaskan voice/valency markers exhibit many of the properties outlined by Hopper and Thompson, as shown in (159).

(159)   MIDDLES
between transitive and intransitive
lowly elaborated participants

CAUSATIVES
highly transitive
two or more participants
overt initiator of event
high potency subject

Athapaskan causatives represent highly transitive situations – addition of the causativizer guarantees two or more participants; introduces an overt causer, or initiator, of an event; it generally involves a volitional subject, or at least a subject that is high in potency. Middles fall between prototypical transitives and prototypical intransitives, as Kemmer (1993) points out. While, for instance, two arguments maybe involved in middles, those arguments have a single semantic referent. Alternatively, participants may be lowly elaborated and non-individuated. I will end with one final property of middles, their aspectual nature.

In (159), we see that middles fall between transitives and intransitives while causatives are highly transitive. It is interesting to note one further characteristic in many Athapaskan languages that differentiates middles (both lexical and productive) from causatives. In a number of Athapaskan languages, prefixally marked perfective morphology differs depending upon whether the verb is a middle or a causative. In particular, in causatives (lexical or productive; also with verbs without an overt voice/valency marker), the perfective prefix is present, while in middles (marked by either *d* or *l*), this prefix is absent, with the verb showing imperfective prefix morphology.

(160)   voice/valency and aspect (e.g. Navajo, Slave, Dogrib, Chipewyan, Sekani) perfective paradigms:

Ø, ł – perfective prefix /ŋ/ surfaces

d, l – perfective prefix is absent; imperfective prefix morphology

It has often been assumed that the perfective marker is present lexically in *d* and *l* voice/valency verbs, and is deleted by a phonological rule (see, for instance, Kari 1976 and Hargus and Tuttle 1997 for treatments in different phonological frameworks). The middle-voice hypothesis provides a different account. As Hopper and Thompson point out, one correlate of low transitivity is atelicity. Verbs in the middle voice are marked for punctuality, telicity and atelicity in Athapaskan languages; it is perfectivity that they lack. However, perhaps the origins of the absence of the perfective prefix in *d* and *l* voice/valency verbs lies in the voice system: in middle-voice verbs, the endpoint is not distinct from the point of initiation, and perfectivity, which requires an endpoint, is less relevant. This absence of the perfective would then be systematic and not a consequence of some idiosyncratic phonological property. This tantalizing hypothesis is worthy of further study; it may be that semantic rather than phonological factors control the appearance of the prefixal perfective marker.

Appendix 1: causatives – language survey

	Ahtna	Koyukon	Slave	Hupa	Carrier	Galice	Mattole	Navajo	Tututni
patientive intransitive	yes	yes	yes	yes	yes	yes	yes	yes	yes
agentive intransitive	yes	yes	no	no?	yes	no?	?	yes	no?
transitive	limited	yes	no	no?	limited	no?	?	limited	no?
possible control by causee	no	yes	no	no	no	?	?	no	?
possible willingness of causee	no	yes	no	no	no	?	?	no	?
causer direct/indirect	direct	direct	direct	direct	direct	?	?	direct	?
causer accidental/intentional	either	either	either	either	either	?	?	either	?
natural/effort	either	either	NA	NA	either	?	?	either	?

Appendix 2: middle voice – language survey

	Ahtna	Koyukon	Slave	Hupa	Carrier	Galice	Mattole	Navajo	Dena'ina	Tsuut'ina	Sekani	Tututni
reflexive	yes	yes	yes	no	yes	?	yes	yes	yes	no	yes	yes
reciprocal	yes	yes	yes	yes	yes	?	?	yes	yes	yes	yes	yes
indirect reflexive (intransitives)	yes	yes	yes (some)	no	?	?	?	yes	yes	?	?	?
indirect recip. (intransitives)	?	yes	yes (some)	yes ('give')	?	?	?	rare	yes	?	yes ('give')	?
self-benefactive	yes	yes	yes	yes	yes	?	?	?	yes	?	?	?
incorporated body parts*	yes	yes	yes	NA	yes	NA	NA	NA	some	yes	?	NA
mediopassive**	yes	yes	yes	yes	yes	?	?	yes	yes	yes	?	?
spontaneous middle	yes	yes	yes	?	yes	?	?	yes	?	?	?	?
passive	no					yes		yes				?
promotional	yes	yes	yes	no	yes		yes	yes	?	yes	yes	
nonpromotional	yes	yes	yes	yes	?		yes	yes	yes	yes	?	
semipassive	no	no	no	?	no	?	?	yes	no	NA	no	
1pl. subject	NA	NA	yes	yes	yes	yes	yes	yes	NA	yes	yes	yes
extension	yes	yes	?	?	?	?	?	yes	?	?	?	?
iterative	yes	yes	yes	yes	yes	?	?	yes	yes	yes	yes	yes
errative	yes	yes	NA	NA	yes	?	?	yes	yes	?	?	?
repetitive/perambulative	no	yes	yes	no	?	?	?	no	no	?	yes	?
perfective prefix in middle?	NA	NA	no	no	NA	no	no	no	NA	NA	no	?

* aspectual conditions

** medioreflexives with *d* (sticklike object – 'arms' and 'legs') or *n* (round object – 'head'); inherent reflexives

References

Aikhenvald, A.Y. Forthcoming. *Classifiers. A typology of noun classification devices.* To be published by Oxford University Press.

Arce-Aranales, M., Axelrod, M. and Fox, B. 1994. 'Active voice and middle diathesis: a cross-linguistic perspective', pp. 1–21 of *Voice: form and function*, ed. B. Fox and P. Hopper. Amsterdam: John Benjamins.

Axelrod, M. 1990. 'Incorporation in Koyukon Athapaskan', *International Journal of American Linguistics* 56.179–95.

1993. *The semantics of time: aspectual categorization in Koyukon Athapaskan.* Lincoln: University of Nebraska Press.

1996. 'Lexis, grammar, and grammatical change: the Koyukon classifier prefixes'. Paper presented at the Milwaukee conference on functionalism vs formalism.

Cook, E.-D. 1984. *A Sarcee grammar.* Vancouver: University of British Columbia Press.

Corbett, G.G. 1991. *Gender.* Cambridge: Cambridge University Press.

Dixon, R.M.W. and Aikhenvald, A.Y. 1997. 'A typology of argument-determined constructions', pp. 71–113 of *Essays on language function and language type*, ed. J. Bybee, J. Haiman and S.A. Thompson. Amsterdam: John Benjamins.

Goddard, P.E. 1905. *The morphology of the Hupa language*, University of California Publications 3. Berkeley: University of California Press.

Golla, V. 1970. 'Hupa grammar'. Ph.D. dissertation. University of California, Berkeley.

1985. *A short practical grammar of Hupa.* Hoopa, Calif.: Hoopa Valley Tribe.

1997. 'The "indefinite" deictic subject pronoun in California Athabaskan'. Talk presented at the Athapaskan Languages Conference, University of Oregon, Eugene, Oregon. May.

Hale, K. and Platero, P. 1996. 'Navajo reflections of a general theory of lexical argument structure', pp. 1–13 of *Athabaskan language studies: essays in honor of Robert W. Young*, ed. S. Midgette, E. Jelinek, K. Rice and L. Saxon. Albuquerque: University of New Mexico Press.

Hargus, S. 1988. *The lexical phonology of Sekari.* New York: Garland.

Hargus, S. and Tuttle, S. 1997. 'Augmentation as affixation in Athabaskan languages', *Phonology* 14.177–220.

Hoijer, H. 1966. 'Galice Athapaskan: a grammatical sketch', *International Journal of American Linguistics* 32.320–7.

Hopper, P.J. and Thompson, S.A. 1980. 'Transitivity in grammar and discourse', *Language* 56.251–99.

Jones, E. and Jetté, J. Forthcoming. *Koyukon Athabaskan dictionary.* Fairbanks: Alaska Native Language Center.

Kari, J. 1976. *Navajo verb prefixing.* New York: Garland.

1990. *Ahtna Athabaskan dictionary.* Fairbanks: Alaska Native Language Center.

Kemmer, S. 1993. *The middle voice*, Typological studies in language 23. Amsterdam and Philadelphia: John Benjamins.

Kibrik, A.A. 1993. 'Transitivity increase in Athabaskan languages', pp. 47–67 of *Causatives and transitivity*, ed. B. Comrie and M. Polinsky. Amsterdam, Philadelphia: John Benjamins.

1996. 'Transitivity decrease in Navajo and Athabaskan: actor-affecting propositional derivations', pp. 259–303 of *Athabaskan language studies: essays in honor of Robert W. Young*, ed. E. Jelinek, S. Midgette, K. Rice and L. Saxon. Albuquerque: University of New Mexico Press.

Krauss, M. 1969. 'On the classification of the Athapaskan, Eyak, and the Tlingit verb', *International Journal of American Linguistics*, Supplement, 35.49–83.

Li F.-K. 1930. *Mattole, an Athapaskan language*. Chicago: University of Chicago Press.

McDonough, J. 1989. 'Argument structure and the Athapaskan "classifier" prefix', *Proceedings of the West Coast Conference on Formal Linguistics* 8.220–45.

Morice, A.G. 1932. *The Carrier language*, Vol. II. St.-Gabriel-Mödling, Austria: Anthropos.

Rice, K. 1989. *A grammar of Slave*. Berlin: Mouton de Gruyter.

    1991. 'Intransitives in Slave (Northern Athapaskan): arguments for unaccusatives', *International Journal of American Linguistics* 57.51–69.

    Forthcoming-a. 'Monadic verbs and argument structure in Ahtna, Navajo, and Slave'. In *Athabaskan language and linguistics*, ed. T. Fernald and P. Platero. Oxford: Oxford University Press.

    Forthcoming-b. *Morpheme order and semantic scope: word formation in the Athapaskan verb*. Cambridge: Cambridge University Press.

Saxon, L. 1990. 'Dogrib passives'. Paper presented at the Conference on Athapaskan Languages and Linguistics, University of British Columbia, Vancouver, British Columbia.

Saxon, L. and Rice, K. 1993. 'On subject-verb constituency: evidence from Athapaskan languages', *Proceedings of the West Coast Conference on Formal Linguistics* 11.434–50.

Stanley, R. 1969. 'The phonology of the Navaho verb'. Ph.D. dissertation, MIT.

Story, G. 1989. 'The Athapaskan first duoplural subject prefix', pp. 487–531 of *Athapaskan linguistics: current perspectives on a language family*, ed. E.-D. Cook and K. Rice. Berlin: Mouton de Gruyter.

Tenenbaum, J. 1978. 'Morphology and semantics of the Tanaina verb'. Ph.D. dissertation. Columbia University.

Thompson, C. 1989a. 'Voice and obviation in Athabaskan and other languages'. Ph.D. dissertation. University of Oregon.

    1989b. 'Pronouns and voice in Koyukon Athabaskan: a text-based study', *International Journal of American Linguistics* 55.1–24.

    1989c. 'Voice and obviation in Navajo', pp. 466–88 of *Proceedings of the Fourth Annual Meeting of the Pacific Linguistics Conference*. Eugene: Department of Linguistics, University of Oregon.

    1996a. 'The Na-Dene middle voice: an impersonal source of the D-element', *International Journal of American Linguistics* 62.351–78.

    1996b. 'The history and function of the yi-/bi- alternation in Athabaskan', pp. 81–100 of *Athabaskan language studies: essays in honor of Robert W. Young*, ed. E. Jelinek, S. Midgette, K. Rice and L. Saxon. Albuquerque: University of New Mexico Press.

Willie, M.A. and Jelinek, E. 1996. 'Navajo as a discourse configurational language'. Paper presented to the Conference on Athabaskan Syntax and Semantics, Swarthmore College, Pennsylvania, April.

Young, R.W. and Morgan, W. 1987. *The Navajo language: a grammar and colloquial dictionary*, 2nd edn. Albuquerque: University of New Mexico Press.

Young, R.W. and Morgan, W. with Midgette, S. 1992. *Analytical lexicon of Navajo*. Albuquerque: University of New Mexico Press.

7 Valency-changing derivations in K'iche'

LYLE CAMPBELL

1 Introduction

In this chapter the principal valency-changing derivations in K'iche' are described, following Dixon and Aikhenvald's (1997) framework. K'iche', spoken by 658,000 in highland Guatemala, is a Mayan language of the K'ichean subgroup.[1] It is particularly relevant for those interested in valency-changing derivations, since it has two distinct passive constructions, two separate antipassive constructions, and an 'instrumental voice' applicative construction, among other things.[2] These various constructions have a range of functions, and some exhibit idiosyncrasies that have proved vexing to formal theories (see, for example, Davies and Sam-Colop 1990; Hale and Storto forthcoming; Larsen 1987; and Trechsel 1982, 1993). In this attempt to characterize K'iche' valency-changing derivations, I present each of these constructions in turn, considering their morphology, basic meaning, syntactic functions and some of the peculiarities that are relevant to understanding them.

2 Transitivity

A grasp of K'iche' verb classes and their morphology is necessary in order to understand the valency-changing constructions; therefore, I begin with a brief

---

[1] K'iche' is also spelled 'Quiché'; 'K'iche'' is the official spelling now used in Guatemala, but 'Quiché' was the general spelling before the 1980s. I gratefully acknowledge helpful feedback on an earlier version of this chapter from Alexandra Y. Aikhenvald and R.M.W. Dixon, though of course they are innocent of any misuse I may have made of their comments.

[2] It should be pointed out that while there is a reasonably large literature on these constructions of K'iche', much of it relies on Mondloch's work, particularly his 1981 dissertation, which is an excellent and extremely thorough treatment of the topic. I have utilized all this literature liberally in this paper, but feel it important to point out Mondloch's special position and unique contribution to these studies.

Figure 7.1. K'iche' cross-referencing Ergative and Absolutive verb prefixes

S/O function (Absolutive, traditionally called 'set B'):

-in-	1sg.ABS	*-ox-* (or *-ux-*)	1pl.ABS[3]
-at-	2sg.ABS (familiar)	*-iš-*	2pl.ABS (familiar)
lah	2sg.ABS (reverential)[4]	*alaq*	2pl.ABS (reverential)
-Ø-	3sg.ABS	*-e:(b')-*	3pl.ABS[5]

A function (Ergative, traditionally called 'set A') pronominal markers have two variants, depending on whether the root they are attached to begins in a consonant or a vowel:

C-initial		V-initial	
in-		*w-/(inw-)*	1sg.ERG
a-		*aw-*	2sg.ERG (familiar)
	lah		2sg (reverential)
u-		*r-*	3sg.ERG
qa-		*q-*	1pl.ERG
i-		*iw-*	2pl.ERG (familiar)
	alaq		2pl (reverential)
ki-		*k-*	3pl.ERG

overview of transitivity in K'iche'. K'iche' is an ergative language, where ergative alignment is signalled through cross-referencing pronominal prefixes on the verb, shown in figure 7.1.

K'iche' exhibits none of the split ergativity characteristic of some ergative languages. Moreover, while basically morphologically ergative, most of its

---

[3] There is variation in the literature about how the 1st person plural absolutive prefix is written. The independent 1st person plural pronoun is invariably *ox*; however, the absolutive prefix seems to vary between *-ox-* and *-ux-*. The dialect represented in Mondloch's work is Nahualá, where it is *-ux-*, and therefore this is the form given in much of the literature on K'iche'. Here, I make no attempt to regularize one or the other of these, but rather simply repeat the variant presented in the sources utilized.

[4] K'iche' has (in most dialects, not all) two sets of 2nd person pronouns; those which I call 'reverential' (*lah* '2sg.REV' and *alaq* '2pl.REV') are sometimes also called 'formal' and 'honorific' in the linguistic literature on the language. Their function is more honorific, reverential, deferential than the typical formal/informal contrast such as in Spanish *tu/usted*; that is, while in European languages the semantic attributes of power and social distance are associated with the formal 2nd person pronouns and solidarity with the informal, in K'iche' the power/solidarity dimension is less important and thus the reverential pronoun may be freely used, for example, with friends and family in ceremonial settings where reverence is in order, with an older person, and with people who are charged with high responsibility in the rotating civil–religious hierarchy. Since the reverential pronouns are never cross-referenced on the verb in any way, but are always present in full form in the sentences which contain them (unlike other independent pronouns, which are optional), they are not represented with a *-Ø-* in the verbal morphology. Since they have no cross-referencing and appear in the same form in A, O, S and oblique contexts, in a few cases it is difficult to determine clearly their role in the clause.

[5] The 3pl.ABS varies in the dialects, with *eb'* (its oldest form) alternating with *e?* or *e:*. In the better-known dialects, it is most frequently *e:*, but shows up also as *eb'* sometimes, for example before vowel-initial morphemes in some cases.

syntactic rules are not sensitive to ergativity, although we will see that it does have a syntactic pivot which gives it a degree of syntactic ergativity (see below).

Some seemingly minor features of the pronominal system are significant for understanding valency-changing derivations in K'iche', and therefore it is necessary to bear three of these in mind.

First, in modern K'iche', *in-* marks 1sg in both Absolutive and Ergative functions, though in Colonial K'iche', 1sg.ERG was *nu-*, which has since shifted to *in-*, making the 1sg.ERG and 1sg.ABS homophonous. This homophony motivates the use of valency derivations to avoid ambiguities in some cases (discussed below). The set of ergative prefixes is identical to the set of possessive pronominal prefixes, except for *nu-* 'my' which occurs with consonant-initial roots; both the Ergative set and the possessives have the two variants, one used with consonant-initial forms and the other with vowel-initial forms (seen in figure 7.1), as illustrated in:

(1)   Consonant-initial
(a)   qa-ts'i:?   (b)   š-Ø-qa-ts'ib'-a:x
      1pl.POSS-dog   ASP-3sg.ABS-1pl.ERG-write-TR
      our-dog   We wrote it

      Vowel-initial
(c)   q-ik   (d)   š-Ø-q-il-oh
      1pl.POSS-chili   ASP-3sg.ABS-1pl.ERG-see-TR
      our-chili   We saw it

Second, K'iche' has reverential 2nd person pronouns (sg and pl), which are distinct from the 2nd person familiar forms (seen in figure 7.1). The reverential 2nd person forms differ from other K'iche' pronouns in that they take no cross-referencing affixes in the verb, neither in S/O function nor in A function (that is, they are marked the same way in transitive and intransitive verbs – i.e. they lack any overt marking). Numerous examples of these are seen throughout this chapter.

Third, it is essentially only human nouns which can bear overt morphological plurals in K'iche', though plurality of a noun can be shown by the 3rd person plural pronominal affixes on verbs which cross-reference a nominal (which itself may bear no formal distinction between singular and plural). However, sometimes singular agreement is also used with semantically plural (but morphologically unmarked) NPs, in which case plurality is determined by context rather than by explicit grammatical marking. For example, in (2) and (3) *le: ts'i?* 'the dogs' / 'the dog' has the same form, where the plurality in (2) and singularity in (3) is conveyed by the difference, not in the NP, but in the verb between the plural (-*e:*-) and singular (-*Ø*-) prefixes:

(2)   š-e:-kam   le: ts'iʔ
        ASP-3pl.ABS-die the dog
        The dogs died[6]

(3)   š-Ø-kam   le: ts'iʔ
        ASP-3sg.ABS-die the dog
        The dog died

Notice in (4) that *le: ačix-a:b'* 'the men', with an overtly marked morphological plural (-*a:b'*), and *le: ts'iʔ* 'the dogs', with no visible marker of plurality, are nonetheless each cross-referenced with 3rd person plural agreement markers in the verb:

(4)   š-e:-ki-kam-isa:-x   le: ts'iʔ le: ačix-a:b'
        ASP-3pl.ABS-3pl.ERG-die-CAUS-TR the dog the man-pl
        The men killed the dogs

2.1   Verb classes

K'iche' has three classes of verbs, TRANSITIVES, INTRANSITIVES and POSITIONALS, each with its own set of morphological markers.

2.1.1   Intransitive

Intransitive verbs are characterized morphologically by (1) pronominal prefixes in the S function (absolutive) and (2) an 'intransitive' suffix, -*ik*, which occurs only when the verb is phrase-final (before a pause), but is not present when the verb is followed by another word, as seen in the comparison of (5) with (6):

---

[6] It may be helpful to point out that K'iche' articles and demonstratives have a visible / not visible distinction; thus *le:* 'the.visible', *ri* 'the.not.visible'. Note also that *are:* 'this, he' is *areʔ* in isolation but *are:* before other words in many K'iche' dialects, though it is *areʔ* everywhere in a few. This word also functions as a focus marker and is translated by many as 'Focus' (FOC) in cleft and similar constructions. In this chapter, I cite the examples taken from other sources by transliterating those written in the practical orthography into linguistic symbols and give the morpheme-by-morpheme glosses in the same format throughout. In some cases, the vowel length of K'iche' comes out inconsistently, though I have tried to make it consistent in these examples, since in a few dialects cited by some linguists (see, for example, Sam-Colop 1988, and Davies and Sam-Colop 1990), most of the long vowels have merged with corresponding short vowels. With respect to articles and demonstratives, sources cite vowel length and presence or absence of glottal stop with considerable variation and often inconsistency, some of it conditioned by legitimate variation within the variety described. A particular difference is that very few forms in K'iche' end in a vowel, though final *h* is difficult to hear and variable, and is often transcribed by non-linguists as absent or as length on the preceding vowel. I have restored the *h* in these forms.

(5)   š-at-war-ik
        ASP-2sg.ABS-sleep-INTR
        You slept

(6)   š-at-war   xela:?
        ASP-2sg.ABS-sleep there
        You slept there[7]

2.1.2   Transitive

Transitive verbs divide into two subclasses, each with its own set of suffixes: root (or non-derived, 'monosyllabic') transitives, traditionally abbreviated 'RTV' in Mayan linguistics, and derived (also called 'polysyllabic'), abbreviated 'DTV'. It is important to keep these two kinds of transitives and their associated morphology in mind in order to understand the valency-changing processes discussed in this chapter. DTVs end in -*x* 'transitive' (both phrase-finally and non-phrase-finally); RTVs take -*oh* (or -*uh* if the vowel of the verb root is *u*) when the verb occurs phrase-finally (as in (7a)), but nothing when the verb is followed by another word in the clause (as in (7b)):

(7) (a)   š-Ø-ki-k'uš-uh
          ASP-3sg.ABS-3pl.ERG-chew-TR
          They chewed it

(b)   š-Ø-ki-k'uš   le: ats'yaq le: č'oh
          ASP-3sg.ABS-3pl.ERG-chew the clothes the mouse
          The mice chewed the clothes

---

[7] One interesting oddity in several Mayan languages is the type of intransitive sentence which seems to exhibit higher transitivity than would be expected of intransitive verbs, sentences which in semantic effect have an A-role NP – albeit signalled obliquely – acting on an S-role NP as though it were an underlying O. These are used quite frequently in Jakalteko, Mam and other Mayan languages of the Huehuetenango region, but somewhat less frequently in K'iche'. Two K'iche' examples are:

(1)   š-Ø-ul   le: wu:x w-uma:l
        ASP-3sg.ABS-arrive the book 1sg.POSS-by
        The book arrived by me/I brought the book
                                    (Larsen and Norman 1979: 349; Kaufman 1990: 77)

(2)   š-Ø-b'e:h   le: wu:x r-uma:l
        ASP-3sg.ABS-go the letter 3sg.POSS-by
        The letter went by her / She sent the letter   (Trechsel 1982: 80)

These are in effect causative sentences in which the intransitive verb exhibits no derivational causative morphology (though K'iche' has a productive causative suffix, -*(i)sa*- (see §5), which could have occurred), but which nevertheless appear to take an agent in an oblique 'by' phrase. The -*uma:l* phrase means 'by, through, because of' (and is used to express the 'by' phrase of real passives – see §3.1), and sentences such as these have the feel of being on their way from an ordinary 'because of' sense towards a grammaticalization of a causative of intransitive verbs.

One constraint on transitive clauses is that a 3rd person A (sg or pl) and a 2nd person reverential O (sg or pl) cannot co-occur; sentences such as (8) and (9) are ungrammatical:

(8)   *k-u-toʔ   lah   ri   ačih
      ASP-3sg.ERG-help 2sg.REV.ABS the man
      The man helps you

(9)   *k-ki-toʔ   alaq   ri   išoq-i:b'
      ASP-3pl.ERG-help 2pl.REV.ABS the women
      The women help you

The simple passive is often used to avoid this problem (see below).

A related constraint is that transitive clauses which would have combinations of 1st person singular *-in-* (ERG or ABS) and 2nd person reverential (sg or pl) as core arguments are avoided and the absolutive antipassive is preferred instead (see below). Thus, (10a) is avoided, generally given instead in the absolutive antipassive counterpart, as shown in (10b) (Mondloch 1979: 173–5):

(10) (a) ?š-in-tsuku-x   lah
          ASP-1sg.ERG-look.for-TR 2sg.REV.ABS
          I looked for you

(b) š-in-tsuku-n   č-e:h   lah
     ASP-1sg.ABS-look.for-ABS.ANT to.3sg.POSS-to 2sg.REV
     I looked for you

These two constraints are seen more clearly in table 7.1 (where '+' means 'can co-occur' and '–' means 'does not co-occur').

Table 7.1. Constraints on transitive clauses

	1O	2Osg.REV	2Opl.REV	3O
1Asg		(–)	(–)	+
1Apl		+	+	+
2A	+			+
3Asg	+	–	–	+
3Apl	+	–	–	+

2.1.3   Positionals

The third class of verbs, positionals, are verbal/adjectival roots whose meaning has to do with positions and shapes. They are distinguished from other verb classes in that: (1) they typically have the semantic property of referring to positions or qualities of objects (e.g. 'sit', 'stand', 'squat', 'lie face up', 'lie face down', 'duck down', etc.); (2) by means of special suffixes which occur only with positional roots, positionals can be derived to form adjectives, intransitive verbs or causatives; (3) all positional roots have the shape CVC; and (4) they do not occur as simple inflected stems without derivational affixes (Norman 1973, Mondloch 1976). Some of the derivational morphology used uniquely with positionals is illustrated in the following:

-V₁l positional adjectives:

$\qquad$ ts'uy-ul   'seated/sitting' (adjective)
$\qquad$ tak'-al   'standing'

-iʔ intransitive inchoative ('to assume position or state X'):

$\qquad$ š-Ø-ts'uy-iʔ-ik   'she sat'
$\qquad$ š-Ø-tak'-iʔ lah   'you (REV) stood'

-V₁-b'aʔ causative:

$\qquad$ k-Ø-u-ts'uyu-b'aʔ   'he seats it'
$\qquad$ k-Ø-u-tak'a-b'aʔ   'he stands it up'

2.1.4   Some categories which K'iche' doesn't have

Given that K'iche' clauses are clearly marked either transitive or intransitive morphologically, surface ambitransitives (verbs used in both intransitive and transitive clauses) are essentially unknown, though the same root can undergo derivational processes whereby it can be encountered in clauses of different valency.[8] K'iche' also has no specific marking for extended transitives; arguments which are not core A, O or S arguments are generally present only in oblique constructions. The oblique constructions in Mayan languages are based on possessed noun roots (possession shown by possessive pronominal prefixes). These constructions are called relational nouns in Mayan (and Mesoamerican) linguistic literature; relational nouns signal the sort of locations and relations that are shown by prepositions in English. A typical example is *č(i)r-e:h* 'to/for him, her, it', made up of *či* 'in, at' + *r-* '3sg.POSS' + *-e:h* 'to' (etymologically from **e:h* 'tooth'; *č(i)r-e:h* is often contracted – unlike most other relational nouns – to *če:h*). In Mayan languages these relational nouns are obligatorily possessed. In the case of underlying core NP arguments of verbs which are placed in oblique phrases through various derivations, 'the nominal that bears the grammatical relation acts as the

---

[8] There is a minor class which is related to the notion of ambitransitives, but to understand its characteristics, it is necessary first to have in mind the valency derivations, especially the antipassives; for that reason, we come back to this topic later.

possessor of the relational noun and is cross-referenced by the appropriate morpheme from the set of ergative [*sic*, read 'possessive'] agreement markers' (Davies and Sam-Colop 1990: 525).

2.2   *Constituent order*

Constituent order in K'iche' is variable but far from entirely free. Much has been written on K'iche' word order; aspects of it are well understood and yet there are differences of opinion concerning some matters. One thing that is clear is that constituent order in K'iche' on the whole is a poor indicator of the semantic roles of NP arguments in transitive clauses. While it is generally agreed that VOA is the most common and most neutral, constituent order is relatively flexible, and all the other logical orders do occur (under conditions of focus and topicalization; see Nik'te' and Saqijix 1993: 131–2; Larsen 1987; Sam-Colop 1988: 8–11).

In reality, transitive clauses with two overt core arguments (overt NPs) are rare. Mondloch (1978b) found only 20 transitive sentences containing both an A and an O nominal NP in 1,380 lines of transcribed narrative, and while VOA was in the lead (7 instances), examples of all the other logically possible orders also occurred (AVO, AOV, OVA, OAV, VAO). Larsen (1987: 40) characterizes K'iche' as both a 'pro-drop' or 'null-subject' and 'null-object' language, since A, S and O can be missing, indicated solely by pronominal cross-referencing prefixes in the verb. This being the case, sentences with external NPs very often are not in the most neutral order (VOA), but reflect processes of focussing or topicalization (see below). Moreover, VOA is not the most frequent order in elicitation, either, but this sort of elicitation creates a discourse context suggestive of emphasis, in which it is necessary to introduce a discourse topic, which tends to appear in preverbal topic position. This, then, often brings forth AVO, which reflects this focus/emphasis (cf. Larsen 1987; more details below). There may be an important fieldwork lesson in this for studies of constituent order (word order) based on direct elicitation, namely, that caution in interpreting data collected in this way is called for.

In sum, constituent order is too flexible to be a reliable gauge for distinguishing A from O in transitive clauses. In most of Mondloch's 20 cases, semantics or context left the sentences clearly unambiguous, but some ambiguous cases are possible – whenever both A and O are 3rd persons of the same number. This is an important point for our interest in valency changing, since one significant function of the antipassives and passives in K'iche' is to disambiguate sentences where the role of the A and O participants is not otherwise clear (see below). Some examples of this ambiguity are:

(11)   š-Ø-u-kuna-x   ri ačih ri išoq
        ASP-3sg.ABS-3sg.ERG-cure-TR the man the woman
        (1)   The woman cured the man
        (2)   The man cured the woman (Mondloch 1978b: 11)

(12)   š-Ø-pe: ri ačih ri š-Ø-u-kuna-x   ri išoq
        ASP-3sg.ABS-come the man REL ASP-3sg.ABS-3sg.ERG-cure-TR the woman
        (1)   The man whom the woman cured came
        (2)   The man who cured the woman came (Mondloch 1978b: 6)

(13)   xači:n š-Ø-u-kuna-x   ri ačih
        who   ASP-3sg.ABS-3sg.ERG-cure-tr the man
        (1)   Whom did the man cure?
        (2)   Who cured the man? (Mondloch 1978b: 6)

After we have seen how the valency derivations work, we will come back to such ambiguous sentences to see how they are typically disambiguated through the use of one of the other valency devices. Also, we will see that there are constraints against some of these possibilities.

In cases where both the A and O person markers in the verb are 3rd persons of the same number and there is a single external NP, this NP is generally interpreted as O, as in (Mondloch 1979: 168):

(14)   š-e:-ki-to?   ri ačix-a:b'
        ASP-3pl.ABS-3pl.ERG-help the man-pl
        They helped the men / (rather than 'the men helped them')

This is consistent with the general claim that new information is introduced through NPs in O (and S) roles, and usually not through A-role NPs.

Finally, K'iche', unlike some languages, is not at all timid about having inanimate As, e.g.:

(15)   k-Ø-u-yak   nu-xolo:m   le: puqla:x
        ASP-3sg.ABS-3sg.ERG-irritate 1sg.POSS-head the dust
        The dust irritates my head [my nose and mouth]

(16)   š-Ø-u-qax-isa:-x   ri ab'i:š   ri saqb'ač
        ASP-3sg.ABS-3sg.ERG-descend-CAUS-TR the cornfield the hail
        The hail knocked down the corn

3   Derivations which remove an argument from the core

3.1   Simple passive

The simple passive is signalled by the morphological markers: -*š* with DTVs, and vowel length in RTVs. Note that the lengthened vowel which marks the passive in the root transitives comes historically from an infixed *-h-* in Proto-K'ichean (and Proto-Mayan). A few examples of RTV active/passive pairs are: *b'it/b'i:t* 'tear / be torn', *b'an/b'a:n* 'do, make / be done, made' *k'ut/k'u:t* 'show / be shown' and *loq'/lo:q'* 'buy / be bought'. (In some dialects, the length is no longer visible before a root-final /ʔ/, *yaʔ* (or *ya:ʔ*) 'give'.) The passive is intransitive in form, permitting only one core argument, S (absolutive), which is interpreted as the underlying O (underlying patient / transitive direct object), and the underlying A is either omitted (as in (17a)) or demoted to an oblique 'by' phrase signalled by the relational noun *-uma:l* 'by' which bears possessive prefixes which indicate the person and number of the underlying A, as in (17b). These two are compared with an active transitive version in (17c):

(17) (a)　k-ox-to:ʔ-ik
　　　　　ASP-1pl.ABS-help.PASS-INTR
　　　　　We are helped

(b)　　　k-ox-to:ʔ　　　　　　k-uma:l
　　　　　ASP-1pl.ABS-help.PASS　3pl.POSS-by
　　　　　We are helped by them

(c)　　　k-ox-ki-toʔ-oh
　　　　　ASP-1pl.ABS-3pl.ERG-help-TR
　　　　　They help us

As for the function/meaning of the simple passive, 'the emphasis is placed on the object with the emphasis on the action done to the object' (Mondloch 1978a: 62). The passives are marked as intransitives by taking S (absolutives) as the only permitted core argument and by the intransitive suffix, phrase-final *-ik*, as in (18) and (19):

(18)　　　š-Ø-ča:p-ik [RTV]
　　　　　ABS-3sg.ABS-grab.PASS-INTR
　　　　　She was caught

(19)　　　k-e:-šib'i-š-ik [DTV]
　　　　　ASP-3pl.ABS-scare-PASS-INTR
　　　　　They were frightened

Compare the active (the (a) sentences) and passive (the (b) sentences) in the following examples:

(20) (a)　š-Ø-u-loq'　　　　　　xun k'aʔa:m r-ule:w ri　w-ika:n
　　　　　ASP-3sg.ABS-3sg.ERG-buy　one cord　his-land the　my-uncle
　　　　　My uncle bought a measure of land (Nik'te' and Saqijix 1993: 135)

(b)   š-Ø-lo:q'   xun k'aʔa:m ule:w r-uma:l   ri w-ika:n
ASP-3sg.ABS-buy.PASS one cord   land 3sg.POSS-by the my-uncle
A measure of land was bought by my uncle (Nik'te' and Saqijix 1993: 136)

(21) (a) š-e:-ki-q'alu:-x   ri ak'al-a:b' ri tixonel-a:b'
ASP-3pl.ABS-3pl.ERG-hug-TR the child-pl the teacher-pl
The teachers hugged the children (Nik'te' and Saqijix 1993: 136)

(b)   š-e:-q'alu-š   ri ak'al-a:b' k-uma:l   ri tixonel-a:b'
ASP-3pl.ABS-hug-PASS the child-pl 3pl.POSS-by the teacher-pl
The children were hugged by the teachers (Nik'te' and Saqijix 1993: 136)

The simple passive is used also when the speaker wishes to ignore the underlying A (transitive subject) or to give it only secondary importance. Compare the following active–passive contrasts illustrated in (22a–c):

(22) (a) š-Ø-u-ti?   ri ak'a:l ri ts'i?
ASP-3sg.ABS-3sg.ERG-bite the child the dog
The dog bit the child

(b)   š-Ø-ti:?   ri ak'a:l r-uma:l   ri ts'i?
ASP-3sg.ABS-bite.PASS the child 3sg.POSS-by the dog
The child was bitten by the dog

(c)   š-Ø-ti:?   ri ak'a:l
ASP-3sg.ABS-bite.PASS the child
The child was bitten

There is an important constraint on the simple passive: if the underlying A (logical transitive subject) is not a 3rd person, the clause cannot be passivized with this construction. That is, for the simple passive, the argument in A role cannot be a 1st or 2nd person form (sg or pl). For example, (23a) has no corresponding simple passive as shown by the ungrammaticality of (23b):

(23) (a) š-Ø-in-č'a:b'e-x   ri ačih
ASP-3sg.ABS-1sg.ERG-speak-TR the man
I spoke to the man

(b)   *š-Ø-č'a:b'e-š   ri ačih w-uma:l
ASP-3sg.ABS-speak-PASS the man 1sg.POSS-by
*The man was spoken to by me (Mondloch 1979: 208–9)

(There is no such constraint on the completive passive, see below.) This is not an uncommon constraint; many languages have passives which cannot apply to underlying 1st or 2nd person As. Since this passive emphasizes underlying Os, and since in the animacy hierarchy 1st and 2nd persons are more frequently As, this constraint is typologically plausible.

Above (§2.1.2), the constraint was pointed out whereby an active transitive clause with a 3rd person A (sg or pl) cannot have a 2nd person reverential (sg or pl) as O. Frequently the simple passive is used to express the equivalent of these clauses. In these instances, the 3rd person A is presented in the oblique 'by' phrase. Compare the following pairs, where the (a) sentences are the acceptable simple passive version, and the (b) sentences are the expected but prohibited and ungrammatical active transitive version:

(24) (a) k-to:ʔ   lah   r-uma:l   ri   ačih
ASP-help.PASS 2sg.REV.ABS 3sg.POSS-by the man
You are helped by the man

(b)   *k-u-toʔ   lah   ri   ačih
ASP-3sg.ERG-help 2sg.REV.ABS the man
*The man helps you

(25) (a) k-to:ʔ   alaq   k-uma:l   ri   išoq-i:bʼ
ASP-help.PASS 2pl.REV.ABS 3pl.POSS-by the woman-pl
You are helped by the women

(b)   *k-ki-toʔ   alaq   ri   išoq-i:bʼ
ASP-3pl.ERG-help 2pl.REV.ABS the woman-pl
*The women helps you

Finally, the simple passive is in no way like the constructions known in some languages – which are sometimes called passive – which are used specifically to keep any A role NP out of the picture (like the Finnish 'impersonal' passive, for example). Rather, it is claimed that K'iche' speakers seem always to have a 'someone' in mind as involved in the action in these passive sentences even when no -*uma:l* 'by' phrase is present to specify the underlying A participant (see Mondloch 1979). This can be seen in the passivized versions of verbs which contain directional prefixes. K'iche' verbs can take the directional prefixes -*ul*- 'hither' (historically from *ul* 'arrive') and -*e:*- 'thither' (historically from *b'e:h* 'go'). In the case of passivized verbs containing these directionals, the 'coming hither' or 'going thither' is attributed to an agent whether or not one is specified overtly in the clause. For example, in (26) it is some unspecified agent who is 'going' in order to get the bench, and not 'the bench' which is cross-referenced with the 3sg.ABS -Ø- marked on the verb that is 'going' (Mondloch 1979: 221). (Note in the following examples, that the directionals require the verb to bear the suffix used in other contexts for dependent clauses (here labelled DEP): -*oq* phrase-finally and its allomorph -*ah* non-phrase-finally.)

(26)   š-Ø-e:-k'a:m-ah   ri   te:m
       ASP-3sg.ABS-DIR.go-get.PASS-DEP the bench
       Someone went to get the bench
       Not: *The bench goes to be gotten

(27)   k-in-ul-sik'i-š-oq
       ASP-1sg.ABS-DIR.come-call-PASS-DEP
       Someone comes to call me (i.e. I get called and someone comes to do that)
       Not: *I come to be called

3.2   Completive passive

The completive passive (which has also been called 'the inchoative-stative passive': Mondloch 1978b) is very different from the simple passive in a number of ways. It is formed by the suffix -*(V)tax* on both RTVs (-*k'ut-utax* 'get shown', -*mes-tax* 'get swept') and DTVs (-*tsuku-tax* 'get looked for', -*kamisa-tax* 'get killed'). The verb is intransitivized, with the underlying O promoted to S and the underlying A-role participant either deleted or demoted to an oblique 'by' phrase. When in phrase-final position, the completive passive verb can take the intransitive morpheme -*ik*, but this is optional (it is not optional with other intransitive roots and derived intransitive verb forms). The completive passive conveys the meaning of the completion of an action (– more *Aktionsart* than 'aspect'). The primary function of the completive passive is to emphasize 'the result of the activity and/or its termination' (Dayley 1981: 24; see also Sam-Colop 1990: 136). Mondloch (1978a: 62) defines it in the following way:

> the spotlight [is] focused on the object of the verb phrase, but now we are not concentrating so much on the action done to it [as in the simple passive] as we are on <u>emphasizing the condition or state of the object</u>, resulting from the action done to it. Therefore, . . . [k-Ø-k'ayi-tax-ik [ASP-3sg.ABS-sell-CMPL.PASS-INTR]] means 'it will get sold', or 'it will finish being sold'. [Completive passive] here emphasizes the 'becoming' (coming-to-be in a state). [Emphasis in the original.]

Sentences (28–30) illustrate this passive:

(28)   š-Ø-kam-isa-tax   le: utiw   q-uma:l
       ASP-3sg.ABS-die-CAUS-CMPL.PASS the coyote 1pl.POSS-by
       The coyote got killed by us

(29)   k-kuna-tax   lah
       ASP-cure-CMPL.PASS 2sg.REV.ABS
       You will get cured

(30)   š-Ø-pili-tax   xun ak'   r-uma:l   le: išoq
            ASP-3sg.ABS-butcher-CMPL.PASS one chicken 3sg.POSS-by the woman
            A chicken got butchered by the woman

As seen in (28) and (29), with the completive passive there is no constraint against an underlying A (logical transitive subject) which is not a 3rd person, as there is with the simple passive (cf. §3.1). Here, the completive passive has no constraint against 1st and 2nd person agents appearing in the -*uma:l* 'by' phrase, as the simple passive does; agents in any person may optionally be expressed in the -*uma:l* 'by' phrase, whether 1st, 2nd or 3rd person, illustrated further in (Mondloch 1979: 240):

(31)   š-Ø-mes-tax   le: u-pa: xa:h w-uma:l
            ASP-3sg.ABS-sweep-CMPL.PASS the 3sg.POSS-interior house 1sg.POSS-by
            The inside of the house got swept by me

(32)   š-ux-tixo-tax   iw-uma:l
            ASP-1pl.ABS-teach-CMPL.PASS 2pl.POSS-by
            We got instructed by you

Compare the following, where (33a) is the completive passive and (33b) is the simple passive counterpart, which is ungrammatical:

(33) (a)   š-in-č'ay-tax   aw-uma:l
            ASP-1sg.ABS-hit-CMPL.PASS 2sg.POSS-by
            I got hit by you

(b)   *š-in-č'a:y   aw-uma:l
            ASP-1sg.ABS-hit.PASS 2sg.POSS-by
            *I got hit by you

As seen in (34), the S cross-referencing affix, -*e:*- 3pl.ABS agrees in person and number with the surface subject (underlying O) of the clause, *ri ak'ala:b'* 'the children (plural)' in this case, and not with the demoted A, *ki-ta:t* 'their father', underlyingly singular in this case:

(34)   š-e:-tsuqu-tax   ri ak'al-a:b' r-uma:l   ki-ta:t
            ASP-3pl.ABS-feed-CMPL.PASS the child-pl 3sg.POSS-by their-father
            The children got fed by their father

Also, as with the simple passives, speakers interpret the completive passive clauses as having an underlying agent even where none is specified by an -*uma:l* 'by' phrase. Thus, just as with the simple passives, when the directional affixes are present in the verb, they are attributed to an agent, to 'someone' or 'somebody', and not to the surface S (underlying object) of the clause, as seen in the comparison of the following two sentences (Mondloch 1979: 249):

(35)   š-in-e:-riqi-tax-oq
       ASP-1sg.ABS-DIR.go-find-CMPL.PASS-DEP
       Someone went to get me found (I got found and someone went to do that)
       Not: *I went to get found

(36)   š-iš-ul-kuna-tax-oq
       ASP-2pl.ABS-DIR.come-cure-CMPL.PASS-DEP
       Someone came to finish curing you (You got cured and someone came to do that)
       Not: *You came to get cured

3.3   Agent-focus antipassive ('agentive voice')

As will soon be clear, this first K'iche' antipassive construction has a rather extensive literature of its own. In form, it has different morphological markers, *-ow* (or one of its allomorphs) for root transitive verbs (RTVs) and *-n* for derived transitive verbs (DTVs). Like the passives, both antipassive constructions are marked intransitively by (1) taking the absolutive pronominal affixes to signal the single cross-referencing personal pronominal affix (though see the important complications discussed below) and (2) by taking the phrase-final intransitive marker *-ik*. The purpose of the agent-focus antipassive is to place emphasis on the A (Mondloch 1978a: 71). The agent-focus antipassive can apply without restriction to transitive verb roots; as we will see below, this is not the case with the 'absolutive' antipassive, where not all transitive verbs permit it. This agent-focus antipassive is employed also when the A-role NP is 'extracted' (and therefore by default focussed) in constructions where it is questioned, relativized or placed in focus (clefted) by preposing: 'Rules such as WH-Questions, relativization and focus may be collectively characterized as extraction rules, since they extract a constituent from its position and move it over an indefinite number of other constituents without however altering its grammatical relation', and in several of the Mayan subgroups these extraction rules must be 'constrained from applying to ergative subjects [A-role NPs]' (Larsen and Norman 1979: 357). In many Mayan languages, an ergative NP cannot be questioned, relativized or clefted (though absolutive NPs can be). Sentences with an underlying A trigger instead a shift to antipassive in these instances (Larsen and Norman 1979: 357; Dayley 1981: 10; see below). Tom Smith-Stark calls this the 'inert ergative constraint' (reported in Dayley 1981: 10). In K'iche' in these extractions, the verb is made intransitive and the underlying A, when it is cross-referenced (see below for conditions), is represented by an absolutive pronominal affix in the verb. Transitive clauses with extracted surface As ordinarily do not occur in the language (Mondloch 1979: 172; see below for exceptions). This is characterized in the following ways: 'The focused subject [underlying A] is always expressed before the verb as a noun or independent pronoun (or some substitute for them)' (Mondloch 1978b: 10); 'In this construction [agent-focus antipassive] the agent (or actor) must be extracted, i.e. it must be focussed . . . the agent OBLIGATORILY precedes the verb' (Davies and Sam-Colop 1990: 525); 'Each of these three types [WH-questions, relativization and focus (clefted)], is characterized by the obligatory presence of an NP or other sentential constituent in the "focus" position immediately preceding the verb and by the obligatory presence of a gap or "empty" constituent in some position following the verb [the NP is no longer there, but preposed]' (Trechsel 1993: 41). Thus, in the agent-focus antipassive construction, the A is de-moted to an S in order to participate in pivot combinations. In order for underlying A arguments of transitive clauses to be questioned, relativized or focussed, A-role arguments ordinarily must first be made accessible by con-verting them into S (absolutives) by means of the agent-focus antipassive. This is described in some detail in this section.

However, in these extraction constructions, though the verb is morpho-logically intransitive in form, the grammatical relations between A and O do not typically change, as they do in the passives and the absolutive antipassive. Though with the agent-focus antipassive the verbs are intransitive morpho-logically, syntactically they can have two core arguments – this will become clearer as we go along.[9] That is, A-role participants (ergative, transitive sub-jects) generally cannot be extracted, and therefore the agent-focus antipassive – which makes underlying A a surface S – is used when A-role arguments are questioned, relativized or focussed; however, neither the A-role nor the O-role NP appears in an oblique construction. (Thus, not every instance of an agent-focus antipassive necessarily results in valency reduction, though most

---

[9] There is some disagreement about whether the agent-focus antipassive is a true antipassive construction or not. Since in general it has the forms, meanings and functions that correspond to antipassives found in other languages, it is considered an antipassive. Like other languages' antipassives, it plays up the role of the agent (A) and eliminates or plays down the role of the object (O), and it shows up as intransitive in form. The hesitation some have in allowing this to be considered a 'true' antipassive is due to the fact that in these extraction contexts (em-phatic focus, relative clauses and content questioning of A), only one situation of several in which it occurs, it appears at times also to be associated with two core arguments, rather than one, neither of which is oblique or optional. (See Larsen 1987, Hale and Storto forthcoming, for different opinions.)

do.) Larsen and Norman (1979: 360) speak of an accessibility hierarchy for these extraction rules (WH-questions, relativization, focussing [clefting]): 'transitive subjects [A] are less accessible . . . than either intransitive subjects [S] or direct objects [O]'. We look at each of these extraction environments in turn.

3.3.1   Agent-focus antipassive with questions

Generally in WH-questions (content questions), the questioned NP is 'extracted' and placed in preverbal position, and this applies freely to S (as seen here in (37)) and O (in (38)) with no morphological changes in the verb:

(37)   xači:n k-Ø-q'ab'ar-ik [S questioned]
        who   ASP-3sg.ABS-get.drunk-INTR
        Who gets drunk? (Mondloch 1979: 176)

(38) (a)   xači:n š-Ø-u-č'ay   le: ačih [O questioned]
           who   ASP-3sg.ABS-3sg.ERG-hit the man
           Whom did the man hit? (Larsen and Norman 1979: 357)

However, an A-role NP normally cannot be questioned in this same way, as seen in (38b) and (39):

(38) (b)   *xači:n š-Ø-u-č'ay   le: ačih *[A questioned]
            who   ASP-3sg.ABS-3sg.ERG-hit the man
            *Who hit the man? (cf. Larsen and Norman 1979: 357)

(Note that (38b) is grammatical in the meaning 'whom did the man hit?', as seen in (38a).)

(39)   *xači:n š-in-r-il-oh *[A questioned]
         who   ASP-1sg.ABS-3sg.ERG-see-TR
         *Who saw me? (Mondloch 1979: 176)

When an A-role NP is to be questioned, the questioned NP is preposed, but also the verb is normally placed in the agent-focus antipassive:

(40)   xači:n š-Ø-č'ay-ow   le: ačih
        who   ASP-3sg.ABS-hit-AF.ANT the man (cf. Larsen and Norman 1979: 358)
        Who hit the man?

(Contrast (40) with (38b).)

(41)   xači:n š-in-il-ow-ik
        who   ASP-1sg.ABS-see-AF.ANT-INTR
        Who saw me? (Mondloch 1979: 176)

(Contrast (39).)

(42) xači:n k-Ø-loq'-ow   r-e:č   ri wiʔč
      who ASP-3sg.ABS-buy-AF.ANT 3sg.POSS-GEN the chick
      Who buys the chicks?[10]

3.3.2   Agent-focus antipassive with relatives

In K'iche', nearly any argument can be relativized.[11] The relative clause follows its head and is introduced by a relative marker which is in effect the
same as the determiners, *le:*, *ri* and *we:* (though the marker is optional in
some very rare circumstances). Just as with WH-questions, the verb form
undergoes no special changes in relative clauses when an NP in S or O role is
extracted, as in (43) and (44a):

(43) š-Ø-inw-il   ri išoq ri š-Ø-q'ab'ar-ik [S relativized]
      ASP-3sg.ABS-1sg.ERG-see the woman REL ASP-3sg.ABS-get.drunk-INTR
      I saw the woman who got drunk

---

[10] In some WH-questions where the agent-focus antipassive is normally required, it is sometimes
not used if no ambiguity would result; for example, both (1) and (2) are possible:

(1) xači:n š-at-u-č'ay-oh
     who ASP-2sg.ABS-3sg.ERG-hit-TR
     Who hit you?

(2) xači:n š-at-č'ay-ow-ik
     who ASP-2sg.ABS-hit-AF.ANT-INTR
     Who hit you? (Larsen 1987)

(This varies across dialects; other similar examples are discussed later in the chapter.)

[11] The only NP that seems inaccessible to relativization is the A NP in a 'by' phrase of the
simple passive, as in the following, neither of which is grammatical:

(1) *le: axkun le: š-Ø-kuna-š   ri ala r-uma:l
     the curer REL ASP-3sg.ABS-cure-PASS the child 3sg.POSS-by
     *the doctor that the child was cured by . . . (Davies and Sam-Colop 1990: 534)

(2) *le: axkun le: š-Ø-kuna-š   ri ala
     the curer REL ASP-3sg.ABS-cure-PASS the child
     *the doctor that the child was cured by . . . (cf. Davies and Sam-Colop 1990: 534)

The S (underlying O-role NP), however, can be relativized in such passive constructions, as
in (3):

(3) ri ala ri š-Ø-kuna-š   r-uma:l   le: axkun
     the child REL ASP-3sg.ABS-cure-PASS 3sg.POSS-by the curer
     The child who was cured by the doctor (cf. Davies and Sam-Colop 1990: 534)

It is possible that this restriction on relativization of the NP from the 'by'-phrase of passives
has to do with the function of passive versus relativization. A function of the passive is to play
down the underlying A and to emphasize the underlying O, whereas, in K'iche', relativization
emphasizes an NP; to relativize the A-role NP of the oblique 'by'-phrase of the passive would
highlight that NP, seemingly conflicting with the passive's demotion of that same element.
The two processes, relativization and passivization, would seem to have opposite purposes to
one another.

(44) (a)   š-Ø-inw-il   le: išoq   le: š-Ø-u-č'ay
ASP-3sg.ABS-1sg.ERG-see the woman REL ASP-3sg.ABS-3sg.ERG-hit
le: ačih [O relativized]
the man
I saw the woman whom the man hit (Larsen and Norman 1979: 357)[12]

However, when an A-role NP is relativized, this same construction, with a regular transitive verb, is not normally possible. Davies and Sam-Colop (1990: 534) report that 'ergative arguments [As] that never bear the absolutive relation [i.e. that do not go through a demotion to S, absolutive case] cannot be relativized in K'iche''. They offer the 'functional perspective' that relates to our pivot (see below): that 'the agentive [agent-focus] antipassive makes the agent accessible to relativization (and extraction in general) by making it an absolutive'. Some examples showing these relations are:

(44) (b)   *š-Ø-inw-il   le: išoq   le: š-Ø-u-č'ay
ASP-3sg.ABS-1sg.ERG-see the woman REL ASP-3sg.ABS-3sg.ERG-hit
le: ačih *[A relativized]
the man
*I saw the woman who hit the man (cf. Larsen and Norman 1979: 357)

(Note that (44b) is grammatical in the meaning 'I saw the woman whom the man hit', as in (44a).) When an A-role NP is extracted in a relative clause, the agent-focus antipassive construction is used:

(44) (c)   š-Ø-inw-il   le: išoq   le: š-Ø-č'ay-ow   le: ačih
ASP-3sg.ABS-1sg.ERG-see the woman REL ASP-3sg.ABS-hit-AF.ANT the man
I saw the woman who hit the man (cf. Larsen and Norman 1979: 358)

(45)   š-Ø-q-il   le: išoq   le: š-Ø-q'oʔ-(o)w
ASP-3sg.ABS-1pl.ERG-see the woman REL ASP-3sg.ABS-embroider-AF.ANT
le: a-poʔt
the 2sg.POSS-huipil
We saw the woman who embroidered your huipil (native blouse)[13]

---

[12] No sexism is intended by the repetition of these examples involving women and men and hitting – these examples were presented before non-sexist guidelines were prepared and are repeated here only because they are now part of the history of argumentation in Mayan linguistics.

[13] This formation extends also to existential clauses, which have no overt relative marker (note that the relative marker is sometimes optional in other cases):

(1)   Ø-k'o: k-Ø-b'an-ow   le: čak
       3sg.ABS-there.is ASP-3sg.ABS-do-AF.ANT the work
       There is someone who will do the work

(2)   e:-k'o: k-e:-kuna-n   le: yawa:b'
       3pl.ABS-there.is ASP-3pl.ABS-cure-AF.ANT the sick.one
       There are those who will cure the sick (person)

In fact, the constraint against extracted As (which are not demoted to S in an agent-focus antipassive construction) is general, but not absolutely required all the time in all the dialects. Some speakers accept sentences such as (46) (Trechsel 1993: 75):

(46)   š-Ø-pe: ri išoq ri š-Ø-u-pil
        ASP-3sg.ABS-come the woman REL ASP-3sg.ABS-3sg.ERG-butcher
        ri ak' [A relativized]
        the chicken
        The woman who butchered the chicken came

In (46), the verb *-pil* is a regular transitive, not the expected *-pil-ow* agent-focus antipassive; in this case, while the head NP (*ri išoq* 'the woman') plays the role of A in the relative clause, rather than the O role that would be expected with the fully active transitive verb form, the semantics make the expected reading, 'the woman whom the chicken butchered', highly unlikely (Mondloch 1978b, Trechsel 1993: 75). The example in (47) is even clearer (Nik'te' and Saqijix 1993: 136):

(47)   ri ts'i? ri š-Ø-u-tix   ri ti?i:x
        the dog REL ASP-3sg.ABS-3sg.ERG-eat the meat
        š-Ø-r-oqata:-x   ri me?s [A relativized]
        ASP-3sg.ABS-3sg.ERG-chase-TR the cat
        The dog that ate the meat chased the cat

Since the meat cannot eat the dog, even though the sentence is in the regular active transitive form with an A as head of the relative clause, the agent-focus antipassive is not absolutely required in this instance. Nevertheless, speakers who accept (46) and (47) as grammatical also accept sentences which they do find ambiguous, such as the following:

(48)   xači:n š-Ø-r-il   ri ačih
        who ASP-3sg.ABS-3sg.ERG-see the man (Trechsel 1993: 75)
        (1) Whom did the man see?
        (2) Who saw the man?

(49)   š-Ø-q-il   le: ak'al le: š-Ø-r-oqata:-x
        ASP-3sg.ABS-1pl.ERG-see the child REL ASP-3sg.ABS-3sg.ERG-chase-TR
        le: ts'i?
        the dog
        (1) We saw the child who chased the dog [A relativized]
        (2) We saw the child whom the dog chased [O relativized] (Trechsel
            1993: 75)

(50) (a) k-Ø-tseʔn   ri ala ri š-Ø-u-tsʼuma:-x   ri ali
        ASP-3sg.ABS-smile the boy REL ASP-3sg.ABS-3sg.ERG-kiss-TR the girl
        (1) The boy who kissed the girl smiles [A relativized!]
        (2) The boy whom the girl kissed smiles [O relativized] (Sam-Colop
             1988: 44)

To avoid the ambiguity of (50a), it is normally put in the agent-focus antipassive, as in (50b), where the second reading is now impossible:

(50) (b) *k-Ø-tseʔn   ri ala ri š-Ø-tsʼuma-n   ri ali
        ASP-3sg.ABS-smile the boy REL ASP-3sg.ABS-kiss-AF.ANT the girl
        (1) The boy who kissed the girl smiles [S relativized]
        *(2) The boy whom the girl kisses smiles *[O relativized] (Sam-Colop
             1988: 45)

3.3.3   Focus function
The focus (cleft) construction is similar to WH-questions and relativization in that in it an underlying A-role argument is taken from its normal neutral position after the verb and preposed, and the verb is placed in the agent-focus antipassive form. Sentences (51–2) show focussed S and O, which require no change in the verb:

(51)   are: ri ačih š-Ø-qʼabar-ik [S focussed]
         FOC the man ASP-3sg.ABS-get.drunk-INTR
         It was the man who got drunk

(52)   are: le: išoq   š-Ø-u-čʼay   le: ačih [O focussed]
         FOC the woman ASP-3sg.ABS-3sg.ERG-hit the man
         It was the woman that the man hit (Larsen and Norman 1979: 357)

In fact in Kʼicheʼ virtually any constituent in the sentence can be focussed (preposed before the verb) in this construction (with the exception of the demoted agent of a passive, see below). However, A cannot be focussed in exactly the same way, as seen in the ungrammaticality of (53a) (Larsen and Norman 1979: 357):

(53) (a) *are: le: ačih š-Ø-u-čʼay   le: išoq [A focussed]
          FOC the man ASP-3sg.ABS-3sg.ERG-hit the woman
          *It was the man that hit the woman

Rather, the verb must be put in the agent-focus antipassive construction in order for an A-role NP to be focussed (clefted) in this way:

(53) (b) are: le: ačih š-Ø-čʼay-ow   le: išoq [A focussed]
         FOC the man ASP-3sg.ABS-hit-AF.ANT the woman
         It was the man that hit the woman (Larsen and Norman 1979: 358)

(54) (a) la at   š-at-kuna-n   le: axkun
        Q 2sg.INDEP.PN ASP-2sg.ABS-cure-AF.ANT the curer
        Was it you who cured the doctor? (Davies and Sam-Colop 1990: 523)

(b)   la are: le: axkun š-at-kuna-n-ik
        Q FOC the curer ASP-2sg.ABS-cure-AF.ANT-INTR
        Was it the doctor who cured you? (Davies and Sam-Colop 1990: 523)

3.3.4 Syntax

In the agent-focus antipassive construction, the A (underlying transitive subject) is first demoted to an S (intransitive subject, absolutive) in order to participate in pivot combinations. In order to question, relativize or focus underlying A arguments of transitive clauses, A-role arguments ordinarily must first be made accessible by being converted into S (absolutives) by means of the agent-focus antipassive. Thus, while on the whole K'iche' is morphologically ergative and most of its syntactic rules are not sensitive to ergativity, we could say that to some degree K'iche' has syntactic ergativity (Mondloch 1979: 58). As Larsen (1987: 44) put it:

> one could claim that Quiché is syntactically ergative by Dixon's criteria. The syntactic rules which form *wh*-questions, relative clauses, and cleft constructions operate in a straightforward way on S and O, but not on A. In order for such rules to apply to A, a NP in underlying A function must first be put into derived S function by means of the [agent-]focus antipassive . . . Thus, it appears that these rules operate on an S/O pivot in Quiché.

A main function of the agent-focus antipassive in these extraction constructions is to convert an underlying A-role NP into a derived S so that it will be accessible for rules which operate only on S and O. In the case of questions, the WH-constituent appears in preverbal position, the focus position, rather than postverbally which is the typical location of non-questioned/non-focussed NPs. The same is true of the relative clauses and the focus construction (clefts – by definition in the case of the clefts).

3.3.5 Disambiguating function

Since *-in-* '1sg', *lah* '2sg.REV' and *alaq* '2pl.REV' are the same (do not have distinct markers) in both ergative and absolutive environments, ambiguities involving combinations of these as participants could arise, but such combinations are avoided (as mentioned in §2.1.2). For example, *kinkunax lah* is ambiguous, meaning either 'I cure you' or 'you cure me'. The structure of the two is as follows, where *-X-* is not intended as either an absolutive or an ergative morpheme, but is employed only to show where such a morpheme would be expected if some other person bearing overt marking were involved.

(55) (a)   k-X-in-kuna-x   lah
        ASP-X.ABS-1sg.ERG-cure-TR 2sg.REV.ABS
        I cure you

(b)   k-in-X-kuna-x   lah
        ASP-1sg.ABS-X.ERG-cure-TR 2sg.REV.ERG
        You cure me

In such instances, if context is unable to disambiguate the sentence, it will be put into another voice, as in (56a) and (56b), where the unambiguous equivalents of (55a) and (55b) are shown in the focussed construction with the agent-focus antipassive:

(56) (a)   in   k-in-kuna-n   lah
        1sg.INDEP.PN ASP-1sg.ABS-cure-AF.ANT 2sg.REV
        It is I who cure you / I myself cure you / I am the one who cures you

(b)   la:l   k-in-kuna-n   lah
        2sg.REV.INDEP.PN ASP-1sg.ABS-cure-AF.ANT 2sg.REV
        It is you who cure me / You yourself cure me / You are the one who cures me

3.3.6   Difficulties for formal theorists

A major problem for some formal theories is encountered in two aspects of the agent-focus antipassive. These complications have been addressed, always with discomfort, in the following theoretical orientations: CATEGORIAL GRAMMAR by Trechsel (1982); GOVERNMENT AND BINDING by Hale and Storto (forthcoming) and Larsen 1987; HPSG by Trechsel (1993); and RELATIONAL GRAMMAR by Davies and Sam-Colop (1990) and Sam-Colop (1988). The first complication stems from the fact that the agent-focus antipassive construction, though it appears morphologically to be intransitive, in certain circumstances behaves syntactically as if it were a transitive clause. 'It is this apparent "mismatch" between the morphological intransitivity of these verb forms and their syntactic and semantic transitivity that presents the most interesting and difficult challenges to linguistic theory' (Trechsel 1993: 33–4). That is, sometimes the clause has both an A (agent) and an O (direct object) as core arguments, even though only one is signalled in the cross-referencing affixes on the verb (an absolutive prefix). Linguists have disagreed over whether these agent-focus antipassive forms are to be considered intransitive or transitive constructions (see Davies and Sam-Colop 1990: 530–1 for a survey of some of the opinions found in the literature).

Let me hasten to add here that, in pointing out the difficulties caused for treatments in various formal approaches by the K'iche' facts discussed in this section, I by no means imply any anti-theoretical bias. Just the opposite: it is facts such as these which drive us to formulate more adequate theories which should help to explain both these facts and others of a similar nature that may show up in other languages.

The problem of a verb marked morphologically as intransitive sometimes syntactically bearing two core arguments is compounded by the second serious complication. The single pronominal affix (always absolutive) sometimes cross-references the A-role NP and sometimes the O-role NP: 'These verbs exhibit an unusual pattern of agreement. In some instances, they agree with the agent; in others, they agree with the patient [O]' (Trechsel 1993: 33). Davies and Sam-Colop (1990: 523) call this 'nonregular agreement in K'iche''. A major issue in theoretical treatments of K'iche' is what determines which of the two arguments – A or O – will be cross-referenced by the single absolutive affix permitted in the agent-focus antipassive verbs (see below). It is generally acknowledged that 'the agreement cannot be accounted for simply by the general agreement rules . . . that are at work elsewhere in the language' (Davies and Sam-Colop 1990: 531; see Mondloch 1979: 319–20). Norman and Campbell (1978) presented a hierarchy for the treatment of these antipassive 'nonregular agreements' found in several Mayan languages:

> The verb which appears in the antipassive construction must by definition be intransitive. For Mayan languages, this entails that only one NP may be cross-referenced on the verb, the other NP remaining as a prepositional [oblique] phrase or a constituent which has no grammatical relation in the clause (a chômeur, in the terminology of relational grammar). Again, from the definition of antipassive one would expect that the verb would be marked for agreement with the NP which represented the deep syntactic [underlying] subject (the formerly ergative NP).
>
> This does not always turn out to be the case in Mayan . . . In languages such as Quiche, which permit one of the NPs in the antipassive to be non-third person, the rules of verb–subject agreement are quite complex . . . :

[1] Are: ri in   š-in-č'ay-ow   le: ačih
     FOC the 1sg.INDEP.PN ASP-1sg.ABS-hit-AF.ANT the man
     I hit the man / It was me that hit the man

[2] Are: ri ačih š-in-č'ay-ow-ik
     FOC the man ASP-1sg.ABS-hit-AF.ANT-INTR
     The man hit me / That's the man who hit me

In both [1] and [2], the verb agrees with the first person constituent, even though that constituent represents an underlying subject [A] in [1] but an underlying object [O] in [2]. In the Quiche antipassive, verb agreement is controlled not by syntactic relations of NPs but by their position on the hierarchy: *non-third person* > *third person plural* > *third person singular*, with special provisions for the second person formal pronoun, which behaves like third person in this case.

To account for the details of K'iche' (rather than Mayan languages generally), this statement needs to be slightly more specific: at least one of the participants must be either a 3rd person (*-Ø-*) or a 2nd person reverential (*lah, alaq*, which take no overt cross-referencing affix) – that is, two overtly marked (non-null) pronominal affixes (i.e. combinations of 1st person (sg or pl) and 2nd non-reverential person (sg or pl) forms) are not permitted to co-occur in this construction. As Mondloch (1978a: 71) puts it, with agent-focus antipassive:

> at least subject [A] or object [O] must be a third person (singular or plural) or *lāl* [*la:l*] or *alak* [*alaq*]. In the event that both subject and object are other than third person or other than *lāl* [*la:l*] or *alak* [*alaq*], then this voice *cannot be used* for emphasizing the subject. [Emphasis in the original.]

Compare the following pairs of agent-focus antipassive sentences, where in the (a) sentences the A-role argument is cross-referenced by the absolutive prefix in the verb, but in the (b) sentences it is the O-role which is cross-referenced:

(57) (a)   at   š-at-riq-ow   le: ak'al-a:b' [*-at-* = A]
         2sg.INDEP.PN ASP-2sg.ABS-find-AF.ANT the child-pl
         You found the children / It was you who found the children (Davies and
         Sam-Colop 1990: 531)

   (b)   e: are: le: ak'al-a:b' š-at-riq-ow   at [*-at-* = O]
         pl FOC the child-PL ASP-2sg.ABS-find-AF.ANT 2sg.INDEP.PN
         It was the children who found you (Davies and Sam-Colop 1990: 531)

(58) (a)   ri   ak'al-a:b' š-e:-tsuqu-w   ri   a   luʔ [*-e:-* = A]
         the child-pl   ASP-3pl.ABS-feed-AF.ANT the HON Peter
         The children fed Peter / It was the children who fed Peter (cf. Davies and
         Sam-Colop 1990: 531)

   (b)   ri   a   luʔ š-e:-tsuqu-w   ri   ak'al-a:b' [*-e:-* = O]
         the HON Peter ASP-3pl.ABS-feed-AF.ANT the child-pl
         Peter fed the children / It was Peter who fed the children
         (cf. Davies and Sam-Colop 1990: 531)

These examples, (57a–58b), illustrate Norman and Campbell's (1978: 150) hierarchy. They propose that the usual K'iche' agreement rule is suspended in this construction: 'verb agreement is controlled not by syntactic relations of NPs but by their position on the [participant] hierarchy' (Davies and Sam-Colop 1990: 524). Larsen (1987: 44) characterizes this as: 'There is a restriction on the focus antipassive construction such that (roughly) either the underlying A or the underlying O or both must be third person.' The following pair of sentences contrasts the focus construction with agent-focus antipassive (in (59a)) with the active transitive counterpart (in (59b)):

(59) (a) are: le: w-a:ts   š-in-to?-ow-ik
          FOC the my-elder.brother ASP-1sg.ABS-help-AF.ANT-INTR
          It was my elder brother who helped me

(b) š-in-u-to?   le: w-a:ts
     ASP-1sg.ABS-3sg.ERG-help the my-elder.brother
     My elder brother helped me

This constraint against cross-referencing two non-null arguments (1st or 2nd non-reverential forms) comes into question only in the focus (cleft) construction, since all the WH-question words are 3rd person and the nouns modified by relative clauses in K'iche' are also 3rd person. In principle it would logically be possible to violate the constraint in the focus construction, which can have two arguments, both non-3rd persons (and non-2nd person reverentials), but this is avoided either by utilizing active voice (with transitive morphology), as in (60a), or by placing the O-role NP in an oblique phrase, as in (60b–61):

(60) (a) in   š-at-in-č'ay-oh
          1sg.INDEP.PN ASP-2sg.ABS-1sg.ERG-hit-TR
          I am the one who hit you (Trechsel 1993: 47)

(b) in   š-in-č'ay-ow   aw-e:h
     1sg.INDEP.PN ASP-1sg.ABS-hit-AF.ANT 2sg.POSS-GEN
     I am the one who hit you (Trechsel 1993: 47)

(61) are: š-Ø-elaq'a-n   q-e:h
      FOC ASP-3sg.ABS-steal-AF.ANT 1pl.POSS-GEN
      He is the one who robbed us (Trechsel 1993: 48)[14]

---

[14] Works on K'iche' focus nearly all contain a note pointing out that examples such as this, with both the agent-focus antipassive morphology and the oblique O, are not found in all K'iche' dialects; they are found in Nahualá, however, the dialect area represented in Mondloch's works, and since Nahualá is a central and typical dialect and because most scholars rely heavily on Mondloch's discussion of these phenomena in K'iche', the literature generally reports these then as relatively unproblematic.

In (60b) the possessed relative noun *aw-e:h* is formally now a 3rd person (in structure a noun), and thus this sentence does not violate the constraint against two non-3rd or non-2nd reverential person NPs, so that the agent-focus antipassive typically used with focus (cleft) is possible (cf. Trechsel 1993: 47).

Ultimately, in spite of the difficulties for various theories which some syntacticians have expressed over the fact that it is sometimes the A-role NP and other times the O-role NP which is cross-referenced by the single absolutive affix in the agent-focus antipassive construction, there is, nevertheless, usually no problem of interpretation because the A-role NP is focussed (clefted) and preposed before the verb (cf. Dayley 1981: 26, 56). That is, we should not lose sight of the help in processing these sentences which this special non-neutral constituent order provides us with in this case. In fact, Dayley, speaking of Mayan languages in general, sees the use of the agent-focus antipassive morphology as specifically fulfilling the role of disambiguating topicalized sentences which have both an A and an O (Dayley 1981: 56):

> if the normal order is V A P [VAO] (or V P A [VOA], for that matter), when one of the NPs is fronted via topicalization[,] the result is NP V NP, and therefore it may not be clear which NP, the agent or the patient [O], has been fronted. The [agent-]focus antipassive may be used to disambiguate in this situation because it explicitly indicates that the NP immediately preceding the verb is the agent.[15]

Given the possibility of two core arguments, A and O, but only one cross-referencing affix (which can sometimes refer to the A argument and sometimes to the O argument in these agent-focus antipassive sentences), it is very important to be able to determine which person-cross-referencing affix will occur and which argument (A or O) it will signal. Which one will occur is easy: whichever of the arguments, A or O, has a non-null absolutive form (not -∅-) is the one which will be cross-referenced in the verb. The combinations permitted are shown in figure 7.2.

---

[15] Trechsel's (1982, 1993) approach to the problem begins with the assumption that transitive sentences in K'iche' assign the patient role to subjects [A] and the agent role to objects [O], 'analyzing absolutive NPs as "subjects" and ergative NPs as "objects"' (1993: 62) (though Trechsel does not insist on this 'inverse' analysis; p. 64). He asserts that 'there is absolutely no reason, other than prejudice and/or convention, to assume that natural languages always and everywhere assign the agent [A] and patient [O] roles in transitive sentences to the subject and object NP, respectively' (p. 64). In spite of the arguments he presents in support of this position, I do not accept it but also do not attempt to present counterarguments, since the typological perspective which maintains a constant A–[Transitive]Subject and O–Object association cross-linguistically – as articulated, for example, by Dixon (1994) and many others – is thoroughly convincing.

Figure 7.2. Permitted A–O combinations in agent-focus antipassive verbs

A	O
1sg/pl (*-in-/-ux-*)	2REV.sg/pl (*-Ø-/-Ø-*)
	3sg/pl (*-Ø-/-Ø-*)
2sg (*-at-*)	3sg/pl (*-Ø-/-Ø-*)
2.REV.sg/pl (*-Ø-*)	1sg/pl (*-in-/-ux-*)
	3sg/pl (*-Ø-/-e:-*)
3sg/pl (*-Ø-/-Ø-(-e:-)*)	1sg/pl (*-in-/-ux-*)
	2sg/pl (*-at-/-iš-*)
	2REV.sg/pl (*-Ø-/-Ø-*)
	3sg/pl (*-Ø-/-Ø-(-e:-)*)

As seen from figure 7.2, A–O combinations of 1sg/pl and 2sg/pl (non-reverential) are excluded. The constraint against two persons with non-null cross-referencing affixes in the focus construction is not an insurmountable problem. If an A is to be extracted for emphasis in an instance where any of these combinations would occur, the active transitive verb forms (and not the agent-focus antipassive) are used, as illustrated in:

(62) are: ri at   š-in-a:-č'ay-oh
      FOC the 2sg.INDEP.PN ASP-1sg.ABS-2sg.ERG-hit-TR
      You were the one who hit me (Larsen 1987: 44)

(63) in   k-at-in-to?-oh
      1sg.INDEP.PN ASP-2sg.ABS-1sg.ERG-help-TR
      I myself will help you

In an A-extraction clause, in order to maintain this constraint against the simultaneous occurrence of two non-Ø pronominal affixes, if a 3rd person plural occurs either as A or O (where *-e:-* '3pl.ABS' would normally be expected in the agent-focus antipassive) in combination with any other non-Ø pronominal affix (anything other than 3sg or 2nd Reverential (singular or plural)), then *-Ø-* is used instead. Examples (64a–c) show *-e:-* 3pl.ABS where there is no clash which would lead to the suppression of the plural pronominal affix:

(64) (a) are: š-e:-riq-ow-ik
          FOC ASP-3pl.ABS-find-AF.ANT-INTR
          He is the one who found them

(b) e: are: š-e:-riq-ow   ri ak'a:l
     pl FOC ASP-3pl.ABS-find-AF.ANT the child
     They are the ones who found the child

(c) e: are: š-e:-riq-ow   ri ak'al-a:b'
     pl FOC ASP-3pl.ABS-find-AF.ANT the children
     They are the ones who found the children

The following pair of sentences shows the ordinary presence of 3rd person plural *-e:-* (in (65a)) contrasted with 3rd person singular *-Ø-* for agreement with the extracted 3rd person singular A NP (in (65b)) (Sam-Colop 1988: 65):

(65) (a)   are: le: ts'i? (le:)   š-e:-riq-ow   le: čix
           FOC the dog (REL) ASP-3pl.ABS-find-AF.ANT the sheep
           It was the dog that found the sheep (plural)

(b)   are: le: ts'i? (le:)   š-Ø-riq-ow   le: čix
           FOC the dog (REL) ASP-3sg.ABS-find-AF.ANT the sheep
           It was the dog that found the sheep (singular)

In contrast to these sentences, (66) illustrates an instance in which the 3rd person plural pronominal affix is suppressed, overridden by the presence of another argument represented by a non-null non-3rd person affix:

(66)   in   š-in-riq-ow   ri   ak'al-a:b'
       1sg.INDEP.PN ASP-1sg.ABS-find-AF.ANT the child-pl
       I am the one who found the children

In (66), the plurality of the O-role argument is not marked in the verb. Since the A-role argument is a non-3rd person singular, the O argument (though underlyingly plural, so that *e:-* would be expected) is treated morphologically as though it were a 3sg.ABS marker (i.e. *-Ø-*) (Mondloch 1979: 322).

Since the 2nd person reverential forms (*lah* and *alaq*) are not cross-referenced by prefixes in the verb, the problem of two non-Ø pronominal markers with the agent-focus antipassive does not arise with the reverential forms. Therefore, the 2nd person reverentials can occur as A or O in combinations with any 1st or 3rd person form, as seen in the following examples:

(67)   in   š-in-č'a:b'e-n   alaq
       1sg.INDEP.PN ASP-1sg.ABS-speak-AF.ANT 2pl.REV
       I am the one who talked to you

(68)   la:l   š-e:-kuna-n   lah
       2sg.REV.INDEP.PN ASP-3pl.ABS-cure-AF.ANT 2sg.REV
       You are the one who cured them

(69)   alaq   š-ux-to?-(o)w   alaq
       2pl.REV.INDEP.PN ASP-1pl.ABS-help-AF.ANT 2pl.REV
       You are the ones who helped us

3.3.7   O-demotion to oblique with agent-focus antipassive

There is one further construction which employs the agent-focus antipassive. In this one, the verb bears the agent-focus antipassive morphology (and is thus intransitive) and cross-references only one argument – the underlying A in this case – with the absolutive verb prefixes, but differs from the extraction constructions above in that the underlying O is demoted to an oblique with the relational noun -e:h/-e:č 'genitive/possessive',[16] as in the following pairs of sentences, where the (a) example is basic and the (b) member of the pair is derived, illustrating the demoted oblique O:

(70) (a) š-Ø-u-čoy   ri če:ʔ ri axča:k pa ri k'iče?la:x [Basic]
ASP-3sg.ABS-3sg.ERG-cut the tree the worker in the forest
The worker cut the tree in the forest (Nik'te' and Saqijix 1993)

(b) are: ri axča:k ri š-Ø-čoy-ow   r-e:č   ri če:ʔ
FOC the worker REL ASP-3sg.ABS-cut-AF.ANT 3sg-POSS.GEN the tree
pa ri k'iče?la:x [Derived]
in the forest
It was the worker who cut the tree in the forest

(71) (a) k-e:b'-u-loq'   ri wiʔč ri w-ika:q' [Basic]
ASP-3pl.ABS-3sg.ERG-buy the chick the my-nephew
My nephew buys the chicks (Nik'te' and Saqijix 1993)

(b) are: ri w-ika:q'   k-Ø-loq'-ow   r-e:č   ri
FOC the my-nephew ASP-3sg.ABS-buy-AF.ANT 3sg.POSS-GEN the
wiʔč [Derived]
chick
It is my nephew who buys the chicks[17]

---

[16] Mayanists typically call this relational noun the 'genitive', since it is used for possession, w-e:č '(it is) mine', r-e:č '(it is) his/hers/its', but it also has the semantic functions of 'dative', 'source', 'instrument' and some other non-core argument notions (cf. Sam-Colop 1988: 18). It is composed of the relational noun root -e:h or -e:č, which are free variants, with no difference in meaning or privilege of occurrence. Etymologically, -e:h comes from the noun root meaning 'tooth' and is used to mean 'to, at'. The locative use usually occurs in the compound form, č(i) 'to, at, on, in, for' (from the noun root meaning 'mouth'), + possessive pronominal prefixes + -e:h/-e:č, as in či-k-e:h 'to/for them', č-w-e:h 'to/for me'. In the 3rd person singular, č-r-e:h alternates with č-e:h, though the latter is more frequent. Not all valency-derivation constructions which utilize the possessed -e:h/-e:č without the preceding compounding či are 'genitive'/'possessive' in nature, as seen where it functions to signal oblique NP roles; nevertheless, I continue to translate these as 'genitive' (GEN), following the tradition in the literature.

[17] There is some variation across K'iche' dialects concerning the general acceptability of this agent-focus antipassive with underlying O demoted to an oblique phrase (see Davies and Sam-Colop 1990: 539).

Also, in some dialects this construction offers another way around the constraint against two non-null pronominal affixes (3rd person or 2nd person reverential forms) with the agent-focus antipassive, where the O-role argument can be demoted to an oblique, though this option is not normally possible in these extractions with other persons:

(1) in   š-in-č'ay-ow   aw-e:h
1sg.INDEP.PN ASP-1sg.ABS-hit-AF.ANT 2sg.POSS-GEN
I am the one who hit you

3.4   'Absolutive' antipassive

The second antipassive is traditionally called the 'absolutive antipassive' (see Smith-Stark 1978). It has the form *-n* with DTVs and *-on* with RTVs (or predictable allomorphs: *-un* if the vowel of the verb root is *u*; *-an* if the root's vowel is *a*). With the absolutive antipassive, unlike in the agent-focus antipassives, the single pronoun, S (absolutive), cross-references the underlying A of an intransitivized verb form, and the underlying O is either demoted to an oblique construction or is omitted. On the whole, it is much more straightforward than the agent-focus antipassive. For example, in (72a) and (72b) the demoted O NP has been omitted, while it is present, but demoted to an oblique phrase, in (73a):

(72) (a)   uts   k-at-b'iša-n
           good ASP-2sg.ABS-sing-ABS.ANT
           You sing well

(b)   k-Ø-mes-on   č-qa-naqa:x
      ASP-3sg.ABS-sweep-ABS.ANT   to-1pl.POSS-near
      She sweeps near us (Trechsel 1982: 60)

(73) (a)   k-at-yoq'-on   č-e:h   ri a-na:n
           ASP-2sg.ABS-mock-ABS.ANT   to.3sg.POSS-GEN the your-mother
           You mock your mother

(Footnote 17 continued)

(2)   iš   š-iš-il-ow   q-e:h
      2pl.INDEP.PN ASP-2pl.ABS-see-AF.ANT 1pl.POSS-GEN
      You are the ones who saw us (Mondloch 1979: 323–8)

The agent-focus antipassive also serves to signal what has been called (inappropriately) 'noun incorporation' in K'iche'. An antipassive construction is employed with noun incorporation in many languages, understandably so, since the antipassive characteristically signals that the verb is formally intransitive (see Mithun 1984). However, the cases which have been called 'noun incorporation' in K'iche' are odd in two ways. (a) They do not actually incorporate a noun into a verb, but rather bear an independent word, albeit a bare nominalization juxtaposed to the verb. (b) They are much more limited than those reported in other languages, even in other Mayan languages such as Yucatec: they are limited essentially to an 'incorporated' nominalization with a few semantically 'light' verbs, like 'do, make', as in (3), where, in this interpretation, the nominalization *č'ax-oʔn* 'washing' is 'incorporated' in the verb *k-Ø-b'an-ow* 'do':

(3)   xun q'i:x k-Ø-b'an-ow   č'ax-oʔn   le: a-na:n
      one day ASP-3sg.ABS-do-AF.ANT   wash-NOMZR   the 2sg.POSS-mother
      Your mother (clothes)washes all day long (lit. all day your mother does washing)

As seen above, an agent-focus antipassive verb in the focus construction is intransitive in form but can have two core arguments associated with it, so that in this case, the so-called incorporation of the nominalization fits this construction in K'iche'. Morever, since the NP in O role in the focus construction need not be non-referential (as the objects incorporated in noun-incorporation constructions in general must be; see Mithun 1984), it is not possible to solve the vexing problem of the two core arguments with an intransitively marked verb through any general appeal to noun-incorporation.

The active counterpart of (73a) is (73b):

(b)   k-Ø-a-yoq'   ri a-na:n
        ASP-3sg.ABS-2sgERG-mock the your-mother
        You mock your mother

In (73a), underlying O has been demoted to an oblique dative construction, *č-e:h ri a-na:n*, the verb is intransitivized, and the underlying A is cross-referenced on the verb by an absolutive affix, *-at-* '2sg.ABS'.

The meaning of the regular active transitive and the absolutive antipassive with underlying O in an oblique construction, while basically the same, is felt to be different by native speakers, with reduced transitivity for the later. Consider the following pair of sentences:

(74) (a) š-Ø-u-č'ay   ri a   lu? ri a   šwa:n
          ASP-1sg.ABS-3sg.ERG-hit the HON Peter the HON John
          John hit Peter

(b)   ri a   šwa:n š-Ø-č'ay-on   č-e:h   ri a   lu?
      the HON John ASP-3sg.ABS-hit-ABS.ANT to.3sg.POSS-to the HON Peter
      John hit Peter

Some speakers prefer to translate (74b) as 'John was fighting with Peter' to show less direct effect by the agent on the derived demoted O – that is, to reflect its lessened transitivity (cf. Larsen 1987).

Unlike the agent-focus antipassive (where sometimes the single absolutive prefix in the verb cross-references either the A-role or the O-role argument), with the absolutive antipassive the single absolutive prefix always unambiguously marks S, the absolutive subject of the intransitivized clause, as in:

(75) š-ux-tsix-on   iw-u:k'
      ASP-1pl.ABS-talk-ABS.ANT 2pl.POSS-with
      We spoke with you

(76) k-e:-q'oxoma-n   le: ala-b'o:m
      ASP-3pl.ABS-play.music-ABS.ANT the boy-pl
      The boys play (a musical instrument)

Unlike the agent-focus antipassive which in effect can have two core arguments, neither of which need visibly be relegated to an oblique phrase, the absolutive antipassive construction can have an underlying O-role NP present only if it is demoted to an oblique. Contrast the following pairs of equivalent sentences, containing agent-focus antipassives (the (a) examples) and absolutive antipassive sentences (the (b) examples), which are contrasted below with ungrammatical counterparts in (77c) and (77d) (Sam-Colop 1988: 95):

(77) (a)   le: axčak-i:b' k-e:-tik-ow   le: ab'i:š
           the worker-pl ASP-3pl.ABS-plant-AF.ANT the cornfield
           The workers plant the cornfield

   (b)   le: axčak-i:b' š-e:-tik-on   č-e:h   le: ab'i:š
           the worker-pl ASP-3pl.ABS-plant-ABS.ANT to.3sg.POSS-to the cornfield
           The workers planted the cornfield

(78) (a)   le: axčak-i:b' š-e:-toʔ-(o)w   le: ala
           the worker-pl ASP-3pl.ABS-help-AF.ANT the boy
           The workers helped the boy

   (b)   le: axčak-i:b' š-e:-toʔb'-an   č-e:h   le: ala
           the worker-pl ASP-3pl.ABS-help-ABS.ANT to.3sg.POSS-to the boy
           The workers helped the boy

Note that (77c), agent-focus antipassive with the underlying O in an oblique phrase, and (77d), absolutive antipassive where the underlying O is not in an oblique phrase, are both unacceptable, at least in the major dialects:

(77) (c)   *le: axčak-i:b' š-e:-toʔ-(o)w   č-e:h   le: ala
           the worker-pl ASP-3pl.ABS-help-AF.ANT to.3sg.POSS-to the boy
           *The workers helped the boy

   (d)   *le: axčak-i:b' š-e:-toʔb'-an   le: ala
           the worker-pl ASP-3pl.ABS-help-ABS.ANT the boy
           *The workers helped the boy

Moreover, in the absolutive antipassive, the oblique phrase (in the relational noun) can optionally be omitted (as in (79a)), but only when it involves a 3rd person singular; compare the following sentences, both of which are grammatical, although the oblique phrase would have been expected also in (79a):

(79) (a)   xači:n š-Ø-čap-an   le: ts'unun
           who   ASP-3sg.ABS-capture-ABS.ANT the hummingbird
           Who caught the hummingbird?

   (b)   xači:n š-Ø-čap-an   č-e:h   le: ts'unun
           who   ASP-3sg.ABS-capture-ABS.ANT to.3sg.POSS-to the hummingbird
           Who caught the hummingbird? (Sam-Colop 1988: 98)

Compare these with the corresponding agent-focus antipassive sentences, where the presence of the oblique makes the sentence (80b) ungrammatical (Sam-Colop 1988: 97, 98):

(80) (a)   xači:n š-Ø-čap-ow   le: ts'unun
           who   ASP-3sg.ABS-capture-AF.ANT the hummingbird
           Who caught the hummingbird?

(b)　　*xači:n š-Ø-čap-ow　　　　　č-e:h　　　le: ts'unun
　　　　who　ASP-3sg.ABS-capture-AF.ANT　to.3sg.POSS-to the hummingbird
　　　　*Who caught the hummingbird?

Absolutive antipassive sentences with 3rd person plurals which lack the oblique are not fully grammatical, though sometimes tolerated by some speakers (as in (81a)), contrasted with grammatical (81b). These are contrasted with the agent-focus antipassive in (81c) and (81d), where (81d) shows the ungrammaticality with the dative oblique:

(81) (a)　?xači:n š-Ø-čap-an　　　　　le: ak'al-a:b'
　　　　　who　ASP-3sg.ABS-capture-ABS.ANT the boy-pl
　　　　　Who caught the boys? (Sam-Colop 1988: 98)

(b)　　xači:n š-Ø-čap-an　　　　　　či-k-e:h　　le: ak'al-a:b'
　　　　who　ASP-3sg.ABS-capture-ABS.ANT to-3pl.POSS-to the boy-pl
　　　　Who caught the boys? (Sam-Colop 1988: 98)

(c)　　xači:n š-e:-čap-ow　　　　　le: ak'al-a:b'
　　　　who　ASP-3pl.ABS-capture-AF.ANT the boy-pl
　　　　Who caught the boys? (Sam-Colop 1988: 98)

(d)　　*xači:n š-e:-čap-ow　　　　　　či-k-e:h　　le: ak'al-a:b'
　　　　who　ASP-3pl.ABS-capture-AF.ANT to-3pl.POSS-to the boy-pl
　　　　Who caught the boys? (Sam-Colop 1988: 98)

3.4.1　Functions

The absolutive antipassive has several functions. One is 'to delete or demote an indefinite, obvious, or insignificant transitive object [underlying O] . . . A speaker at times . . . chooses to use the absolutive [antipassive] rather than the active [transitive] voice because he does not consider the direct object as important as the action and the subject/agent who performs it' (Mondloch 1979: 275). Some additional examples of absolutive antipassive with omitted underlying Os are:

(82)　　k-Ø-loq'-on　　　　　ri w-ika:q'
　　　　ASP-3sg.ABS-buy-ABS.ANT the my-nephew
　　　　my nephew buys

(83)　　sib'alax　k-iš-yax-an-ik
　　　　very.much ASP-2pl.ABS-scold-ABS.ANT-INTR
　　　　You really scold a lot

In some cases the omitted O-role NP is a predictable or prototypical O, as 'song' for the verb 'sing' in (84) (Davies and Sam-Colop 1990: 525):

(84)   k-e:-b'iša-n   le: ak'al-a:b' pa xa:h
ASP-3pl.ABS-sing-ABS.ANT the child-pl   in house
The children sing indoors

3.4.2   Disambiguating function

As seen above (§2.2), sometimes when both the A and O are 3rd persons of
the same number (both singular or both plural), the active transitive sentence
is ambiguous. Also, where one of the arguments is *-in-* '1st person singular'
(which does not distinguish between 1sg.ABS and 1sg.ERG) and the other
participant is a 2nd person reverential form (sg or pl), the active transitive
sentence would be ambiguous (see above). In these situations, K'iche' prefers
the absolutive antipassive as one mechanism for disambiguating these. Thus,
for example, (85a) and (86a) would be ambiguous:

(85) (a) k-in-to?   lah
(1)   ASP-1sg.ERG-help 2sg.ABS.REV
          I helped you

(2)   ASP-1sg.ABS-help 2sg.ERG.REV
          You helped me

(86) (a) š-in-kuna-x   alaq
(1)   ASP-1sg.ERG-cure-TR 2pl.ABS.REV
          I cured you

(2)   ASP-1sg.ABS-cure-TR 2pl.ERG.REV
          You cured me

These are shifted to absolutive antipassive to disambiguate them:

(85) (b)
(1)   k-in-to?b'-an   č-e:h   lah
          ASP-1sg.ABS-help-ABS.ANT to.3sg.POSS-to 2sg.REV
          I helped you

(2)   k-to?b'-an   lah   č-w-e:h
          ASP-help-ABS.ANT 2sg.REV.ABS to-1sg.POSS-to
          You helped me

(86) (b)
(1)   š-in-kuna-n   č-e:č alaq
          ASP-1sg.ABS-cure-ABS.ANT to-to 2pl.ABS.REV
          I cured you

(2)   š-in-kuna-n   alaq   č-w-e:h
          ASP-1sg.ABS-cure-ABS.ANT 2pl.REV.ABS to-1sg.POSS-to
          You cured me

3.4.3 Hierarchy-linked function

In K'iche', there is a constraint (mentioned above, see §2.1.2) on transitive clauses: 'a third person subject [A] and a second person formal [reverential] object [O] cannot co-occur in an active [transitive] clause . . . such a combination will frequently be expressed in an absolutive antipassive construction'. This constraint is linked to the pronoun/animacy hierarchy. To accommodate the hierarchy restriction, sentences such as the unacceptable (87a) and (88a) are put in the absolutive antipassive, as in (87b) and (88b), to make them acceptable:

(87) (a) ?k-ki-to?   lah
           ASP-3pl.ERG-help 2sg.ABS.REV
           ?They help you

(b)   k-e:-to?b'-an   č-e:h   lah
           ASP-3pl.ABS-help-ABS.ANT to.3sg.POSS-to 2sg.REV
           They help you[18]

(88) (a) *k-u-tsuku-x   lah
           ASP-3sg.ERG-look.for-TR 2sg.REV.ABS
           *He looks for you

(b)   k-Ø-tsuku-n   č-e:h   lah
           ASP-3sg.ABS-look.for-ABS.ANT to.3sg.POSS-to 2sg.REV
           He looks for you

3.5 *Ambitransitive-like matters and semantic wrinkles*

Let us now return to the topic of ambitransitives – verbs which can be used in both transitive and intransitive clauses. While strictly speaking these do not occur in K'iche', there is a related phenomenon involving unexpected semantic and syntactic outcomes of some verbs when they occur with the 'absolutive' antipassive suffix. In a very few cases, the transitive verb root in antipassive form has a meaning more like a medio-passive than the antipassive, where the single core argument (absolutive) seems to function more as underlying O (or reflexive), rather than as an underlying A, as in:

(89) (a) š-Ø-wuli-n   le: xa:h
           ASP-3sg.ABS-collapse-ABS.ANT the house
           The house fell down (Mondloch 1979: 273, 289)

(b)   š-Ø-wuli-n   le: čoma:l aw-uma:l
           ASP-3sg.ABS-collapse-ABS.ANT the meeting 2sg.POSS-by/because
           You wrecked the meeting (lit. The meeting came apart because of you / on your account) (Mondloch 1979: 273, 289; -*wuli* is translated variously as 'to crumble, collapse, dismantle, take apart, wreck')

---

[18] In this case, -*to?* and -*to(?)b'*- are merely allomorphs of the verb 'to help'.

Contrast this with the fully active transitive in (89c) (Davies and Sam-Colop 1990: 529):

(89) (c)　le: kab'raqan　š-Ø-u-wuli-x　　　　　　　le: xa:h
　　　　　the earthquake ASP-3sg.ABS-3sg.ERG-collapse-TR the house
　　　　　The earthquake crumbled the house

Sentence (89a) does not mean 'the house collapsed/crumbled something', as would normally be expected if it were derived from an active transitive form, illustrated in (89c). Some other examples of such seemingly medio-passive verbs are seen in the following pairs which compare the sentences which have antipassive morphology (in the (a) examples) with the active transitive sentences (in the (b) examples):

(90) (a)　k-Ø-raqi-n　　　　　　　　le: pu:puh
　　　　　ASP-3sg.ABS-break-ABS.ANT the balloon
　　　　　The balloon will break [explode] (Mondloch 1979: 273, 289)

(b)　　　le: q'a:q'　š-Ø-u-raqi-x　　　　　　le: pu:pux
　　　　　the fire　ASP-3sg.ABS-3sg.ERG-break-TR the balloon
　　　　　The fire broke the balloon (Davies and Sam-Colop 1990: 537)

(91) (a)　š-Ø-ts'api-n　　　　　　　le: u-či?　　　　　xa:h
　　　　　ASP-3sg.ABS-close-ABS.ANT the 3sg.POSS-mouth house
　　　　　The door closed (Trechsel 1982: 65)

(b)　　　le: išoq　š-Ø-u-ts'api-x　　　　　　le: u-či?　　　　　xa:h
　　　　　the woman ASP-3sg.ABS-3sg.ERG-close-TR the 3sg.POSS-mouth house
　　　　　The woman closed the door (Trechsel 1982: 65)

(92) (a)　k-Ø-č'ax-an　　　　　　　　le: po?t
　　　　　ASP-3sg.ABS-wash-ABS.ANT the huipil
　　　　　The huipil (native blouse) runs (is not colour-fast) (Mondloch 1979: 273, 289)

(b)　　　k-Ø-u-č'ax　　　　　　　le: po?t le: ali
　　　　　ASP-3sg.ABS-3sg.ERG-wash the huipil the girl
　　　　　The girl washes the huipil (native blouse)

(93) (a)　la k-e:-tix-ow　　　　　　le: raqantiš
　　　　　Q ASP-3pl.ABS-eat-AF.ANT the elephant
　　　　　Are elephants eaten? (Davies and Sam-Colop 1990: 527)

(b)　　　la k-e:-ki-tix　　　　　　le: raqantiš le: ačix-ab'
　　　　　Q ASP-3pl.ABS-3pl.ERG-eat the elephant the man-pl
　　　　　Do the men eat the elephants?

The verbs of these (a) sentences have been variously called 'pseudopassives', 'inactives' and 'middles' (Davies and Sam-Colop 1990: 527; cf. Mondloch

1979, Norman and Campbell 1978). Norman's and Campbell's (1978: 151–2) discussion of these is frequently cited; they say:

> Apparently these suffixes [antipassive suffixes in Mayan languages] can occur in simple intransitive sentences which have no relation to antipassive constructions. To take an example, both -*Vn* and -*ow* are employed in Quiche antipassive constructions, but they may also derive verb stems which occur in simple intransitive clauses. It is interesting that the verbs derived with these suffixes include both actives and inactives. Examples of actives are plentiful (cf. *kinxojowik* 'I dance' [k-in-šox-ow-ik [ASP-1sg.ABS-dance-AF.ANT-INTR]], *kintz'iib'anik* 'I write' [k-in-ts'i:b'a-n-ik [ASP-1sg.ABS-write-AF.ANT-INTR]]); examples of inactives include *katijowik* 'it is eaten' [k-Ø-tix-ow-ik [ASP-3sg.ABS-eat-AF.ANT-INTR]], *kayub'uwik* 'it is spongy' [k-Ø-yub'-uw-ik [ASP-3sg.ABS-extinguish/tighten-AF.ANT-INTR]], *katz'inowik* 'it is silent' [k-Ø-ts'in-ow-ik [ASP-3sg.ABS-be.silent/desolate-AF.ANT-INTR]], *kawulinik* 'it collapses' [k-Ø-wuli-n-ik [ASP-3sg.ABS-fall.apart-AF.ANT-INTR]], *kajat'inik* 'it is too tight' [k-Ø-xat'i-n-ik [ASP-3sg.ABS-be.tied-AF.ANT-INTR]], *karich'inik* 'it tears' [k-Ø-rič'i-n-ik [ASP-3sg.ABS-tear-AF.ANT-INTR]].
>
> In Quiche . . . one could argue that -*Vn* . . . and -*ow* . . . are neutral voice suffixes which derive a class of neutral intransitive stems whose subjects could be active or inactive, depending on the syntactic construction and the semantic features of the subject and the verb root.

Davies and Sam-Colop, in their relational grammar account of K'iche' antipassives, stress these cases where 'antipassives and "inactives" take the same voice morphology' (1990: 527); they analyse the 'inactives' as 'unaccusatives' (that is, lacking underlying A so that underlying O shifts to surface S; 1990: 535; cf. Sam-Colop 1988: 136). They also argue that K'iche' has 'a small number of bivalent verbs' (1990: 537; as illustrated by the (a–b) pairs in the sentences above: (90a–93b)). However, I agree with Dayley (1981: 25) in treating these as 'a few derived I[ntransitive] V[erb]s that are formally like absolutive antipassives; however, they have been lexicalized so that their Ss refer to the P[atient, i.e. O] of the underlying T[ransitive] V[erb], not the A'.[19]

---

[19] A few verbs have special unexpected meanings, some of which vary from dialect to dialect, when put in the absolutive antipassive, e.g.:

č'ax 'to wash'	č'axa-n 'to wash oneself, for colours to run'
elesa:-x 'to remove, take out'	elesa-n 'to take after (a chip off the old block)'
(from *e:l* 'leave' + -*sa*-'causative')	
k'am 'to get, receive'	k'am-on 'to receive, become habitual'
tix 'to eat'	tix-on 'to eat people' (Proto-K'ichean *tix* 'eat meat')
tsaq 'to drop (let fall)'	tsaq-an 'to abort'
ts'uma:-x 'to kiss'	ts'uma-n 'to nurse, suckle'
	(Mondloch 1979: 291–2; Trechsel 1982: 64)

It should also be noted that a few RTVs can form alternative simple passive forms, either as expected with lengthened root vowel or through suffixing -*ow*:

4   Reflexives

Reflexives are rather straightforward and do not change the valency of the sentence. K'iche' reflexives consist of a regular transitive verb followed by the relational noun -*i:b'* 'self' as the O-role argument, with no argument-transferring derivations. They are unambiguously transitive in structure, with -*i:b'* 'self' following the verb and agreeing in person and number with the A-role verb marking, signalled by the possessive prefixes; since this reflexive word is an external NP, it is cross-referenced by 3sg.ABS in the verb:

(94)   š-Ø-qa-kuna:-x   q-i:b'
        ASP-3sg.ABS-1pl.ERG-cure-TR 1pl.POSS-REFL
        We cured ourselves

(95)   k-Ø-a-tixo-x   aw-i:b'
        ASP-3sg.ABS-2sg.ERG-teach-TR 2sg.POSS-REFL
        You teach yourself

One interesting fact about the reflexives is that they are an exception to the general rule that A-role participants (ergative, transitive subjects) cannot be extracted when questioned, relativized or focussed in normal transitive verbs but must be cast in the agent-focus antipassive as absolutives (above). With reflexives, the A (ergative, transitive subject) can readily be extracted in order to be relativized, questioned or focussed with no voice change in the verb necessary:

(96) (a) š-Ø-w-il   ri ačih ri š-Ø-u-sok
          ASP-3sg.ABS-1sg.ERG-see the man REL ASP-3sg.ABS-3sg.ERG-wound
          r-i:b'
          3sg.POSS-REFL
          I saw the man who wounded himself

(Footnote 19 continued)

č'i:x/č'ix-ow	'to be tolerated/withstood'
q'i(:)ʔ/q'iʔ-ow	'to be tolerated/withstood'
ti:x/tix-ow	'to be eaten'
k'i:s/k'is-ow	'to be finished/ended'
ri:q/riq-ow	'to be reached'
ko:l/kol-ow	'to be defended/rescued/saved'

The -*ow* suffix marks the agent-focus antipassives; however, here these are taken to be passives and not antipassives, since they occur with passive meaning and syntax. For example (1a) and (1b) show the two passive alternatives, with the same meaning and with the 'by' phrase:

(1) (a) š-Ø-k'is-ow   xuntir le: wah k-uma:l
         ASP-3sg.ABS-finish-PASS   whole the tortilla 3pl.POSS-by
         The tortillas were completely finished off by them

    (b) š-Ø-k'i:s   xuntir le: wah k-uma:l
         ASP-3sg.ABS-finish.PASS   whole the tortilla 3pl.POSS-by
         The tortillas were completely finished off by them

If it were a non-reflexive external NP in A role in the subordinate clause being relativized, we would expect the agent-focus antipassive, which in this case turns out to be ungrammatical:

(96) (b) *š-Ø-w-il   ri ačih ri š-Ø-sok-ow
          ASP-3sg.ABS-1sg.ERG-see the man REL ASP-3sg.ABS-wound-AF.ANT
          r-i:b'
          3sg.POSS-REFL
          *I saw the man who wounded himself

The same is true of the focus (cleft) sentences, where those with agent-focus antipassive and reflexive together are ungrammatical (Trechsel 1993: 48):

(97) (a) *in   š-in-sok-ow   w-i:b'
          1sg.INDEP.PN ASP-1sg.ABS-wound-AF.ANT 1sg.POSS-REFL
          *I am the one who wounded myself

     (b) *in   š-Ø-sok-ow   w-i:b'
          1sg.INDEP.PN ASP-3sg.ABS-wound-AF.ANT 1sg.POSS-REFL
          *I am the one who wounded myself

This must be expressed with regular active transitive morphology (Trechsel 1993: 49):

(97) (c) in   š-Ø-in-sok   w-i:b'
          1sg.INDEP.PN ASP-3sg.ABS-1sg.ERG-wound 1sg.POSS-REFL
          I am the one who wounded myself[20]

---

[20] Mondloch (1981) and Trechsel (1993: 49) report that the constraint against agent-focus antipassives with reflexives may be more general, since the agent-focus antipassive is also not permitted when the focussed NP is coreferential with the possessor of a NP in O role, as seen in the following:

(1) *are: le: a šwa:n š-Ø-k'at-ow   r-aqan
     FOC the HON John ASP-3sg.ABS-burn-AF.ANT 3sg.POSS-foot
     *John$_1$ is the one who burned his$_1$ foot

(2) *e: xači:n š-e:-tsaq-ow   ki-xasta:q
     pl who   ASP-3pl.ABS-lose-AF.ANT 3pl.POSS-thing
     *Who$_1$ are the ones who lost their$_1$ things?

(3) *š-Ø-in-č'ab'e-x   le: ačih le: š-Ø-xač-ow
     ASP-3sg.ABS-1sg.ERG-speak-TR the man REL ASP-3sg.ABS-divorce-AF.ANT
     r-išoqi:l
     3sg.POSS-wife
     *I talked to the man$_1$ who divorced his$_1$ wife (Trechsel 1993: 49)

The only way to express these grammatically is with an active transitive verb inflected with both ergative and absolutive affixes.

Another somewhat odd piece of behaviour in the K'iche' reflexive is the fact that reflexive clauses can be passivized in the completive passive:

(98)   k-Ø-č'ax-tax   w-i:b'   w-uma:l
        ASP-3sg.ABS-wash-CMPL.PASS 1sg.POSS-REFL 1sg.POSS-by
        I will finish washing myself (lit. Myself gets washed by me, i.e., I get washed by myself)

(99)   š-Ø-kuna-tax   aw-i:b'   aw-uma:l
        ASP-3sg.ABS-cure-CMPL.PASS 2sg.POSS-REFL 2sg.POSS-by
        You finished curing yourself (lit. Yourself got cured by you, i.e., You got cured by yourself)[21]

Reciprocals are straightforward and essentially like reflexives, as seen in:

(100)   Ø-ki-tere-b'a-l-o?m   k-i:b'
        3sg.ABS-3pl.ERG-follow-CAUS-Rapid.action-PERF 3pl.POSS-REFL
        They are following one after another

One reciprocal construction – an indefinite 'they' – used only for indefinite persons, is essentially merely a passivized version of the transitive reflexive clause, though with no possessive prefixes on the relational noun *i:b'* 'self', which otherwise normally does not occur unpossessed, and with the verb ordinarily only in incomplete aspect (*k-*):

(101)   k-Ø-to:?   i:b'
        ASP-3sg.ABS-help.PASS REFL
        They (indefinite) help each other (lit. self is helped)

(102)   k-Ø-loq'o-š   i:b'
        ASP-3sg.ABS-love-PASS REFL
        They (indefinite) love each other (lit. self is loved) (Mondloch 1979: 211)

---

[21] However, according to Ayres (1980: 56), 'the relational noun [*r-uma:l* 3sg.POSS-by] may not be used in conjuction with the reflexive in such passives', as seen, as he reports, in grammatical (1) and (2), but ungrammatical (3) with completive passive and the 'by'-phrase:

(1)   š-Ø-č'ax-tax   r-uma:l   le: ačih
       ASP-3sg.ABS-wash-CMPL.PASS 3sg.POSS-by the man
       It got washed by the man / The man finished washing it

(2)   š-Ø-č'ax-tax   r-i:b'   le: ačih
       ASP-3sg.ABS-wash-CMPL.PASS 3sg.POSS-REFL the man
       The man finished washing himself (lit. himself got washed by the man)

(3)   *š-Ø-č'ax-tax   r-i:b'   r-uma:l le: ačih
       ASP-3sg.ABS-wash-CMPL.PASS 3sg.POSS-REFL 3sg.POSS-by the man
       *The man finished washing himself (lit. himself got washed by the man)

Essentially it is A-role NPs (transitive subjects) which control reflexivization (oblique NPs do not control reflexivization in K'iche'; Larsen and Norman 1979: 349), but the statement of the constraint must be refined to take into account the reciprocal construction in (101) and (102) in which the reflexive can be passivized. Here it would appear that the former O-role reflexive relational noun has been placed in S-role (subject of the intransitivized passive verb); however, in this case the reflexive *i:b'* is unusual, since relational nouns characteristically bear a possessive pronominal prefix reflecting the person and number of the controlling A-role NP, but in this reciprocal construction lack this prefix.

5   Adding an argument to the core: causatives

Causative morphology in K'iche' is rather straightforward and reasonably productive. The suffix *-(i)sa-* derives transitive verbs from intransitives, as seen in the following pairs of sentences:

(103) (a) š-e:-kam-ik
         ASP-3pl.ABS-die-INTR
         They died

(b)   š-e:-qa-kam-isa:-x
         ASP-3pl.ABS-1pl.ERG-die-CAUS-TR
         We killed them

(104) (a) š-Ø-atin-ik
         ASP-3sg.ABS-bathe-INTR
         He bathed

(b)   š-Ø-r-atin-isa:-x
         ASP-3sg.ABS-3sg.ERG-bathe-CAUS-TR
         She bathed him

The causative of positional stems is signalled by the suffix *-b'aʔ*, as in:

(105)   š-qa-t'uyu-b'aʔ   lah
         ASP-1pl.ERG-sit-CAUS 2sg.ABS.REV
         We seated you

(106)   ri tina š-Ø-u-q'oyo-b'aʔ   ri r-a:l   pa ri č'a:t
         the Tina ASP-3sg.ABS-3sg.ERG-lie.down-CAUS the 3sg.POSS-child in the bed
         Tina lay her child in the bed

6   Argument-manipulating derivation

K'iche' has only one argument-manipulating derivational construction, which
is called instrumental voice (but is in fact an instrumental applicative, in
the terms of Dixon and Aikhenvald 1997). In the construction Mayanists call
'instrumental voice' or 'instrument advancement', transitive verbs take the
suffix -*b'e*-, which promotes the underlying instrument to a derived O (direct
object), and the logical O (underlying direct object) is marked obliquely with
a relational noun (-*e:h*/-*e:č*) 'possession' [GEN]). Compare the following pairs
of sentences, where the (a) example is a regular active transitive and the (b)
example is in instrumental voice:

(107) (a) š-Ø-u-rami-x   le: če:ʔ le: ačih č-e:h   xun č'i:č
       ASP-3sg.ABS-3sg.ERG-cut-TR the tree the man to.3sg.POSS-to a   metal
       The man cut the tree with a machete

    (b) č'i:č' š-Ø-u-rami-b'e-x   le: ačih r-e:h   le: če:ʔ
       metal ASP-3sg.ABS-3sg.ERG-cut-INSTR-TR the man 3sg.POSS-GEN the tree
       The man used a machete to cut the tree / A machete is what the man used to
       cut the tree

(108) (a) š-at-in-č'ay   či   če:ʔ
       ASP-2sg.ABS-1sg.ERG-hit with wood
       I hit you with a stick

    (b) če:ʔ š-Ø-in-č'aya-b'e-x   a:w-e:h
       wood ASP-3sg.ABS-1sg.ERG-hit-INSTR-TR 2sg.POSS-GEN
       I used a stick to hit you

In (108b), *če:ʔ* 'wood, tree, stick' is promoted to O (direct object) and is
cross-referenced in the verb by -*Ø*- '3sg.ABS', while 'you' (the underlying O,
as in (108a)) is relegated to an oblique, here as *a:w-e:h* (Sam-Colop 1988:
70).

The NP promoted by the instrumental voice need not 'be a "pure instrument" [though usually it is], but a means of doing something. Thus, it can
be a person, an adverb, or a sentence' (Sam-Colop 1988: 104; see Mondloch
1981: 296). For example (Sam-Colop 1988: 121):

(109)   e: are: q-axa:w k-Ø-ki-toq'i-b'e-x   r-e:h   ri pwaq
       pl FOC our-lord ASP-3sg.ABS-3pl.ERG-ask.for-INSTR-TR 3sg.POSS-GEN the money
       They used God to ask for money

The -*b'e*- instrumental suffix can also be used with intransitive verb stems
to make a non-A/non-O NP (i.e. instrument, locative) into a core argument of
the verb, as, for example, in:

(110)   le: ačih le: b'o:la:x   š-Ø-u-t'uy-uli-b'e-x
        the man the block.of.wood ASP-3sg.ABS-3sg.ERG-sit-POSI-INST-TR
        The man sat on a block of wood / The man used a block of wood to sit on

(111)   Ø-tak'-al   le: ačih č-u-wa   xa:h
        3sg.ABS-stand-POSI the man to-3sg.POSS-before house
        š-Ø-r-oki-b'e-x   le: ts'i? pa xa:h
        ASP-3sg.ABS-3sg.ERG-enter-INST-TRthe dog in house
        (While) the man (was) standing in front of the house, the dog entered the
        house / (The dog used the man's standing before the house to enter the
        house) (Kaufman 1990: 79)

It is possible with the *-b'e-* instrumental voice also to topicalize another NP
which is not the underlying instrument, as seen in (Kaufman 1990: 79):

(112)   le: ačih xukub' k-Ø-u-wa?oq-isa-b'e-x   r-e:h
        the man trough ASP-3sg.ABS-3sg.ERG-eat-CAUS-INST-TR 3sg.POSS-GEN
        le: a:q
        the pig
        As for the man, a trough is what he used to feed the pigs

A NP advanced in the instrumental construction can also be relativized and
questioned (Kaufman 1990: 100):

(113)   le: mu:ruh le: š-Ø-u-rami-b'e-x   le: če:? le: ačih
        the machete REL ASP-3sg.ABS-3sg.ERG-cut-INST-TR the tree the man
        The machete with which the man cut the wood . . .

(114)   xa:čike: mu:ruh š-Ø-u-rami-b'e-x   le: če:? le: ačih
        which   machete ASP-3sg.ABS-3sg.ERG-cut-INST-TR the tree the man
        With which machete did the man cut the wood?

Otherwise, K'iche' has no special derivational properties for non-A and
non-O participants; all other clauses which in some languages mark a valency
of more than two core arguments mark non-A and non-O obliquely as relational nouns in K'iche', as seen in the three-place predicate of (115):

(115)   le: alah š-Ø-u-ya: le: ya:k č-e:č   le:
        the youth ASP-3sg.ABS-3sg.ERG-give the fox to.3sg.POSS-to the
        r-ači?il
        his-companion
        The boy gave the fox to his friend / The boy gave his friend the fox

7   Summary

Figure 7.3 summarizes some of the verbal morphology involving transitivity,
verb class and valency derivation:

Figure 7.3. Verb-class morphology in K'iche'

	INTRANS	DTV	RTV	POSI
active	*-ik* (phrase-final)	*-x* (phrase-final)	*-oh* (phrase-final)	*-iʔ(-ik)*
simple passive		*-š*	*V:* (in root)	
completive passive		*-(V)tax*	*-(V)tax*	
AF.ANT		*-n*	*-ow*	
ABS.ANT		*-(o)n*	*-n*	
causative		*-(i)sa-*	*-(i)sa-*	*-bʼa-*

Figure 7.4 summarizes the choices involved in determining voice markers and valency derivations in K'iche':

Figure 7.4. Voice markers and valency derivation decisions

CLAUSE WITH BOTH A AND O? No = intransitive (*-ik* phrase-final markers)
Yes:
    FOCUS ON RESULT? Yes = *-(V)tax* completive passive
    No:
        1ST AND 2ND PERS INFORMAL ARGUMENTS? Yes = active TR (*-x/-oh* phrase-final markers)
        No:
            AGENT FOCUS? Yes = *-n/-ow* agent-focus antipassive
            No:
                O FOCUS? Yes = *V/-š:* simple passive
                No:
                    ACTION FOCUS; REDUCED TRANSITIVITY? Yes = (*-(o)n/-n*) absolutive antipassive
                    No = active TR (*-x/-oh* phrase-final markers)

References

Ayres, G. 1980. 'A note on Mayan reflexives', *Journal of Mayan Linguistics* 2.53–9.
Davies, W.D. and Sam-Colop, L.E. 1990. 'K'iche' and the structure of antipassive', *Language* 66.522–49.
Dayley, J.P. 1981. 'Voice and ergativity in Mayan languages', *Journal of Mayan Linguistics* 2.3–82.
Dixon, R.M.W. 1994. *Ergativity*. Cambridge: Cambridge University Press.
Dixon, R.M.W. and Aikhenvald, A.Y. 1997. 'A typology of argument-determined constructions', pp. 71–113 of *Essays on language function and language type*, ed. J. Bybee, J. Haiman and S.A. Thompson. Amsterdam: John Benjamins.
Hale, K. and Storto, L. Forthcoming. 'Agreement and spurious antipassives'. In *ABRALIN, Boletim da Associação Brasileira de Lingüística*.

Kaufman, T. 1990. 'Algunos rasgos estructurales de los idiomas mayances con referencia especial al K'iche'', pp. 59–114 of *Lecturas sobre la lingüística maya*, ed. N.C. England and S.R. Elliott. Guatemala: Centro de Investigaciones Regionales de Mesoamerica.

Larsen, T.W. 1987. 'The syntactic status of ergativity in Quiché', *Lingua* 71.33–59.

Larsen, T. and Norman, W.M. 1979. 'Correlates of ergativity in Mayan grammar', pp. 347–70 of *Ergativity: towards a theory of grammatical relations*, ed. F. Plank. London: Academic Press.

Mithun, M. 1984. 'The evolution of noun incorporation', *Language* 60.847–94.

Mondloch, J.L. 1976. 'Positional roots in Quiché'. Unpublished Master's essay. University of Rochester, Rochester, N.Y.

1978a. *Basic Quiché grammar*, Institute for Mesoamerican Studies 2. Albany: State University of New York.

1978b. 'Disambiguating subjects and objects in Quiché', *Journal of Mayan Linguistics* 1.3–19.

1979. 'Case marking mechanisms in Mayan languages'. Doctoral qualifying examination essay. Department of Anthropology, State University of New York, Albany.

1981. 'Voice in Quiché-Maya'. Ph.D. dissertation. State University of New York, Albany.

Nik'te' (M.J. Sis Iboy) and Saqijix (C.D. López Ixcoy). 1993. *Gramática pedagógica K'ichee' [Oxlajuuj Keej Maya' Ajtz'iib]*. Guatemala: Universidad Rafael Landívar, Programa para el Desarrollo Integral de la Población Maya.

Norman, W.M. 1973. 'Positional and transitive roots in Quiché'. Paper presented at the annual meeting of the American Anthropological Association.

Norman, W.M. and Campbell, L. 1978. 'Toward a Proto-Mayan syntax: a comparative perspective on grammar', pp. 136–56 of *Papers in Mayan linguistics, II*, ed. N. England, Miscellaneous Publications in Anthropology 6. Columbia: Museum of Anthropology, University of Missouri.

Sam Colop, L.E. 1988. 'Antipassive and the 2 to 3 retreat in K'iche''. Unpublished Master's thesis. University of Iowa.

1990. 'Bosquejo de algunos temas de la gramática K'iche'', pp. 127–44 of *Lecturas sobre la lingüística maya*, ed. N.C. England and S.R. Elliott. Guatemala: Centro de Investigaciones Regionales de Mesoamerica.

Smith-Stark, T. 1978. 'The Mayan antipassive: some facts and fictions', pp. 169–87 of *Papers in Mayan linguistics, II*, ed. N. England, Miscellaneous Publications in Anthropology 6. Columbia: Museum of Anthropology, University of Missouri.

Trechsel, F.R. 1982. *A categorial fragment of Quiché*, Texas Linguistics Forum 20. Austin, Tex.: Department of Linguistics, University of Texas at Austin.

1993. 'Quiché focus constructions', *Lingua* 91.33–78.

8 Valency-changing derivations in Dulong/Rawang

RANDY J. LAPOLLA

1 Introduction

Dulong/Rawang is a Tibeto-Burman language spoken on both sides of the China/Myanmar (Burma) border just south and east of Tibet. In China, the people who speak this language for the most part live in Gongshan county of Yunnan province, and belong either to what is known as the 'Dulong' nationality (pop. 5,816 according to the 1990 census), or to one part (roughly 6,000 people) of the Nu nationality (those who live along the upper reaches of the Nu River – the part of the Salween within China). Another subgroup of the Nu people, those who live along the lower reaches of the Nu River (in China), speak a language called 'Anung' which seems to be the same as, or closely related to, the Kwinpang dialect spoken in Myanmar, so should also be considered a dialect of Dulong/Rawang.[1] Within Myanmar, the people who speak the Dulong/Rawang language (possibly up to 100,000 people) live in northern Kachin State, particularly along the Mae Hka ('Nmai Hka) and Maeli Hka (Mali Hka) River valleys. In the past they had been called 'Hkanung' or 'Nung', and have often been considered to be a subgroup of the Kachin (Jinghpaw). Among themselves they have had no general term for the entire group; they use their respective clan names to refer to themselves. This is true also of those who live in China, although these people have accepted the

I'd like to thank all those who gave me comments on the draft of this chapter presented at the International Workshop on Valency-changing Derivations (Canberra, 1997), and also the editors of this volume and Tasaku Tsunoda for comments on the written version.

[1] See Sun (1988) for a brief description of the Anung language. See Lo (1945), Sun (1982), Liu (1988), Dai et al. (1991) and LaPolla (1995b) for descriptions of Dulong dialects. Barnard (1934) is a description of the Wvdamkong dialect of Rawang, though it does not mark tones or glottal stops, and the structures presented there seem to have been influenced by the working language (Jinghpaw) used for the elicitation.

exonym 'Dulong' (or 'Taron', or 'Trung'), a name they were given because they mostly live in the valley of the Dulong (Taron/Trung) River.[2]

Recently, speakers of this language in Myanmar have begun a movement to use the name /rəwaŋ/ (spelled 'Rvwang' in the Rawang orthographies, but 'Rawang' for this chapter) to represent all of its speakers. This name is said to be an abbreviation for *rvmèwàng* 'middle river', as the Rawang people are said to have come down from the north along the middle river (the Mekong). The speakers in China, though, continue to use the name 'Dulong'. For this reason I refer to the language as Dulong/Rawang.[3] In this chapter, I will be using data of the Mvtwang (Mvt River) dialect, which is considered the most central of those dialects in Myanmar and so has become something of a standard for writing[4] and intergroup communication, though most of the phenomena we will be discussing are general to dialects in both China and Myanmar.[5] I will use the short form 'Rawang' in referring to this dialect.

2   Verb classes

In Rawang there are three classes of verb: intransitives, which can be used transitively only when they take valency-increasing morphological marking

---

[2] The name 'Nung' ~ 'Anung' (< Rawang *Nòng*) seems to be related to one of the Rawang names for the Salween, *Tinòng* 'Brown River', a place where the Rawang people are said to have settled for quite some time before moving further west. In the past, the Dulong River, particularly the upper stretches, was known in Chinese as the Qiu River, and the Dulong people were known as the Qiu, Qiuzi, Qiupa or Qiao.

[3] The actual number of dialects of Dulong/Rawang that exist and the relationships among them still need to be worked out, but it seems there are at least seven major dialects: Mvtwang, Wvdamkong, Longmi, Dvru (Ganung), Dulong, Tangsarr and Kwinpang (Anung). Within the Dulong dialect it is also possible to distinguish at least four subvarieties: First Township, Third Township, Fourth Township and Nujiang Dulong. The differences among these subvarieties are rather minor, and so all are mutually intelligible. The dialect picture is actually not neatly divided between Chinese and Myanmar dialects, as Third Township Dulong and Dvru (spoken in Myanmar) are both very conservative phonologically, while the First Township, Fourth Township and Nujiang varieties of Dulong share phonological innovations with other dialects in Myanmar.

[4] A system of writing using the Roman alphabet and a few other symbols was developed by the American missionary Robert H. Morse (see Morse 1963 for an analysis of Rawang phonology), and is in common use among the Rawang people. This system will be used in this chapter. Most letters represent the standard pronunciations of English, except that *i* = [i], *v* = [ə], *a* = [ɑ], *ø* = [ɯ], *q* = [ʔ] and *c* = [s] or [ts] (free variation; historically [ts]). Tones are marked as follows (using the letter *a* as a base): high tone, *á*; mid tone, *ā*; low tone, *à*. All syllables that end in a stop consonant (-p, -t, -ʔ, -k) are in the high tone. Open syllables without a tone mark are unstressed. A colon marks non-basic long vowels.

[5] The data used for this chapter are from a number of different speakers, though mainly from James Khong Sar Ong and Meram Rawang, both native Mvtwang speakers from Kachin State, Myanmar. I would like to thank them for their assistance.

(e.g. *ngōē* 'to cry');[6] transitives, which can be used intransitively only when they take valency-reducing morphological marking (e.g. *rìòē* 'to carry (something)'); ambitransitives (labile verbs), which can be used as transitives or intransitives without morphological derivation (*v̀mòē/v̄mē* 'to eat').[7] The citation form for verbs is the 3rd person non-past affirmative/declarative form; intransitives take the non-past affirmative/declarative particle (*ē*) alone, while transitives take the non-past 3rd person O marker (*ò*) plus the non-past affirmative/declarative particle (*ē*). A second difference between intransitive and transitive verbs is that in transitive clauses the agentive marker generally appears on the NP representing the A argument.[8] In past-tense clauses (with 3rd person O arguments), transitives can be distinguished from intransitives by the appearance of the transitive past-tense marker (*-à*) instead of the intransitive past-tense marker (*-ì*). We will discuss derived transitives and intransitives below.[9]

Ambitransitive verbs are verbs that can be used either as transitives (and so take the 3rd person transitive tense markers) or as intransitives (and take the intransitive past-tense marker), without requiring any other morphological derivation. There are both S = O types and S = A types. With the S = O type, as in (1), below, adding an A argument creates a causative, without the need to use the causative prefix. With the S = A type, use of the intransitive vs the transitive form marks a difference between a general or habitual situation and a particular situation respectively. The choice is due partly to the nature of

---

[6] Some stative intransitive verbs can take an oblique argument marked by the locative/dative marker *sv̀ng*, e.g. *svrē* 'to be afraid', where the stimulus is marked as an oblique argument:

> ngà vgīsv̀ng svrēngē
> ngà vgī-sv̀ng svrē-ng-ē
> 1sg dog-LOC afraid-1sg-N.PAST
> I'm afraid of dogs

[7] I have found one case where there are two verbs with the same meaning, one transitive and the other intransitive. These are the verbs for 'arrive': *hōq (høqòē)* is transitive, *tuq (tuqē)* is intransitive: *ngà tukngē* 'I arrived'; *ngài Yānggūng hōk yǹngà* 'I have been to Yangon'. This shows that transitivity is a salient grammatical category in this language, unlike in many other Sino-Tibetan languages (e.g. Chinese, Lahu; see Matisoff 1976: 413 on the non-salience of transitivity as a grammatical category in Lahu).

[8] Morse (1965: 348) analysed the appearance of the verbal suffix *-ò* as a necessary criterion for a clause to be transitive, and so argued that only clauses with 3rd person O arguments were transitive. I have chosen to analyse this suffix as marking a 3rd person O argument (from a comparison with other dialects, it seems this form comes from the 3rd person form of the verb 'to do'), and consider clauses that do not have 3rd person O arguments as transitive if the NP representing the A argument can take the agentive marker. To avoid confusion, I have generally used examples involving 3rd person O arguments in this chapter.

[9] The transitive verb marking can also be added to some nouns to make transitive cognate noun–verb combinations, e.g. *(àng)chēr chēròē* 'grow wings', *pvlū pvlūòē* 'lay out a mat'. (Neither the causative nor applicative markers are used to make verbs from nouns.)

the O, and partly to the nature of general vs specific action. I.e. if the O is specific, then the transitive form must be used, but if the O is non-specific, it is not necessary to use the intransitive form. If no O is mentioned, then usually the intransitive form is used. Some examples are given in (2):

(1)   S = O type
(a)   gvyaqē   'be broken, destroyed'   gvyaqòē   'break, destroy'
(b)   gvyøpmē   'be crumpled'   gvyø:pmòē   'crumple'
(c)   dvtnē   'be broken, snapped (thread)'   da:tnòē   'break, snap' (vt)
(d)   bvløpmē   'be folded'   bvlø:pmòē   'fold' (vt)
(e)   dvchøpmē   'be capped'   dvchø:pmòē   'put cap on'

(f)   mèsògøm jaqē
        mèsògøm jaq-ē
        paper   have.holes-N.PAST
        The paper has holes in it

(g)   à:ngí mèsògøm jaq bǿà
        àng-í   mèsògøm jaq   bǿ-à
        3sg-AGT paper   make.holes PFV-3+TR.PAST
        He made holes in the paper

(2)   S = A type
(a)   àng v̄mē
        àng v̄m-ē
        3sg eat-N.PAST
        He's eating / He eats

(a')   à:ngí yālòng v́mpà á:mòē
        àng-í   yā-lòng v́mpà v́m-ò-ē
        3sg-AGT this-CL rice   eat-3+TR.N.PAST-N.PAST
        He is eating this rice

(b)   àng pé zvtnē
        àng pé   zvt-ē
        3sg basket weave-N.PAST
        He weaves baskets (general or habitual sense)

(b')   à:ngí pé tiqchv̀ng za:tnòē
        àng-í   pé   tiq-chv̀ng zvt-ò-ē
        3sg-AGT basket one-CL   weave-3+TR.N.PAST-N.PAST
        He is weaving a basket

Rawang seems to have only two lexical ditransitive (extended transitive) verbs: *zí* 'give' (3a) and *v̄l* 'tell' (3b). All other ditransitive verbs, such as another form of 'tell' (3c), *dvtānòē* 'show' (< *vtānē* 'be clearly visible'), *shvríòē* 'send' (< *rí* 'carry'), etc., are all derived using the causative construction (see (a) in §3.2.1). In both lexical and derived ditransitives, the Recipient takes Dative/Goal (Locative) marking, while the Gift is unmarked. The Donor usually takes the agentive marker. It is not possible to use the causative prefix on *zí* 'give'; for a causative sense, the analytical causative construction must be used (see (b) in §3.2.1). There is also no construction analogous to English 'dative shift'. The order of the NPs may vary according to the information structure, but there is no change in the morphological marking.

(3) (a)   Vpūngí Vdǿsv̀ng lègābok zíòē
    Vpūng-í   Vdǿ-sv̀ng lègā-bok zí-ò-ē
    Vpung-AGT Vdeu-LOC book-CL give-3+TR.N.PAST-N.PAST
    Vpung is giving Vdeu the book

(b)   àngkaq ngà zòngsv̀ng dìám èā:lòé
    àng-kaq ngà zòng-sv̀ng dì-ám è-v̄l-ò-é
    3sg-LOC 1sg school-LOC go-DIR N.1-tell-3+TR.N.PAST-exc
    Tell him I went to school

(c)   àngkaq ngà zòngsv̀ng dìám wā dètáò
    àng-kaq ngà zòng-sv̀ng dì-ám wā   dv-è-tá-ò
    3sg-LOC 1sg school-LOC go-DIR COMP CAUS-N.1-hear-3+TR.N.PAST
    Tell him I went to school

There are also at least three verbs that may be considered extended intransitives: *mvyǿ* 'to want, to like', *vdá* 'to have, to own' and *wā* 'to say' ('see', 'look at', 'hear' and 'listen to' all pattern as normal transitives). They are always intransitive, in that they cannot take the transitive tense suffixes, and the NP representing the A argument does not take the agentive marker, but they generally take two arguments, the A argument and an O argument (a clause (propositional argument) in the case of *mvyǿ* and *wā*), neither of which takes any kind of role marking (though the initial NP can take topic marking). Examples are given in (4):[10]

(4) (a)   ngà kédān lún mvyǿngē
    ngà kédān lún   mvyǿ-ng-ē
    1sg pen   have want-1sg-N.PAST
    I want to have a pen

[10] The verb *mvyǿ* 'to want' only takes a clausal argument. For wanting of an object rather than a propositional argument, usually the verb *shòng* 'to love, like' is used, e.g.:

    (nà) kāpà èshòngē
    (nà) kā-pà   è-shòng-ē
    (2sg) Q.PN-thing N.1-like/love-N.PAST
    What do you want?

The verb *vdá* can be used without the O argument, but then has the meaning 'to be rich'.

(b)　ngà pv̄ngdāngsv̀ng dī mvyǿngē
　　ngà pv̄ngdāng-sv̀ng dī mvyǿ-ng-ē
　　1sg below-LOC　　go want-1sg-N.PAST
　　I want to go downstairs/below

(c)　nōngmaq (nō) rǿmnv̄ng ànglí tiqcégǿ vdáiē
　　nōngmaq nō rǿmnv̄ng ànglí tiq-cé-gǿ vdá-ì-ē
　　1pl　　TOP friend　　old　one-ten-CL have-1pl-N.PAST
　　We have ten old friends

(d)　ngà laq dī wāē
　　ngà laq　dī wā-ē
　　1sg should go say-N.PAST
　　He says I should go

The locative postposition in (4b) is on an argument of the embedded clause, not the matrix clause. The matrix verb *mvyǿ* follows the verb of the embedded clause directly, and no directional or other post-verbal morphology can intervene. That is, there is no tense, nominalization or person marking on the embedded clause. The intransitive nature of the verb *wā* can be seen clearly when contrasted with the homophonous verb *wā* 'to do', which is transitive:[11]

(4) (e)　àng wàapmì
　　　àng wà-ap-ì
　　　3sg say-TMdys-3+INTR.PAST
　　　He said something [< wāē]

(f)　à:ngí wàapmà
　　àng-í　wà-ap-à
　　3sg-AGT do-TMdys-3+TR.PAST
　　He did something [< wāòē]

3　Argument-transferring derivations

There are a number of constructions for increasing or reducing the valency of verbs in Rawang, but there is no passive or antipassive construction.

---

[11] The verb *wā* 'to say' can also have the sense of a hearsay particle, as in the following two examples:

(1)　nà èdì bǿì wāē
　　nà è-dì　bǿ-ì　　　　wā-ē
　　2sg N.1-go PFV-3+INTR.PAST say-N.PAST
　　I heard you went (just now)

(2)　dārì dvgvp àngnōngnv̄m vshǿmpè ā:lē　　　wāē
　　dārì dvgvp àngnōngnv̄m vshǿm-pè v̄l-ē　　　wā-ē
　　past time brothers　　three-M　exist-N.PAST say-N.PAST
　　It is said that in the past there were three brothers

3.1   *Valency-reducing derivations*

There are two ways that transitive verbs can be intransitivized. One is by use of the intransitivizing prefix *v-*. The other is by using the reflexive/middle-marking suffix *-shì*.

3.1.1   The intransitivizing prefix

The main function of the prefix *v-* is intransitivization, as in (5a–b), but if the single direct argument of the derived intransitive is a plural animate argument, then the meaning is reciprocal, as in (5c–f):

(5) (a)   tá:lòē   >   vtv̄lē
          tv́l-ò-ē   v-tv́l-ē
          roll-3+TR.N.PAST-N.PAST   PREF-roll-N.PAST
          to roll (vt)   to roll (vi)

    (b)   ngaqòē   >   vngaqē
          ngaq-ò-ē   v-ngaq-ē
          push.over-3+TR.N.PAST-N.PAST   PREF-push.over-N.PAST
          push over   fall over

    (c)   àngmaq vshvtnē
          àng-maq v-shvt-ē
          3pl   PREF-hit/kill-N.PAST
          They are arguing/fighting

    (d)   àngmaq vyv̀ng kēē
          àng-maq v-yv̀ng-kē-ē
          3pl   PREF-see-RECIP-N.PAST
          They are looking at each other

    (e)   àngmaq shàv́m kēē
          àng-maq shv-v-v́m   kē-ē
          3pl   CAUS-PREF-eat RECIP-N.PAST
          They are feeding each other

    (f)   àngmaq tāsv̀ng tālē dà-zà-kē-ē
          àng-maq tā-svng tā-lē dv̀-v-zà   kē-ē
          3pl   (to.each.other) CAUS-PREF-feel.ill/pain RECIP-N.PAST
          They are hurting each other

In (5c), the *v-* prefix is used alone for the reciprocal meaning. This is the normal pattern in Dulong/Rawang in general, but in the Mvtwang dialect, the verb *kē ~ ké* 'eat (meat), bite' has grammaticalized into an auxiliary reciprocal marker, and generally the two markers are used together. This usage is shown in (5d–f). In (5e–f) we have a combination of the causative prefix (both allomorphs; see §3.2.1(a)) and the reciprocal use of the intransitivizing prefix. See that when two non-basic prefixes combine, in this case *shv-* ~ *dv-* and *v-*, the result is that the vowel becomes [ɑ-], and it takes on a full tone. In (5f) we also have a 3rd marker of reciprocity, *tāsv̀ng tālē*, a phrase meaning 'to each other'.[12]

The *v-* prefix can function to intransitivize in order to create something like a noun incorporation structure or to mark an unexpected or unintentional action ('just happened to . . .'):[13]

(6)	ríòē	>	cv̀mré vrīv́mì
	rí-ò-ē		cv̀mré v-rī-v́m-ì
	carry-3+TR.N.PAST-N.PAST		child PREF-carry-DIR-3+INTR.PAST
	to carry		to have become pregnant
(7)	zòmòē	>	vzōmv́mì
	zòm-ò-ē		v-zōm-v́m-ì
	hold-3+TR.N.PAST-N.PAST		PREF-hold-DIR-3+INTR.PAST
	to hold		to happen to grab (as when grabbing for something when slipping down a hill)

The *v-* prefix is also used in some cases to derive nouns from verbs, such as *vngǿ* 'someone who likes to cry a lot', from *ngōē* 'to cry'; *vkǿ* 'thief', from *kōē* ~ *kǿòē* 'to steal'.[14] In these cases there is also a change to high tone on the derived noun.

3.1.2 The reflexive/middle marker

The verbal suffix *-shì* in Rawang functions in a similar way to the reflexive construction in French, in that it marks true reflexives, as in (8a–b), and also middles, as in (8c–d):

(8) (a)	àng (nṑ àng) vdipshìē
	àng nṑ àng vdip-shì-ē
	3sg TOP 3sg hit-R/M-N.PAST
	He is hitting himself

---

[12] I am unclear on the meaning of *tā*, as it only appears in this expression; *sv̀ng* is the locative/allative/dative marker in Rawang, and *lē* is possibly cognate with the allative/dative marker *le³¹* found in some of the Dulong dialects.

[13] As is common in Tibeto-Burman languages, the directional particles are often used to mark a change of state, e.g. *tē-ē* 'big', *té-lú:ng-ì* 'big-up-3+INTR.PAST' ('became big; grew up'); *dṑ* 'dark', *dṑ-daq-ì* 'dark-down-3+INTR.PAST' ('became dark (of the sky)'); *cv́m-ē* 'small', *cv́m-á:m-ì* 'small-away-3+INTR.PAST' (or *cv́m daq-ì*) ('became small'). It may be that in these examples what the directional particles are doing is marking a change of state, e.g. that in (6) and (7) the meanings are closer to 'come to be baby-carrying' and 'come to be holding' respectively.

[14] As 'to steal' is an ambitransitive verb, it may be that the noun is derived from the intransitive form of that verb, and so the rule of *v-* derivation would be that when the *v-* prefix is added to a transitive verb it forms a derived intransitive, and when added to an intransitive forms a derived noun.

(b) àng mūgwàí kupshìē
     àng mūgwà-í   kup-shì-ē
     3sg plastic.raincoat-INST cover-R/M-N.PAST
     He is covering himself with a plastic raincoat

(c) àng léshì bǿì
     àng lé-shì   bǿ-ì
     3sg cross-R/M PFV-3.INTR.PAST
     He went out.

(d) àng vhø̄shìē
     àng vhø̄-shì-ē
     3sg laugh/smile-R/M-N.PAST
     He is laughing (or smiling)

In most reflexives it is possible to add a pronoun representing the O argument, which will be understood as coreferential with the clause-initial NP, as in (8a). The pronoun used for this is a normal pronoun; there are no special reflexive pronouns, only special emphatic pronouns, e.g. *vdè* 'oneself' (in the sense of 'do something oneself', not 'to oneself').

The direct reflexive and the middle are semantically similar in that one and the same referent is performing and being affected by the action, but in the case of middles these two semantic aspects of the referent or the action are not as clearly distinct as for direct reflexives. Kemmer (1993) characterizes middles as involving a 'low elaboration of participants in an event' (ch. 3), or, more generally, a 'low elaboration of events' (ch. 6) relative to direct reflexives. There is a formal difference in that for middle verbs the marking is often obligatory for a certain meaning. That is, having or not having the marker on the verb will involve a change in the meaning of the verb, e.g. *lē* 'to cross' and *cv̀n* 'to follow' vs *léshì* 'to go out' and *cv̄nshì* 'to learn', while with direct reflexives the addition of the marker only changes the relationship between the two participants in the action. In Dulong/Rawang the semantic types of situations that are coded with the reflexive/middle marker include those that are marked with middle-voice marking in languages that have unique middle-voice marking, e.g. Old Norse, Russian and Dutch. These types include changes in body posture, emotions, cognitive actions, grooming actions and spontaneous events.[15]

The reflexive/middle marking is generally added only to transitive verbs, and makes them intransitive, in that the A argument can no longer take the

---

[15] See Kemmer (1993) for an in-depth discussion of middles and the categories often marked by middle marking. For more on the use of the reflexive/middle marker in Dulong/Rawang using data from the Third Township Dulong dialect, see LaPolla (1995b), and for more on middle marking in other Tibeto-Burman languages, see LaPolla (1996).

agentive suffix and the verb cannot take the transitive tense markers. Though the resulting verb is intransitive, it contrasts with intransitives formed by the intransitivizing prefix (*v-*) in that the verbs with the intransitive prefix express an action that is unintentional, while those marked with the reflexive/middle marker express an action that is intentional. Compare the examples in (9a–c) with the derived intransitives in (5a–c).

(9) (a) tv́lshìē
     tv́l-shì-ē
     roll-R/M-N.PAST
     to roll oneself (on purpose; intransitive, but with intentionality)

(b) ngaqshìē
     ngaq-shì-ē
     push.over-R/M-N.PAST
     fall over (on purpose)

(c) yv́ngshìē
     yv̀ng-shì-ē
     see/look.at-R/M-N.PAST
     look at oneself/make oneself visible, manifest oneself (such as a spirit)[16]

While clauses with reflexive/middle-marked verbs are formally intransitive, an unmarked NP (representing an O argument) may appear in the clause, as in (10a–b):

(10) (a) àng nə̄l tutshìē
     àng nə̄l   tut-shì-ē
     3sg fingernail cut-R/M-N.PAST
     He is cutting his fingernails

(b) àng mv́r zv́lshìē
     àng mv́r zv́l-shì-ē
     3sg face wash-R/M-N.PAST
     He is washing his face

These examples represent situations that seem to be transitive events, and in languages, such as English and Chinese, that do not have middle marking and represent some middle situations with prototypical transitive forms, these examples would be coded as transitives. The possessive relationship between the A argument and the bodypart must be overtly coded in English with a

---

[16] In the Dulong dialects there is a formal difference between the two meanings given for this example (which generally only holds for perception verbs): for the meaning 'look at oneself', only the reflexive/middle marker is used, i.e. $\int \partial \eta^{55}$-ςu^{31}, while for the more stativized meaning 'be visible, manifest oneself', the intransitivizing prefix is also added to the verb, i.e. ∂-$\int \partial \eta^{55}$-ςu^{31}. If a perceiver must be mentioned in the clause, it is marked with the locative/dative postposition (le^{31} in the Third Township Dulong dialect, *svng* in the Mvtwang dialect).

genitive construction, as in the free translations given above. In Chinese, the relationship between the possessor and possessed bodypart is not overtly coded at all, and so must be inferred, as in the following example:

(11)   wǒ yào xǐ   liǎn
        1sg want wash face
        I want to wash (my) face

In Rawang, the possessor–possessed relationship must be marked by the reflexive/middle marker.

Where the O argument represented by the unmarked NP is not a bodypart, the referent will be understood as something that has some sort of strong connection with the referent of the A argument. Consider the examples in (12) to (14):

(12) (a)   àng tvwv̀n vchaqòē
           àng tvwv̀n vchaq-ò-ē
           3sg snow brush-3+TR.N.PAST-N.PAST
           He is brushing the snow off (something)

    (b)   àng tvwv̀n vchaqshìē
           àng tvwv̀n vchaq-shì-ē
           3sg snow brush-R/M-N.PAST
           He is brushing the snow off (himself)

(13) (a)   à:ngí shvmǿ sha:tnòē
           àng-í   shvmǿ   shvt-ò-ē
           3sg-AGT mosquito kill-3+TR.N.PAST-N.PAST
           He is killing a mosquito

    (b)   àng shvmǿ shvtshìē
           àng shvmǿ   shvt-shì-ē
           3sg mosquito kill-R/M-N.PAST
           He is killing a mosquito (on him)

(14) (a)   àng laqtūn wv̄nòē
           àng laqtūn wv̄n-ò-ē
           3sg clothing buy-3+TR.N.PAST-N.PAST
           He is buying clothing

    (b)   àng laqtūn wv̄nshìē
           àng laqtūn   wv̄n-shì-ē
           3sg clothing buy-R/M-N.PAST
           He is buying himself clothing

In these cases, the sense of the reflexive/middle is more like a benefactive, doing something FOR oneself rather than TO oneself. There is still an overlapping of roles on one referent, but instead of the two roles being A and O, they are Λ and Benefactive.

In some cases there is a difference of tone on the verb in a direct reflexive situation as opposed to an indirect reflexive. In these cases a high tone marks a direct reflexive, while a mid tone marks an indirect reflexive. This can be seen by comparing the (a) and (b) examples in (15–16):

(15) (a) àng nō̄ àng vdǿrshìē
      àng nō̄ àng vdǿr-shì-ē
      3sg TOP 3sg hit-R/M-N.PAST
      He's hitting himself

(b) àng nō̄ àng vdō̄rshìē
      àng nō̄ àng vdō̄r-shì-ē
      3sg TOP 3sg hit-R/M-N.PAST
      He is hitting his own (child, etc.)

(16) (a) nà nō̄ nà èwáshì bǿì
      nà nō̄ nà è-wá-shì bǿ-ì
      2sg TOP 2sg N.1-do-R/M PFV-3+INTR.PAST
      You did it *to* yourself

(b) nà nō̄ nà èwāshì bǿì
      nà nō̄ nà è-wā-shì bǿ-ì
      2sg TOP 2sg N.1-do-R/M PFV-3+INTR.PAST
      You did it *for* yourself

In (15b) the form is that of a direct reflexive except for the tone on the verb, which marks the action as NOT a direct reflexive, so the object hit must be something other than the actor, but something closely related to the actor. In (16a–b) again the forms differ only in terms of the tone, but this makes the difference between the actor as O and the actor as Benefactive (with possibly some other assumed O).

A subtype of this indirect reflexive is when the reflexive/middle marker is used to show an alienable possessive relationship between the A and O arguments, as in (17).

(17) Vpūng (nō̄) Vdǿsv̀ng lègābok zīshìē
      Vpūng nō̄ Vdǿ-sv̀ng lègā-bok zī-shì-ē
      Vpung TOP Vdeu-LOC book-CL give-R/M-N.PAST
      Vpung gave his (own) book to Vdeu

In the case of some auxiliary verbs, the reflexive/middle marker is used on the auxiliary simply to intransitivize it to match the matrix verb in terms of transitivity. Compare the two sentences in (18).

(18) (a) à:ngí shǿng rímā:nòē
      àng-í shǿng rí-mv̄n-ò-ē
      3sg-AGT tree/wood carry-continue-3+TR.N.PAST-N.PAST
      He is continuing to carry the wood

(b)   àng yøpmv̄nshìē
       àng yøp-mv̄n-shì-ē
       3sg sleep-continue-R/M-N.PAST
       He is continuing to sleep

In (18a), the main verb, *ríòē* 'carry', is transitive, and so the auxiliary verb, *mv̄nòē* 'continue', is also transitive, but in (18b), the main verb, *yøpmē* 'sleep', is intransitive, and so *mv̄nòē* takes the reflexive/middle marker to make it intransitive. A number of other auxiliary verbs, such as *dv́nòē* 'be about to', *mūnòē* 'be used to', *dv́ngòē* 'be finished', *pv́ngòē* 'begin to' and *nēòē* 'be willing to', also follow this pattern. These verbs follow this pattern even with the different forms of the ambitransitive verbs, that is, when the ambitransitive main verb is used as an intransitive, the auxiliary verb takes *-shì*, but if the ambitransitive main verb is used as a transitive verb, then *-shì* is not used. Compare (19a–b), for example:

(19) (a)   àng v́mdv́ngshì bǿì
           àng v́m-dv́ng-shì bǿ-ì
           3sg eat-finish-R/M PFV-3+INTR.PAST
           He finished eating [intransitive v̄mē 'eat']

(b)   à:ngí v́mpàlòng v́mdv́ng bǿà
       àng-í   v́mpà-lòng v́m-dv́ng bǿ-à
       3sg-INST food-CL   eat-finish PFV-3+TR.PAST
       He has finished eating the food [transitive v́mòē 'eat']

The pattern is also followed when the main verb is nominalized, as in (20):

(20)   vngaqlv́m dv́nshìē
        v-ngaq-lv́m   dv́n-shì-ē
        PREF-push-INF about.to-R/M-N.PAST
        It seems like it is about to fall down

The reflexive/middle marker can also be used when one wants to stress that some expression represents a general situation or existing state rather than a specific event. Compare (21a) and (21b) below:

(21) (a)   à:ngí àngsv̀ng shvngōòē
           àng-í   àng-sv̀ng shvngō-ò-ē
           3sg-AGT 3sg-LOC hate-3+TR.N.PAST-N.PAST
           He hates him

(b)   àng nø̄ shvngōshìē
       àng nø̄   shvngō-shì-ē
       3sg TOP hate-R/M-N.PAST
       He's hateful

Example (21a) expresses the idea that the referent feels hate towards a specific individual, while (21b) expresses the idea that he is hateful in general, not that he hates any one person in particular.[17] Compare now (22a) and (22b).

(22) (a) àng shv̀m pēshìē
       àng shv̀m pē-shì-ē
       3sg sword hang.on.shoulder-R/M-N.PAST
       He is wearing a sword

(b) à:ngí shv̀m péòē
     àng-í   shv̀m pé-ò-ē
     3sg-INST sword hang.on.shoulder-3+TR.N.PAST-N.PAST
     He is putting on or wearing a sword

In (22a), the situation is expressed as an on-going state rather than an action or event, while in (22b) the action is a transitive event which could involve either the putting on or the wearing of the sword (notice in English we use two different verbs for these two meanings). There is a privative opposition between the two forms, in that the transitive form can be used for either meaning, while the reflexive/middle-marked verb has only the state-like meaning. To express the meaning 'put on' without ambiguity, it is possible to use the causative prefix (see §3.2.1(a) below) together with the reflexive/middle marker, as in (22c):

(22) (c) àng shv̀m dvpēshìē
       àng shv̀m dv-pē-shì-ē
       3sg sword CAUS-hang.on.shoulder-R/M-N.PAST
       He is putting on a sword

As discussed in LaPolla (1995a), it seems that the reflexive/middle marker may have at first been used only for direct reflexives, then came to be used more and more to express middle situations, i.e. came more and more to be associated with situations where there is a 'low elaboration of events', and then, when used on transitive verbs, came to have a function similar to that of a 'stativizer': diminishing the conceptual separation of the events and participants involved, making the overall event more like a state.

3.2   Valency-increasing derivations
There are six different ways that the valency of a clause can be increased in Rawang. There are two types of causative construction, an applicative

---

[17] Because this is also the reflexive form of the verb, it is ambiguous between the general meaning and the reflexive meaning, so for the reflexive meaning a second pronoun is often added after the topic marker: *àng nō àng shvngōshìē* 'He hates himself'.

benefactive, a -*t* suffix, non-use of the reflexive/middle marker on 'deponent' verbs, and the use of the verb *kéòē* 'eat (meat), bite' as an adversative marking auxiliary verb. We will discuss each construction in turn.

3.2.1   Causative constructions

There are two unrelated types of causative marking: a verbal prefix (*shv- ~ dv-*) and an analytical (periphrastic) causative construction involving the verb *dvzvr* 'send'.

(a) The causative prefix   The main morphological means for deriving causative verbs is adding the causative prefix (*shv- ~ dv-*).[18] The verb in a causative involving the causative prefix can represent a state, a process or an action, and can be intransitive or transitive, but not ditransitive. A causative formed by the verbal prefix can generally be either a direct causative (actually bringing about a change of state or directly causing or helping a causee perform an action) or an indirect causative (having someone do something, but without the causer being physically involved as in the direct causative). There is no difference whether the causee is willing to perform the action or not, whether the action was accidental or not, or whether the causee is in control or not. The causative of an intransitive verb becomes a transitive verb, taking on the transitive tense marking, and the NP representing the A argument can take the agentive marking. In some cases a locative-marked argument in the intransitive takes the instrument marker in the causativized form (see (28a–b) for example). With the causative of a transitive verb, the NP representing the causer can take the agentive marker, the NP representing the A argument (the causee) often takes the dative/locative marker, and the NP representing the O argument is unmarked. The causative prefix is not used for applicatives or to derive verbs from nouns, and it is not used on ditransitives (though it is used to create ditransitives). The analytical causative

---

[18]   In the Dulong dialects of Dulong/Rawang, there is clear phonetic conditioning on the two forms of the causative prefix (*tu³¹-* and *su³¹-*): the form *tu³¹-* is used before voiceless fricative initials, while *su³¹-* is used before all other initials. I have not found any such phonetic conditioning in the Rawang dialects. I have also not found Morse's (1965: 348) statement that *dv-* is used mainly on intransitives to be correct. One factor that may be involved is that some verbs can take both prefixes, but then only *shv-* has a causative meaning, while *dv-* has the sense of 'able to [Verb]', e.g. *lēē* 'to cross (a stream, etc.)', *dv-lēē* 'to be able to cross', *shv-léòē* 'make (him) cross' (it can be seen from these examples that when *dv-* has this meaning it does not transitivize the verb). The causative prefix clearly derives from the Proto-Sino-Tibetan causativizing/transitivizing **s-* prefix (see for example Benedict 1972: 105–6; Mei 1989), but the origin of this prefix in Sino-Tibetan is not clear. The analytical causative is a relatively late development, and paralleled in many other Sino-Tibetan languages (see LaPolla 1994).

construction must be used for causatives of ditransitives. There is generally no way for the verb to remain intransitive and yet have an A argument represented, e.g. as a peripherally marked NP. The only exception to this is the possible addition of an experiencer/perceiver argument using the locative/dative postposition to certain derived intransitives of perception (see note 16). I have not found any particular syntactic or discourse functions associated with use of the causative aside from the semantic function of adding an A argument. Following are some examples:

(23) nǿē   > shvnǿòē
      nǿ-ē   shv-nǿ-ò-ē
      be.tame-N.PAST   CAUS-tame-3+TR.N.PAST-N.PAST
      be tame   to tame (an animal) (vt)

(24) vmv̄ngngē   > shvmá:ngòē
      vmv̄ng-ē   shv-vmv̄ng-ò-ē
      be.lost-N.PAST   CAUS-be.lost-3+TR.N.PAST-N.PAST
      be lost   to lose (something)

(25) lǿmmē   > shvlǿ:mòē
      lǿm-ē   shv-lǿm-ò-ē
      be.warm-N.PAST   CAUS-be.warm-3+TR.N.PAST-N.PAST
      be warm   to warm (something)

(26) vshatnē   > dvshatnòē
      vshat-ē   dv-vshat-ò-ē
      wake.up-N.PAST   CAUS-wake.up-3+TR.N.PAST-N.PAST
      wake up   wake (someone) up

(27) vhǿmmē   > dvhǿmòē
      vhǿm-ē   dv-vhǿm-ò-ē
      meet-N.PAST   CAUS-meet-3+TR.N.PAST-N.PAST
      meet   gather, get together

(28) (a) shvrì tiqgō tvwátaq wá apì
          shvrì tiq-gō tvwá-taq   wá   ap-ì
          deer one-CL trap(n.)-LOC be.trapped TMdys-3+INTR.PAST
          A deer was caught in a trap

(b)   shvrì tiqgō tvwái shvwá apà
      shvrì tiq-gō tvwá-í   shv-wá   ap-à
      deer one-CL trap(n.)-INST CAUS-be.trapped TMdys-3+INTR.PAST
      (He) caught a deer in/with a trap

In the causative forms in (24), (26) and (27), even though there is a combination of *shv-* ~ *dv-* and *v-*, the resulting vowel is still [ə], and not [ɑ-], as the *v-* here is inherent to the root form and not a derivational prefix. Only a combination of two derivational prefixes causes the vowel change. In the intransitive (28a) ('to be caught in a trap'), the NP *tvwá* 'trap(n.)' takes locative marking, while in the causativized version in (28b) ('cause to be trapped') the same NP has instrumental marking. This example also shows that cognate verbs function morphosyntactically the same as verbs formed in other ways (see note 9). Examples (29a–c) are causatives of transitive verbs, and (29d) is an example of an intransitive verb that becomes ditransitive after causativization (the only example of this I have):

(29) (a)   ... mvshv̄ngshícèní sv̀ng dvkéòē, wā
             mvshv̄ng-shí-cè-ní-sv̀ng dv-ké-ò-ē   wā
             human-seed-son-du-LOC CAUS-eat-3+TR.N.PAST-N.PAST say
             ... (and it is said he) fed the original people (the child's flesh)

(b)   à:ngí Vpūng sv̀ng laqtūn dvgwāòē
             àng-í   Vpūng-sv̀ng laqtūn   dv-gwā-ò-ē
             3sg-AGT Vpung-LOC   clothing CAUS-put.on/wear-3+TR.N.PAST-N.PAST
             He made (or helped) Vpung put his clothes on

(c)   à:ngí (àng sv̀ng) shvrī mā:nòē
             àng-í   àng-sv̀ng shv-rī   mv̄n-ò-ē
             3sg-AGT 3sg-LOC CAUS-carry continue-3+TR.N.PAST-N.PAST
             He makes (him) continue carrying (not 'send' here, but 'help carry')

(d)   à:ngí ngà sv̀ng Yangon dètān yv̀ngà
             àng-í   ngà-sv̀ng Yangon də-è-vtān   yv̀ng-à
             3sg-AGT 1sg-LOC Yangon CAUS-N.1-visible TMyrs+1sg-3+TR.PAST
             He showed me Yangon (Rangoon)

As mentioned above, generally the derived causative can be direct or indirect, but if the causation is very indirect, such as in a situation where, for example, one might be said to have 'killed' someone by not saving that person when s/he was drowning, then the word for 'cause to die' (see (30a)) would not be used directly, but would be used in a paraphrastic construction meaning 'it was as if I killed him', as in (30b):

(30) (a)   dvshǿng bǿngà
             dv-shí-ng   bǿ-ng-à
             CAUS-die-1sg PFV-1sg-3+TR.PAST
             I caused him to die (Direct action)

(b)   ngàí dvshíò də̄ íá:mì
             ngà-í   dv-shí-ò   də̄ í-ám-ì
             1sg-AGT CAUS-die-3+TR.N.PAST ADV be-DIR-3+INTR.PAST
             It is like I caused him to die

(b) The analytical causative/permissive The analytical (phrasal) causative construction involves the use of the verb *dvzýr* 'send' after the main verb. This construction only has an indirect causative sense, without direct involvement of the causer, of having or letting someone do something, and the causing/letting must be purposeful, not accidental, with the causee in control, but the causee may be willing or unwilling.[19] The verb involved can be intransitive, transitive or ditransitive, and generally represents an action or process that requires some effort rather than a state, for which the causative prefix is more generally used. The analytical causative can also be used together with the direct causative to express a double causative or permissive and causative. Examples of the three causative possibilities are given in (31) for intransitives and (32a–c) for transitives. The marking of noun phrases is the same as that with the causative prefix: the causer (optionally) takes agentive marking, and the causee takes the locative/allative marker (but see discussion of reflexive causatives below); (32d–e) are examples with NPs to show their marking.

(31) (a)   dí dvzá:ròē
       dí dvzýr-ò-ē
       go send-3+TR.N.PAST-N.PAST
       to let/make (him) go

(b)   dvdìòē
       dv-dì-ò-ē
       CAUS-go-3+TR.N.PAST-N.PAST
       to make (him) go/walk

(c)   dvdí dèzá:rò
       dv-dí   è-dv̀zýr-ò
       CAUS-go N.1-send-3+TR.N.PAST
       You let him make him go

---

[19] There is another way to express one type of having or letting someone do something, by use of the prefix *laq-*. This construction is formally a subtype of the imperative, and so functions differently from the analytical causative. Compare the two sentences below:

(1)   Vpū:ngí bǿ laqdǿ:rò
     Vpūng-í   bǿ   laq-dǿr-ò
     Vpung-AGT rice INDTV-pound-3+TR.N.PAST
     Let Vpung pound the rice [imperative]

(2)   Vpū:ngí bǿ dǿr dèzá:ròē
     Vpūng-í   bǿ dǿr   è-dvzýr-ò-ē
     Vpung-AGT rice pound N.1-send-3+TR.N.PAST-N.PAST
     You let Vpung pound the rice [non-imperative]

(32) (a) ́vm dèzá:rò
    ́vm è-dvźvr-ò
    eat N.1-send-3+TR.N.PAST
    Let him eat

(b)   shvá:mòē
    shv-́vm-ò-ē
    CAUS-eat-3+TR.N.PAST-N.PAST
    He feeds him

(c)   shv́vm dvzá:rò
    shv-́vm dvźvr-ò
    CAUS-eat send-3+TR.N.PAST
    Let him feed him

(d)   à:ngí Vpūng sv̀ng mūgwàí dvrèrì wv̄m dvzá:ròē
    àng-í Vpūng-sv̀ng mūgwà-í   dvrè-rì   wv̄m
    3sg-AGT Vpung-LOC raincoat-INST luggage-pl cover
    dvźvr-ò-ē
    CAUS-3+TR.N.PAST-N.PAST
    He is making Vpung cover the luggage with the raincoat

(e)   à:ngí àng sv̀ng shv̀m lv́ng dvza:ròē
    àng-í   àng-sv̀ng shv̀m lv́ng dvźvr-ò-ē
    3sg-AGT 3sg-LOC knife hold CAUS-3+TR.N.PAST-N.PAST
    He is making him hold the knife

(c) The interaction between causatives and reflexives   We have looked at reflexives, and we have looked at causatives, and have seen one example ((22c)) of how they can be used together. In this section we discuss a few more examples to see how the two derivations interact. Compare the three examples in (33):

(33) (a) à:ngí laqtūn dvshúòē
    àng-í   laqtūn dv-shū-ò-ē
    3sg-INST clothing CAUS-be.dry-3+TR.N.PAST-N.PAST
    He is drying clothes

(b)   àng dvshúshìē
    àng dv-shū-shì-ē
    3sg CAUS-be.dry-R/M-N.PAST
    He is drying himself

(c)   àng laqtūn dvshūshìē
    àng laqtūn dv-shū-shì-ē
    3sg clothing CAUS-be.dry-R/M-N.PAST
    He is drying his clothes

In (33a) we have a causative based on the intransitive verb *shūē* 'be dry', with distinct A and O arguments, and it means simply that the person is drying clothes on a line or somewhere else. In (33b) we have a causative-reflexive with no other O argument and a high tone, so the meaning is that the person is drying him or herself, for example by standing next to a fire. In (33c) an O argument is mentioned, and the verb is followed by the reflexive/middle marker and has a mid tone rather than a high tone, so what is being dried is the clothing, and not the person (in a sense FOR the person), but the drying of the clothes must be while the person is wearing them.

We saw above that adding the causative prefix to a transitive verb can create an indirect causative where the causer causes (or helps) the causee perform an action that is not directed at the causer, as in (34).

(34)   àːngí Vpūng sv̀ng laqtūn dvgwàòē
        àng-í   Vpūng-sv̀ng laqtūn dv-gwā-ò-ē
        3sg-AGT Vpung-LOC   clothing CAUS-put.on/wear-3+TR.N.PAST-N.PAST
        He made (or helped) Vpung put his clothes on

Considering only the use of the causative prefix and the reflexive/middle marker, there is then a four-way contrast:

    (a)   gwá-ò-ē   'to put on' or 'to wear'
    (b)   gwā-shì-ē   'to wear'
    (c)   dv-gwā-ò-ē   'to dress someone'
    (d)   dv-gwā-shì-ē   'to get oneself dressed' or 'to cause/make some-
                             one else get dressed'

The causative form, as in (34), can also be made reflexive/middle, but different dialects of Dulong/Rawang vary somewhat in what they allow. In the Third Township Dulong dialect, if the reflexive/middle-marking suffix is also added to the verb in this construction, there are two possible outcomes, depending on whether another animate referent is mentioned or assumed in the clause. Compare (35a) and (35b) (from LaPolla 1995b):

(35) (a) $aŋ^{53}$ Jɔʔ $suɯ^{31}$-gua^{55}-$ɕuɯ^{31}$
           3sg cloth CAUS-put.on-R/M
           He (causes himself to) put his clothes on

    (b) $aŋ^{53}$ $aŋ^{53}$-mei^{53}-le^{31} Jɔʔ $suɯ^{31}$-gua^{55}-$ɕuɯ^{31}$
           3sg 3sg-mother-LOC cloth CAUS-put.on-R/M
           He had his mother put his clothes on him

In (35a), as no other causee is mentioned or assumed, then the interpretation is that the causer causes himself or herself to perform the action, in this case, put clothes on. In (35b), which could be said of a small child, an animate causee is mentioned, and the reflexive/middle marker limits the interpretation of the situation to one where the action performed by the causee (which has been caused by the causer) is directed at or in some way affects the causer, not necessarily the causee.

It is also possible to add the reflexive/middle marking to a periphrastic causative construction, with the effect that the causer causes the causee to do something to him or herself, as in (36), where it is Pung's face that is to be washed:

(36)   aŋ⁵³-mi⁵⁵ puŋ⁵⁵-(le³¹) məɹ⁵⁵ tɕiʔ-ɕɯ³¹ dʐɯːɹ⁵⁵
       3sg-AGT Pung-LOC face wash-R/M cause
       He made Pung wash his face

A second causative can also be added to a construction such as that in (36) if the verb involved is a basic intransitive, as in (37):

(37)   aŋ⁵³-mi⁵⁵ puŋ⁵⁵-(le³¹) ɟɔʔ⁵⁵ sɯ³¹-kam⁵⁵-ɕɯ³¹ dʐɯːɹ⁵⁵
       3sg-AGT Pung-LOC cloth CAUS-dry-R/M cause
       He made Pung dry his clothes (with Pung wearing them)

Here Pung is made to dry the clothes that he is wearing; the analytic causative expresses the idea that Pung is made to do something, while the inflectional causative expresses the idea that Pung causes the clothes to become dry, and the reflexive marker expresses the idea that the clothes being dried are the ones being worn by Pung at the time of the action.

In the Mvtwang (Rawang) dialect, the equivalent of (35a) is possible (see (38a)), but for the meaning where the causer has the causee do something to the causer, the analytical causative must be used, as in (38b).

(38) (a)   àng laqtūn dvgwāshìē
          àng laqtūn dv-gwā-shì-ē
          3sg clothing CAUS-wear-R/M-N.PAST
          He's putting his clothes on

(b)   àng nō̄ àngmèí laqtūn dvgwā dvzv́rshìē
      àng nō̄ àng-mè-í laqtūn dv-gwā dvzv́r-shì-ē
      3sg TOP 3sg-mother-AGT clothing CAUS-wear send-R/M-N.PAST
      He had his mother put his clothes on him

An interesting difference between the two dialects is that, while both dialects can express the difference between the causer having the causee doing something to the causee and the causer having the causee doing something to the causer, the way they express these two differs. In the Dulong dialect the difference between the two types of causative is in the use of the analytical causative with the reflexive/middle marker on the main verb to express the former meaning (see (36)), and the causative prefix and the reflexive/middle marker on a transitive verb for the latter meaning (see (35b)), while in the Mvtwang dialect both meanings are expressed using the analytical causative construction, with the difference being expressed by whether the reflexive/middle marker appears on the main verb or on the causative auxiliary verb. Compare (39a) (and also (38b)) with (39b):

(39) (a) àng nō̄ Vpūngí mv́r zv́l dvzv́rshìē
       àng nō̄ Vpūng-í mv́r zv́l dvzv́r-shì-ē
       3sg TOP Vpung-AGT face wash send-R/M-N.PAST
       He is making Vpung wash his face (causer's face, not Vpung's)

(b) à:ngí Vpūngsv̀ng mv́r zv́lshì dvzá:ròē
      àng-í Vpūng-sv̀ng mv́r zv́l-shì dvzv́r-ò-ē
      3sg-AGT Vpung-LOC face wash-R/M send-3+TR.N.PAST-N.PAST
      He is making Vpung wash his (Vpung's) face

The marking of the NPs in the clause differs according to the placement of the reflexive/middle marker. The NP representing the A argument of whichever verb is not marked by the reflexive/middle marker can take the agentive marker, while the NP representing the A argument of a reflexive/middle-marked verb cannot take the agentive marker, but may take the locative/dative marker (and may take the topic marker if it is in initial position).

The equivalent of (37) in the Mvtwang dialect is (40):

(40) à:ngí Vpūngsv̀ng laqtūng dvshūshì dvzá:ròē
      àng-í Vpūng-sv̀ng laqtūng dv-shū-shì dvzv́r-ò-ē
      3sg-AGT Vpūng-LOC clothing CAUS-dry-R/M send-3+TR.N.PAST-N.PAST
      He is making Vpung dry his clothes (while Vpung is wearing them)

The causative can also be used with the reflexive in situations where the reflexive/middle marker indicates a possessive relation between the A and the O (see (17) above). In example (41), below, the reflexive/middle marker indicates the fact that the book that Vpung is letting/making Vdeu hold belongs to Vpung.

(41) Vpūng (nō̄) Vdǿí lègābok shvlv̄ngshìē
      Vpūng (nō̄) Vdǿ-í lègā-bok shv-lv̄ng-shì-ē
      Vpung TOP Vdeu-AGT book-CL CAUS-hold-R/M-N.PAST
      Vpung is letting Vdeu hold his book

3.2.2   Applicative benefactive

The only applicative construction in Rawang is the benefactive construction marked by the verbal suffix *-ā*. This form cannot be used for causative or other functions, such as for making an instrumental or locative phrase a direct argument.[20] It also cannot be used for comitatives.[21] The benefactive can apply to both transitives and intransitives. As adding the benefactive argument increases the transitivity of the verb, intransitive verbs become formally transitive, though the original S does not take agentive marking. With transitives the old O stays unmarked, and the new argument (the benefactive) is marked with the benefactive postposition (*dvpvt*)[22] or the locative/dative postposition *sv̀ng* (as with the other arguments, it may not be expressed as a noun phrase if it is recoverable from the context or person marking). Examples are given in (42a–c):

---

[20] Nouns representing instruments are marked with the agentive–instrumental–adverbial suffix (*-i*), and those representing locatives with one of the locative postpositions. For alternations of the 'spray/load' type, different verbs would be used in Rawang:

(1)   kvlángí mōdōchv̀ng dv̀n dvz∂ngòē
       kvláng-í mōdō-chv̀ng dv̀n   dv-z∂ng-ò-ē
       hay-INST truck-CL   fullness CAUS-full-3+TR.N.PAST-N.PAST
       I fill the truck with hay

(2)   mōdōchv̀ngtaq kvláng dv̀n zv́ngòē
       mōdō-chv̀ng-taq kvláng dv̀n   zv́ng-ò-ē
       truck-CL-LOC   hay   fullness put-3+TR.N.PAST-N.PAST
       I put hay onto the truck

[21] For comitatives, the comitative postposition *nv̀ng* is used. How it is used, together with the person marking on the verb, determine whether the added referent is treated as part of a single direct argument of the verb or as a separate oblique argument:

(1)   ngà àngnv̀ng rūngē
       ngà àng-nv̀ng rūng-ē
       1sg 3sg-COMIT sit-N.PAST
       I am sitting with him

(2)   ngà nv̀ng àng tiqdō rúngshìē
       ngà nv̀ng àng tiq-dō   rúng-shì-ē
       1sg COMIT 3sg one-ADV sit-du-N.PAST
       He and I are sitting together

In (1), the comitative postposition appears after the second NP, and the verb agreement is singular, while in (2) the comitative postposition comes between the two NPs and the verb agreement is dual.

[22] The benefactive postposition can sometimes be used without adding the benefactive suffix to the verb, as in the following example:

       yākōng v́mpà n∂ vsh∂mg∂ dvpvt luqē
       yā-kōng v́mpà n∂ vsh∂m-g∂ dvpvt luq-ē
       this-CL rice TOP three-CL for   be.enough-N.PAST
       This bowl of rice is enough for three people

(42) (a) ngàí (àng-sv̀ng/dvpvt) shǿng rǿngàngòē
ngà-í   àng-sv̀ng/dvpvt shǿng rí-ng-ā-ng-ò-ē
1sg-AGT 3sg-LOC/for[23]   wood carry-1sg-BEN-1sg-3+TR.N.PAST-N.PAST
I'm carrying wood for him

(b)   àng dvpvt rvmáhv́ng shvláāòē
àng dvpvt rvmá-hv́ng shvlá-ā-ò-ē
3sg for   field-field be.good-BEN-3+TR.N.PAST-N.PAST
The fields are good for him

(c)   àngtaq yādùng bèlaq mvnøklá téāòē
àng-taq yā-dùng bèlaq   mvnøklá té-ā-ò-ē
3sg-LOC this-CL upper.garment too   be.big-BEN-3+TR.N.PAST-N.PAST
This shirt is too big for him

If there is an auxiliary verb, such as *mv̄nòē* 'to continue' or *dv́ngòē* 'to finish', then the benefactive suffix appears after the auxiliary verb, as in (42d):

(42) (d) à:ngí rímv̄nāòē
àng-í   rí-mv̄n-ā-ò-ē
3sg-AGT carry-continue-BEN-3+TR.N.PAST-N.PAST
He continues carrying for someone else

In some cases the benefactive suffix has the meaning 'instead of', as in (43). If the name of the person in whose place the action is performed needs to be mentioned, then it is followed by either the benefactive postposition (*dvpvt*) or by *tvlē* 'exchange'.

(43)   (Vpūng tvlē) àngsv̀ng ngø̄tnāngòē
Vpūng tvlē   àng-sv̀ng ngø̄t-ā-ng-ò-ē
Vpung exchange 3sg-LOC mourn-BEN-1sg-3+TR.N.PAST-N.PAST
I mourn him (instead of Vpung mourning him)

Although the suffix -*ā* generally has the function of adding a benefactive argument, in two cases from the Rawang Creation Story and one elicited example the use of the suffix does not seem to have the meaning of doing the action 'for someone', but more the sense of possession. These are given in (44):

---

[23] This postposition is only used for the benefactive sense of English *for*; the purposive sense of *for* in, for example, 'I work for money' is expressed by *rvt* 'because' of:

gv̀msùng rvt bv̀nlì wv̄ngē
gv̀msùng rvt bv̀nlì wā-ng-ē
money   for work do-1sg-N.PAST
I work for money

(44) (a)   shv̄ngbéí vgō vshvpmā yà:ngà rvt vpú vgō vdv́mē, wāē
       shv̄ngbē-í vgō vshvp-ā yàng-à   rvt   vpú vgō
       all-AGT   head rub-BEN TMyrs-3+TR.PAST because owl head
       vdv́m-ē   wā-ē
       flat-N.PAST say-N.PAST
       It is said that because everyone rubbed his head (rubbed him on the head after he said something wise), the owl's head is (now) flat

(b)   vnō dvbøp hv́m gō èlv̄māòē
       vnō dvbøp hv́m   gō è-lv̄m-ā-ò-ē
       bean rotten basket also N.1-step.on-BEN-3+TR.N.PAST-N.PAST
       You stepped on (someone's) basket of fermented beans

(c)   yābok lègā kāgǿ íāòē
       yā-bok lègā kā-gǿ í-ā-ò-ē
       this-CL book Q.PN-CL be-BEN-3+TR.N.PAST-N.PAST
       Who does this book belong to?

In (44a), *vshvp* 'rub' could have been used without the -*ā* suffix and have basically the same meaning. It seems that the benefactive suffix is used here because the actual direct argument (which could be marked by the locative/dative marker *svng*) is *vgō* 'head', but the person/animal to whom the head belongs is affected as well. In (44b), the benefactive is used to emphasize that the deer stepped on someone else's beans. In (44c) the benefactive suffix makes the copula transitive, giving it the sense of 'this belongs to' rather than 'this is'.

Aside from the applicative benefactive, there are other ways that a benefactive sense is accomplished. We saw above that the reflexive/middle marker in some cases has a benefactive sense, though it is unlike the applicative benefactive in that it is transitivity-reducing and limited to cases where the benefactive and the A are the same referent. The benefactive in that construction cannot take the benefactive postposition (*dvpvt*).

A third type of benefactive that is also a type of indirect reflexive developed from the grammaticalization into auxiliary verbs of the two words for 'to eat': *v̄m(ò)ē* 'to eat (rice, vegetables)', *kē(ò)ē* 'to eat (meat), bite'. These verbs are used after the main verb for an indirect reflexive sense when the action expressed by the main verb relates to doing something to or with a domestic animal (*kē*) or non-animal food (*v̄m*) that is eaten. The auxiliary verbs follow the pattern of transitive for specific actions and intransitive for general or regular, continuing actions (such as actions done for one's livelihood; see §2, and noted in (b) below). This is also a type of benefactive, but not applicative, as it does not increase the transitivity of the clause. Following are examples of this usage with different types of activities.

(45) (a)   àng kwá tiqyờm róng kēē

        àng kwá tiq-yờm róng   kē-ē

        3sg bee one-hive put.in.hole eat-N.PAST[24]

        He is raising bees for himself

(b)   àng waq nākēē

        àng waq nā-kē-ē

        3sg pig feed-eat-N.PAST

        He feeds the pigs for himself[25]

(c)   àng ngā mit kē-ē

        àng ngā mit kē-ē

        3sg fish catch eat-N.PAST

        He catches fish for himself

(d)   àng lávmē

        àng lá-v̄m-ē

        3sg cut.down-eat-N.PAST

        He cuts down (banana trees) to get the fruit for himself

(e)   tì kvpmv́m á:mìē

        tì   kvp-v́m ám-ì-ē

        water get-eat DIR-1pl-N.PAST

        We go get water for ourselves

(f)   ngàmaq yúng kvtná:mì

        ngàmaq yúng   kvt-v̄m-ì

        1pl   vegetables grow-eat-1pl

        We grow vegetables for ourselves

(g)   àng v́mpà wv̄nv̄mē

        àng v́mpà   wv̄n-v̄m-ē

        3sg rice/food buy-eat-N.PAST

        He is buying himself rice/food[26]

---

[24] The larvae of the bees are eaten, so *kēē* and not *v̄mē* is used; the verb *róng* 'put in a hole' is used because bees are raised in a hole in a tree.

[25] Compare this example with (45b):

     à:ngí waq nākēòē

     àng-í   waq nā-kē-ò-ē

     3sg-AGT pig feed-eat-3+TR.N.PAST-N.PAST

     He is feeding the pigs (right now)

Here, as the main verb is used transitively (due to the fact that it is a specific action/event rather than a general one), the auxiliary is also transitive.

[26] Contrast this with the use of the reflexive/middle marker for the same situation, but involving non-edible objects:

     ngà laqtūn wv̄nshờngē

     ngà laqtūn   wv̄n-shì-ng-ē

     1sg clothing buy-R/M-1sg-N.PAST

     I am buying myself clothes

(h)   àng nǒ wāv̄mē
       àng nǒ   wā-v̄m-ē
       3sg wine make/do-eat-N.PAST
       He is making wine for himself

In terms of the benefactive sense, there is then a four-way contrast:

- (a) kvtshìē   'to grow something (not eaten) for oneself' (reflexive)
- (b) kvtnv̄mē   'to grow something (eaten) for oneself' (food-benefactive)
- (c) kvtnāòē   'to grow something for someone else' (benefactive)
- (d) vkvtnā kēē   'to grow something for one another' (reciprocal-benefactive)

3.2.3   Transitivization by addition of final *-t*

A second form of transitivization is not productive. This is transitivization by the addition of a final *-t* to an intransitive form. I have only one example of this type, though I believe there should be other examples, as this form of transitivization is found in closely related languages, such as Jinghpaw, and is an old Sino-Tibetan trait (see Dai and Xu 1992; Benedict 1972: 98–102; Michailovsky 1985; van Driem 1988).

(46) (a) ngǭ-ē 'to cry' > ngøt-ò-ē 'to cry over/mourn someone'

(b)   ngàí àng ngøtnòē
       ngà-í   àng ngø-t-ò-ē
       1sg-AGT 3sg cry-transitivizer-3+TR.N.PAST-N.PAST
       I am crying over (mourning) him

3.2.4   Other ways of increasing transitivity

There are two other ways that the transitivity of a verb can be increased. One is by NOT using the reflexive/middle marker on a verb for which the reflexive/middle form is the statistically unmarked form. This has the same effect as the applicative in some other languages. For example, *vhøshìē* 'laugh' has the middle as its statistically unmarked form, even though it has the intransitivizing prefix and the reflexive/middle-marking suffix, while the formally unmarked (but statistically marked) form *hǭòē* 'laugh at someone' (e.g. *à:ngí àngsv̀ng hǭòē* 'He is laughing at him') is statistically and semantically more marked.

In situations where there is an adversative sense of something happening to someone that is beyond their control, the verb *kéòē* 'eat (meat), bite' can be used, often with the causative prefix as well, and this can make the sentence partly transitive, as in (47a–c). It is only partly transitive because there is no A argument that can take the agentive marker (though in some cases there is an instrumental argument, as in (47c)), as the cause of the action is generally unknown. Semantically then, it is like a passive in emphasizing affectedness and lack of control, but syntactically it is not valency-reducing, the way passives are.

(47) (a) àng dvgøq kéòē
àng dv-gøq ké-ò-ē
3sg CAUS-hiccup eat-3+TR.N.PAST-N.PAST
He's hiccuping (uncontrollably) (normally àng gøqē)

(b) (pòyaq) chapgá (gá) cv̀mré shvngǿ kéòē
pòyaq chapgá gá cv̀mré shv-ngǿ ké-ò-ē
all.night morning bright child CAUS-cry eat-3+TR.N.PAST-N.PAST
The children are / have been crying (all night) until morning (light)

(c) àng vléí mvdǿng kéòē
àng vlé-í mvdǿng ké-ò-ē
3sg vlé-INST stuck eat-3+TR.N.PAST-N.PAST
He has vlé stuck in his throat (vlé is a kind of rough food)

This usage is actually a subtype of a more general usage of the verb *ké ~ kē* 'eat (meat), bite' for an adversative sense shown in (48). It can be used for any situation where the speaker has a negative attitude towards the referent involved in the action/situation or the action/situation itself. This can be used to show empathy with someone suffering a negative situation, and so is said to be more polite in some instances, such as (48d), and also has something of a passive sense, emphasizing affectedness (e.g. (48a), where the word order marks the receiver of the scolding as the topic). In these cases the form of the verb is always transitive.

(48) (a) àng(sv̀ng) vpèí ngv̄n kéòē
àng-sv̀ng v-pè-í ngv̄n ké-ò-ē
3sg-LOC 1-father-AGT scold eat-3+TR.N.PAST-N.PAST
He is being scolded by my father

(b) àng svmǐí gáng kéòē
àng svmī-í gáng ké-ò-ē
3sg fire-INST hot eat-3+TR.N.PAST-N.PAST
He's hot from the fire

(c) à:ngí pàgø̄ mà-shvbǿn kéò
àng-í pà-gø̄ mà-shv-bǿn ké-ò
3sg-AGT thing-also NEG-CAUS-be.possible eat-3+TR.N.PAST
He's incapable of doing anything

(d) àngsv̀ng tvp ké bǿà
àng-sv̀ng tvp ké bǿ-à
3sg-LOC be.arrested eat PFV-3+TR.PAST
He was arrested

(e)   àng nō nə̀ mvnøklá aq dárì rvt (nə̀í) vrù kéòē

        àng nō nə̀   mvnøklá aq   dár-ì   rvt   nə̀-í

        3sg TOP wine too   drink TMhrs-3+INTR.PAST because wine-INST

        vrù   ké-ò-ē

        drunk eat-3+TR.N.PAST-N.PAST

        He drank too much and so is/got drunk (from the wine)

4   Conclusions

We have seen that in Rawang, unlike in many other Sino-Tibetan languages, the coding of transitivity and the use of transitive vs intransitive constructions to convey different meanings are important aspects of the grammar. Aside from the different uses of the two forms of ambitransitive verbs, there are two morphological means for decreasing the valency of clauses, and six means for increasing their valency. We have also seen that a speaker may employ several different valency-increasing and valency-decreasing morphemes in the same clause to achieve different meanings through their interaction.

References

Barnard, J.T.O. 1934. *A handbook of the Rawang dialect of the Nung language.* Rangoon: Superintendent of Government Printing and Stationery.

Benedict, P.K. 1972. *Sino-Tibetan: a conspectus* (J.A. Matisoff, contributing ed.). New York: Cambridge University Press.

Dai Qingxia, Huang Bufan, Fu Ailan, Renzengwangmu and Liu Juhuang. 1991. *Zàng-Miǎnyǔ shíwǔ zhǒng (Fifteen Tibeto-Burman languages)*. Beijing: Yanshan Chubanshe.

Dai Qingxia and Xu Xijian. 1992. *Jǐngpōyǔ yǔfǎ (The grammar of the Chinghpaw language)*. Beijing: Zhongyang Minzu Xueyuan Chubanshe.

Driem, G. van. 1988. 'Reflexes of the Tibeto-burman *-t directive suffix in Dumi Rai', pp. 157–67 of *Prosodic analysis and Asian linguistics: to honour R.K. Sprigg*, ed. D. Bradley, E.J.A. Henderson and M. Mazaudon, Pacific Linguistics C 104. Canberra: Australian National University.

Kemmer, S. 1993. *The middle voice*, Typological studies in language 23. Amsterdam and Philadelphia: John Benjamins.

LaPolla, R.J. 1994. 'Parallel grammaticalizations in Tibeto-Burman: evidence of Sapir's "drift"', *Linguistics of the Tibeto-Burman Area* 17.61–80.

    1995a. 'On the utility of the concepts of markedness and prototypes in understanding the development of morphological systems', *Bulletin of the Institute of History and Philology* (Academia Sinica) 66.1149–85.

    1995b. 'Reflexive and middle marking in Dulong/Rawang.' Paper presented to the 28th International Conference on Sino-Tibetan Languages and Linguistics.

Charlottesville, Va., 6–9 October. To appear in *Himalayan linguistics*, ed. G. van Driem. Berlin: Mouton de Gruyter.

1996. 'Middle voice marking in Tibeto-Burman languages.' *Pan-Asian linguistics: proceedings of the Fourth International Symposium on Languages and Linguistics*. Vol. V. Thailand: Mahidol University.

Liu Juhuang. 1988. 'Dúlóngyǔ dòngcí yánjiū (Studies on the Dulong verb)'. *Yǔyán yánjiū* 1988.1.176–91.

Lo Ch'ang-p'ei. 1945. 'A preliminary study of the Trung language of Kung Shan', *Harvard Journal of Asiatic Studies* 8:343–8.

Matisoff, J.A. 1976. 'Lahu causative constructions: case hierarchies and the morphology/syntax cycle in a Tibeto-Burman perspective', pp. 413–42 of *The syntax of causative constructions*, ed. M. Shibatani. New York: Academic Press.

Mei Tsu-lin. 1989. 'The causative and denominative functions of the *s- prefix in Old Chinese.' *Proceedings of the Second International Conference on Sinology*. Taipei: Academia Sinica.

Michailovsky, B. 1985. 'Tibeto-Burman dental suffixes: evidence from Limbu (Nepal)', pp. 334–43 of *Linguistics of the Sino-Tibetan area: the state of the art. Papers presented to Paul K. Benedict for his 71st birthday*, ed. G. Thurgood, J.A. Matisoff and D. Bradley, Pacific Linguistics C 87. Canberra: Australian National University.

Morse, R.H. 1963. 'Phonology of Rawang', *Anthropological Linguistics* 5.17–41.

1965. 'Syntactic frames for the Rvwang (Rawang) verb', *Lingua* 15.338–69.

Sun Hongkai. 1982. *Dúlóngyǔ jiǎnzhì (A sketch of the Dulong language)*. Beijing: Minzu Chubanshe.

1988. 'Notes on a new language: Anong', *Linguistics of the Tibeto-Burman Area* 11.27–63.

9 Valency-changing and valency-encoding devices in Amharic

MENGISTU AMBERBER

1 Introduction

Amharic belongs to the Ethio-Semitic subgroup of the Semitic language family.[1] As a typical Semitic language, it employs root-and-pattern morphology as its main word-formation strategy.[2] It is a nominative–accusative language with a mixture of head- and dependent-marking. The verb shows subject (S/A) and object / indirect object (O/IO) agreement. Subject agreement is obligatory, whereas object and indirect object agreement is often optional.

Accusative case depends on definiteness: only definite object NPs take the accusative suffix. In fact, definite object NPs must take the accusative suffix. Subject NPs are not marked for case. The indirect object is marked by a prepositional particle which also marks the beneficiary peripheral argument.

Number distinction (singular and plural) is made in all persons (1st, 2nd and 3rd), whereas gender distinction (masculine and feminine) is made in 2nd and 3rd person singular only.

---

[1] I would like to thank Sasha Aikhenvald, Bob Dixon, Debbie Hill and two anonymous referees for their useful suggestions and comments on an earlier draft of this chapter. I would also like to thank the participants of the International Workshop on Valency-changing Derivations, Canberra, 1997, for their insightful comments and questions. Of course, I am responsible for remaining shortcomings.

[2] ROOT-AND-PATTERN morphology is a typical Semitic word-formation strategy. It is basically characterized by a ROOT which consists of consonantal radicals and a PATTERN which comprises vowels. In general, the roots encode lexical meaning, whereas the patterns encode grammatical meaning. For example, the verb *səbbərə* 'he broke (tr)' consists of the triradical root √sbr 'break', and the pattern $C_1 \partial C_2 \partial C_3 \partial$ encodes the perfect conjugation with the 3rd person masculine. The infinitive of √sbr 'break' is *məsbər* 'to break' which is formed by attaching the prefix *mə-* to the pattern -$C_1 C_2 \partial C_3$. Traditionally, Amharic verbs are classified into three morphological (conjugational) classes – Type A, Type B and Type C – on the basis of the vocalic pattern of the stem and gemination: whether or not the 2nd radical of the root is geminated throughout the conjugation (cf. Leslau 1995: 280ff.).

The language makes a distinction between basic intransitive and transitive verbs. The relevant transitivity classes are listed in (1):[3]

(1) (a) INTRANSITIVE
    (i) Unaccusative   k'omə   'stand'
    (ii) Unergative   č'əffərə   'dance'
(b) TRANSITIVE   səbbərə   'break (tr)'
(c) AMBITRANSITIVE   bəlla   'eat'
(d) EXTENDED TRANSITIVE   sət't'ə   'give'

There are two sets of intransitive verbs which I will refer to as 'unaccusative' and 'unergative'. The unaccusative class includes verbs which encode state (e.g. *k'omə* 'stand'), change of state (e.g. *k'əllət'ə* 'melt') and motion (e.g. *mət't'a* 'come'); the unergative class includes verbs which encode activities such as *č'əffərə* 'dance'. There is a small set of ambitransitive (or 'labile') verbs of the S = A subtype which almost exclusively contains ingestive verbs such as *bəlla* 'eat' and *t'ət't'ə* 'drink'. Extended transitive (or ditransitive) verbs which have three core arguments include verbs such as *sət't'ə* 'give'. In addition, Amharic has copula clauses which express equation, possession, attribution and identity, among other things.

In this chapter, I will discuss valency-changing and valency-encoding devices of Amharic. Essentially, my aim is to make three main points. First, I will show that the lexical semantic distinction between unergatives and unaccusatives is crucial in the organization of transitivity classes in Amharic.

Second, I will argue that the presence of an external causer in bringing about an event is an important parameter in determining whether a verb can have the anticausative form or not.

Third, I will demonstrate that at a descriptive level a distinction should be made between two types of morphosyntactic devices: those which change valency and those which encode valency.

The chapter is organized as follows. In §2 and §3, argument-reducing and argument-adding derivations are discussed respectively. In §4, the reflexive and reciprocal derivations are briefly examined. In §5 valency-encoding devices and bound verbs are discussed. In §6, the valency of complex predicates is addressed.

2   Argument-reducing derivations

There are three types of argument-reducing derivations which are derived by attaching the detransitivizer prefix *tə-* (*t-* before a vowel), to a basic transitive

---

[3] The citation form of the verb is inflected in the 3rd person masculine perfect which is the unmarked conjugation.

stem (see also Demoz 1964). They are: (a) the passive, (b) the anticausative and (c) the reflexive. In this section, the derivation of the passive and the anticausative is discussed. As a reflexive clause can also be derived without the use of the detransitivizer prefix, the derivation of the reflexive is discussed in §4 with that of the reciprocal.

2.1   Passive

	TRANSITIVE		PASSIVE	
(2) (a)	k'orrət'ə	'cut'	tə-k'orrət'ə	'be cut'
(b)	mətta	'hit'	tə-mətta	'be hit'
(c)	gənəbba	'build'	tə-gənəbba	'be built'

In the passive, the O argument of the transitive verb becomes S and the A argument is either omitted or placed in a prepositional phrase (headed by *bə-* 'by') as shown in (3b):

(3) (a)   aster gəməd-u-n   k'orrət'ə-čč
          A.   rope- DEF-ACC cut+PERF-3F
          Aster cut the rope

(b)   gəməd-u [bə-aster] tə-k'orrət'ə
      rope-DEF (by-A.)   PASS-cut+PERF+3M
      The rope was cut (by Aster)

Typically, the passive does not apply to intransitive verbs:

	INTRANSITIVE		PASSIVE
(4) (a)	hedə	'go'	*tə-hedə
(b)	təñña	'sleep'	*tə-təñña
(c)	mət't'a	'come'	*tə-mət't'a

However, a passive-like derivation of intransitive verbs is acceptable with a special shade of meaning: it expresses irony or sarcasm (cf. Leslau 1995: 467). Thus, consider the following example:

(5)   wədə bet   tə-hedə
      to   home PASS-go+PERF+3M
      So you are going home!

The sarcastic passive has a special rising intonation and is often employed to address the 2nd person. Note that the verb has the default 3rd person masculine agreement.

2.2   *Anticausative*

	TRANSITIVE		ANTICAUSATIVE	
(6) (a)	səbbərə	'break (tr)'	tə-səbbərə	'break (intr)'
(b)	kəffətə	'open (tr)'	tə-kəffətə	'open (intr)'
(c)	bəttənə	'scatter (tr)'	tə-bəttənə	'scatter (intr)'

The anticausative simply derives intransitive verbs: the O argument of the transitive verb becomes S and there is no A (either demoted or implicitly implied).

The distinction between the passive and the anticausative can be subtle as the same formal strategy (the detransitivizer prefix *t(ə)-*) is used to derive both constructions. Thus, for instance, the verb *tə-səbbərə*, like all of the anticausative verbs in (6), can have either a passive reading ('be broken') or an anticausative reading ('break (intr)'). However, it is possible to force a passive reading syntactically as in (7):

(7)   t'ərmus-u bə-lïǰ-u   tə-səbbərə
        bottle-DEF by-boy- DEF PASS-break+PERF+3M
        The bottle was broken (by the boy)

In (7), the presence of the agent (occurring in the peripheral 'by'-phrase) forces the passive reading alone. Furthermore, it is possible to force the passive reading by placing agent-oriented adverbial phrases like *bə-t'ïnïk'k'ak'e* 'with care, with attention':

(8) (a) bər-u   tə-kəffətə
        door-DEF ANTC/PASS-open+PERF+3M
        The door opened / was opened

(b)   bər-u   bə-t'ïnïk'k'ak'e   tə-kəffətə
        door-DEF with-care/attention PASS-open+PERF+3M
        The door was opened with care

The question of which verbs allow the anticausative derivation and which verbs do not largely depends on the notion of external causation (for a similar notion, see Levin and Rappaport 1995). The relevant generalization is stated in (9):

(9)   If an event encoded by a transitive predicate can be conceptualized as taking place without the intervention of an external causer, the event can be cast in the anticausative.

Thus, by examining the lexical semantic content of the basic verb, it is generally possible to predict whether the anticausative is possible or not. Consider the verbs in (10):

(10) (a)   sənət't'ək'ə   'split'   tə-sənət't'ək'ə   'split (intr)'
(b)   k'əddədə   'tear'   tə-k'əddədə   'tear (intr)'

The events encoded by the transitive verbs *sənət't'ək'ə* 'split' and *k'əddədə* 'tear' have an external causer that brings about the event. However, the events can also come about without the intervention of an external causer. For instance, consider the verb *sənət't'ək'ə* 'split' in (11):

(11) (a)   anas'i-w   t'awla-w-in   sənət't'ək'ə
            carpenter-DEF plank-DEF-ACC split+PERF+3M
            The carpenter split the plank

(b)   t'awla-w   tə-sənət't'ək'ə
            plank-DEF ANTC/PASS-split+PERF+3M
            The plank split / was split

The event of 'a plank splitting' can come about by an external causer as in (11a), or can happen naturally, for example due to excessive heat. Thus, (11b) can have an anticausative or a passive reading. On the other hand, consider the semantically close verb *fəllət'ə* in (12), which refers to the splitting of wood as a result of using an instrument such as an axe (it also has the meaning 'chop (wood)' and 'quarry (stone)'):

(12) (a)   anas'i-w   t'awla-w-in   fəllət'ə
            carpenter-DEF plank-DEF-ACC split+PERF+3M
            The carpenter split the plank

(b)   t'awla-w   tə-fəllət'ə
            plank-DEF PASS-split+PERF+3M
            The plank was split

The event encoded by the verb *sənət't'ək'ə* 'split' differs from that of *fəllət'ə* 'split/chop' in one crucial respect: the latter cannot come about without an external causer and as a result it cannot be cast in the anticausative.

The same contrast pertains to a number of verbs in other languages such as English. For instance, as pointed out by Haspelmath (1993: 93), in English the event encoded by *cut* requires an 'agent-oriented meaning component' (usually involving a sharp object as an instrument). On the other hand, the event encoded by the verb *tear* can occur without the involvement of an external causer. Thus, the intransitive ('inchoative') form of the verb *cut* is ungrammatical – e.g. **the cloth cut* – as opposed to the intransitive form of the verb *tear* – e.g. *the pants tore*.

Most verbs of creation such as *s'afə* 'write' and *gənəbba* 'build' do not allow the anticausative interpretation. This follows directly from the assumption that such verbs require the involvement of an external causer. Thus, *tə-s'afə* can only have the passive meaning 'be written'.

It appears that if a verb allows the anticausative, it also allows the passive but not vice versa. Hence: anticausative implies passive.

3   Argument-adding derivations

3.1   *Causatives*

There are two types of causatives: (a) morphological causatives and (b) the periphrastic causative. In morphological causatives, explicit derivational affixes are employed to increase the valency of a verb: a one-place predicate becomes a two-place predicate and a two-place predicate becomes a three-place pre-dicate. In the periphrastic causative an independent causative verb is used to introduce a causer argument. In addition, there are lexical causatives (also referred to as the 'suppletive' causative (cf. Haspelmath 1993)), i.e., verbs whose intransitive and transitive forms are morphologically unrelated. Typical examples of lexical causatives in Amharic are presented in (13):

(13) (a)   wəddək'ə   'fall'   t'alə   'drop (tr)'
(b)   motə   'die'   gəddələ   'kill'

In this chapter, I will not discuss lexical causatives as they are not relevant to the issue of valency-changing derivations. The following two sub-sections will deal with morphological and periphrastic causatives.

3.1.1   Morphological causatives

There are two types of productive causative prefixes. They are: (a) the causat-ive *a-* and (b) the causative *as-*, exemplified in (14a) and (14b) respectively:

(14) (a)   mət't'a   'come'   a-mət't'a   'bring'
(b)   kʼʷərrət'ə   'cut'   as-kʼʷərrət'ə   'make x cut y'

The distribution of the two causative prefixes is, by and large, predictable from the lexical semantics of the basic verb.

(a) Causative a-   In general, the causative *a-* attaches only to unaccusatives, as in (15), and not to unergatives as in (16):

(15) (a)   k'omə   'stand (intr)'   a-k'omə   'stand (tr)'
(b)   k'əllət'ə   'melt (intr)'   a-k'əllət'ə   'melt (tr)'

(16) (a)   č'əffərə   'dance'   * a-č'əffərə
(b)   sak'ə   'laugh'   * a-sak'ə

More examples of unaccusative verbs (including verbs of state, change of state, and motion) which take the causative *a-* are presented in (17–19). The category labels for the verb classes are taken from Levin's (1993) study of English verb classes.

(17)   Verbs of Inherently Directed Motion[4]
       gəbba   'enter (intr)'   a-gəbba   'insert'
       wərrədə   'descend'   a-wərrədə   'bring down'
       wət't'a   'exit'   a-wət't'a   'take out'

(18)   Verbs of Emission
(a)   LIGHT   nəddədə   'burn (intr)'
                  a-nəddədə   'burn (tr)'
(b)   SOUND   fənədda   'explode (intr)'
                  a-fənədda   'explode (tr)'
(c)   SMELL   t'ənəbba   'stink (intr)'
                  a-t'ənəbba   'stink (tr)'
(d)   SUBSTANCE   dəmma   'bleed (intr)'
                  a-dəmma   'bleed (tr)'

(19)   Verbs of Existence and Appearance
       norə   'exist'   a-norə   'let exist, put'
       bək'k'ələ   'grow'   a-bək'k'ələ   'grow (tr)'

In the causative *a-*, the causee does not have control over the event (see Dixon's discussion of the semantic parameters of causatives in chapter 2 of this volume). The causer acts directly and may achieve the result volitionally or non-volitionally. The causer is always involved in the event and can be initiating a natural process or may exert effort.

The alignment of arguments in the causative *a-* is quite straightforward: the newly introduced argument and the old S are realized as A and O respectively:

(20) (a)   k'ɨbe-w   k'əllət'ə
          butter-DEF melt+PERF+3M
          The butter melted

(b)   aster k'ɨbe-w-ɨn   a-k'əllət'ə-čč
      A.   butter-DEF-ACC CAUS-melt+PERF+3F
      Aster melted the butter

---

[4] The reader should keep in mind that the meaning given in the gloss of a given verb is only the central meaning amongst a number of possible related meanings. For instance, the verb *a-gəbba*, which is the causative of *gəbba* 'enter', can have a range of meanings including: 'bring in', 'insert', 'take a spouse (in marriage)', among others.

As already mentioned, the causative *a-* does not attach to unergatives, nor to transitives. However, there is one systematic exception to this generalization. A small class of transitive verbs which express ingestion, such as *bəlla* 'eat' and *t'ət't'ə* 'drink', can take the causative *a-*. Consider the verb *bəlla* 'eat' in (21):

(21) (a) lïj-u   dabbo bəlla
child-DEF bread eat+PERF+3M
The child ate some bread

(b)   aster lïj-u-n   dabbo a-bəlla-čč-ïw
A.   child-DEF-ACC bread CAUS-eat+PERF-3F-3MO
Aster fed the child some bread

Notice in (21b) that when the verb *bəlla* 'eat' takes the causative *a-*, it essentially becomes a three-place predicate with the meaning 'feed' (or 'give to eat').

Interestingly, these same verbs exhibit special behaviour in a number of languages including Berber (Guerssel 1986: 36ff.), Chichewa (Baker 1988: 461n.31) and Malayalam (Mohanan 1983: 105–6).

(b) Causative as-   The causative *as-* has a wider distribution – it applies to transitive and (both unaccusative and unergative) intransitive verbs:

(22) (a) k^{1w}ərrət'ə   'cut'   as-k^{1w}ərrət'ə   'cause to cut'
(b)   mət't'a   'come'   as-mət't'a   'cause to come'
(c)   č'əffərə   'dance'   as-č'əffərə   'make dance'

With intransitive verbs, the new argument introduced by the causative *as-* becomes the A of the derived verb, and the old S of the intransitive verb becomes O:

(23) (a) aster č'əffərə-čč
A.   dance+PERF-3F
Aster danced

(b)   ləmma aster-ïn as-č'əffər-at
L.   A.-ACC CAUS-dance+PERF+3M-3FO
Lemma made Aster dance

In the case of transitive verbs, the new argument introduced by the causative *as-* becomes the A of the derived verb and the old A becomes the new O. The O of the basic verb is either retained or omitted:

(24) (a) aster sïga-w-ïn   k'orrət'ə-čč
A.   meat- DEF-ACC cut+PERF-3F
Aster cut the meat

(b)   ləmma aster-in (siga) as-k'orrət'-at
L.   A.-ACC (meat) CAUS-cut+ PERF+3M-3FO
Lemma made Aster cut (some meat)

When the O of the basic verb is retained, it is often realized as indefinite, due to a tendency to avoid double-accusative NPs (though this does not mean that a clause with double-accusatives is ungrammatical). Note that the causee is always definite and thus obligatorily marked as accusative.

In some cases, omitting the object of the basic verb may cause ambiguity. For instance, in (24b), if the NP *siga* 'meat' is omitted, the construction could mean either: (a) 'he made her cut (something unspecified)' or (b) 'he had her be cut (by someone)'.[5]

The causer of the causative *as-* may act directly or indirectly, volitionally or non-volitionally. Although typically the causer of the causative *as-* exerts force, it need not be coercive. However, the causer itself is often not involved in the event. This property of the causer of the causative *as-* is in marked contrast to that of the causative *a-* where the causer is always directly involved in the event. Consider the verb *wət't'a* 'exit/leave' in (25):

(25) (a)   aster wət't'a-čč
A.   exit+PERF-3F
Aster exited

(b)   ləmma aster-in a-wət't'a-t
L.   A.-ACC CAUS-exit+PERF+3M-3FO
Lemma took Aster out (as in 'out of the house')

(c)   ləmma aster-in as-wət't'a-t
L.   A.-ACC CAUS-exit+PERF+3M-3FO
Lemma made Aster exit
Lemma let Aster exit

In (25b), with the causative *a-*, the causer is directly involved in the event, e.g. the causer physically transports the causee. In (25c), with the causative *as-*, the causer is not directly involved in the event, e.g. the causer can simply issue an order.

Notice that the causative *as-* can also have a permissive interpretation ('let') where the causer is conceptualized as helping the causee, or at least not obstructing the efforts of the causee.

---

[5] It is possible to analyse the causative *as-* as a three-place predicate (as argued in Alsina 1992 for Chichewa) with an agent, a causee (an affected object) and an event, where the causee is also an argument of the basic verb. The causee can be identified either with the subject or the object of the basic verb. It is when the causee is identified with the object of the basic verb that the subject takes an oblique position.

3.1.2   Periphrastic causative

The periphrastic causative is formed by the independent verb *adərrəgə* 'make'. The semantically basic verb is marked by a complementizer particle:

(26)   aster ləmma wədə bet   ind-i-hed   adərrəgə-čč
        A.   L.   to   home COMP-IMPERF+3M-go+IMPERF make+PERF-3F
        Aster made Lemma go home

The periphrastic can apply to both intransitive and transitive verbs and its meaning is often indistinguishable from the causative *as-*. However, one important difference between the periphrastic causative and the causative *as-* is seen with negation. Consider the examples in (27):

(27) (a)   kasa aster ɨnd-a-ti-hed   adərrəgə
            K.   A.   COMP-NEG-IMPERF+3F-go+IMPERF make+PERF+3M
            Kasa prevented Aster from going (lit. he made her not go)

(b)   kasa aster-ɨn al-as-hed-at-ɨmm
       K.   A.-ACC NEG-CAUS-go+PERF+3M-3FO-NEG
       Kasa did not make Aster go

As (27a) shows, the periphrastic causative allows for the polarity of the embedded verb to be different from that of the matrix verb. Thus, negation can have scope over the embedded verb alone. In the causative *as-*, on the other hand, negation has scope over the entire clause.

3.2   *Applicative*

Amharic has one type of construction which can be described as applicative. Consider the examples in (28–29):

(28)   aster bə-mət'rəgiya-w dəĵĵ   t'ərrəgə-čč-[ɨbb-ət]
        A.   with-broom-DEF doorway sweep+PERF-3F-(with-3MO)
        Aster swept a doorway with the broom

(29)   aster mət'rəgiya-w-ɨn dəĵĵ   t'ərrəgə-čč-ɨbb-ət
        A.   broom-DEF-ACC doorway sweep+PERF-3F-with-3MO
        Aster swept a doorway with the broom
        (lit. Aster, the broom, she swept a doorway with it)

In (28), the instrumental NP occurs with the prepositional element *bə-* 'with' (which also has a range of different prepositional meanings including 'by', 'at', 'on'). The verb is optionally marked by the form *-bb-*, which is similar to the prepositional form *bə-*, followed by a pronominal agreement suffix which cross-references the instrumental NP (see also Haile 1970). In this construction, the form *-bb-* and the pronominal suffix that follows it occur as a unit, i.e., one cannot occur without the other.

Notice that (29) is different from (28) in two important ways: (a) the instrumental NP occurs without the prepositional particle *bə-* and is marked by the accusative suffix, and (b) the prepositional suffix *-bb-* and the pronominal agreement suffix that follows it are no longer optional. Although the term 'applicative' has not been used in the description of Amharic, it is used here to refer to constructions such as (29) where an erstwhile peripheral argument occurs as a core argument. For ease of exposition, the prepositional suffix in (29) will be glossed as the applicative marker as in (30):

(30)   aster mət'rəgiya-w-in dəǰǰ   t'ərrəgə-čč-<u>ibb</u>-ət
         A.   broom-DEF-ACC doorway sweep+PERF-3F-<u>APPLIC</u>-3MO
         Aster swept a doorway with the broom

The applicative is quite productive in that it applies to both transitive and intransitive verbs as the following examples show:

(31) (a) k'ʷərrət'ə   'cut'   k'ʷərrət'ə-bb-ət   'cut with/on'
(b)   sak'ə   'laugh'   sak'ə-bb-ət   'laugh at'
(c)   wəddək'ə   'fall'   wəddək'ə-bb-ət   'fall on'

Thus, the applicative derivation applies to a range of peripheral arguments including instrument, malefactive and locative. There is another prepositional suffix, namely *-ll-* (similar to the prepositional particle *lə-* 'for', 'to'), which often occurs with beneficiary arguments as in (32):

(32)   aster-in fərrədə-ll-at
         A.-ACC judge+PERF+3M-APPLIC-3FO
         He judged in Aster's favour (i.e., he acquitted her)

In general, the applicative marker *-ll-* marks a beneficiary argument, thus paradigmatically contrasting with *-bb-* which can mark the malefactive. This contrast can be seen by comparing (32) with (33):

(33)   aster-in fərrədə-bb-at
         A.-ACC judge+PERF+3M-APPLIC-3FO
         He judged to the disadvantage of Aster (i.e., he convicted her)

The applicative marker *-bb-* has a wider distribution, marking the instrumental, locative and malefactive arguments, whereas *-ll-* is generally restricted to benefactive arguments.

There is an interesting interaction between the malefactive applicative and the two types of intransitive verbs. Consider the unergative verb *sak'ə* 'laugh' in (34):

(34) (a)   astemari-wa   bə-lɨj-u   sak'ə-čč
              teacher-DEF+F at-boy-DEF laugh+PERF-3F
              The teacher laughed at the boy

(b)   astemari-wa   lɨj-u-n   sak'ə-čč-ɨbb-ət
              teacher-DEF+F boy-DEF-ACC laugh+PERF-3F-APPLIC-3MO
              The teacher laughed at the boy

In (34a), the malefactive argument occurs with its prepositional marking. In (34b), which is the applicative construction, the malefactive argument is marked as accusative, as expected. Now, consider the unaccusative verb *təsəbbərə* 'break (intr)' in (35):

(35) (a)   *t'ərmus-u   bə-aster tə-səbbərə
              bottle-DEF on-A.   ANTC-break+PERF+3M
              (for 'the bottle broke to the disadvantage of Aster')
              (OK as: 'the bottle was broken by Aster')

(b)   aster-(ɨn) t'ərmus-u   tə-səbbərə-bb-at
              A.-(ACC) bottle-DEF ANTC-break+PERF+3M-APPLIC-3FO
              The bottle broke to the disadvantage of Aster

Notice that there are two important differences between (34) and (35). First, unlike the malefactive of the unergative verb *sak'ə* 'laugh', the malefactive of the unaccusative verb *təsəbbərə* 'break (intr)' cannot occur in the prepositional phrase (marked by *bə-*) as shown in (35a). Note that the construction is grammatical only as a passive, i.e., if the preposition *bə-* is interpreted as 'by'.

Second, the malefactive argument occurs with an (optional) accusative case and occupies a clause-initial position as shown in (35b). If the malefactive argument of the unaccusative verb does not occur in a clause-initial position, the construction becomes ungrammatical as shown in (36):

(36)   *t'ərmus-u aster-(ɨn) tə-səbbərə-bb-at
              bottle-DEF A.-(ACC) ANTC-break+PERF+3M-APPLIC-3FO

This structural pattern of unaccusative verbs is quite productive. In fact, it occurs even with unaccusatives which do not normally take any referential argument. Consider the verb *məššə* 'become night' (or 'become dark') in (37):

(37)   aster-(ɨn) məššə-bb-at
              A.-(ACC) become.night+PERF+3M-APPLIC-3FO
              It became night (it got dark) to the disadvantage of Aster
              (lit. Aster, it became night on her)

Normally, the verb *məššə* 'become night' does not take any referential argument. However, through the applicative construction, the event can be cast as adversely affecting someone as shown in (37).

Hence, the question is: what is the cause of the variation between the two intransitive predicates? A detailed analysis of the phenomenon is beyond the scope of this chapter. However, I believe that the key to the solution resides in the lexical semantics and argument structure of the predicates in question. The malefactive argument has a different conceptual status depending on the lexical semantics of the basic predicate along the following lines:

(38) (a)   The malefactive of unergatives is an implicit argument which specifies the stimulus of the event.
(b)   The malefactive of unaccusatives is an experiencer ('undergoer') argument.

Thus, consider the event encoded by the verb *sak'ə* 'laugh'. When someone laughs, there is often a stimulus for the event. I suggest that the malefactive argument specifies that stimulus. On the other hand, with unaccusatives, the malefactive is simply an experiencer (or 'undergoer') argument.

The difference between the malefactive of the two predicates (unergative vs unaccusative) can be highlighted by content questions:

(39) (a)   Who was she laughing at?
(b)   Who was affected by the breaking of the bottle?

If you see somebody laughing, you can ask the question in (39a). This question is normal, because the malefactive argument is implicitly part of the lexical semantics of the basic verb – it is an argument which elaborates the activity event.

On the other hand, if you see a bottle breaking, the question in (39b) is quite odd, at least without prior background information. This is so because the malefactive argument is not part of the lexical semantics of the basic verb.

We have seen that the malefactive of the unaccusative verb occurs with an optional accusative marker and is cross-referenced by an obligatory object pronominal suffix on the verb. I argue that this fact is connected to the experiencer status of the malefactive argument. The evidence for this assumption comes from the argument structure of the so-called 'impersonal' verbs of sensation, emotion and perception which have quirky subjects. Consider the verbs *ammamə-* 'be/become ill', *raba-* 'be/become hungry' and *bərrədə* 'be/become cold' in (40):

(40) (a)   aster-(ɨn) amməm-at
           A.-(ACC) be/become.ill+PERF+3M-3FO
           Aster is/became ill (lit. it pained Aster)

(b)   aster-(ɨn) rab-at
           A.-(ACC) be/become.hungry+PERF+3M-3FO
           Aster is/became hungry (lit. it hungered Aster)

(c)   aster-(ɨn) bərrəd-at
           A.-(ACC) be/become.cold+PERF+3M-3FO
           Aster is/became cold (lit. it chilled A.)

It is obvious that the arguments of the impersonal verbs are undergoing a physical and/or mental experience. Notice that the arguments occur with an optional accusative case and control obligatory object agreement, exactly like the malefactive arguments of the unaccusatives. The argument which controls subject agreement can be regarded as the physical and/or mental state itself which is represented by *it* in the literal English translations.

It is interesting to note that the experiencer arguments of the impersonal verbs and the malefactive argument of the unaccusative verbs lack volitional control over the event. Thus, sentences such as (35b) can be employed to express events that are accidental or unexpected – for example, if the bottle broke after slipping out of one's grip.

4   Reflexives and reciprocals

4.1   Reflexives
The reflexive applies to transitive verbs. The prefix *t(ə)-*, which we have seen in the passive and anticausative, is also used to derive the reflexive:

(41) (a)   aster t-at't'əbə-čč
           A.   REFL-wash+PERF-3F
           Aster washed herself

(b)   ləmma tə-lač'č'ə
           L.   REFL-shave+PERF+3M
           Lemma shaved himself

Note that, as in the anticausative, the reflexive verb can have a passive interpretation as well. However, with verbs such as *at't'əbə* 'wash' and *lač'č'ə* 'shave' which express events that normally affect a bodypart, the preferred reading is that of the reflexive.

A reflexive clause can be derived without applying a valency-changing derivation. Amharic has a strategy of reflexivization which maintains the valency of the predicate and employs reflexive pronouns. The reflexive pronouns are formed by the root *(i)ras* 'self' (which also means 'head') plus possessive pronominal suffixes.

(42)　ləmma ras-u-n　　　　mətta
　　　L.　self-POSS+3M-ACC hit+PERF+3M
　　　Lemma hit himself

Notice that the reflexive pronoun occurs in the O slot and is marked by the accusative suffix. The verb *mətta* 'hit' can take the prefix *tə-* as in *tə-mətta* but it has only the passive interpretation. Thus, there is no reflexive of *mətta* 'hit':

(43)　*ləmma tə-mətta
　　　　L.　　REFL-hit+PERF+3M
　　　(for 'Lemma hit himself')
　　　(OK as: 'Lemma was hit')

Thus, verbs which do not take the reflexive prefix occur with reflexive pronouns to form the reflexive. The set of transitive verbs which take the prefix *t(ə)-* but do not have a reflexive meaning include verbs such as *mətta* 'hit' and *gəddələ* 'kill'. On the other hand, the set of transitive verbs which take the the prefix *t(ə)-* and have a reflexive meaning include verbs such as *at't'əbə* 'wash' and *lač'č'ə* 'shave'. Thus, the reflexive verbs refer to actions that are normally performed on one's own bodypart.

Interestingly, with verbs which encode events that affect parts of the body, the reflexive verb can take an accusative-marked argument:

(44)　ləmma ras-u-n　　　　　tə-lač'č'ə
　　　L.　head-POSS+3M-ACC REFL-shave+PERF+3M
　　　Lemma shaved his head
　　　(*for 'Lemma shaved himself')

However, note that the sentence in (44) is acceptable only if the form *(i)ras* is interpreted as 'head' (instead of as 'self'). Thus, the equivalent of 'he shaved his beard' involves the relevant body part in the O slot as in (45):

(45)　ləmma si'm-u-n　　　　　tə-lač'č'ə
　　　L.　beard-POSS+3M-ACC REFL-shave+PERF+3M
　　　Lemma shaved his beard

It is also important to note that the reflexive pronouns can have an emphatic function and occur in subject or object position:

(46) (a) ɨras-u   mət't'a
         self-POSS+3M come+PERF+3M
         He (not anyone else) came

(b)   aster ɨras-u-n   ayyə-č-ɨw
         A.   self-POSS+3M-ACC see+PERF-3F-3MO
         Aster saw him (not anyone else)

4.2   Reciprocals

Reciprocity is expressed by the prefix *t(ə)-* plus a special reduplicative stem inflected in the plural. For a triradical verb such as *nəkkəsə* 'bit', the reduplicative pattern is *tə+C_1əC_2aC_2C_2əC_3$-*:

(47)   wɨšš-očč-u tə-nəkakkəs-u
         dog-pl-DEF RECIP-bit+RECIP+PERF-3pl
         The dogs bit each other

In addition to the reciprocal stem, there are reciprocal pronouns formed by the stem *ɨrsbərs* plus a plural possessive suffix:

(48)   səww-očč-u ɨrsbərs-aččəw   tə-dəbaddəb-u
         person-pl-DEF each.other-POSS+3pl RECIP-hit+RECIP+PERF-3pl
         The people hit each other

The reciprocal pronoun cannot take the accusative case suffix:

(49)   *səww-očč-u ɨrsbərs-aččəw-ɨn   tə-dəbaddəb-u
          person-pl-DEF each.other-POSS+3pl-ACC RECIP-hit+RECIP+PERF-3pl

The absence of an accusative-marked NP in the O slot indicates that the reciprocal derivation always reduces valency.

5   Valency-encoding devices

In Amharic, one has to distinguish strictly valency-changing devices from valency-encoding devices.

Valency-changing devices are involved in directional alternation (in the sense of Haspelmath 1993: 91), i.e., either an intransitive form is formally basic and the transitive is derived from it or else the transitive is basic and the intransitive is derived from it. In addition to this pattern, we need to recognize non-directed alternation, or what Haspelmath (1993) calls 'equipollent alternation' in which both the intransitive and transitive forms of a verb are derived from a common stem by employing different affixes or auxiliary verbs.

Amharic and other Ethio-Semitic languages have a number of verbs which do not occur in their basic forms despite their phonological well-formedness. Such verbs can be described as bound because they are not well formed unless they occur with a derivational prefix. Consider the following examples:

(50) (a)   tə-dəssətə   'be pleased, be happy'
           as-dəssətə   'please (tr), make happy'
           (*-dəssətə)

(b)   tə-k'əmmət'ə   'sit (intr), be placed'
           as-k'əmmət'ə   'sit (tr), put'
           (*-k'əmmət'ə)

Both the transitive and intransitive verbs are derived by attaching the relevant prefix to the same bound form. Thus, bound verbs occur with valency-encoding prefixes. Note that it is not possible to predict the class of verbs that require valency-encoding prefixes on morphophonological or lexical semantic grounds.

6   The valency of complex predicates

A study of transitivity classes in Amharic would not be complete without examining the valency of complex predicates. There is a productive complex predicate which essentially involves the juxtaposing of the verb *alə* 'say' or the verb *adərrəgə* 'make/do' with a verbal noun:

(51)   t'ərmus-u sɨbbɨr   alə
           bottle-DEF break+VN say+PERF+3M
           The bottle broke

In (51), it is only the verb *alə* 'say' that is inflected for tense/aspect and pronominal agreement. The element which co-occurs with the verb *alə* 'say' takes no verbal inflection. I will employ the terms 'verbal noun' (VN) and 'simple verb' (SV) to refer to the non-inflected constituent of the predicate (e.g. *sɨbbɨr* 'break+VN') and the inflected verb (e.g. *alə* 'say') respectively. The latter is sometimes known by the term 'light verb' – a term familiar from the study of similar constructions in languages such as Japanese (cf. Grimshaw and Mester 1988). See also Reid's chapter in this volume for a similar complex verb formation in Ngan'gityemerri and other Daly/Kimberley languages.

Although the verbal noun does not have the usual verbal inflection, it occurs with distinct templates. In a typical triradical root, the VN appears in two different templates, which can be identified as intensive and attenuative respectively (cf. Beyene 1972):

(52) (a) Intensive: $C_1iC_2C_2iC_3$
(b)   Attenuative: $C_1\partial C_2\partial C_3$

Although the intensive and attenuative templates encode a range of related meanings, the most common meaning component has to do with the manner in which the event is realized: for instance, whether the patient argument is completely affected or not or whether the action is more intense or not. Thus, in (51) where the predicate occurs with the intensive template, there is a sense in which the action is rather intense.

Synchronically, there are a number of constructions in which the position of the VN is filled with onomatopoeic items:

(53) (a) zɨnab-u t'əbb t'əbb alə
       rain-DEF 'drip'   say+PERF+3M
       The rain dripped
       (lit. the rain said: 't'əbb t'əbb')

(b)   gomma-w sit'it't'   alə
       tyre-DEF   'squeak' say+PERF+3M
       The tyre squeaked
       (lit. the tyre (of a car) said: 'sit'it't'')

Interestingly, the complex predicate formed by the verb *alə* 'say' occurs only in intransitive clauses. Thus, the simple verb *alə* 'say' cannot occur in transitive clauses:

(54) (a) *aster t'ərmus-u-n   sɨbbɨr   alə-čč
       A.   bottle-DEF-ACC break+VN say+PERF-3F
       (for 'Aster broke the bottle')

(b)   *anas'i-w   t'awla-w-ɨn   sɨnt't'ɨk' alə
       carpenter-DEF plank-DEF-ACC split+VN say+PERF-3F
       (for 'the carpenter split the plank')

The transitive variants of the above constructions involve another simple verb, namely the verb *adərrəgə* 'make/do':

(55) (a) aster t'ərmus-u-n   sɨbbɨr   adərrəgə-čč
       A.   bottle-DEF-ACC break+VN do+PERF-3F
       Aster broke the bottle

(b)   anas'i-w   t'awla-w-in   sint't'ik' adərrəgə
         carpenter-DEF plank-DEF-ACC split+VN do+PERF+3M
         The carpenter split the plank

Notice that the same verbal noun can occur with either *alə* 'say' or *adərrəgə* 'make/do' with a corresponding difference in transitivity. For instance, compare (54a) with (55a). In both clauses, the verbal noun (*sibbir* 'break+VN') is constant and the valency of the predicate is indicated by the simple verbs. Thus, the simple verbs are valency-encoding devices parallel to the valency-encoding prefixes discussed in §5.

7   Conclusion

In this chapter, I have discussed valency-changing and valency-encoding devices in Amharic.

First, I showed that the lexical semantic distinction between unergatives and unaccusatives is important in determining transitivity. Second, I argued that the presence of an external causer in bringing about an event is a crucial lexical semantic notion that is responsible for the presence of the anticausative derivation. Third, I suggested that at a descriptive level valency-encoding devices should be recognized as distinct from valency-changing devices.

Excluding the applicative,[6] the morphological derivations which we have seen so far can be categorized into two broad classes: (a) micro-derivations and (b) macro-derivations. Micro-derivations apply to a relatively restricted class of verbs and are more sensitive to the lexical semantic property of the basic predicate (for instance, whether or not the event can come about without the involvement of an external causer). Macro-derivations are relatively free in their application:

(56) (a) Micro-derivations
          (i)   anticausative
          (ii)   causative *a-*
          (iii) reflexive/reciprocal

     (b) Macro-derivations
          (i)   passive
          (ii)   causative *as-*

---

[6] For the applicative, one has to examine the interaction between the peripheral arguments (including locative, benefactive, malefactive, instrumental) on the one hand, and transitivity classes on the other – a task which is beyond the scope of this chapter.

It can be argued (as pointed out to me by Masayoshi Shibatani) that the anticausative, the passive and the reflexive can be grouped in one class under the label 'middle' (see also Kemmer 1993):

(57) middle
      (a) anticausative
      (b) passive
      (c) reflexive

The grouping of these three derivations under the label 'middle' can be justified mainly on morphological grounds: the prefix *t(ə)-* is employed in all cases. (Note that the reciprocal is excluded from the class because it requires reduplication in addition to the prefix.)

However, from a syntactico-semantic perspective, the verbs that take the prefix *t(ə)-* hardly constitute a homogenous ('middle') class in Amharic. Indeed, we have seen that the anticausative applies only to a restricted class of transitive verbs, whereas the passive applies to any basic transitive verb. The reflexive typically applies to events that normally affect a bodypart. Unlike the anticausative and the passive, the reflexive does not necessarily reduce valency because the bodypart NP can occur in the O position.

Needless to say, a chapter of this size cannot cover all of the intricacies of valency-changing and valency-encoding devices in Amharic. However, I hope that the chapter presents a general overview of the transitivity designs of the language which would be of interest for linguistic typology.

References

Alsina, A. 1992. 'On the argument structure of causatives', *Linguistic Inquiry* 23.517–56.

Baker, M. 1988. *Incorporation: a theory of grammatical function changing*. Chicago: University of Chicago Press.

Beyene, T. 1972. 'Aspects of the verb in Amharic'. Ph.D. dissertation. Georgetown University, Washington, D.C.

Demoz, A. 1964. 'The meaning of some derived verbal stems in Amharic', Ph.D. dissertation. UCLA.

Grimshaw, J. and Mester, A. 1988. 'Light verbs and θ-marking', *Linguistic Inquiry* 19.205–32.

Guerssel, M. 1986. *On Berber verbs of change: a study of transitivity alternations*, Lexicon Project Working Papers 9. Cambridge, Mass.: Lexicon Project, Center for Cognitive Science, MIT.

Haile, G. 1970. 'The suffix pronouns in Amharic', pp. 101–11 of *Papers in African linguistics*, ed. Chin-Wu Kim and H. Stahlke. Edmonton: Linguistic Research.

Haspelmath, M. 1993. 'More on the typology of inchoative/causative verb alterna-tions', pp. 87–120 of *Causatives and transitivity*, ed. B. Comrie and M. Polinsky. Amsterdam: John Benjamins.

Kemmer, S. 1993. *The middle voice*, Typological studies in language 23. Amsterdam and Philadelphia: John Benjamins.

Leslau, W. 1995. *Reference grammar of Amharic*. Wiesbaden: Otto Harrassowitz.

Levin, B. 1993. *English verb classes and alternations*. Chicago: University of Chi-cago Press.

Levin, B. and Rappaport, M. 1995. *Unaccusativity: at the syntax–semantics interface*. Cambridge, Mass.: The MIT Press.

Mohanan, K.P. 1983. 'Move NP or lexical rules? Evidence from Malayalam causativ-ization', pp. 47–111 of *Papers in Lexical–Functional Grammar*, ed. L. Levin *et al*. Bloomington: Indiana University Linguistics Club.

10 Complex verb collocations in Ngan'gityemerri: a non-derivational strategy for encoding valency alternations

NICHOLAS REID

This chapter investigates the range of constructions in Ngan'gityemerri[1] that can be thought of as involving shifts in the associated argument structure of verbs. The major contribution of this chapter is to highlight the fact that some languages have at their disposal morphosyntactic mechanisms that encode valency, without necessarily needing morphological derivations to achieve the same kinds of valency shifts that derivations are good for. Ngan'gityemerri's main strategy, a system of complex verb formation, is of the morphosyntactic type. However, it does additionally make use of some minor but genuinely morphological derivations, including a presentative applicative derived from an incorporated bodypart noun.

1 Preliminaries

There are two parameters around which Australian languages vary. Firstly, most employ suffixes, but in northern Australia there is a large bloc of languages that also use prefixes. These latter 'prefixing' languages mostly have A, S and O bound pronominals as prefixes to the verb. Ngan'gityemerri requires the obligatory cross-referencing of core arguments by bound pronominals on

---

[1] Ngan'gityemerri is a prefixing language spoken in the Daly River region of the Northern Territory of Australia by about 150 people. The two varieties of this language, known as Ngan'gikurunggurr and Ngen'giwumirri, share a 90+% cognacy rate, the same phoneme inventory, and near-identical morphosyntactic structuring. For the purposes of this chapter there is no real need to distinguish between these dialects, so reference is made to Ngan'gityemerri throughout, while most of the data is from Ngen'giwumirri. Note that in the Ngan'gityemerri orthography ng represents a velar nasal, whereas n'g is a hetero-organic cluster of alveolar nasal plus velar stop.

This chapter has benefited from editorial criticism from Sasha Aikenvald and Bob Dixon, and useful comments from Ian Green, Mark Harvey, Emily Knight and William McGregor.

the verb in strictly nominative/accusative patterning. However it is unusual amongst prefixing languages in marking A and S as prefixes, but O as a suffix.

Secondly, some Australian languages have many simple inflecting verbs and few complex verbs, while others have few simple inflecting verbs and large numbers of complex verbs. Ngan'gityemerri is of the latter type. One of its most distinctive typological features, shared by many languages in northern parts of Western Australia and the Northern Territory, is that it has only a handful of simple inflecting verbs, and thousands of 'complex verbs' made up of two component lexical elements. Complex verbs combine one of a smallish class of finite verbs which carry most of the affixation, with a non-inflecting verb stem.[2] This is no homogenous phenomenon: there is considerable variation in the the the ordering of and degree of binding between, these two elements. And, unsurprisingly, a wide range of terminological conventions have been used to label the constituent elements of a complex verb. Throughout this chapter I refer to the small class of affix-bearing finite verbs as 'finite verbs', and to the non-inflecting lexical verb stems as 'coverbs'.[3] A sample Ngan'gityemerri verb showing these structural characteristics is given below, where '+' divides the finite verb from the coverb.

(1)[4]   nga-rim-Ø+pawal
           1sgA-Poke-3sgO+spear
           I speared it

The range of strategies in Ngan'gityemerri for manipulating valency all hinge on the interaction between these two elements of the complex verb. §2 presents a more detailed overview of verbal structure, noting in particular that both finite verbs and coverbs can be independently assigned transitivity/valency values. §3 examines the various possibilities for constructing complex verbs through different finite verb and coverb combinations. The choice of finite verb to combine with a coverb is shown to be a strategy that achieves the same kinds of valency shifts that are achieved by derivations in most of

---

[2] For a more detailed discussion of complex verbs as an areal phenomenon, see Reid (forthcoming).
[3] Examples include 'preverbs and generic verbs' (Schultze-Berndt, p.c.), 'verbals and classifiers' (McGregor 1990), 'auxiliary and verb root' (Reid 1990). Other labels for the lexical verb stem include 'verbal particle' (Merlan 1989), 'gerund' (Capell 1976), 'participle' (Cook 1987). In more recent literature there appears to be some convergence on the term 'coverb', and to the extent that this class of morpheme can be identified across a variety of languages, this appears to be a useful term in assuming no positional characteristics, and in appropriately conveying a sense of the shared contribution that these lexical stems make to the complex verb's meaning. For these reasons I happily adopt this term here.
[4] Example glosses employ the conventional abbreviations set out at the beginning of the volume. Additionally, finite verbs are given a semantically based label, e.g. 'Sit', 'Lie', 'Go', 'Do', 'Hands', 'Poke', etc. Readers should also be aware that I have simplified glossing in a number of ways intended to make the morphological complexity of Ngan'gityemerri words more digestible. In particular I have sacrificed the marking of tense, aspect and mood information.

the languages presented in this volume. Also discussed in this section is the 'impersonal verb' construction in Ngan'gityemerri, involving a mismatch between formal transitivity of a complex verb on the one hand, and its associated argument structure on the other. Impersonal verbs are a fairly restricted set of transitive verbs carrying non-referential fixed A marking, and with only a single argument, coded as O. §4 examines two minor valency-manipulating strategies involving genuine morphological derivation of coverbs, where Ngan'gityemerri has developed presentative and locative applicatives. Intriguingly, the presentative applicative is shown to have developed this derivational function from an unlikely source – from the syntactically incorporated bodypart morpheme meaning 'eye'.

Given the crucial role that the complex verb type plays in each of these valency-manipulating strategies, some slightly more detailed investigation of verb structure and transitivity will be essential preliminaries.

2   Overview of verbal structure

There are two types of verb in Ngan'gityemerri: simple and complex. Simple verbs consist of just a finite verb which inflects for TAM categories (irrealis, present, past perfective, past imperfective), and which hosts a prefix cross-referencing its A/S and a suffix cross-referencing its O. There are only twelve such verbs in this language, seven intransitive and five transitive, so they can simply be listed exhaustively. Table 10.1 sets out these simple verbs, showing

Table 10.1. *The twelve 'simple' verbs in Ngan'gityemerri*

INTRANSITIVE		
sit	*ngi-rim*	I'm sitting.
stand	*ngi-rribem*	I'm standing.
lie	*yi-bem*	You're lying down.
go	*ya-ganim*	You're going.
travel[5]	*yi-rripin*	She's travelling.
perch	*wi-tyibem*	It's perching.
arrive	*ye-menggeng-ngindi*	You arrived to me.
TRANSITIVE		
say/do/think	*ngi-m-Ø*	I did it.
see	*ngi-nyirri-nyi*	I'll see you.
take	*ya-wang-ngi*	Take me!
inscribe, write	*nga-rim-Ø*	I'm writing it.
spread, smear	*ngu-pun-Ø*	I'm spreading it.

[5] 'Travel' differs from 'go' in implying more motivated goal-oriented movement.

sample subject prefixes and object suffixes. The simple verb 'arrive' demonstrates the possibility of optionally suffixing non-core arguments such as 'goals', while 'see' and 'take' demonstrate O-marking on transitive simple verbs.

Beyond these twelve, every other verb in Ngan'gityemerri is complex, consisting of a finite verb in combination with a lexical coverb, mostly in that order.[6] Finite verbs and lexical verbs in combination constitute a single word in terms of both phonological and morphological criteria. In total there are thirty-one finite verbs, including the twelve listed above. Thus each of the simple verbs listed in table 10.1 can also occur in combination with a coverb, as demonstrated in table 10.2. I refer to these twelve verbs as 'finite verbs' in discussing their complex verb role, and as 'simple verbs' in discussing their independent occurrence. (Note that the simple verbs 'write' and 'spread' are glossed as 'Poke' and 'Slash' when functioning as finite verbs.) In table 10.2 the finite verbs above the dotted line are those which can also function as simple verbs, those below it can only co-occur with coverbs. Note that the transitive finite verbs are broadly concerned with how things are manipulated at the interface between the human body and other objects. The remaining ten are the monovalent reflexes of transitive finite verbs.

Finite verbs are a small closed class of verbs that inflect for TAM categories and index the person/number categories of core participant roles. Critically, finite verbs contribute to the semantics of the resultant whole verb in some way.

These two-part verbal systems are found in a bloc extending from the Kimberley region of northern Western Australia across towards the Gulf of Carpentaria on the eastern side of the Northern Territory. As a general observation, for those languages with larger finite verb systems (say between twenty and thirty-five) such as the southern Daly languages, finite verb semantics tend to be more lexical, whereas for those languages with smaller finite verb systems, such as the eastern Daly languages and the Kimberley languages, finite verb semantics tend to involve more generalized semantic categorizations and vaguer distinctions in aspect and transitivity (see for example McGregor's 1990 (557–72) discussion of 'extendible classifiers' and 'accomplishment classifiers' in Gooniyandi). The Ngan'gityemerri system is

---

[6] There is a small subset of verbs (mostly those employing the 'Say/Do' finite verb) that have these constituents ordered 'coverb – finite verb'. This subset of verbs has no relevance to the topic of this chapter. See Reid (forthcoming) for an analysis of such ordering as a retention of the dominant verb order in a prior stage of this language.

Table 10.2. *Meanings of the thirty-one finite verbs in Ngan'gityemerri*

INTRANSITIVE

Sit	carried out in a sitting posture
Stand	carried out in a standing posture
Lie	carried out in a lying posture
Go	carried out in motion
Travel	carried out in motion
Perch	carried out up off the ground
Arrive	involving arrival/emergence

TRANSITIVE

Say/Do	speech and unspecified doing (do things, say things)
See	performed with the eyes (look at, watch, keep an eye on)
Take	taking/bringing things
Poke	using long thin things in point contact (stab, prod)
Slash	using hinged trajectory and edge-on contact (sweep, slice)

Hands	holding things within the grasp of the hands (grab, hold, grip)
Feet	holding things down with the feet (tread on, kick, walk on)
Mouth	holding things within the mouth (chew, suck, some speech verbs)
Bash	using vertical trajectory and lumpy contact (thump, crash)
Move	moving things to a different place (shift, throw, push)
Heat	applying heat (burn, melt, warm, light)
Suck	ingesting things (eat, drink)
Pull	pulling things (pull, tow, lever up)
Snatch	acquiring things (get, pick up)

REFLEXIVE DETRANSITIVE

Hands.REFL	reflexive activity holding things within the grasp of the hands
Feet.REFL	reflexive activity holding things down with the feet
Mouth.REFL	reflexive activity holding things within the mouth
Poke.REFL	reflexive activity using long thin things in point contact
Move.REFL.DYN	reflexive activity by moving things to a different place DYNAMIC
Move.REFL.STAT	reflexive activity by moving things to a different place STATIVE
Bash.REFL	reflexive activity using vertical trajectory and lumpy contact
Heat.REFL	reflexive activity by applying heat
See.REFL	reflexive activity performed with the eyes (look at your own reflection)
Say/Do.REFL	reflexive speech (talk to yourself, mutter under your breath)

at the more lexical end of this range – there is generally no real difficulty in determining the semantic contribution that a finite verb brings to a complex verb. Their contrasting semantics are readily accessible because many finite verbs co-occur with the same coverb, e.g.:

(2) (a)   ngi-rim-fifi
           1sgS-Sit-smoke
           I'm smoking (sitting)

(b)   ngi-rribem-fifi
           1sgS-Stand-smoke
           I'm smoking (standing)

(c)   ngi-bem-fifi
           1sgS-Lie-smoke
           I'm smoking (lying)

(3) (a)   nge-rim-Ø-kalal
           1sgA-Hands-3sgO-rustle
           I rustled it (using my hands)

(b)   nga-nan-Ø-kalal
           1sgA-Feet-3sgO-rustle
           I rustled it (using my feet)

(c)   nge-m-Ø-kalal
           1sgA-Mouth-3sgO-rustle
           I rustled it (using my mouth, e.g. by blowing)

(4) (a)   nga-rim-Ø-gurrgurr
           1sgA-Poke-3sgO-miss
           I missed an attempted 'Poke' contact (a prod or stab with a long thin weapon)

(b)   nge-rim-Ø-gurrgurr
           1sgA-Hands-3sgO-miss
           I missed an attempted 'Hands' contact (a pinch or grab)

(c)   ngu-pun-Ø-gurrgurr
           1sgA-Slash-3sgO-miss
           I missed an attempted 'Slash' contact (a swinging slap or chop)

(d)   nge-ben-Ø-gurrgurr
           1sgA-Bash-3sgO-miss
           I missed an attempted 'Bash' contact (a heavy thud with a lump-like object)

However, in addition to these semantically transparent examples, it should be noted that there are many verbs in Ngan'gityemerri where the finite verb's contribution to the meaning of the complex verb involves a high degree of abstraction. That the verb meaning 'to catch flu' ('Hand':grab) is formed with the 'Hands' finite verb, can be fairly easily viewed in terms of metaphorical extension – flu grabs hold of you in much the same way as a policeman does, and 'holds on' longer than you'd want. However it is less apparent why a verb meaning 'want', or 'give a speech', or 'be jealous' or 'travel in a plane', etc., should be formed with the 'Hands' finite verb.

Lexical verbs are an open class of typically uninflecting roots. Several hundred lexical verbs can usually be identified, and the class is typically open in the sense that additions to the class come about through some derived use of adjectives and nouns as lexical coverbs, through the combination of finite verbs with English/Kriol lexical verbs, and through, usually limited, morphological derivation (often marking location), etc. They are often phonotactically distinct from nominal roots, often being (closed) monosyllabic and allowing initial or final consonants not found in other word classes.

Finite verbs contribute to the semantics of the whole verb complex in terms of the kinds of meanings listed here, and they can usefully be thought of as having a classificatory function, in the sense that they provide further specification of the manner in which the action specified by the coverb is performed (posture, instrumental bodyparts, contact type, etc.). However, finite verbs do not provide a basis for the division of lexical verbs into disjoint classes. That is, the class of lexical verbs cannot be divided up into disjoint subclasses according to their finite verb combination. Across a finite verb system there is typically wide variation in degrees of productivity and semantic transparentness. While some lexical verbs will occur in combination with only a single finite verb, more typically there will be lexical verbs which combine with a number of different finite verbs. Also, some finite verbs will be highly productive and combine with hundreds of different lexical verbs, while others will be relatively unproductive. Looking back at the list of finite verbs in table 10.2, we can observe, for instance, that 'Hands', 'Poke', 'Slash', 'Bash' and 'Move' are all highly productive and textually common, whereas 'Snatch', 'Pull', 'Suck' and 'Perch' are both rare and unproductive.

2.1 Transitivity

Transitivity is a bit messy in Ngan'gityemerri. In the case of the simple verbs (those 12 that don't combine with a coverb) we can readily divide them into transitive and intransitive classes, as shown in table 10.1. However, it is when we turn to complex verbs that things get a bit more complicated.

Ultimately the transitivity of a Ngan'gityemerri verb is a property of the whole complex verb, and the criterion for verbal transitivity is quite simple: transitive verbs require obligatory cross-referencing of objects, intransitive verbs do not allow cross-referencing of objects. Note though that this simple formula is clouded in practice by the fact that 3sg objects have Ø marking, and by the fact that non-human referents generally don't qualify for pronominal cross-referencing at all. It is thus only possible to formally demonstrate the transitivity of those Ngan'gityemerri verbs that have human non-3sg objects.

However, the two elements that combine to produce complex verbs, the finite verb and the coverb, can each usefully be thought of as having associated transitivity/valency values. Throughout this discussion I refer to the distinct transitivity values of finite verbs and coverbs using the terms 'transitive' and 'intransitive' in quotation marks, and transitivity values assigned to the whole complex verb as transitive or intransitive (without quotation marks). So where does it get messy? Generally speaking it can be observed that finite verb 'transitivity' is a good predictor of verbal transitivity, but not absolutely so. By the end of this chapter we'll see that Ngan'gityemerri allows a rich and varied array of strategies when it comes to mixing and matching finite verbs and coverbs. Among other possibilities, low transitive verbs can be formed with 'intransitive' finite verbs, while monovalent coverbs can be paired up with 'transitive' finite verbs. Before we examine the semantic consequences of these strategies, let's look at the morphosyntactic categories of verbal indexing.

2.2   *Pronominal cross-referencing on the verb*
In Ngan'gityemerri there are clearly intransitive verbs, which only have subjects. There are clearly transitive verbs which obligatorily have both subjects and objects. A and S pronouns are prefixes to the finite verb root, while O pronouns are suffixes to it. These two basic types are exemplified in (5) and (6) below.

(5)   ngi-rim-fifi
        1sgS-Sit-smoke
        I'm smoking

(6)   ngi-nyinggin-nyi-kerrety
        1sgA-See-2sgO-watch
        I'm looking after you

The verb structure additionally allows for the coding of several other types of argument. Firstly there are 'goal' or 'indirect object' pronominals which appear in the same position as direct O marking, and over-ride it. Compare (6) above with (7) below. This outranking of O is generally explicable in terms of the likelihood of goals being higher on the animacy hierarchy, though G still outranks O where they have the same animacy value.

(7)   ngi-nyinggin-mbi-kerrety
        1sgA-See-2sgGOAL-watch
        I'm looking after (it/them) for you

Further there is another set of bound pronominals, restricted to intransitive verbs, which code peripheral arguments typically in the role of maleficiary. These are suffixed, not to the finite verb, but to the coverb, e.g.:

(8)   da-gum-felfil-nginde
       3sgS-Feet-run.away-1sgMAL
       (My wife) she ran away on me

As there are only two core roles obligatorily marked on the verb, three-argument verbs have one argument that fails to qualify for coding on the verb, but which can be tacked on as a free-form noun. 'Give' and 'show', for example, mark agent as A, recipient as O, and gift appears only as an uncasemarked free noun, and is not targeted for coding on the verb.

(9)   yibe nga-Ø-nyi-fime-pe   mani
       later 1sgA-Poke-2sgO-give-FUT money
       I'll give you the money later

2.3   Finite verb transitivity

As demonstrated in table 10.2 the thirty-one Ngan'gityemerri finite verbs can be divided into three groups. The seven posture/motion finite verbs are all intransitive in their simple function, and in their complex function they typically combine with monovalent coverbs, forming intransitive complex verbs. These two functions are contrasted in Table 10.3.

Table 10.3. Simple and complex functions of the posture/motion finite verbs

Sit	*ngi-rim*	I'm sitting
	ngi-rim-fifi	I'm smoking
Stand	*ngi-rribem*	I'm standing
	ngi-rribem-tyalak	I'm standing upright
Lie	*yi-bem*	You're lying down
	yi-bem-tyerrakul	You're talking (lying)
Go	*ya-ganim*	You go
	ya-ganim-lalirr	You eat
Travel	*yi-rripim*	She's going somewhere
	yi-rripin-syety	She's afraid
Perch	*wi-tyibem*	It's hanging
	wi-tyibem-filkity	It's whirling (parrot on branch)
Arrive	*ye-menggeng*	You arrived
	ye-menggeng-tasat	You emerged

Of the subset of 'transitive' finite verbs, those five that occur as simple verbs can be demonstrated to form transitive verbs. The remaining nine can be usefully thought of as 'transitive', most typically forming transitive verbs, and, to the extent that the semantic nature of finite verbs can be independently characterized, they can be shown to be 'transitive/bivalent' in their concerns for the contact/trajectory details of objects manipulated by potent agents. Three common 'transitive' finite verbs are demonstrated in (10–12) below:

(10)   'See'   ngi-nyirri-nyi-kerrety
                 1sgA-See-2sgO-watch
                 I'll look after you

(11)   'Poke'   nga-rim-nyi-pawal
                 1sgA-Poke-2sgO-spear
                 I speared you

(12)   'Slash' ngu-pun-nyi-fulirr
                 1sgA-Slash-2sgO-rub
                 I'm rubbing you

2.4   Coverb valency/transitivity

Just as it is possible to assign transitivity values independently to finite verbs, so we can assign transitivity/valency values to coverbs in Ngan'gityemerri. Verb stems are either monovalent or bivalent. Verbs formed with monovalent coverbs can be either simple intransitives or else transitive causatives, depending on the finite verb choice. Bivalent verb stems specify activities that have two participants (in the sense of Hopper and Thompson 1980). One subclass of bivalent coverbs has low transitivity value, its members specifying activities where patient nouns are barely affected and frequently non-individuated. The other subclass of bivalent coverbs has high transitivity value, its members specifying activities where potent As carry out highly telic actions on individuated and highly affected Os. The relationship between participant number and transitivity is thus rather loose, with two-participant clauses not necessarily being strongly transitive. We will pick up this issue in the following sections. Sample coverbs of each of these three classes are set out in table 10.4.

Table 10.4. Transitivity/valency classes of coverbs

monovalent: (du 'sleep', wap 'sit', wurr 'enter', etc.)
bivalent low transitive: (pup 'rub', wuty 'pour', tip 'pick up', etc.)
bivalent high transitives: (pawal 'spear', kerrety 'grasp', etc.)

3 Finite verb plus coverb combinations

Of the nine combinatorial possibilities for finite verbs and coverbs, eight are attested, and each of these combinations has predictable semantic effect. The following section examines each of the various combinations in some detail, but they are summarized in table 10.5.

Table 10.5. *Summary of finite verb + coverb combinations*

'Intransitive'	+	Monovalent	=	intransitive verb
finite verbs	+	Bivalent low transitive	=	(in)transitive with S/A focus
	+	Bivalent high transitive	=	intransitive anticausative
'Transitive'	+	Monovalent	=	transitive causative
finite verbs	+	Bivalent low transitive	=	low transitive with O focus
	+	Bivalent high transitive	=	high transitive
'Reflexive'	+	Monovalent	=	intransitive, causative/reflexive
finite verbs	+	Bivalent low transitive		(unattested)
	+	Bivalent high transitive	=	intransitive, reflexive

3.1 *'Intransitive' finite verbs plus monovalent coverbs*
Monovalent coverbs combine with 'intransitive' finite verbs, forming simple intransitive verbs. The single core arguments of such verbs are cross-referenced as S and may fill agentive roles as in (13–15), or patientive roles as in (16–17):

(13)   Nga-ganim-du
        1sgS-Go-sleep
        I slept

(14)   Ya-ni-wurr pagu!
        2sgS-Go-enter hither
        (You) come in!

(15)   Ngi-ni-tyutytyurr-tye
        1sgS-Sit-swim-PAST
        I was swimming

(16)   Ye-nim-purity
        3sgS-Go-slip
        He slipped

(17)   Wi-rribem-gulirr
        3sgS-stand-spin
        It (cassette) is spinning round

3.2   'Transitive' finite verbs plus monovalent coverbs (causative effect)
The same monovalent coverbs can also be freely combined with 'transitive'
finite verbs, forming transitive causative verbs. Functionally then, these verbs
are analogous to the valency-increasing causative derivations discussed in
other contributions to this volume. Compare (13–17) above with (18–22)
below, which involve the same coverbs:

(18)   Ngirrngirr ngu-dum-birrki-du
        sleep   1sgA-Move-3duO-sleep
        I put them to sleep

(19)   Yu-di-Ø-wurr   yerrwasyanderri
        2sgA-Move-3sgO-enter sack
        (You) put it in the sack!

(20)   Walipan ngu-dum-Ø-tyurr
        clothes 1sgA-Move-3sgO-swim
        I immersed the clothes in water

(21)   Ngu-di-nyi-purity-pe
        1sgA-Move-2sgO-slip-FUT
        I'll make you slip

(22)   Tuwa nge-riny-Ø-gulirr
        door 1sgA-Hands-3sgO-spin
        I turned the door handle

The combination of monovalent coverbs with 'reflexive' finite verbs is taken
up in §3.7 below.

3.3   'Intransitive' and 'transitive' finite verbs plus low transitive
        bivalent coverbs
Looking now at low transitive bivalent coverbs, we note that they can freely
combine with both 'intransitive' and 'transitive' finite verbs. For the moment,
we'll set aside the question of the transitivity of these verbs, and consider the
differences in their focus. In (23–25) the (a) examples have 'intransitive'
finite verbs, while the (b) examples have 'transitive' finite verbs.

(23) (a) ngi-rim(-Ø)-pup   (palayin)
          1sgS/A-Sit(-3sgO)-rub (firesticks)
          I'm rubbing firesticks [Intransitive aux: focus on subject posture/activity]

     (b) nga-rim-Ø-pup   (palayin)
          1sgA-Poke-3sgO-rub (firesticks)
          I'm rubbing firesticks [Transitive aux: focus on how object is manipulated]

(24) (a)   nga-ganim(-Ø)-wuty   (kuru)
           1sgS/A-Go(-3sgO)-pour (water)
           I poured the water out [Intransitive aux: focus on subject movement/activity]

(b)   ngu-dupun-Ø-wuty   (kuru)
           1sgA-Move-3sgO-pour   (water)
           I poured the water out [Transitive aux: focus on how object is manipulated]

(25) (a)   wi-rribem(-Ø)-tiptip   ngan'gi nyinyi
           3sgS/A-Stand(-3sgO)-pick up word   2sg
           It (taperecorder) is recording your speech [Intransitive aux: focus on sub-
           ject activity]

(b)   wa-mumu-ninggi de-m-burr-tiptip   (wurrum)
           M-taboo-AGT   3sgA-Hands-3plO-pick up (3pl)
           The policeman arrested them [Transitive aux: focus on how object is
           manipulated]

In general we are able to specify the distinction between the choice of
'intransitive' and of 'transitive' finite verbs in these complex verbs in terms
of focus. 'Transitive' finite verb choice brings focus to the affected patientive
role of the object. Thus (24b) focusses on a subject walking along engaged in
activity that makes water get splashed out, and it is the effect on the water
that is highlighted. 'Intransitive' finite verb choice on the other hand brings
focus to the activity that the subject is engaged in. Thus (24a) focusses on a
subject walking along engaged in the act of pouring.

Now what of the transitivity of these verbs? The (b) sentences above
(formed with 'transitive' finite verbs) are uncontroversially transitive. They
have A function subject pronouns, and O function object pronouns, which
may be overt, as in (25b). They also have object nouns optionally includable
in free form, as shown by the bracketed constituents in (24b) and (25b).

But what are we to make of the transitivity of the (a) sentences in (23–25)?
Where 'intransitive' finite verbs are paired with low transitive bivalent
coverbs, we find subject focus; but are the subjects Ss or As? (Note that the
glosses provided allow for either interpretation.) Note that the (a) sentences,
like the (b) sentences, also allow 'object' nouns optionally includable in free
form. For example, (24a) includes a noun (*kuru*) that is a non-individuated
and essentially unaffected patient. But what is the status of these nouns
with respect to the argument structure of the verb? There are at least two
possibilities here. Verbs constructed with 'intransitive' finite verbs and low
transitive bivalent coverbs could be transitive, with their failure to show overt
O marking explicable in terms of the non-individuated status of those objects.

Alternatively, these verbs could have a different grammatical structure to the (b) sentences, being essentially intransitives with 'cognate objects'. Hopper and Thompson (1980: 254), in presenting transitivity as a continuum, note that the presence of a patient noun that is a 'poor patient' is not a crucial component of transitivity, and that many languages use intransitive verbal morphology in coding two-participant events that lack their proposed high-transitivity features.

The criterion of formal O-marking on the verb might be expected to provide grounds for choosing between these analyses, but it fails us here because 3sg objects are Ø-marked and there are no examples where we find overt O cross-referencing on these verbs.[7] This in itself is not proof of intransitivity; it is precisely because these 'subject-focus' verbs have non-individuated second participants that it is generally not possible to get 1st or 2nd person overt object marking (shifters like pronouns being typically individuated). But it is at least suggestive of intransitivity, and we note that there are no other types of verb construction involving 'intransitive' finite verbs where the resultant verbs are not intransitive.

3.4   *'Transitive' finite verbs plus high transitive coverbs*

Next we need to consider the second type of coverb, which we label 'high transitive'. High transitive bivalent coverbs typically combine with 'transitive' finite verbs, yielding high transitive verbs with A and O cross-referencing. This is statistically the most common type of complex verb in Ngan'gityemerri.

(26)   da-m-burrki-pawal
        3sgA-Poke-3duO-spear
        He speared those two

(27)   wu-m-ngi-pi-ket
        3sgA-Slash-1sg-head-cut
        She cut my hair

(28)   da-m-ngi-syi-bang
        3sgA-Poke-1sgO-nose-pierce
        He pierced my nose

(29)   ye-mi-ngi-me-kerrety
        2sgA-Hands-1sgO-hand-grasp
        Grab hold of my hand!

---

[7] There is a construction where 'intransitive' finite verbs bear overt 1st and 2nd person objects; however, these are presentative and locative applicatives, and are distinguished by derived verb stems. See examples (74), (76), (77) and (78) in §4.1 and §4.2.

3.5 *'Intransitive' finite verbs plus high transitive coverbs*
(anticausative effect)

However, high transitive coverbs can also combine with 'intransitive' finite verbs, producing an intransitive verb with a subject corresponding to the object of the transitive verb. Consider the pairs below:

(30) (a) nge-rim-Ø-pal
1sgA-Hands-3sgO-break
I broke it

(b) ye-nim-pal
3sgS-Go-break
It is broken

(31) (a) nge-rim-Ø-tum
1sgA-Hands-3sgO-bury
I sank it

(b) ngi-rim-tum
1sgS-Sit-bury
I'm sinking

(32) (a) ngu-dupun-Ø-tyerr-ket   mudiga
1sgA-Move-3sgO-mouth-cut car
I bogged the car

(b) ngir-rim-tyerr-ket
1pl.excS-Sit-mouth-cut
We're bogged

(33) (a) da-ngim-Ø-baty
3sgA-Poke-3sgO-sew
She's sewing it

(b) ye-nim-baty
3sgS-Go-sew
He's twisted up (draped over something)

(34) (a) kuru ngi-nem-Ø-purrngpurrng
water 1sgA-Heat-3sgO-boil
I'm boiling the water

(b) kuru di-m-purrngpurrng nyine
water 3sgS-Sit-boil   FOC
The water is boiling now

The (b) examples (30–34) above function as agentless counterparts to the transitive (a) sentences on the left. This is a kind of anticausative construction which allows the undergoer of a highly transitive verb to function as an intransitive S. Functionally then, these verbs are analogous to the valency-decreasing agentless passive derivations discussed in other contributions to this volume. Several dozen such verbs have been recorded and they seem to form a semantic class involving totally (and usually negatively) affected patients.

3.6 *'Reflexive' finite verbs plus bivalent high transitive coverbs*

As discussed in §1, all complex verbs in Ngan'gityemerri are constructed from a finite verb in combination with a coverb. Of the set of thirty-one finite verbs, there is a subset of eleven finite verbs that are transitive and their semantics specifically concern how objects are manipulated (what parts of the body are used to contain them, what kind of patterns of contact and trajectory are involved, etc.). For nine of these transitive finite verbs, we find another subset of finite verbs that are their reflexive equivalents. That is, the finite verb system allows for the specification of reflexive verbs through the mechanism of finite verb choice. All complex verbs formed with 'reflexive' finite verbs are formally intransitive, being unable to cross-reference objects on the verb. While their transitive equivalents have distinct A and O roles, reflexive verbs have role coreference, and this triggers a switch to an intransitive verb with only a single role formally marked. That is, the S of a reflexive verb encodes the original $A_i = O_i$ relationship. The selection of 'reflexive' finite verbs is thus a reduced-valency alternation.

The relationship between verbs constructed with 'transitive' finite verbs and 'reflexive' finite verbs is demonstrated in the contrasted pairs below. Note that there are two 'reflexive' finite verbs that are semantically related to the 'transitive' finite verb 'Move'. The difference between these is aspectual, coding a dynamic vs stative contrast. The 'Move' finite verb triplet are contrasted in example (40).

(35) (a) 'Hands' transitive
          nge-riny-Ø-syirr
          1sgA-Hands-3sgO-scratch
          I scratched her

     (b) 'Hands' Reflex
          nge-meny-syirr
          1sgS-Hands.REFL-scratch
          I scratched myself

(36) (a) See transitive
          di-nyinggin-ngi-kerrety
          3sgA-See-1sgO-watch.over
          She looks after me

     (b) SeeReflex
          di-nyerrem-kerrety
          3sgS-See.REFL-watch.over
          He's looking after himself now

(37) (a) Move transitive
          ngu-dum-Ø-fel. ball
          1sgA-Move-3sgO-bounce.ball
          I bounced the ball

     (b) MoveReflex dynanic
          ngu-dem-fel
          1sgS-Move.REFL-bounce
          I jumped (lit. I bounced myself)

(38) (a) 'Mouth' transitive
          we-yim-ngiti-figulgul
          3sgA-Mouth-1sg.GOAL-stir
          He talked me into it

     (b) 'Mouth' Reflex
          di-weny-figulgul
          3sgS-Mouth.REFL-stir
          He psyched himself up

(39) (a) Poke transitive
          nga-rim-Ø-fipal
          1sgA-Poke-3sgO-bend.back
          I bent it (a reed so the two
          ends touch)

     (b) PokeReflex
          nga-rany-fipal
          1sgS-Poke.REFL-bend.back
          I returned

(40) (a) Move transitive
          ngu-dum-Ø-garri-fityi
          1sgA-Move-3sgO-leg-roll
          I crossed his legs

     (b) MoveReflex dynamic
          ngu-deny-garri-fityi
          1sgS-Move.REFL.DYN-leg-roll
          I crossed my legs

(c)   MoveReflex stative
           ngi-n-garri-fityi
           1sgS-Move.REFL.STAT-leg-roll
           I am crosslegged

3.7   *'Reflexive' finite verbs plus monovalent coverbs*

We noted above that 'transitive' finite verbs can be combined with mono-valent coverbs to produce causative readings. Consistent with this patterning, we also find that 'reflexive' finite verbs combine with monovalent coverbs to produce reflexive causatives. The combination of the monovalent coverb *wurr* 'enter' with 'intransitive' finite verb 'Go', with 'transitive' finite verb 'Move', and with 'reflexive' finite verb 'Move.REFL', giving intransitive, causative and reflexive-of-a-causative readings respectively, are set out in (41–43) below:

(41)   Nga-ganiny-wurr
        1sgS-Go-enter
        I entered

(42)   Ngu-dum-Ø-wurr   debi-werre
        1sgA-Move-3sgO-enter leg-ASSOCIATIVE
        I dressed him (I put him in trousers; causative)

(43)   Ngu-deny-wurr   debiwerre.
        1sgS-Move.REFL.DYN-enter leg-ASSOCIATIVE
        I got dressed (I put myself into trousers; causative and reflexive)

3.8   *Impersonal verbs: monoreferential transitive complex verbs*

Ngan'gityemerri has a complex verb construction that is formally transitive, morphologically coding both A and O with verbal affixes, but which is essen-tially monoreferential, having only a single semantic argument. These are verbs of emotion and experience of physical, cognitive and psychological states and processes, and they are formed exclusively with a small subset of 'transitive' finite verbs ('Bash', 'Hands', 'Poke', 'Mouth', 'See'). Such verbs have 'fixed' 3sg A-marking which is non-referential, and undergoer/experiencer O-marking. This construction type is typical of 'impersonals' in having a foregrounded O, but O remains marked as O. However, this cannot be thought of as a subject-backgrounding construction, because of the non-referentiality of the subject.

(44)   danging-ngi-ge-da   (45)   de-m-ngi-pi-yiri
        3sgA.Poke-1sgO-belly-hit   3sgA-Hands-1sgO-head-numb
        I'm feeling sad   I feel shamed

(46)   be-nging-ngi-perrety
       3sgA-Bash-1sgO-cold/dead
       I'm cold

(47)   be-nging-ngirr-ge
       3sgA-Bash-1pl.excO-belly
       We're happy

(48)   we-Ø-ngi-ge-wurr
       3sgA-Mouth-1sgO-belly-enter
       I need to get my breath back

(49)   be-ngim-ngi-dirr
       3sgA-Bash-1sgO-teeth
       I've got a toothache

(50)   di-nyinggin-ngi-ngini-pup
       3sgA-See-1sgO-body-rub
       I feel ill at ease (sense unease
       in my body, feel something is
       wrong)

(51)   de-nging-ngirr-tyerr-yiri
       3sgA-Hands-1pl.excO-mouth-numb
       We feel uncomfortable talking
       together (being sisters)

Impersonal verbs can conceivably be thought of as having vague 'causers' (the 'Law' makes us uncomfortable talking, the temperature/wind makes me cold, etc.), but these constructions cannot include overt agentive NPs. As is evident from the examples above, many impersonal verbs include incorporated bodypart terms, which denote 'locus of sensation' in the undergoer O's body. These bodypart morphemes also cannot be interpreted as the As of this construction. Bodypart terms can be agents of verbs which have the whole/owner cross-referenced as O, as in (52) below, but bodyparts in agentive roles are blocked from incorporation.

(52)   tyi-ninggi   da-ngim-ngi-(*tyi)pawal-nyine
       breast-AGT   3sgA-Poke-1sgO-(breast)spear-FOC
       My breasts are starting to poke out now (lit. starting to spear me)

Some difficulties do arise in determining whether a given verb is impersonal, but there are two criteria we can draw on. The best criterion is monoreferentiality. Verbs of this type are never translated by Ngan'gityemerri speakers into English using 3sg transitive subjects, but rather using corresponding intransitive undergoer/experiencer-as-S constructions, or agentless passives (as suggested by the translations provided above). There can be difficulties in applying this test though. For instance Ngan'gityemerri speakers are prone to translating transitive verbs, with distinctly referential A and O, by passive constructions, or by switching to a verb with a completely different argument structure (especially where O is 1st person). Thus example (53) below which has 2sg Agent and 1sg Object was freely translated by my dictionary co-compiler as 'I can't take it from you any more'.

(53)   yu-dupung-ngi-ge-wirr
       2sgA-Move-1sgO-belly-enter
       You've pushed me too far (I can't take it from you any more)

Note though that even where speakers provide such reworkings, they maintain reference to two arguments. In contrast 'impersonal' verbs are only ever strictly monoreferential.

The second criterion is that 'impersonal' verbs cannot sustain manipulation of the person or number category of A. Non-referential A is fixed as 3sg. Thus some verbs that might first appear to be candidates for impersonal verbs, such as (54):

(54)   da-nging-ngi-da
         3sgA-Poke-1sgO-itch
         It's itching me (I'm itchy?)

turn out to be demonstrably not impersonal verbs because they can have plural A (because A has referents):

(55)   war-ring-ngi-da
         3plA-Poke-1sgO-itch
         They're itching me (i.e. Some 'itchy grubs' are itching me)

4   Morphological derivations

4.1   Adding a presentative argument by giving the verb an 'eye'
As noted in §1 (and already evidenced in examples (27–29)), many verb stems in Ngan'gityemerri are compounds made up of coverbs and incorporated bodypart terms. There is a set of about thirty-five bodypart terms that undergo incorporation, and this is a pervasive and highly distinctive feature of Ngan'gityemerri morphosyntax. Analysis of the contemporary Ngan'gityemerri verb stem benefits from a distinction between lexical and syntactic incorporation of bodypart morphemes.

Lexical incorporation is a compounding process that takes a bodypart morpheme and a coverb, and from them derives a new verb stem. Lexical incorporation is non-productive, cannot be paraphrased by having the bodypart noun appear outside the verb, and the meaning of lexical bodypart+coverb stems is typically compositional and implicit, and not amenable to description in terms of syntactic relations. Thus *tyeribaty* in (56) below is a lexically compounded verb stem meaning 'listen', so *tyeri* is not omittable, nor can it be productively substituted by any other bodypart morphemes.

(56)   ngi-bem-mbi-tyeri-baty
         1sgS-Lie-2sg.GOAL-ear-hold
         I'm listening to you

Syntactic incorporation on the other hand, is 'optional', in the sense that the construction can be paraphrased by extracting the bodypart noun and having it appear as a free-form noun external to the verb. Syntactic incorporation is productive, and constrained to where certain predictable grammatical relations hold between the incorporated nominal and predicate (prototypically, where bodypart possessors are the objects or locatives of transitive verbs). Thus, in (57) below, *panmi* either could appear outside the verb, or indeed could be substituted by *firr* 'foot', *garri* 'leg', *purr* 'bottom', etc.:

(57)　　da-ngim-fi-panmi-tyat　　　　(da-panmi)
　　　　3sgA-Poke-APPLIC-crotch-place (BP-crotch)
　　　　He placed it in the fork (of the tree)

The discourse function of syntactic incorporation is essentially a backgrounding one. For a fuller description of bodypart incorporation in Ngan'gityemerri, readers are referred to Reid (1990), while general description of the distinction between lexical and syntactic incorporation can be found in Evans (1996: 72–3). For the purpose of this discussion, we can set aside lexical incorporation, and look at the set of syntactically incorporable bodypart terms.

One of the set of bodypart terms that is available for syntactic incorporation is *muy* 'eye', which reduces to *mi* under incorporation.[8] In some cases incorporated *mi* can be fairly readily shown to have the usual object/locative kinds of argument relations with the verb, cropping up in verbs where 'eye' is demonstrably syntactically incorporated in an undergoer/patient type of role.

(58)　　wu-dupung-ngi-mi-pit
　　　　3sgA-Move-1sgO-eye-rub
　　　　He rubbed ash in my eye

(59)　　di-nging-ngi-mi-wul
　　　　3sgA-Mouth-1sgO-eye-water
　　　　It made my eye water

Incorporated *mi-* extends metaphorically from reference to 'eye' as a bodypart specifically, to the 'face' more generally,[9] and then to reference to activity involving 'spots' – that is, activity that involves seeds or other small round eye-like things generally, activity that takes place in holes in the ground or places that represent foci of human activity (freshwater springs, hearths, etc.).

---

[8] Cross-linguistically, morphological reduction or suppletion is common under incorporation. However, *mi-* is the only one of the thirty-five Ngan'gityemerri bodypart terms available for syntactic incorporation that undergoes such reduction.

[9] E.g. *Minde nginyingginy-nyi-mi-yilil* 'I didn't recognize your face'. The independent noun *muy* 'eye' also extends to reference to the face, but does not extend to the other meanings available to *mi-*. However, *muy* does frequently crop up in compounds denoting seeds, small eye-like things, holes in the ground, etc.

(60) ngu-pun-Ø-mi-wuty
      1sgA-Slash-3sgO-eye-throw
      I threw (tealeaf) into the billy (where 'eye' is the round open top of the billy)

(61) di-nem-Ø-mi-ferr
      3sgA-Heat-3sgO-eye-warm
      She warmed the food in the fire (fire is the 'eye')

(62) da-ngim-Ø-mi-tuntum   yewirr
      3sgA-Poke-3sgO-eye-bury tree
      He planted a row of trees (each hole is an 'eye')

Indeed, there are many examples where both literal and extended senses of incorporated *mi-* are readily available. Thus we need only remove the specific 1sgO pronoun from example (58) to allow the 'small round eye-like thing' reading in addition to the literal 'eye as location' reading:

(63) wu-dupung-Ø-mi-pit
      3sgA-Move-3sgO-eye-rub
      either: He rubbed ash in her eye
      or: He rubbed up a ball (e.g. of chewing tobacco; where this ball is the 'eye')

The verb in (63) is thus vague, with the interpretation of *mi-* on a scale of literal to metaphorical readings being entirely context-dependent. This kind of process, whereby incorporated bodypart terms develop a range of extended meanings, is typical across the range of syntactically incorporable bodypart terms in Ngan'gityemerri. As our interest is in *mi-* specifically, there is no need to discuss here the full range of extended meanings for all thirty-five incorporable bodypart terms. For a fuller account see Reid (1990), but there is a short list in table 10.6 to give an indication of the kinds of meaning extension involved:

Table 10.6. *Extended senses of some incorporable bodypart terms*

backs:	humps, ridges, outsides of buildings
chest:	hollows, riverbeds, insides of buildings
neck:	pathways, intersecting trajectories
bladder:	rupturable things, animal guts, balloons, etc.
nose:	extended points, bonnet of car, headland, etc.
mouth:	openings, lids, doorways, etc.
arm:	creeks, small rivers
shins:	cylindrical things, tree trunks, etc.

Where *mi-* is functioning simply as an incorporated bodypart term with 'eye' or 'eye-extended' semantics, then it appears to not interact with the transitivity of the verb, simply adding locative/patient-type information. Consider the pair of verbs below, both transitive, where the addition of *mi-* to the coverb *wuty* 'throw' means 'throw into a round thing', i.e. it specifies the 'location/shape of target' of the verb 'throw', but the addition of *mi-* has no effect on transitivity:

(64)   ngu-pun-Ø-wuty
        1sgA-Slash-3sgO-throw
        I threw it out

(65)   ngu-pun-Ø-mi-wuty
        1sgA-Slash-3sgO-eye-throw
        I threw it into the billycan

However, there are clearly cases where *mi-* has moved in the direction of doing grammatical work coding an increase in valency. From its 'eye/face' semantics, *mi-* has come to specify activity that is somehow performed 'face-to-face' with another person, carried out 'in the sight of' or 'in the presence of' some other person. In many such cases *mi-* has no effect on the formal transitivity of the verb. In §3.2 we saw that monovalent coverbs can combine with 'transitive' finite verbs and cross-reference their objects within the verb, without the need for *mi-* derivation. In a sense, then in examples like (67) and (69), the presence of *mi-* is redundant as a potential marker of transitivity, and here perhaps its 'face-to-face' semantics is its primary contribution to the verb.

(66)   yi-rin-di
        2sgS-Sit-cry
        You cried

(67)   nge-rin-nyi-mi-di
        1sgA-Hands-2sgO-eye-cry
        I made you cry

(68)   wi-rribem-fafala
        3sgS-Stand-wave
        She's waving

(69)   wu-pun-ngi-mi-fafala
        3sgA-Slash-1sgO-eye-wave
        She's signing to me

This sense that applicative *mi-* brings, of activity carried out 'in person' in the presence of some other entity, is not unique to its incorporated role. There is in Ngan'gityemerri a free nominal expression *damuy-ninggi* (eye-INSTR) with precisely this meaning. Thus example (71) below can be more fully worded as example (70):

(70)   da-muy-ninggi ngu-dupun-Ø-mi-wul
        BP-eye-INSTR   1sgA-Move-3sgO-eye-return
        I personally took him back. (in contrast to arranging more indirectly for him to be taken back; lit. I took him back using my eyes)

There are, however, several other more explicit indicators that *mi-* increases the transitivity of the verb. Firstly, we noted above that verbs with 'transitive' finite verbs and bivalent coverbs can be made reflexive through the substitution of a 'reflexive' finite verb. Such verbs are formally intransitive, and semantically lose the sense of 'face-to-face' interaction because they are single-argument verbs. With this shift in transitivity, applicative *mi-* is dropped from all reflexive verbs.

(71)	ngu-dupun-Ø-mi-wul	(72)	wu-dem-wul
	1sgA-Move-3sgO-eye-return		3sgS-Move.REFL.DYN-return
	I took him back		He went back (lit. He took himself back)

Secondly, in several cases applicative *mi-* prefixes monovalent coverbs in combination with 'low transitive' finite verbs, forming verbs which, while formally transitive, involve low patient affectivity and have subject focus. These cases appear to involve genuine derivation, where the affixation of *mi-* to a monovalent coverb derives a transitive bivalent verb stem and it is in this sense that 'eye' can be shown to have developed a function that is valency-changing. Consider (73) below, where *wap* is a coverb meaning 'sit/camp/live', and (75) where *tyerr* is a coverb meaning 'halt'. The verbs in (73) and (75) are intransitive, each combining an 'intransitive' finite verb and a monovalent coverb. In (74) and (76) the *mi-*derived bivalent coverbs *miwap* 'sit/camp/live in the presence of (someone else)' and *mityerr* 'stop in the presence of (someone)' are transitive. Each of these verbs now codes its promoted O by the expected object suffixes to the finite verb.

(73)	ye-nim-wap wunu	(74)	ye-nim-ngi-mi-wap
	3sgS-Go-sit there		3sgA-Go-1sgO-PRSNTV.APPLIC-sit
	She lives there		She lives with me (She's married to me)

(75)	nga-ni-tyerr-pe	(76)	nga-ni-nyi-mi-tyerr-pe
	1sgS-Go-halt-FUT		1sgA-Go-2sgO-PRSNTV.APPLIC-halt-FUT
	I'm going to pull up		I'm going to pull up in front of you

Recall that combining an 'intransitive' finite verb with a low transitive bivalent coverb produces low transitive verbs characterized by barely affected patients. Those *mi-*derived verbs formed with 'intransitive' finite verbs are quite consistent with this.

It isn't always easy to distinguish between *mi-* functioning as a bodypart and *mi-* functioning as an applicative. Examples (67) and (69) above demonstrate this difficulty most clearly. While *mi-* is argued here to have derived a new function as an extension of its bodypart-term semantics, *mi-* nevertheless occupies the same morphological slot within the complex verb structure as incorporated bodypart morphemes. Further, it is probably true that *mi-* functioning as an applicative can still be thought of as retaining its bodypart-term semantics to at least some extent.[10]

In summary, *mi-* can be incorporated into the verb with literal bodypart semantics, and it has further developed the extended senses of: face, seeds, balls, spots, etc. From the extended 'face' semantics, *mi-* has come to specify verbal activity carried out 'face-to-face' or 'in the presence of' another person. Furthermore, there are examples of *mi-* doing clearly grammatical work in altering the valency of verb stems by promoting presentative arguments for object-marking. This data seems to demonstrate the development in Ngan'gityemerri of a presentative applicative verbal derivation from an incorporated bodypart term, which cross-linguistically is not a common source of applicatives.

4.2   *Locative applicative bodypart coverbs*

There is a minor construction in Ngan'gityemerri which has direct parallels with the 'eye-derived' construction. Low transitive bivalent coverbs can be derived by the locative applicative morpheme *ngan-* being prefixed to bodypart terms. This allows for the promotion of an additional argument into the object slot. All such derived verbs involve being positioned with respect to someone else's body, and that someone else is the promoted object, e.g.:

(77)   ngi-rim-nyi-ngan-wanytyirr
        1sgA-Sit-2sgO-LOC.APPLIC-armpit
        I'm sitting at your side [focus on subject posture/location]

(78)   yi-m-ngi-ngan-derri
        2sgA-Lie-1sgO-LOC.APPLIC-back
        Spoon up behind me! [focus on subject posture/location]
        (i.e. Lie curled up behind me with your chest to my back)

As noted for *mi-*derived verbs, combining an 'intransitive' finite verb with a low transitive bivalent verb root produces low transitive verbs characterized by barely affected patients. These *ngan-*derived verbs formed with 'intransitive' finite verbs are also consistent with this patterning.

---

[10] In working through all the Ngan'gityemerri verbs with *mi-*derived verb stems with linguistically sophisticated native speakers, in every case they attempted to construct an explanation of the role of *mi-* in terms of the meaning 'eye' (or at least in terms of its extended bodypart senses – orifice, fire, etc.). Thus, even in the case of verbs like that in example (74), speakers explain that 'being married to someone' is having the kind of relationship where you 'keep an eye on each other'.

5 Conclusion

In §4 we saw that Ngan'gityemerri does indeed have some minor but genuine morphological derivations that increase valency. Specifically it has developed presentative and locative applicatives that allow for the promotion of O arguments into verbs that are otherwise intransitive. However, beyond these minor applicatives, the main strategies for encoding and manipulating valency in verbal constructions are non-derivational ones.

Ngan'gityemerri's system of 'complex verbs' means that all verbs are constructed by pairing a non-inflecting coverb with one of the set of thirty-one finite verbs. Among the set of finite verbs, some are clearly intransitive, others are transitive, and a third subset are the intransitive reflexive equivalents of some of the transitive ones. In §3 we saw that a given coverb can be fairly freely combined with different finite verbs, and that these collocational possibilities signal alternations in the valency of complex verbs. However, it is important to note that coverbs have no independent occurrence, and that there is little clear evidence suggesting that certain finite verb + coverb combinations are privileged or basic in any sense. The criteria for derivation employed by Dixon and Aikenvald (1997) include formal morphological marking and an underlying construction from which another construction type can be got to (i.e. the notion of 'direction' in derivation). With respect to Ngan'gityemerri, it should be clear that finite verb + coverb collocations represent alternative strategies, none morphologically derived from another.

Are there any other criteria for determining 'basicness'? In some cases there is a temptation to view one construction type as more basic in terms of semantic complexity. For example, in §3.2 we discussed a construction where a monovalent coverb can combine with both 'transitive' and 'intransitive' finite verbs. Combination with an 'intransitive' finite verb (as in example (79)) produces a regular intransitive verb. Combination with a 'transitive' finite verb produces a causative verb (as in example (80)).

(79)	nga-ganiny-wurr	(80)	ngu-dum-Ø-wurr
	1sgS-Go-enter		1sgA-Move-3sgO-enter
	I went in		I put it in (caused it to enter)

Here it is tempting to argue for 'basicness' in terms of semantic complexity, i.e. to view causatives as being derived by virtue of their representing a kind of 'macro situation' involving two micro-situations, one of which is the intransitive construction. This view of causatives (put forward by Comrie

1981 (158), Frawley 1992 (159) and others) has been reworked by Dixon (chapter 2, this volume) who defines causatives as 'the specification of an additional argument, a causer, onto a basic clause . . . That is, a causative derivation involves the addition of a new argument in A function.' With respect to Ngan'gityemerri, it should be clear that the morphology of the language lends no support to such a resolutely derivational definition. As Dixon mentions in chapter 2, Ngan'gityemerri employs a syntactic strategy – of exchanging auxiliaries – which is functionally equivalent to the causative derivation in other languages.

In other cases we find finite verb+coverb combinations that have limited distribution. For example, the pairing of 'intransitive' finite verbs with high transitive bivalent coverbs (§3.5), which corresponds to a valency-reducing anticausative, is only found with a small subclass of high-impact coverbs ('break', 'sink', 'boil', etc.). Likewise the impersonal verb construction (§3.8) can readily be thought of as 'marked' by virtue of the strict restrictions applying to A person/number-marking categories (3rd singular), and to the small range of verb types (emotions, experience of physical and psycho-logical states and processes) that it applies to. However, markedness does not imply non-basicness (where 'non-basic' is understood to involve derivation from some underlying structure). Indeed it is not at all clear what kind of underlying structure 'impersonal verbs' could possibly derive from.

'Reflexive' finite verb choice can also readily be thought of as 'marked' on fairly compelling distributional grounds if not on morphological ones, i.e. verbs selecting 'reflexive' finite verbs involve the kinds of activity that usually involve distinct NPs in A and O roles, but reflexive verbs are a subset of such verbs where A and O are coreferential (triggering a switch to formal intransitivity). Constructions with limited distribution, such as anticausatives, reflexives and impersonals, may then provide some marginal evidence in support of the markedness of some construction types, but say nothing about their (non-)basicness. Moreover, for the bulk of Ngan'gityemerri verbs, especially those where low transitive bivalent coverbs combine with either 'transitive' or 'intransitive' finite verbs, we find no change to argument structure, and no unambiguously determinable difference in transitivity – just varying focus on the degree of patient affectivity. In this sense then, Ngan'gityemerri has a rich array of devices for encoding valency and transitivity, but this is achieved through alternate finite verb and coverb collocations, not through directed morphological derivation from underly-ing forms.

References

Capell, A. 1976. 'Rapporteur's introduction and summary to simple and compound verbs: conjugation by auxiliaries in Australian verbal systems', pp. 615–25 of *Grammatical categories in Australian languages*, ed. R.M.W. Dixon. Canberra: Australian Institute of Aboriginal Studies.

Comrie, B. 1981. *Language universals and linguistic typology*. Chicago: University of Chicago Press.

Cook, A. 1987. 'Wagiman Matyin: a description of the Wagiman language of the Northern Territory'. Ph.D. thesis. La Trobe University, Melbourne.

Dixon, R.M.W. and Aikenvald, A.Y. 1997. 'A typology of argument-determined constructions', pp. 71–113 of *Essays on language function and language type*, ed. J. Bybee, J. Haiman and S.A. Thompson. Amsterdam: John Benjamins.

Evans, N. 1996. 'The syntax and semantics of bodypart incorporation in Mayali', pp. 65–109 of *The grammar of inalienability*, ed. H. Chappell and W. McGregor. Berlin: Mouton de Gruyter.

Frawley, W. 1992. *Linguistic semantics*. Hillsdale, N.J.: Lawrence Erlbaum.

Hopper, P.J. and Thompson, S. 1980. 'Transitivity in grammar and discourse', *Language* 56.251–99.

McGregor, W. 1990. *A functional grammar of Gooniyandi*, Studies in Language Companion Series 22. Amsterdam: John Benjamins.

Merlan, F. 1989. *Mangarayi*. London: Routledge.

Reid, N. 1990. 'Ngan'gityemerri: a language of the Daly River region, Northern Territory of Australia'. Ph.D. thesis. Canberra, Australian National University.

forthcoming, 'Phrasal verb to synthetic verb: recorded morphosyntactic change in Ngan'gityemerri'. In *Proceedings of the Conference on Non PamaNyungan Linguistics*, ed. N. Evans. Canberra: Pacific Linguistics.

11 Valency-changing derivations in Tsez

BERNARD COMRIE

1 Introduction and background

Tsez, also known as Dido, is one of the Tsezic languages spoken in western Daghestan in the Caucasus, by about 7,500 speakers in the Tsez villages of western Daghestan and perhaps a further 6,500 speakers in lowland areas of Daghestan. A traditional view of the genetic relations of the Tsezic languages within the larger framework of Daghestanian and Nakh-Daghestanian (also called North-East Caucasian, East Caucasian) languages is presented in (1), although many details are subject to revision as more intensive work on the comparative linguistics of the Daghestanian languages proceeds.

(1)   Nakh-Daghestanian (North-East Caucasian, East Caucasian)
           Nakh
               Chechen, Ingush, Tsova Tush
           Daghestanian
               Avar–Andi–Tsez
                   Avar
                   Andic
                   Tsezic
                       Tsez, Hinukh, Khwarshi, Bezhta, Hunzib
               Lak–Dargwa
                   Lak, Dargwa
               Lezgic (incl. Lezgian)

The Nakh-Daghestanian languages in general are not noted for having grammatical voice systems, and Tsez is in this respect by no means atypical. Tsez does, however, have a number of lexical derivations that change valency.

The body of this chapter is devoted to the description and analysis of such phenomena.[1]

In order to understand the discussion of clause types and diathesis in the body of the chapter, some preliminary information relating to Tsez morphology is necessary. Tsez has four noun classes. Noun class is a covert category, showing itself in agreement, in particular in agreement prefixes on (nearly all) vowel-initial verbs. (Other verbs show no agreement whatsoever. Verbs that show agreement can only agree with an argument in the absolutive case.) The agreement prefixes are set out in (2), together with a rough semantic characterization of each of the four classes. Note that in the plural there is only a two-way distinction, between class I and classes II–IV.

(2)   sg   pl

		sg		pl
I	Ø-	male human		b-
II	y-	female human; some inanimate	⎫	
III	b-	animals; some inanimate	⎬	r-
IV	r-	inanimate	⎭	

Two rules recur throughout Tsez phonology. One drops a vowel before another vowel, e.g. *uži* 'boy', ergative *už-ā*. The other inserts the vowel *e* to break up consonant clusters, other than clusters of two consonants intervocalically, e.g. *is* 'bull', lative *is-er* (cf. *uži* 'boy', lative *uži-r*). Also related to syllable structure is a morphologically conditioned rule whereby certain suffixes, including both nominal and verbal suffixes, have the shape CV except word-finally after a vowel, when they have the shape C, e.g. super (expressing location on) *-λ'(o)*, past unwitnessed *-s(i)*.

Tsez nouns have a rich case system, in addition to a singular–plural number opposition; to avoid unnecessary complications, only singular nouns are considered here. The absolutive case is used as the citation form. Some nouns simply attach case inflections to a stem identical to the absolutive case, e.g. *uži* 'boy', lative *uži-r*. Other nouns have an oblique stem distinct from the absolutive, e.g. *kid* 'girl', ergative *kidb-ā*. The richness of the case system

---

[1] This material is based upon work supported by the National Science Foundation under Grant SBR-9220219, and includes material contributed by Maria Polinsky and Ramazan Rajabov. Note that the trio S, A, P is used in this chapter rather than the S, A, O of most other contributions, to avoid a terminology that could be misinterpreted as saying that the prototypically patient-like argument of a two-place predicate is necessarily, or even prototypically, a syntactic object; see further Comrie (1978). While this distinction does reflect a significant difference in philosophical standpoint, for the purposes of this chapter the two sets of terms can be taken as notationally equivalent. To avoid confusion between noun class I and the 1st person singular pronoun, the latter is glossed as 'me'.

resides primarily in the local cases, many of which combine morphemes for up to three spatial parameters, for instance orientation and direction, as in super:lative *besuro-λ'o-r* 'fish-SUPER-LAT', i.e. 'onto the fish', where *-λ'(o)* indicates orientation (super, 'on top of'), and *-r* indicates direction (lative, 'to'); compare super:ablative *besuro-λ'-āy* 'off the fish' (ablative, 'from') and super:essive (essive, 'at') *besuro-λ'*; note that the essive series has no overt formative. Labels such as 'super:lative' with an internal colon mean orientation 'super' and direction 'lative'. A further point relative to noun declension is that Tsez has two genitive cases, genitive-1 in *-s* used when the genitive is dependent on a noun in the absolutive case, genitive-2 in *-z* when the genitive is dependent on a noun in any other case.

Most issues relevant to verb morphology will occur in the body of the chapter, but one preliminary note is necessary concerning the shape of Tsez verb stems, i.e. the forms to which verbal inflectional morphemes are added. Tsez verb stems may only end in a consonant or the vowels *i* or *u*. Stems that would otherwise end in some other vowel take a final *d*, which appears as *y* syllable-finally. Thus, the root of the verb 'see' is *ikʷa-*, as can be seen in its causative *ikʷa-r* 'show', but its stem is *ikʷad-*, as in the infinitive *ikʷad-a* and the present *ikʷay-xo*.

For a fuller account of the above phenomena, and of Tsez grammar more generally, reference may be made to Bokarev (1959), Imnajšvili (1963) and Comrie, Polinsky and Rajabov (forthcoming).

2   Clause types

Constituent order in Tsez is grammatically free, although there is a tendency towards SOV order, and this order has been generalized in the examples used in this chapter.

The intransitive construction has a single argument (S) in the absolutive case. If the verb belongs to the class of vowel-initial verbs that take an agreement prefix, then the verb will agree in class with that single argument. No distinction is made according to the degree of control, agentivity, volitionality, etc., of the single argument, as is illustrated in sentences (3–4).

(3)   is   b-exu-s
        bull.ABS III-die-PAST.WIT
        The bull died

(4)   ečru žek'u   qoqoλi-s
        old   man.ABS laugh-PAST.WIT
        The old man laughed

The basic construction for two-place predicates is the ergative construction, in which A stands in the ergative,[2] P in the absolute, and the verb, if capable of showing agreement, agrees with the P in the absolutive case. This is illustrated in (5), in which *biš^{w}a* is a class IV noun.

(5)   žek'-ā   biš^{w}a   r-ac'-xo
       man-ERG food.ABS IV-eat-PRES
       The man eats the food

The 1st person singular pronoun *di* and the 2nd person singular pronoun *mi* exceptionally use the citation form not only for S and P, but also for A, as illustrated in (6).

(6)   di mi žek'-si
       me you hit-PAST.WIT
       I hit you

Most ditransitive verbs in Tsez are causatives, and will thus be dealt with below in §3. The verb 'give', however, is a non-causative ditransitive verb. It takes its A in the ergative, its P (the gift) in the absolutive, and the recipient in either the lative (if the transfer is permanent) or the poss:lative (if the transfer is temporary), as in (7–8).[3]

(7)   ʕal-ā   kidb-er surat   teλ-si
       Ali-ERG girl-LAT picture.ABS give-PAST.WIT
       Ali gave a picture to the girl (for good)

(8)   ʕal-ā   kidb-eqo-r surat   teλ-si
       Ali-ERG girl-POSS-LAT picture.ABS give-PAST.WIT
       Ali gave a picture to the girl (as a loan)

There is one further kind of transitive construction worthy of mention, and illustrated in (9).

(9)   žek'-ā   gulu-z   (gugyo-λ') čuret   b-ok'-si
       man-ERG horse-GEN2 back-SUPER whip.ABS III-hit-PAST.WIT
       The man hit the horse (on the back) with the whip

---

[2] Most nouns have the ergative in -*ā*, identical to the in:essive. However, some nouns with an oblique stem ending in *o* have a zero ending in the ergative, e.g. *gut'* 'smoke', genitive *gut'yo-s*, ergative *gut'yo*. The fact that some nouns have an ergative distinct from the in:essive (and all other case forms) justifies recognizing a distinct ergative case.

[3] The orientation series glossed POSS has a literal local interpretation 'attached to a vertical surface or to a downward facing horizontal surface', as in 'on the wall', 'on the ceiling'. However, in actual discourse it is much more frequently used to express the possessor in 'have' constructions, whence the choice of abbreviation in glossing this morpheme.

The version of (9) including the parenthetical material is unproblematic, and could be translated literally as 'the man hit the whip on the horse's back'. Note that since 'back' is in an oblique case, the genitive-2 of 'horse' is required (see §1). However, it is possible to omit the parenthetical material, in which case the sense is 'the man hit the horse with the whip', with no particular part of the horse in mind. Despite the peculiarity of having a genitive-2 without any apparent understood head, the construction is clearly a sub-type of the ergative construction, having an A in the ergative, a P in the absolutive, and, for verbs of the appropriate class, agreement in class, with the P.

The same verbs as occur in the ergative construction can also occur in another two-place predicate construction, the bi-absolutive construction, in which both A and P occur in the absolutive case. The choice between ergative and bi-absolutive constructions is determined by aspect. The ergative construction is the basic choice. The bi-absolutive construction occurs only with certain periphrastic verb forms; verb forms that are capable of agreeing do so as follows: the lexical verb agrees with the P, the auxiliary verb agrees with the A. In one periphrastic construction, with the imperfective converb of the lexical verb and the auxiliary verb 'be', the bi-absolutive construction is preferred, but the ergative construction is also possible, as in (10). In the other periphrastic construction, with the imperfective converb of the lexical verb, the resultative participle of the auxiliary verb 'become', and the auxiliary verb 'be', only the bi-absolutive construction is possible, as in (11).

(10)   žek'u/žek'-ā   biš^wa   r-ac'-xo   zow-si
       man.ABS/man-ERG food.ABS IV-eat-IMPFV.CVB be-PAST.WIT
       The man was eating the food

(11)   žek'u žin biš^wa   r-ac'-xo   Ø-ič-āsi   yoł
       man.ABS still food.ABS IV-eat-IMPFV.CVB I-become-RES be.PRES
       The man is still engaged in eating the food

One of the characteristics of the Daghestanian languages is the existence of a separate affective (or experiencer) construction, comprising two-place predicate constructions in which the typically animate argument, often expressing an experiencer, stands in an oblique case other than the ergative, the other argument in the absolutive; if the verb is capable of taking agreement in class, then it agrees with the absolutive argument. In Tsez, the experiencer stands in the lative case, as in (12).

(12)   aħo-r   meši   b-ik^way-si
       shepherd-LAT calf.ABS III-see-PAST.WIT
       The shepherd saw the calf

There are other constructions similar to the affective construction, in that they have a typically animate argument in an oblique case other than the ergative and another argument in the absolutive. One of these constructions is the potential of transitive verbs. The potential is formed by adding the suffix *-l* to the verb stem. If the verb is intransitive, then the construction remains an intransitive construction, with its single argument in the absolutive. If, however, the verb is transitive, then the agent-like noun phrase appears not in the ergative, but in the poss:essive, as in (13).

(13) k'et'u-q ɣˤay ħaλu-ł-xo
      cat-POSS milk.ABS drink-POT-PRES
      The cat can drink the milk

In the accidental construction, the verb is lexically intransitive, but the clause includes reference to the inadvertent agent by means of a noun phrase in the poss:essive case, as in (14).

(14) uži-q č'ikay y-exu-s
      boy-POSS glass.ABS II-break-PAST.WIT
      The boy accidentally broke the glass

It must be emphasized that the verb *exu-* that appears in (14) is intransitive; its transitive equivalent would be the causative *exu-r*; compare (15) and (16).

(15) č'ikay y-exu-s
      glass.ABS II-break-PAST.WIT
      The glass broke

(16) už-ā č'ikay y-exu-r-si
      boy-ERG glass.ABS II-break-CAUS-PAST.WIT
      The boy broke the glass

The bi-absolutive, potential and accidental constructions all illustrate ways of ringing changes on the meaning of what would otherwise be an ergative clause by changing case marking. But the differences among the three constructions are substantial. In the bi-absolutive construction, there is no evidence of any valency change and there is no extra derivational morphology relative to the ergative construction; the difference in case correlates with the choice of periphrastic construction.[4] In the potential construction, there is a derivational morpheme, the potential suffix *-l*, which triggers the change in

---

[4] One might argue that the bi-absolutive construction is bi-clausal, the upper clause being intransitive with an S, the lower clause ergative with an expressed P and an understood A. However, application of syntactic tests suggests on balance that the construction is mono-clausal. It may well, of course, derive historically from a bi-clausal construction.

case marking. In the accidental construction, although the resultant clause is two-place, the lexical verb is one-place.

3   Transitivity and the lexicon

In the literature on Daghestanian languages, it is often said that so-called labile verbs are characteristic of these languages, i.e. verbs that can be used either intransitively or transitively, like English *melt* (*the ice melted, John melted the ice*) with intransitive S corresponding to transitive P (S = P), or *eat* (*Mary eats, Mary eats the pizza*) with intransitive S corresponding to transitive A (S = A). Tsez, however, does not share in this. Tsez has no labile verbs of the S = P type, and we have found no clear instances of labile verbs of the S = A type either. Although this section will concentrate on S = P relations, an instance of absence of S = A can be seen by comparing sentence (5) above with (17).

(17)   ʕali   Ø-iš-xo
         Ali.ABS I-eat-PRES
         Ali eats

Tsez has morphologically unrelated stems *ac'* 'eat (vt)' and *iš* 'eat (vi)'.

For S = P pairs, Tsez usually has morphologically related verbs. There are three possibilities. First, both transitive and intransitive verbs may have distinct suffixes, as in (18). In such pairs, the transitive suffix is always *-k'*, the intransitive suffix either *-ł* or *-x*, lexically determined. This pattern is particularly common where the verbs are derived from some other part of speech.

(18)   Transitive (-k')   Intransitive (-ł, -x)   Compare
         at'i-k' 'make wet'   at'i-ł 'become wet'   at'iy 'wet'
         bito-k' 'move away (vt)' bito-x 'move away (vi)'   bittay 'over there'
         łic'o-k' 'mix (vt)'   łic'o-x 'mix (vi)'

Second, the intransitive member of the pair may be formed from the transitive member by adding the suffix *-nad*, which thus serves as an anticausative suffix, as in (19–20).[5] (Recall from §1 that verbs whose stems end in *d* shift this to *y* when syllable-final. The root 'wash' is *esa-*, extended to *esad-* before inflectional suffixes, and this last form is modified to *esay-* syllable-finally.)

(19)   pat'-ā   uži   Ø-esay-xo
         Fatima-ERG boy.ABS I-wash-PRES
         Fatima is washing the boy

---

[5] This same suffix also serves to derive frequentative forms of some transitive and agentive intransitive verbs, without any valency change, e.g. *cax-* 'write', *cax-nad-* 'write frequently', *k'ešad-* 'play', *k'eša-nad-* 'play frequently'.

(20)　　pat'i　　　ker-ā　　y-esa-nay-xo
　　　　Fatima.ABS river-IN II-wash-DETR-PRES
　　　　Fatima is washing in the river

　　But by far the most common pattern in Tsez is for the transitive member of the pair to be derived from the intransitive member, by means of the productive causative suffix *-r*. Indeed, in terms of the typology set up by Haspelmath (1993), Tsez is clearly a language that prefers basic intransitive inchoative verbs and derived transitive causative verbs corresponding to them. For instance, Tsez has a basic intransitive verb *esu-* 'be found', from which the transitive *esu-r-* 'find' is derived; contrast the formal markedness relation shown by the English translations, or the more clearly derivational relation between Russian transitive *naxodit'* 'to find' and intransitive *naxodit'-sja* 'to be found'.

　　As indicated, the causative formation in Tsez, with the suffix *-r* (which will appear as *-er* to avoid impermissible consonant clusters, following the generalization stated in §1), is productive. Addition of *-r* to an intransitive verb in the intransitive construction produces a corresponding transitive verb in the ergative construction, as in (21–22):

(21)　　meši　　b-exu-s
　　　　calf.ABS III-die-PAST.WIT
　　　　The calf died

(22)　　aħ-ā　　　　meši　　b-exu-r-si
　　　　shepherd-ERG calf.ABS III-die-CAUS-PAST.WIT
　　　　The shepherd killed the calf

　　The construction as in (22) behaves like an ordinary transitive construction. Thus, in the appropriate aspectual forms it will show up as a bi-absolutive construction. Addition of the potential suffix after the causative suffix will give rise to a potential-construction clause. (It is thus possible to form potentials of causatives. It is not, however, possible to form causatives of potentials.)

　　However, it is also possible to form causatives of already transitive verbs, thereby adding a further argument to express the causee. Such a causee appears in the poss:essive case, as in (24) – note that this case is distinct from that used for recipients of 'give', as in (7–8).

(23)　　čanaqˁan-ā zey　　žek'-si
　　　　hunter-ERG bear.ABS hit-PAST.WIT
　　　　The hunter hit the bear

(24)   aħ-ā   čanaqˤan-qo zey   žek'-er-si
        shepherd-ERG hunter-POSS bear.ABS hit-CAUS-PAST.WIT
        The shepherd made the hunter hit the bear

The question of causatives of affective verbs is more complex, and this is one respect in which affective verbs may not all behave uniformly. The verb *ikʷa-* 'see', as illustrated in (12), normally requires overt expression of both its arguments.[6] In the causative *ikʷa-r-* 'show', the agent is in the ergative and the causee is in the poss:essive, just as if *ikʷa-* were an ordinary transitive verb, i.e. (25) parallels (24). Note again that the case of 'shepherd' in (25) is distinct from that of the recipient of a basic ditransitive verb like 'give'.

(25)   ʕal-ā   aħo-q   meši   b-ikʷa-r-si
        Ali-ERG shepherd-POSS calf.ABS III-see-CAUS-PAST.WIT
        Ali showed the calf to the shepherd

The verb *esu-* 'find' may also appear in the affective construction, but here expression of the experiencer is optional, so that both (26) and (27) are possible.

(26)   meši   b-esu-s
        calf.ABS III-be.found-PAST.WIT
        The calf turned up

(27)   aħo-r   meši   b-esu-s
        shepherd-LAT calf.ABS III-be.found-PAST.WIT
        The shepherd came across the calf

The causative of *esu-* 'find' is derived from the intransitive construction as in (26), to give an ordinary ergative construction as in (28).

(28)   aħ-ā   meši   b-esu-r-si
        shepherd-ERG calf.ABS III-be.found-CAUS-PAST.WIT
        The shepherd (sought and) found the calf

Another complication that needs to be considered is that some causative verbs in Tsez have apparently been lexicalized. Thus, *egir-* 'send' seems, on the basic of comparative evidence, to be historically the causative of *egi-*,

---

[6] Tsez has the phenomenon of zero anaphora (null anaphora), so that it is not necessarily trivial to establish which noun phrases are required by a predicate, given the problem of distinguishing between an optional noun phrase and a noun phrase that can be omitted under conditions of zero anaphora. But there does seem to be a clear semantic distinction between a sentence like *meši b-esu-s* 'the calf turned up', which is felt to be complete in isolation, and *meši b-ikʷay-si* '. . . saw the calf', the latter only being possible where the experiencer is retrievable from the context.

although the latter means 'fade' in contemporary Tsez. If a verb has been lexicalized, its valency may no longer reflect that of productively derived causatives, and this might be an additional factor leading to differential behaviour of what are apparently causatives of affective verbs.

Finally, it should be noted that it is possible to have two causative suffixes in sequence in Tsez, the semantic interpretation being the causative of a causative, as in (29).

(29)   učitel-ā   uži-q   kidb-eq keč'   qˤaλi-r-er-si
       teacher-ERG boy-POSS girl-POSS song.ABS sing-CAUS-CAUS-PAST.WIT
       The teacher made the boy make the girl sing a song

Note that both causees stand in the poss:essive case, given that the base verb *qˤaλi-* is transitive. A textual example, slightly modified in irrelevant ways, involving the causative of the causative of an intransitive verb is given in (30).

(30)   di žek'u-q reλ'a   r-iti-re-r-āčin
       me man-POSS hand.ABS IV-touch-CAUS-CAUS-FUT.DEF.NEG
       I will not allow the man to let his hand touch (me)

The verb *iti-* 'touch' is intransitive; the thing touched, if expressed, would be in the poss:essive case.

4   The syntactic structure of Tsez clause types

So far, material has been presented on the morphological encoding of predicates and arguments in various constructions, and it is now time to turn to criteria for the syntactic structure of these constructions. Three tests are considered below: word order, reflexives and obligatory coreferential noun phrase deletion. With each test, the question posed is which noun phrase, if any, has a privileged position with respect to the syntax, i.e. which noun phrase is singled out as trigger or target of a particular syntactic phenomenon. It should be emphasized that these three syntactic phenomena – word order, reflexives, obligatory coreferential noun phrase deletion – are discussed here only in so far as they provide evidence for the syntactic structure of the constructions discussed in §3.

4.1   *Word order*
Given that Tsez word order is relatively free from a syntactic viewpoint, and is largely determined by pragmatic factors (such as topic and focus status), arguments for syntactic structure based on word order must be used with caution. Nonetheless, it does seem to be the case that the word orders presented

in the examples in this chapter reflect the least marked order of constituents. The noun phrase that is privileged for initial position in the clause would thus seem to be the absolutive noun phrase (S) in the intransitive construction, the ergative (A) noun phrase in the ergative construction, the A absolutive noun phrase in the bi-absolutive construction, the lative (experiencer) noun phrase in the affective construction, and the poss:essive (most agentive) noun phrase in the potential and accidental constructions. Preposing of the absolutive noun phrase in the two-place constructions (of the P absolutive noun phrase in the bi-absolutive construction) seems to be pragmatically marked, involving topicalization of that noun phrase.

4.2   Reflexives

The discussion of reflexivization below is derived from that of Comrie and Polinsky (1997), concentrating on those points that are relevant to the syntactic structures of different clause types. Incidentally, reciprocals behave like reflexives in the relevant respects.

Tsez has two reflexive formations, both involving repetition of the personal pronoun. In the first, the pronoun appears first in the ergative, then in the case appropriate for the syntactic–semantic role of the reflexive. In the second, available for all cases other than the absolutive, the pronoun appears first in the case appropriate for the syntactic–semantic role of the reflexive, then in the absolutive. Selected morphological forms are given in (31). In the remainder of this section, only the first type of reflexive will be exemplified, but both have identical syntactic behaviour.

(31)

	Class I		Classes II–IV	
absolutive	nes-ā že	(*že že)	neł-ā že	(*že že)
genitive	nes-ā nesi-s	nesi-s že	neł-ā neło-s	neło-s že
lative	nes-ā nesi-r	nesi-r že	neł-ā neło-r	neło-r že
super:essive	nes-ā nesi-λ'	nesi-λ' že	neł-ā neło-λ'	neło-λ' že

The question relating to privileged syntactic position with reflexives is the following: what noun phrase(s) can function as the antecedent for reflexive pronouns in the various clause types? In the intransitive construction, the S serves as antecedent, as in (32).

(32)   pat'i   neł-ā   neło-λ'   qoqoλi-x
       Fatima.ABS she-ERG she-SUPER laugh-PRES
       Fatima is laughing at herself

In the ergative construction, in general it is the A noun phrase in the ergative case that serves as antecedent, as in (33–34). Note that it makes no difference whether the target of reflexivization is the P, as in (33), or some other constituent, as in (34).

(33)   ʕal-ā   nes-ā   že   žek'-si
       Ali-ERG he-ERG he.ABS hit-PAST.WIT
       Ali beat himself

(34)   ʕal-ā   nes-ā   nesi-ł-āy   keč'   b-oy-si
       Ali-ERG he-ERG he-AMG-ABL song.ABS III-make-PAST.WIT
       Ali wrote a song about himself

Things are, however, a little more complex when there is another potential antecedent for the reflexive in an ergative clause, as in (35).

(35)   ʕal-ā   wacʕal-qo-r   nes-ā   nesi-ł-āy   Ø-aλ'i-s
       Ali-ERG cousin-POSS-LAT he-ERG he-AMG-ABL I-talk-PAST.WIT
       Ali talked to his cousin about himself

By far the preferred interpretation is to take the reflexive pronoun as coreferential with the ergative noun phrase. However, at least for some speakers, there is a less preferred secondary interpretation with the reflexive pronoun coreferential with 'cousin'. This secondary interpretation is subject to heavy restrictions that do not apply to the primary interpretation; for instance, the possibility of the secondary interpretation disappears if the reflexive pronoun is moved before *wacʕal-qo-r*, while the primary interpretation remains if the reflexive pronoun is moved before *ʕal-ā*. But it remains true that only the ergative noun phrase is unconditionally available as an antecedent to the reflexive pronoun in the ergative construction. Likewise in the bi-absolutive construction, it is the A which serves as antecedent, as in (36).

(36)   ʕali   nes-ā   že   žek'-xo   Ø-ič-āsi zow-si
       Ali.ABS he-ERG he.ABS beat-IMPFV.CVB I-be-RES be-PAST.WIT
       Ali was engaged in beating himself

A more complex picture is presented by the affective construction. Consider first an example where the coreferential noun phrases are the experiencer in the lative and the other argument noun phrase in the absolutive, as in (37). Here, the antecedent is necessarily the absolutive noun phrase, and the reflexive shows up in the lative. This is critically different from the ergative construction, and indeed from the evidence suggested in §4.1 using word order. But note the word order in (37): the usual word order in the affective construction is for the experiencer to precede the absolutive argument, but here the preferred order is the inverse; preposing the lative noun phrase would have the effect of topicalizing it (or of focusing *pat'i*). Thus, reflexivization in the affective construction seems to assign syntactic priority to the absolutive noun phrase.

(37)   pat'i   neł-ā   neło-r   y-eti-x
       Fatima.ABS she-ERG she-LAT II-love-PRES
       Fatima loves herself

But before accepting this conclusion, consider further an example where one of the coreferential noun phrases is neither the experiencer nor the absolutive noun phrase, as in (38). Here, the antecedent is the experiencer noun phrase in the lative case.

(38)   ʕali-r   nes-ā   nesi-de puħo t'aqˤ r-ikʷay-si
       Ali-LAT he-ERG he-APUD beside knife IV-see-PAST.WIT
       Ali saw a knife beside him

The overall behaviour of reflexivization in the affective construction suggests that the experiencer is privileged except when it is coreferential with the absolutive noun phrase, in which case the latter is privileged. This shift of assignment of privilege is not found with the ergative construction.

   Summarizing the behaviour of reflexives, we can say that the privileged noun phrase, i.e. the antecedent of the reflexive, is usually the same as is identified by word order, namely the absolutive noun phrase in the absolutive construction, the ergative noun phrase in the ergative construction, and the A absolutive noun phrase in the bi-absolutive construction, and even the experiencer in the affective construction when the reflexive pronoun is not absolutive. The one exception concerns the relative ranking of experiencer and absolutive noun phrases (and only these) in the affective construction, since word order suggests that the experiencer is syntactically privileged, while reflexives suggest that the absolutive noun phrase is privileged.

4.3   *Obligatory coreferential noun phrase omission*

The omission of noun phrases in Tsez is largely determined by pragmatic factors, as would be expected in a language that allows zero anaphora. However, under certain highly restricted circumstances coreferential noun phrases must be omitted, and it is this obligatory omission of coreferential noun phrases that provides a test for the syntactic structure of clauses. Tsez typically combines clauses into complex sentences by using non-finite forms, with the semantically and syntactically most neutral being the various converbs (gerunds). In examples (39–42), the main clause is finite and in sentence-final position, preceded in each example by a non-finite, converbal clause. (But note that in (42) the dependent clause *guz pˤoλi-r-λ'orey* is internal to the main clause.)

In such constructions, under conditions of coreference Tsez sometimes requires that one noun phrase be omitted. Such an obligatorily omitted noun phrase is always in the dependent clause. However, it is the syntactic status of the coreferential noun phrase in the main clause that determines the obligatory omission. In the intransitive construction, the S of the main clause requires omission of a coreferential noun phrase in the dependent clause, as in (39).

(39) keč' qˤaλi-x, kid iduɣor y-ik'i-s
      song.ABS sing-IMPFV.CVB girl.ABS home II-go-PAST.WIT
      Singing songs, the girl went home

In the ergative construction, it is the ergative A noun phrase in the main clause that determines obligatory omission of a coreferential noun phrase in the dependent clause, as in (40).

(40) is žek'-no, ʕomoy-ā neło-r sis ʕaq'lu b-oy-no
      bull.ABS beat-PFV.CVB donkey-ERG it-LAT one advice-ABS III-do-PAST.UNW
      The donkey beat up the bull, and then gave it a piece of advice

In the bi-absolutive construction, the A noun phrase again determines such obligatory omission of a coreferential noun phrase in the dependent clause, as in (41).

(41) keč' qˤaλi-x, kid uži žek'-xo y-ič-āsi yoł
      song.ABS sing-IMPFV.CVB girl.ABS boy.ABS beat-IMPFV.CVB II-be-RES be.PRES
      Singing songs, the girl is engaged in beating the boy

In the affective construction, the noun phrase in the main clause that triggers obligatory coreferential deletion is the experiencer in the lative case, as in (42).

(42) ʕali-r aħo, guz pˤoλi-r-λ'orey, Ø-esu-s
      Ali-DAT shepherd.ABS rock.ABS explode-CAUS.CVB I-find-PAST.WIT
      While (Ali was) blowing up the rock, Ali found a shepherd

The results of applying the obligatory coreference noun phrase omission test are thus parallel to those obtained from word order. The syntactically privileged noun phrase, in this case the noun phrase in the main clause that requires deletion of a coreferential noun phrase in the dependent clause, is the absolutive noun phrase in the absolutive construction, the ergative noun phrase in the ergative construction, the A absolutive noun phrase in the bi-absolutive construction, and the experiencer noun phrase in the affective construction.

4.4   Summary of syntactic tests

The material in §4 can be summed up as follows. The choice of privileged noun phrase in Tsez is in general independent of the morphology, in particular there is no general principle of selecting absolutive noun phrases. The absolutive noun phrase is normally only selected in the intransitive construction, while elsewhere the most typically agentive or human noun phrase is selected. The only exception concerns the very local relation between experiencer and absolutive arguments in the affective construction, which may, as suggested in Comrie and Polinsky (1997), reflect a stricter grammaticalization in this local domain (arguments of the same predicate) on the basis of the morphology.

5   Conclusions

Although Tsez is not rich in the more obvious kinds of valency-changing derivations that are found in most of the languages discussed in this volume, it does present interesting material relating to the more general question of valency. Different constructions are used depending on the valency and semantics of the predicate; the differences are most noticeable at the morphological level, though the constructions also have interesting syntactic properties that do not always coincide with the morphological distribution. And the potential and accidental constructions do show how the valency of a given lexical predicate can be altered for semantic effect. Even languages that have rather little valency-changing derivation can nonetheless throw light on this problem.

References

Bokarev, E.A. 1959. *Cezskie (didojskie) jazyki Dagestana* [*The Tsezic (Didoic) languages of Daghestan*]. Moscow: Izd-vo AN SSSR.

Comrie, B. 1978. 'Ergativity', pp. 329–94 of *Syntactic typology: studies in the phenomenology of language*, ed. W.P. Lehmann. Austin: University of Texas Press.

Comrie, B. and Polinsky, M. 1997. 'Reflexivization in Tsez'. Paper presented at NSL-10, University of Chicago, May 1997, and submitted to the proceedings.

Comrie, B., Polinsky, M. and Rajabov, R. Forthcoming. 'Tsezian languages'. In *Caucasian languages*, ed. A. Harris and R. Smeets. London: Curzon Press.

Haspelmath, M. 1993. 'More on the typology of inchoative/causative verb alternations', pp. 87–120 of *Causatives and transitivity*, ed. B. Comrie and M. Polinsky. Amsterdam: John Benjamins.

Imnajšvili, D.S. 1963. *Didojskij jazyk v sravnenii s ginuxskim i xvaršijskim jazykami* [*The Dido language in comparison with Hinukh and Khwarshi*]. Tbilisi: Izd-vo AN Gruzinskoj SSR.

12   Creek voice: beyond valency

JACK B. MARTIN

In chemistry, VALENCY refers to the capacity of an atom or group of atoms to combine in specific proportions with other atoms or groups of atoms.[1] The French linguist Lucien Tesnière is generally credited with introducing this term to linguistics, where it is used metaphorically for the capacity of a verb to combine with distinct arguments or valents (Crystal 1985). A verb like *rain*, which has no referential noun phrases associated with it, is said to be ZERO-PLACE or AVALENT; a verb like *disappear*, which takes only a subject argument, is said to be ONE-PLACE or MONOVALENT; verbs like *devour* and *give* are said to be TWO-PLACE (BIVALENT) and THREE-PLACE (TRIVALENT), respectively.

This chemical metaphor has had a pervasive influence in linguistics: causative and applicative morphemes are now described as 'adding arguments', while passives and middles are described as 'suppressing' or 'deleting' arguments, respectively. Entire sections of grammars are devoted to 'valency-changing', 'valency-increasing' or 'valency-reducing' processes, suggesting that the primary function of these grammatical processes is to regulate the number of arguments in clauses.

---

[1] The title of this chapter extends a chain begun by Barber (1975) and continued by Croft (1994). The phonemic transcription used here for Creek is based on Mary R. Haas's work. The phonemes are /p t c k f s ł h m n w l y i i· a a· o o·/. /c/ is a voiceless palatal affricate; /ł/ is a voiceless lateral fricative. As a diphthong, /ay/ is pronounced and written /ey/; V· is a long vowel. Primary stress (realized as the last high-pitch syllable in a word) is written with an acute accent; ˆ and ˇ indicate falling tone and rising tone, respectively; ⁿ indicates nasalization; ' indicates a stressed word-initial syllable (usually resulting from aphaeresis).

I am grateful to Margaret McKane Mauldin and George Bunny for help with the Creek data cited in this chapter, to Bob Dixon and Sasha Aikhenvald for organizing the workshop at which these ideas were developed, and to Ann Reed and two anonymous reviewers for comments. All mistakes are mine.

The chemical metaphor contrasts with an older tradition that distinguishes just two classes of predicates – TRANSITIVE and INTRANSITIVE – and a category of VOICE. Passive voice and middle voice are seen within this tradition as altering the 'point of view' or 'centre of interest' (Jesperson 1924: 167) within a clause rather than applying mathematical operations to it, and causatives and applicatives are sometimes included in, and sometimes excluded from, the traditional range of voice-related phenomena.

There are important issues here that need to be researched and clarified. One point distinguishing the theories of voice and valency, for example, is the issue of the degree to which grammars have the ability to COUNT. As an analogy, one commonly reads descriptions of stress systems in which accent is said to be placed on the third or fourth syllable from an edge, but these have generally been replaced by more restrictive theories in which rhythm operates in prosodic units of different sizes. In discovering this, we learn an important fact about language: that while counting may be a basic human cognitive process, it plays virtually no role in grammar.

To an extent, then, voice and valency are competing theories of clause structure.

(a) The theory of valency claims that there are at least four distinct grammatical classes of predicate (zero-, one-, two- and three-place). The capacity of a predicate to occur with different numbers of noun phrases can itself be taken as a grammatical diagnostic of class membership, of course, but it is not clear whether these classes have any independent motivation in grammars. Given the four-way classification, we might expect that only one-place verbs would be allowed as complements of causatives in a particular language, for example, or that a certain allomorph of the past tense would be limited to three-place verbs.[2] In contrast, the traditional theory predicts that these phenomena might be sensitive to transitivity.

(b) By stating that a process is 'valency-reducing', linguists are further claiming that there is something in common among the various processes that create intransitives from transitives. A two-place verb in a clause like *John is cooking the rice* can in some languages be converted to what Dixon and Aikhenvald (chapter 1) call an S = O intransitive (*The rice is cooking*) or an S = A intransitive (*John is cooking*). If valency reduction is a valid linguistic concept, we might expect that the same affix could be used in some language to derive both of these one-place clauses. An account appealing to voice,

---

[2] An example that comes close to this is Dixon's (chapter 2) claim that Sonrai, Basque and Abkhaz allow causativization of intransitive and simple transitive verbs, but not of ditransitives.

however, predicts that different grammatical devices will be used for these two detransitivizing processes, since the S = A intransitive has the agent as the centre of interest, while the S = O intransitive altogether avoids reference to an external cause.

(c) Similarly, the theory of valency leads us to assume that causatives and applicatives are essentially similar in functioning to increase the number of arguments in a clause. Hence, we might expect that the same affix would commonly signal both of these functions.[3] If causatives and applicatives are treated within a theory of voice, however, we would expect that they would normally be signalled by different grammatical processes, since causation manipulates the starting point of an event, while applicatives manipulate the endpoint.

This chapter has two interrelated goals: (a) to provide a description of phenomena within the traditional categories of voice and valency in Creek; and (b) to argue that the concept of voice better describes the Creek system than the concepts of valency increase or valency reduction. Creek is ideally suited for such a study because it has a number of morphological operations that can be thought of as changing voice or valency:

(1) (a)	ta·c-ís	's/he is cutting it'	Active
(b)	táck-i·-s	'it is cut'	Middle -k-
(c)	tácho·y-ís	'they/people are cutting it'	Impersonal plural -ho-
(d)	ín-ta·c-ís	's/he is cutting it for him/her'	Dative applicative im-
(e)	ís-ta·c-ís	's/he is cutting it with it'	Instrumental applicative is-
(f)	tac-ípeyc-ís	's/he is making him/her cut it'	Indirect causative -ipeyc-

The processes deriving (1b–c) from (1a) could be called 'valency-reducing': while two full noun phrases are possible in (1a), only a subject is possible in (1b) and only an object is possible in (1c). Similarly, the processes in (1d–f) could be called 'valency-increasing' because the addition of these affixes allows the basic verb to sanction an additional argument. I will argue instead that a speaker does not use the processes in (1b–f) to change the capacity of a verb to combine with noun phrases, however, but to shift the centre of interest in a clause. On this view, the middle in (1b) leads to a shift in attention from the cause to the effect; the impersonal plural in (1c) shifts attention away from the cause; the applicatives in (1d) and (1e) shift attention from an effect to a secondary effect and manner, respectively; and the indirect

---

[3] Indeed, Comrie (1989: 183) makes the claim that the suffix -al in Wolof is 'a general indicator of increase in valency', serving both to indicate a causative ('I will make the child sit') and to add an indirect object ('He is reading his book to the pupils'). A similar claim is made for Tolkapaya by Munro (1996).

causative in (1f) shifts attention to a primary cause. An approach of this kind, which supports and extends Croft's (1994) conception of voice, leads to the conclusion that changes in valency are side-effects of changes in point of view. We include or omit noun phrases in clauses according to our ability to incorporate them into a particular event view: valency is the codification of that ability.

In §1 I provide an overview of Creek grammar and transitivity. §§2–7 describe the voice-related affixes in (1). §8 examines the interaction of these markers.

1   Background

Creek, along with Chickasaw, Choctaw, Alabama, Koasati, Apalachee and Hitchiti-Mikasuki, is a member of the Muskogean family of languages of the southeastern United States. Creek literacy developed in the middle of the nineteenth century. The description in this chapter has been aided by the existence of a large number of letters, laws and stories written by Creek speakers and by extensive field work by Mary R. Haas and others (see, e.g. Haas 1940; Nathan 1977; Booker 1984; Hardy 1988, 1994).

The neutral word order in Creek is subject – object – verb. Subjects and objects are commonly omitted when they are clear from context. Creek has a nominative/non-nominative ('oblique') system of case marking in which *-t* occurs at the end of a subject noun phrase and *-n* occurs at the ends of non-subject noun phrases within a clause:

(2) (a)   ifá-<u>t</u>   wo·hk-ís
           dog-NOM bark:LGR-INDIC
           A dog is barking

    (b)   ifá lást-i·-<u>t</u>   fítta-<u>n</u>   hôy<del>l</del>-is
           dog black-DUR-NOM outside-OBLQ stand:FGR-INDIC
           A black dog is standing outside

    (c)   ifá-<u>t</u>   pó·si lást-i·-<u>n</u>   á·ssi·c-ís
           dog-NOM cat   black-DUR-OBLQ chase:LGR-INDIC
           A dog is chasing a black cat

In colloquial speech, nominative *-t* and oblique *-n* are sometimes omitted.

Related suffixes *-it* and *-in* indicate same-subject and different-subject switch-reference marking of subordinate clauses:

(3) (a)   ifá-t   wo·hk-<u>ít</u>   pó·si-n á·ssi·c-ís
           dog-NOM bark:LGR-SS cat-OBLQ chase:LGR-INDIC
           The dog is barking and chasing the cat

(b)   ifá-t   wo·hk-ín   pó·si-t   á·ssi·c-ís
            dog-NOM bark:LGR-DS cat-NOM chase:LGR-INDIC
            The dog is barking and the cat is chasing him

In (3a), *-it* indicates that the subject of the first clause extends to the second clause; in (3b), the use of *-in* signals a break that is often interpreted as a shift from one subject to another.

Creek verb stems occur in one of several GRADES characterized by suprasegmental changes that usually signal a change in aspect. Grades in Creek include the zero-grade (e.g. *wanáy-as* 'tie it!'), the level-pitch grade (*wana·y-ís* 's/he is tying it'), the h-grade (*wanáhy-is* 's/he tied it (just now)') and the falling-tone grade (*wanâ·y-is* 's/he has tied it').

Creek has two series of person markers corresponding most closely to a distinction in agency (Martin 1991b). Because there are irregularities in the semantics, I follow Munro and Gordon (1982) in labelling the two series types I and II:

(4)   TYPE I (AGENTIVE)   TYPE II (NONAGENTIVE)

na·fk-éy-s	'I am hitting it/him/her'	ca-na·fk-ís	'S/he is hitting me'
hî·c-ey-s	'I see it/him/her'	ca-hî·c-is	'S/he sees me'
li·tk-éy-s	'I am running'	ca-híc-i·-s	'I can see'
lêyk-ey-s	'I am sitting'	ca-láw-i·-s	'I am hungry'
latêyk-ey-s	'I fell (on purpose)'	ca-latêyk-is	'I fell (accidentally)'
kô·m-ey-s	'I think' / 'I want it'	ca-yá·c-i·-s	'I need it'

As the first column in (4) reveals, type I person-marking is typically used for most transitive subjects and for agentive (volitional) intransitive subjects. Type II person-marking is used for most transitive objects and for nonagentive intransitive subjects. A few transitive nonagentive verbs (e.g. *ca-yá·c-i·-s* 'I need it') use type II person-marking for their subjects.

While I have resorted to the terms 'transitive' and 'intransitive' in the previous paragraph, Creek lacks obvious diagnostics for these categories. In English, a transitive verb is generally defined as a verb that can take a direct object (e.g. *John sees the town*), while an intransitive verb is one that cannot (**John is going the town*). This distinction is not so clear-cut in Creek. Consider the following:

(5)   cá·ni 'taló·fa-n   hî·c-is
            John town-OBLQ see:FGR-INDIC
            John sees the town

(6)   cá·ni 'taló·fa-n   ay-áha·n-ís
            John town-OBLQ go:sg-FUT:LGR-INDIC
            John is going to town

Since both of these verbs occur with objects in Creek, there is little motivation for placing them in different classes.

There is an important distinction in Creek between a verb like *ay-* 'go (of one)' and *litk-* 'run (of one)', however: as (6) shows, when *ay-* occurs with an object, the object can be interpreted as a destination. The verb *litk-* does not allow this:

(7)   *cá·ni 'taló·fa-n   lítk-aha·n-ís
        John town-OBLQ run:sg-FUT:LGR-INDIC
        John is running to town

The sentence in (7) could only mean that the activity will take place *in* town, as in a race. This locative reading is available to almost any predicate, however:

(8)   tálsi-n   o·sk-acók-s
        Tulsa-OBLQ rain:LGR-EVID-INDIC
        It is raining in Tulsa

To express destination with the verb *litk-*, the object must be mediated through an applicative prefix (9a) or a postposition-like element (9b):

(9) (a) cá·ni 'taló·fa-n   a-lítk-aha·n-ís / oh-lítk-aha·n-ís
         John town-OBLQ at-run:sg-FUT:LGR-INDIC / on-run:sg-FUT:LGR-INDIC
         John is running to town

(b)   cá·ni 'talo·f-fácca-n   lítk-aha·n-ís
         John town-toward-OBLQ run:sg-FUT:LGR-INDIC
         John is running toward town

The distinction between the verbs *ay-* 'go (of one)' and *litk-* 'run (of one)' in this respect is similar to the distinction between transitive and intransitive verbs in English. One might therefore suggest that transitive verbs in Creek assign specific thematic interpretations to their noun phrase objects, while intransitive verbs do not:

(10)   VERBS NOT ASSIGNING INTERPRETATIONS TO THEIR OBJECTS
        osk- 'rain', litk- 'run'
        VERBS ASSIGNING INTERPRETATIONS TO THEIR OBJECTS
        ay- 'go', hic- 'see', a-litk- 'run to', oh-litk- 'run to'

This semantic distinction appears not to have entered the grammar of Creek, however.

One might distinguish predicates based on the number of arguments they allow or imply:

(11)   ZERO-PLACE PREDICATES
       osk- 'rain', atokyiha·tt- 'flash lightning', hayatk- 'get to be day, dawn'
       ONE-PLACE PREDICATES
       litk- 'run', atotk- 'work'
       TWO-PLACE PREDICATES
       ay- 'go', hic- 'see', a-litk- 'run to', oh-litk- 'run to', homp- 'eat', nafk- 'hit'
       THREE-PLACE PREDICATES
       im- 'give', acca·y- 'lean (one) against', hompeyc- 'feed'

Such a classification is based on the meanings assigned to noun phrases, however, and the classification is not independently motivated in the grammar.

From this discussion, it appears that Creek is a language that lacks clear diagnostics for transitive and intransitive verbs (and hence for the labels 'S', 'O' and 'A' used in some of the chapters in this volume). There are, however, a number of voice-related derivational processes in the language whose side-effect is an increase or reduction in valency. These are treated in the following sections.

2   Middle *-k-*

Creek has a suffix *-k-* appearing on many one-place verbs and often deriving one-place verbs from two-place verbs, as in (12):

(12) (a)   hopóywa-t ifá-n   i·h-ís
        child-NOM dog-OBLQ hide:LGR-INDIC
        The child is hiding the dog

(b)   ifá-t   i·hk-ís
        dog-NOM hide:MID:LGR-INDIC
        The dog is hiding

Hardy (1988, 1994) labels Creek *-k-* in examples like (12b) the 'middle' voice. Following work by Kemmer (1993), he suggests that *-k-* records 'affected subjects of events of very low elaboration'. I will adopt the term 'middle' here, though I will claim that affectedness and valency reduction in middle voice forms are consequences of a more fundamental shift in event view from cause to effect.

(a) Historically, Creek *-k-* derives from an auxiliary (Haas 1977). In its origin and structure, then, it shares more with the English *get*-passive (as in *He got fired*) than with the reflexive middles found in French, Spanish, Italian, Icelandic and Russian.

(b) A large number of middle verbs in Creek are deponents: the presence of -*k*- can only be determined in these forms through internal reconstruction (by applying morphological diagnostics).[4]

(c) Adding -*k*- to a stem usually has the effect of reducing the number of arguments in the clause, so that an *n*-place predicate becomes an *n*-1-place predicate. Usually, the middle derives a one-place predicate from a two-place predicate, as in (12), though it may also occasionally derive a two-place predicate from a three-place predicate:

(13)   acca·k̲-itá 'to lean against'   cf. acca·y-itá 'to lean (one) against'

In one instance, a zero-place predicate occurs in the middle, however:

(14)   hayatk̲-itá 'to dawn'   cf. hayatí·c-a 'morning star',
                                            lit. 'one that makes it dawn'

The middle is also occasionally added to one-place predicates without reducing valency:

(15)   hopoɫink̲-itá 'to gain wisdom'   cf. hopoɫin-í· 'sensible, wise'
         tikínk̲-i·   'on tip-toe'   cf. tikinn-itá 'to tip-toe'

While valency-reduction is thus a common side-effect of the Creek middle, it is not a necessary consequence of it.

(d) The use of a reflexive or reciprocal does not lead to use of the middle in Creek:

(16)   i·-hic-áhk-is
         REFL-see-pl:HGR-INDIC
         They saw themselves (just now)

(17)   iti-hic-áhk-is
         RECIP-see-pl:HGR-INDIC
         They saw each other (just now)

A decrease in elaboration (the number of referentially distinct arguments) therefore does not trigger use of -*k*- in Creek.

(e) As the case marking in (12a–b) shows, the argument interpreted as changed or affected is case-marked as a non-subject in the active voice form, but as a subject in the corresponding middle voice form. Similarly, selectional restrictions associated with the theme or patient shift from the non-subject to

---

[4] The tests used in this chapter are absence of -*k*- in direct causative or plural forms of verbs or alternation of -*k*- with -*y*-. When internal reconstruction has been used to establish the presence of the middle, 'cf.' is placed before the related form.

the subject. Many motion verbs and positional verbs, for example, supplete in Creek for the number of the theme or patient. This means that in active forms, they supplete for a non-subject, while in middle forms they supplete for the subject:

(18)   pasat<u>k</u>-itá 'to die (of two or more)'   cf. pasat-itá 'to kill (two or more)'

(f) There is no implicit argument in the middle, as there is in the English passive or in Creek impersonals. Example (12b) is thus better translated as 'the dog is hiding' than as 'the dog is being hid'.

(g) As (12b) shows, the subject of the middle may be agentive or nonagentive. The function of Creek -*k*- is thus not to avoid ascribing agency; instead, the event is 'self-contained' and any patient or theme argument, whether or not it is also agentive, becomes the 'centre of interest'.

(h) Creek middles may in principle occur in one of several aspects. These include the imperfective (or 'level-pitch grade', used for progressives), the durative perfective (used for states) and the durative imperfective (used for habits or generic statements), among others:

(19) (a)   ahópank-ís (IMPERFECTIVE)
            break:MID:LGR-INDIC
            It is breaking

(b)   ahopánk-i·-s (DURATIVE PERFECTIVE)
            break:MID-DUR-INDIC
            It is broken

(c)   ahópank-í·-s (DURATIVE IMPERFECTIVE)
            break:MID:LGR-DUR-INDIC
            It breaks (routinely)

Many nonagentive middle verbs show a marked preference for the durative perfective aspect, however. In this aspect, middles indicate a state resulting from the activity described by the verb. This use is commonly observed with verbs describing procedures:

(20)   USE OF THE MIDDLE WITH PROCEDURAL VERBS:

ahó<u>l</u>k-i·	'sewn'	aho<u>l</u>-itá	'to sew'
akhót<u>k</u>-i·	'closed, shut'	akhott-itá	'to close, shut'
háw<u>k</u>-i·	'open'	cf. hawic-itá	'to open'
hóc<u>k</u>-i·	'pounded'	hoc-íta	'to pound'
hotán<u>k</u>-i·	'braided'	hotan-itá	'to braid, plait'
kác<u>k</u>-i·	'snapped, broken'	kac-íta	'to snap (one)'
láf<u>k</u>-i·	'cut open, gashed'	laff-itá	'to cut open'
lím<u>k</u>-i·	'plucked'	li·m-itá	'to pluck'

łató·s<u>k</u>-i·	'unfolded (of a quilt, etc.)'	cf. łato·sic-íta	'to unfold'
łicáp<u>k</u>-i·	'loose, untied'	łicap-itá	'to untie, release'
mót<u>k</u>-i·	'cropped, bobbed'	mot-íta	'to crop, bob'
pikíc<u>k</u>-i·	'pleated'	pikic-itá	'to pleat'
tác<u>k</u>-i·	'cut'	tac-íta	'to cut'
táł<u>k</u>-i·	'woven, knitted'	tał-íta	'to weave'
wocót<u>k</u>-i·	'chopped (as of wood)'	wocot-itá	'to chop'
wokóc<u>k</u>-i·	'smashed, shattered'	wokoc-itá	'to crush, smash, shatter'

The use of the middle is thus tied in part to aspect, with verbs in this class favouring a context in which states result from a procedure of some kind.

(i) There is no simple way in Creek to predict whether a verb will be active or middle based on the meaning of the verb. Thus, predicates differing only in number may differ in whether they are middles or not:

(21)   il-íta   'to die (of one)'   pasat<u>k</u>-itá   'to die (of two or more)'

Antonyms may also differ:

(22)   hitót-i·   'frozen'   sití·f<u>k</u>-i·   'thawed'

(j) There are a few semantic generalizations emerging from the data, however. First, verbs describing simple movement without implying a specific manner or special effort tend NOT to be middles:

(23)   LACK OF THE MIDDLE WITH BASIC MOTION VERBS:
        ał-íta   'to go about (of one)'   hoyan-itá   'to go by (of one)'
        at-íta   'to come (of one)'   (i)ci·y-itá   'to go in (of one)'
        ay-íta   'to go (of one)'   oss-itá   'to go out (of one)'

Verbs describing manner of motion or more energetic motion DO tend to be middles:[5]

(24)   USE OF THE MIDDLE WITH MANNER-OF-MOTION VERBS:

acim<u>k</u>-itá	'to climb (of one)'	cf. acimic-íta	'to climb (of three or more)'
hal<u>k</u>-itá	'to crawl (of one)'	halic-itá	'to crawl (of three or more)'
kawap<u>k</u>-itá	'to rise, go up (of one)'	kawap-itá	'to lift, raise'
lit<u>k</u>-itá	'to run (of one)'	cf. liticeyc-itá	'to run off, make (one) run'
sofo·t<u>k</u>-itá	'to drag oneself'	cf. sofo·tic-íta	'to drag'

---

[5] One exception is *yakap-itá* 'to walk'.

solo·t<u>k</u>-itá	'to slide, slip (of one)'	cf. solo·ticeyc-itá	'to make (one) slide'
tam<u>k</u>-itá	'to fly (of one)'	cf. tamiceyc-itá	'to flush (one bird)'
ta·s<u>k</u>-itá	'to jump (of one)'	cf. ta·sic-íta	'to jump (of three or more)'

Verbs describing movement into a specific posture or the adoption of a position also tend to be middles:[6]

(25) USE OF THE MIDDLE WITH POSTURE VERBS OR POSITIONALS:

a·-coko·<u>k</u>-itá	'to get on piggyback'	a·-coko·y-itá	'to carry piggyback'
apey<u>k</u>-itá	'to get or be inside (of one)'	cf. apeyc-itá	'to have added on'
apo·<u>k</u>-itá	'to sit (of three or more)'	apo·y-itá	'to set (three or more)'
ka·<u>k</u>-itá	'to sit (of two)'	ka·y-itá	'to set (two)'
ley<u>k</u>-itá	'to sit (of one)'	cf. leyc-itá	'to set (one)'
siho·<u>k</u>-itá	'to stand (of two)'	siho·y-itá	'to stand (two)'
wak<u>k</u>-itá	'to lie (of one)'	cf. wakic-itá	'to lay (one) down'

There are several differences between the middles in (24) and (25) and those in (20): the middles derived from procedural verbs (20) usually have nonagentive subjects, generally refer to states resulting from activities, are derived morphologically through affixation of -*k*- to the active voice form, and are formed fairly freely. In contrast, the manner-of-motion verbs and positional verbs usually have agentive subjects, usually refer to events, are generally not derived by simple affixation and are not formed productively.

(k) Middle -*k*- is fairly common: a recent dictionary (Martin and Mauldin ms.) contains approximately 144 verbs that can be shown to include -*k*-. There are restrictions on the shape of the root to which it attaches, however. Thus, active verbs cannot form middles if adding -*k*- would produce an illicit consonant cluster. A verb like *afast-itá* 'to take care of' thus has no corresponding middle **afastk-* 'taken care of', and posture verbs that end in consonant clusters (e.g. *hoyɬ-itá* 'to stand (of one)') cannot occur in the middle even though other verbs in this semantic class are middle verbs.[7]

Based on (a–k) above, it seems unlikely that a description of Creek -*k*- in terms of valency reduction, affectedness or elaboration will be successful. Describing -*k*- as valency-reducing fails to explain why -*k*- does not create

---

[6] Verbs in this class may refer to the act of assuming a position or to the state resulting from that act depending on the aspect the verb is placed in.

[7] In some instances, the weight of a root may be adjusted, however, to permit the formation of a middle.

S = A intransitives (e.g. *John cooks*). Describing *-k-* in terms of subject-affectedness would fail to explain its use with manner-of-motion verbs (rather than 'basic' motion verbs) and zero-place verbs like 'to dawn'. Describing it in terms of low elaboration fails to explain why it is not required with reflexives and reciprocals.

It seems more promising to describe Creek *-k-* as framing the clause from the endpoint.[8] A shift in point of view would then effect changes in valency, transitivity, aspect and affectedness, though none of these is obligatory when *-k-* is present. These tendencies are shown in (26).

(26)   EFFECTS OF THE CREEK MIDDLE

	BASE FORM		DERIVED FORM
EXT. ORIENTATION	cause (actor)	→	effect (undergoer)
INT. ORIENTATION	(no change)		
CAUSE AVOIDANCE	explicit external cause	→	self-contained event (no external cause)
ASPECT	activity	→	resulting state or inchoative
SUBJ. AFFECTEDNESS	usually not affected	→	often affected
VALENCY	*n*-place predicate	→	*n*-1-place predicate
TRANSITIVITY	transitive	→	intransitive
	ditransitive	→	transitive

In this table and in tables to follow, I distinguish between EXTERNAL orientation (roughly, the orientation of the subject or starting point at the clause-level) and INTERNAL orientation (the orientation of the object or endpoint at the predicate-level). In this sense, external orientation is close to what Klaiman (1988) refers to as 'diathesis' or to the traditional restriction of voice to the point of view of the subject in a clause. In the base or active form, the external orientation is towards a cause (actor), while in the derived form, the external orientation is towards the effect (undergoer). In the base form, there is typically an explicit external cause, while the derived form avoids mention of this entity. The base form is typically an activity, while the derived middle is usually a resulting state or inchoative. The subject of the derived middle is usually affected, and both valency and transitivity are reduced.

What the table in (26) and subsequent tables attempt to describe is the fact that a single morphological process can have several historically or functionally related grammatical effects. It is far from obvious that change in valency

---

[8] The characterization of the Creek middle as signalling the endpoint differs from Croft's (1994) characterization of middles cross-linguistically as inchoatives. While Creek middles can have inchoative readings, they more commonly refer to resulting states.

has any special status. If the approach to the Creek middle outlined here can be generalized to other derivational processes, then 'valency' and 'valency reduction' – to the extent that these terms are even significant linguistically – may be consequences of larger decisions speakers make about the organization of event view.

3   Impersonal plural -*ho*-

Creek has an affix -*ho*- used when the specific identity of a subject is felt to be unimportant. The affix also has plural uses in clauses allowing overt subjects, but in the impersonal use leads to subjectless clauses in which a patient receives greater attention. The Creek impersonal plural can therefore be seen as a voice marker (because it increases the prominence of a patient) as well as a valency-reducing marker (because overt noun phrase subjects are disallowed).

(a) One common use of -*ho*- is to make statements that refer to people in general:

(27)   hĭ·ⁿc-itá   tó·ko-··-t   ô·ⁿw-i·-s
       see:NGR-INF be:not-DUR-SS be:FGR-DUR-INDIC
       má·ho·k-at-í·-t   ôn-ka
       say:IMPERS.pl:LGR-PAST-DUR-SS be:FGR-SO
       'You're not supposed to stare at it', they/people used to say, so . . . (1992a)

(28)   heyyô·ⁿwa·t-ta·t i·kaná kɨɬ-is-ikó··   fá·ka
       now-TOP   land   know-exist-not-DUR hunting
       apiy-ípho·y-â·t
       go:triplural-CMPL:IMPERS.pl:LGR-TOP
       But now, they/people go hunting on unfamiliar lands . . . (1992b)

This use is nonanaphoric in the sense that it does not refer back to any character in the narrative.

(b) Impersonal plural -*ho*- may also refer back to characters who have already been established in a narrative, however, if the speaker is not concerned with the identity of the individuals (1992c):

(29)   hompeyc-ak-í·-s máhk-it   ifá-ta·t hompeyhóhc-in
       feed-pl-DUR-INDIC say:HGR-SS dog-TOP feed:IMPERS.pl:HGR-DS
       Saying 'Let's feed him', they (two minor characters in the story) fed the
       dog . . .

The use of -*ho*- is not just for generic subjects, then, but for subjects that the speaker chooses to background.

(c) Impersonal plural *-ho-* is always grammatically plural. If a verb has distinct forms for singular, dual and triplural (three or more), the triplural form is used, though the sense may be singular (30) or triplural (31) (1939):

(30)   cofí-n   akál-ała·n-ít   s-ohh-apí·ho·y-â·n
        rabbit-OBLQ pour-FUT:LGR-SS INST-on-go:triplural:IMPERS.pl:LGR-TOP
        when <u>he/they</u> (a minor character) went up to pour it on Rabbit . . .

(31)   pa·n-ít   fólho·y-at-í·-s
        dance:LGR-SS go.about:triplural:LGR-PAST-DUR-INDIC
        . . . <u>they/people</u> were dancing about

(d) Because impersonal plural *-ho-* functions to deemphasize a subject, it is the preferred way to translate the English passive (Matthew 9: 25):

(32)   mô·meysísti   sosséyho·c-ô·f . . .
        but   people cast.out:triplural:IMPERS.pl:LGR-when
        But when the people were put forth . . .

(e) The Creek impersonal plural differs from a passive, however, in that objects continue to be coded as objects, with oblique *-n* (1939):

(33)   oymó·łki-<u>n</u>   yahá-<u>n</u>   akálho·y-ín
        boiling.water-OBLQ wolf-OBLQ pour.on:IMPERS.pl:LGR-DS
        . . . <u>they</u> pour boiling water on Wolf . . .

(f) An impersonal clause cannot normally occur with an overt subject:

(34) (a) sókca-n   óywa-n   acánho·y-ís
        bag-OBLQ water-OBLQ pour.in:IMPERS.pl:LGR-INDIC
        They/people are pouring water into bags

(b)   *ísti   sókca-n   óywa-n   acánho·y-ís
        person bag-OBLQ water-OBLQ pour.in:IMPERS.pl:LGR-INDIC
        People are pouring water into bags

With an overt subject, a true plural form must be used:

(35)   ísti   sókca-n   óywa-n   acán-a·k-ís
        person bag-OBLQ water-OBLQ pour.in-pl:LGR-INDIC
        People are pouring water into bags

(g) Not all verbs are compatible with impersonal *-ho-*. The semantic class of verbs that occurs with the impersonal has not been researched extensively, though agentive predicates appear to be favoured.

While it seems clear that the creation of subjectless clauses in Creek is a change in valency, it is also clear that a description of the impersonal plural as 'valency-reducing' would capture only a small part of its grammar. The Creek impersonal plural functions to background the role of the subject in a clause, so that the role of a cause (actor) is acknowledged by the speaker without being activated in the hearer's mind. The point of view can therefore be described as being away from the cause, though any patient or theme will consequently receive greater attention. These side-effects are charted in (36):

(36)   EFFECTS OF THE CREEK IMPERSONAL PLURAL

	BASE FORM		DERIVED FORM
EXT. ORIENTATION	cause	→	away from cause
INT. ORIENTATION	patient	→	greater topicality
CAUSE AVOIDANCE	explicit external cause	→	implicit external cause
ASPECT	(no change)		
SUBJ. AFFECTEDNESS	(no change)		
VALENCY	*n*-place predicate	→	*n*-1-place predicate
TRANSITIVITY	(no change)		

4 Dative applicative *im-*

Creek has a prefix *im-* (or *in-* before nonlabial consonants) whose function appears to be that of adding an 'indirect object' to the verb it attaches to (generally a benefactive or malefactive, but also, depending on the verb, a goal, source or possessor). Observing similarities to a construction in Bantu, Baker (1988: 472–3) proposed referring to the Chickasaw and Choctaw cognate as an 'applicative', a term that has since been adopted by some Muskogeanists.

For Baker, applicatives are incorporated adpositions. Like prepositions or postpositions, then, applicatives add noun phrases to clauses. An alternative conception of applicatives is found in Croft (1994: 95–6), where it is observed that:

> ... derived applicatives have the effect of assigning to direct object role some participant other than the 'patient' (endpoint of the verbal segment) of the basic verb form ... The benefactive/malefactive represents the one situation in which a resulting state can cause something else to happen: a person's mental state can be altered by an otherwise static state of affairs. The mental state itself, being another state, is easily construed as the new endpoint of the event.

For Croft, subjects and objects represent the starting point and endpoint of the segment of a causal network represented by each verb (1994: 92). Within this framework, dative applicatives are a shift in conceptualization from the patient as endpoint to the dative as endpoint. The 'valency-increasing' function of applicatives would then be a side-effect of a conceptual shift to datives as endpoints.

(a) The dative applicative agrees with the object it adds to a verb's argument structure:

(37)   án-yaheyk-ís   's/he is singing for <u>me</u>'
       cín-yaheyk-ís   's/he is singing for <u>you</u>'
       ín-yaheyk-ís   's/he is singing for <u>him/her</u> (another)'
       pón-yaheyk-ís   's/he is singing for <u>us</u>'

(b) The dative applicative in Creek often adds an argument to a clause. With active verbs, the added argument is often interpreted as a benefactive:

(38) (a) cá·ni-t   istaha·kocí-n ha·y-ís
          John-NOM doll-OBLQ   make:LGR-INDIC
          John is making a doll

(b)   cá·ni-t   cími-n   istaha·kocí-n <u>ín</u>-ha·y-ís
      John-NOM Jim-OBLQ doll-OBLQ   DAT-make:LGR-INDIC
      John is making a doll for Jim

(c) The dative applicative may also add an argument that is adversely affected by the activity:

(39)   acani·y-itá 'to peek'   <u>im</u>-acani·y-itá 'to peek at (someone)'
       akiɬ-itá   'to cheat'   <u>im</u>-akiɬ-itá   'to cheat on, deceive'

In many cases it is difficult to decide whether the added argument benefits from, or is harmed by, the activity, however:

(40)   ti·f-itá 'to take off (two or   <u>in</u>-ti·f-itá 'to take (two or more shoes or
       more shoes or socks)'   socks) off of (someone else)'

The dative applicative thus serves to add a new endpoint: whether the endpoint benefits or is harmed by the activity is left to pragmatics.

(d) The benefactive and malefactive uses lead to a 'possessive' reading, most often seen when the patient is a bodypart (Martin ms.):

(41)   mo·mín ca-háɬpi-ów   <u>an</u>-litáf-aɬ-i··-t-o·k
       and   1sgII-skin-too 1sg.DAT-tear.up-FUT-DUR-SS-say:LGR
       and it will tear my skin, too (1936)

In examples like these, the dative applicative is commonly offered because the whole (possessor) is naturally affected by action on the part.

(e) The possessive reading may have led to a partitive reading seen in examples like the following:

(42) acan-itá 'to fill' im-acan-íta 'to fill (a part of something, such as a gas tank)'

(f) The benefactive reading leads to a goal reading in some verbs:

(43) yaheyk-itá 'to sing'   in-yaheyk-itá 'to sing for, to'
      oponay-íta 'to talk'   im-oponay-itá 'to talk for, to'
      laks-itá   'to tell a lie'   in-laks-itá   'to tell a lie to'
      onay-itá   'to tell (a story)' im-onay-íta   'to tell to'
      atot-itá   'to send'   im-atot-íta   'to send to'

The goal use of the dative applicative is usually limited to transmission of an object to the added argument rather than movement of a subject to a destination. The dative applicative is thus not used to translate sentences like *John is walking to school* in which the agent undergoes movement.

(g) Instead, the dative applicative adds a source to verbs of motion:

(44) litk-itá 'to run (of one)'ᶜ in-litk-itá 'to run from (someone, of one)'

It seems contradictory to construe a source as an 'endpoint' in Croft's framework, but becomes more plausible if one considers that the source may benefit or be adversely affected by removal. This effect is more easily seen in examples like the following:

(45) kapak-itá 'to separate' in-kapak-itá 'to leave (a person or place)'
      akoyk-itá 'to move'   im-akoyk-itá 'to move out of the way of'

There are many other uses of the dative applicative (signalling the reference point of a comparison, an argument collaborating in the performing of an action, etc.). In general, though, we have seen that the dative applicative adds a noun phrase in most uses and therefore can be described as valency-increasing. Yet such a description does little to explain the use of Creek *im-*. If *im-* were simply valency-increasing, it might add agents to stative verbs (like a causative), instruments or patients. The specific uses of *im-* are better explained if *im-* is described in Croft's terms as shifting the point of view to the secondary effect of an activity. Such an account explains the use of *im-* in benefactives and malefactives, possessive readings with inalienable objects, goal readings with verbs involving transmission, and even source readings when movement deprives or benefits a location.

(46)   EFFECTS OF THE CREEK DATIVE APPLICATIVE

	BASE FORM		DERIVED FORM
EXT. ORIENTATION	(no change)		
INT. ORIENTATION	patient	→	secondary effect
CAUSE AVOIDANCE	(no change)		
ASPECT	(no change)		
SUBJ. AFFECTEDNESS	(no change)		
VALENCY	n-place predicate	→	$n+1$-place predicate
TRANSITIVITY	intransitive	→	transitive
	transitive	→	ditransitive

5   Instrumental applicative *is-*

In addition to the dative applicative, Creek has an instrumental applicative *is-* (relating historically to *is-íta* 'to take, hold') that often adds an argument to a clause. I will argue that *is-* is better treated as shifting the internal orientation towards the manner in which the event takes place, and is thus better treated in terms of 'point of view' than in terms of valency.

(a) One use of the prefix *is-* in Creek is to add an instrumental object to a clause:

(47) (a)   Bill có·ka-n   hó·cceyc-ís
           Bill letter-OBLQ write:LGR-INDIC
           Bill is writing a letter

(b)   Bill isho·ccéycka có·ka-n   is-hó·cceyc-ís
           Bill pen   letter-OBLQ INST-write:LGR-INDIC
           Bill is writing a letter with a pen

In this use it is valency-increasing: an n-place predicate becomes an $n+1$-place predicate.

(b) The prefix *is-* is not limited to instrumental readings, however. The instrumental is often added to a verb if the patient or theme of the verb is 'complex' (consisting of salient parts):

(48) (a)   siskitá-n   î·s-ey-s
           cup-OBLQ hold:sg:FGR-1sgI-INDIC
           I'm holding a cup (one that's empty)

(b)   siskitá-n   (i)s-î·s-ey-s
           cup-OBLQ INST-hold:sg:FGR-1sgI-INDIC
           I'm holding a cup (one that contains something)

The implication here is that the object is being held with something else (possibly inside it). Some objects are conventionally treated as being complex. Books, for example, often trigger the instrumental because they contain pages:

(49)   có·ka-n   (i)s-î·s-ey-s
book-OBLQ INST-hold:sg:FGR-1sgI-INDIC
I'm holding a book

Similarly, frames, pictures, dentures, eyeglasses, a harness (on a horse) and watches often trigger use of the instrumental because they have salient parts. This use of the instrumental applicative is not valency-increasing, however.

(c) The use of the Creek instrumental applicative is sensitive to the degree to which a speaker wishes to draw attention to an object that is secondarily involved in the event. While it is customary to use the instrumental for pictures, books, etc., other objects may or may not trigger the instrumental. A speaker may use the instrumental in speaking of an apron, for example, if the apron has a large pocket or a salient splotch of batter on it, or might use the instrumental in a sentence like 'Look at him sitting there!' if a man is sitting with his pants unzipped (Margaret Mauldin, p.c.).

(d) The instrumental applicative is often used with verbs of motion when the object undergoing motion is accompanied by another argument:

(50)   litk-itá 'to run (of one)'   is-litk-itá 'to run off with (something, such as a book, or bearing something, as of a horse, of one)'

The object undergoing motion must be in control of the activity, however.

There are a number of other uses of the instrumental applicative that could be described with more space. The data examined here are sufficient to show that a description of the prefix in terms of valency alone fails to explain uses where it is not valency-increasing. In their close proximity to verbs, applicatives thus appear to enter the event structure of predicates, and thus differ semantically from adpositions. The effects of the instrumental applicative are summarized in the following chart:

(51)   EFFECTS OF THE CREEK INSTRUMENTAL APPLICATIVE

	BASE FORM		DERIVED FORM
EXT. ORIENTATION	(no change)		
INT. ORIENTATION	patient	$\rightarrow$	manner
CAUSE AVOIDANCE	(no change)		
ASPECT	(no change)		
SUBJ. AFFECTEDNESS	(no change)		
VALENCY	n-place predicate	$\rightarrow$	$n(+1)$-place predicate
TRANSITIVITY	intransitive	$\rightarrow$	(in)transitive
	transitive	$\rightarrow$	(di)transitive

6   Direct causative -*ic*-

A direct causative is often described as adding an agent to a verb's argument structure, converting an *n*-place predicate to an *n*+1-place predicate. Creek has a suffix -*ic*- (-·*c*-, -*yc*-, -*iceyc*-, -*yci*·*c*-) that appears to have this same function.

Like the other processes discussed in this chapter, the direct causative can be viewed in terms of voice rather than in terms of valency, however. Croft (1994: 94), for example, characterizes direct causative derivation as shifting the conceptualization of the starting point in a clause to a prior cause in a chain of causation. Direct causatives are commonly found with states because states 'can be easily construed as a final endpoint of a causal chain'.

(a) The direct causative is common in Creek, though most of the examples of the suffix are almost certainly learned rather than created spontaneously. For this reason, I do not separate the direct causative with a hyphen. The direct causative is most commonly applied to nonagentive states or inchoatives:

(52) | | | | |
|---|---|---|---|
| asl-itá | 'to go out (of a fire)' | asli·c-itá | 'to put out (a fire, a light), erase' |
| cákh-i· | 'sticking in (of one)' | cakhi·c-itá | 'to stick (one) in' |
| call-itá | 'to roll (as of a tyre)' | calli·c-itá | 'to roll (a tyre, etc.)' |
| cá·t-i· | 'red' | ca·ti·c-itá | 'to redden (something)' |
| fikhonn-itá | 'to stop' | fikhonneyc-itá | 'to stop (something)' |
| hic-íta | 'to see' | hiceyc-itá | 'to show' |
| hoyɬ-itá | 'to stand (of one)' | hoyɬeyc-itá | 'to stand (one)' |
| il-íta | 'to die (of one)' | ili·c-itá | 'to kill (of one)' |
| káɬp-i· | 'dry' | kaɬpi·c-itá | 'to dry (something)' |
| kancap-í· | 'low' | kancapoyc-itá | 'to lower' |
| kiɬɬ-itá | 'to know' | kiɬɬeyc-itá | 'to inform' |
| lomh-itá | 'to lie (of three or more)' | lomheyc-itá | 'to lay (three or more)' |
| ɬákk-i· | 'big' | ɬakkoyc-itá | 'to enlarge' |
| noɬ-íta | 'to be cooked' | noɬeyc-itá | 'to cook (something)' |

A vowel appearing before a direct causative is generally derived from a verb-final vowel historically. The appearance of this vowel is extremely limited in Creek outside the direct causative and its quality is partially predictable.[9]

---

[9] The stem-vowel is generally /a/ (raising to /e/ before tautosyllabic /y/) when the preceding vowel is /i/ or /o/; the stem-vowel is generally /i/ when the preceding vowel is /a/. An /i/ stem-vowel sometimes rounds to /o/ after /k/ and /p/ for some speakers. Thus, *kancapV-ic-itá* 'to lower' surfaces as *kancapoyc-itá*.

(b) As the translations in (52) suggest, the Creek direct causative is commonly used when there is a single event effected by an intentional causer acting directly to manipulate a causee who is portrayed as having virtually no control over the event, as being completely affected, and possibly as being an unwilling partner in the event. Direct causatives are commonly formed from one-place states, though two-place verbs and activities are also possible base forms:

(53)   homp-itá   'to eat'   hompeyc-itá   'to feed'
       isk-itá   'to drink'   iskoyc-itá   'to give drink'
       linta·pp-itá 'to stumble'   linta·ppoyc-itá 'to trip'

Because the causee is at the complete mercy of the new agent in the direct causative, the direct causative could alternatively be called a transitivizer. Just as the semantics of one-place middle verbs is indistinguishable from one-place intransitive verbs, the semantics of two-place direct causatives is indistinguishable from two-place transitives.

(c) Deponent middles delete -*k*- before the direct causative. In this case, there is no stem vowel:

(54)   fáck-i·   'full'   facic-itá   'to fill'
       fásk-i·   'sharp'   fasic-itá   'to sharpen'
       fink-itá   'to blaze'   finic-itá   'to light (a fire), turn on
                                                       (a lamp)'
       hasátk-i·   'clean'   hasatic-íta   'to clean'
       hátk-i·   'white'   hatic-itá   'to whiten'
       háwk-i·   'open'   hawic-itá   'to open'
       leyk-itá   'to sit (of one)'   leyc-itá   'to set (one)'
       tánk-i·   'empty'   tanic-itá   'to void'
       wakk-itá   'to lie (of one)'   wakic-itá   'to lay (one)'

Deletion of the middle in deponent verbs presumably arose because these events were no longer self-contained, and thus no longer middle in point of view.[10]

(d) The causee is case-marked like other objects, with oblique -*n*:

(55)   honánwa-t istocí-n   hómpeyc-ís
       male-NOM baby-OBLQ eat:DIRECT.CAUS-INDIC
       The man is feeding the baby

(e) The direct causative suffix -*ic*- also has a pluralizing function. With verbs having a theme or patient as subject, -*ic*- indicates a triplural theme or patient (three or more):

---

[10] The reflexive middle in Italian is also deleted under causativization (Martin 1991a).

(56)   somk-itá 'to disappear (of one)'   som<u>ic</u>-itá 'to disappear (of three or more)'
       tamk-itá 'to fly (of one)'   tam<u>ic</u>-itá 'to fly (of three or more)'

With verbs having a theme or patient as object, -*ic*- is combined with reduplication to yield a plural theme or patient (two or more):

(57)   halat-itá 'to hold (one)'   halathe<u>yc</u>-itá 'to hold (two or more)'
       ton-íta 'to trim (one)'   tonto<u>yc</u>-itá 'to trim (two or more)'

The plural use of -*ic*- is clearly related to the direct causative use. Note that deponent middles lose -*k*- in the plural forms in (56), just as in direct causatives.

The plural use of -*ic*- appears to take priority over the direct causative use, however. When a given verb has a triplural reading attached to -*ic*-, a direct causative must be formed another way. In this case, Creek has a special long form -*iceyc*- (-*yci·c*-) to indicate a direct causative:

(58)   somk-itá 'to disappear (of one)'   som<u>iceyc</u>-itá 'to lose (one)'
       tamk-itá 'to fly (of one)'   tam<u>iceyc</u>-itá 'to make (one) fly, flush'

The nature of the connection between number and causation is difficult to explain, though not without precedent (see, for example, Breen 1981 (339) for a similar case of polysemy in Margany).

(f) In two or three instances, the direct causative appears to add an object. Thus, *apil-itá* 'to laugh' has a related form *apileyc-itá* that means 'to laugh at' rather than 'to make laugh'. In these exceptional examples, the primary object has been reinterpreted as a secondary object (see also Dixon's description of Yidiny, in §1 of chapter 2).

The effects associated with causativization are charted in (59):

(59)   EFFECTS OF THE CREEK DIRECT CAUSATIVE

	BASE FORM		DERIVED FORM
EXT. ORIENTATION	usually patient or theme	→	cause
INT. ORIENTATION	(usually not present)	→	causee
CAUSE AVOIDANCE	(no change)		
ASPECT	usually state or inchoative	→	activity
SUBJ. AFFECTEDNESS	sometimes affected	→	usually affected
VALENCY	*n*-place predicate	→	*n*+1-place predicate
TRANSITIVITY	intransitive	→	transitive
	transitive	→	ditransitive

In most instances, the direct causative in Creek serves to assign responsibility for a state or inchoative to an external cause, thereby portraying the causee as a patient. This leads to aspectual shifts as well as shifts in valency and transitivity. These side-effects can be understood in terms of a shift in point of view to a prior starting point, however, while describing the process as valency-increasing fails to distinguish the direct causative from an applicative and fails to link causation to aspect.

7   Indirect causative *-ipeyc-*

In addition to the direct causative discussed in §6, Creek has an indirect causative formed by adding *-ipeyc-* (or *-ipoyc-* for some speakers) to the verb root. Grayson (1885) records the following examples:[11]

(60)   cími-t   cá·ni-n   náfk-ipoyc-ís
        Jim-NOM John-OBLQ hit-make:LGR-INDIC
        James is causing John to strike

(61)   paksankí·-n   cató-n   aweyk-ipôyc-ay-ank-s
        yesterday-OBLQ stone-OBLQ throw-make:FGR-1sgI-PAST-INDIC
        I caused him to throw a stone yesterday

(62)   páksi-n   'kapotóka-n ohhompitá-n
        tomorrow-OBLQ hat-OBLQ   table-OBLQ
        oh-leyc-ipóyc-á·ɬ-i·-s
        on-set:sg-make-1sgI:FUT-DUR-INDIC
        I will cause him to put his hat on the table tomorrow

As these translations suggest, the indirect causative adds a higher causative predicate and agent to the clause structure. The added causer is marked in the nominative, and the causee and all other non-subjects are marked in the oblique.

(a) The indirect causative is semantically distinct from the direct causative, as the following translations suggest:

(63)   honánwa-t istocí-n   hómpeyc-ís
        male-NOM baby-OBLQ eat:DIRECT.CAUS:LGR-INDIC
        The man is feeding the baby (as by spooning food into the baby's mouth)

(64)   honánwa-t istocí-n   hómp-ipeyc-ís
        male-NOM baby-OBLQ eat-make:LGR-INDIC
        The man is making the baby eat (perhaps by commanding the baby)

In the direct causative, the causee has no control over the event. In the indirect causative, the causee retains control over the activity while losing ultimate responsibility for the action. In the direct causative (63), the act of

---

[11] George Washington Grayson was Principal Chief of the Creek Nation from 1917 to 1920. I have phonemicized his orthography.

causation and the state effected are virtually inseparable. In the indirect causative (64), the two activities are separable to a degree. These differences can be shown by examining the use of the instrumental (Martin 1991a: 216):

(65) (a)   *istocí ínki-n   is-hómpe-yc-éy-s
           baby 3:hand-OBLQ INST-eat-DIRECT.CAUS:LGR-1sgI-INDIC
           lit. I'm feeding the baby with his hand

(b)   istocí ínki-n   is-hómp-ipeyc-éy-s
           baby 3:hand-OBLQ INST-eat-make:LGR-1sgI-INDIC
           I'm making the baby eat with his hand

As (65a) shows, an instrumental cannot be construed with the secondary predicate of a direct causative because there is not enough separation between the events and the causee lacks control. In the indirect causative in (65b), however, the causee can be construed as using an instrument to effect a secondary event.

(b) Anaphora points to a further difference between the direct and indirect causatives. The direct causative (66a) is just like a transitive verb (66b) in disallowing a pronominal prefix to be coreferent with a subject in the same clause:

(66) (a)   *ca-híceyc-éy-s
           1sgII-see:DIRECT.CAUS:LGR-1sgI-INDIC
           lit. I'm showing me

(b)   *ca-na·fk-éy-s
           1sgII-hit:LGR-1sgI-INDIC
           lit. I'm hitting me

An indirect causative allows a pronominal prefix to be coreferent with the matrix subject, and in this respect acts as though there are two clauses in the structure:

(67)   cími-n   ca-náfk-ipeyc-éy-s
           Jim-OBLQ 1sgII-hit-make:LGR-1sgI-INDIC
           I'm making Jim hit me

This grammatical contrast supports the claim that the contrast between direct and indirect causatives involves the separation of events.

(c) The causee in the indirect causative need not have any control over the secondary event – in fact, zero-place predicates may be causativized in this way:

(68)   ósk-ipeyc-ís
           rain-make:LGR-INDIC
           S/he is making it rain (as perhaps through the use of sorcery)

The form in (68) confirms that it is conceptualizing the event as two causally related activities that triggers the indirect causative rather than agency or valency.

There are many other details involved in the indirect causative, but the basic properties can be charted as in (69):

(69) EFFECTS OF THE CREEK INDIRECT CAUSATIVE

	BASE FORM		DERIVED FORM
EXT. ORIENTATION	usually cause	→	prior cause
INT. ORIENTATION	patient	→	causee
CAUSE AVOIDANCE	(no change)		
ASPECT	activity	→	activity
SUBJ. AFFECTEDNESS	usually not affected	→	usually affected by prior cause
VALENCY	n-place predicate	→	$n+1$-place predicate
TRANSITIVITY	intransitive	→	transitive
	transitive	→	ditransitive

The indirect causative can thus be seen as a shift in point of view from one starting point to a prior starting point through the addition of the causative activity.

8   Interaction of voice-related processes

A rough description of the interaction of the processes discussed in this chapter can be captured in the form of a formula:

(70)   [INSTR-DAT-[*verb*-MIDDLE-DIRECT.CAUS]-INDIR.CAUS.]-IMPERS

As (70) suggests, the impersonal plural may apply to actives and middles (71) as well as direct and indirect causatives (72):

(71) (a)   í·hho·y-ís (ACTIVE)
          hide:IMPERS.pl:LGR-INDIC
          They/people are hiding it

(b)   í·hho·k-ís (MIDDLE)
      hide:MID:IMPERS.pl:LGR-INDIC
      They/people are hiding

(72) (a)   hompéyho·c-ís (DIRECT CAUSATIVE)
          eat:DIRECT.CAUS:IMPERS.pl:LGR-INDIC
          They/people are feeding it

(b)   homp-ipéyho·c-ís (INDIRECT CAUSATIVE)
      eat-make:IMPERS.pl:LGR-INDIC
      They/people are making him eat

A clause with an impersonal plural subject may not be causativized, however:

(73)   *nafhok-ípeyc-ís
         hit:IMPERS.pl-make:LGR-INDIC
         S/he makes them/people hit

The formula in (70) also captures the fact that middles are never formed from causatives:

(74)   *hompéyc-k-i·
         eat:DIRECT.CAUS-MID-DUR
         fed

A middle voice form is also sometimes judged to be odd as the complement of an indirect causative:

(75)   *í·hk-ipeyc-ís
         hide:MID-make:LGR-INDIC
         S/he is making him/her hide

The dative, instrumental, impersonal and causative are all compatible with each other, occurring in the order predicted by (70):

(76)   (i)s-in-tac-ipéyho·c-ís
         INST-DAT-cut-make:IMPERS.pl:LGR-INDIC
         They/people are making him/her cut it for him/her with it

When other applicative processes are taken into consideration, we find that derivation in Creek can add as many as four arguments to a clause, in principle allowing seven-place verbs to be derived from basic three-place verbs.

It is important to examine the interaction of these voice-related processes to see whether there is any grammatical evidence in Creek that they form a single system. We have already seen that there is close interaction between the middle and the direct causative, because the middle usually deletes in the presence of the direct causative as shown in (54). It is further possible to distinguish the preverbal and postverbal affixes, however: the former shift point of view within the verb phrase to a new object; the latter revolve around the status of the subject. Instead of claiming there is a single, overarching category of voice or valency in Creek then, it seems that there are two grammatical systems dealing with the information status of objects and subjects.

9   Conclusion

Two systems of orientation operate in Creek at the external (clause) level and at the internal (predicate) level. At the external level, predicates are either oriented towards the cause or towards an effect or state. Postverbal elements (suffixes or infixes) are used to create changes in this basic orientation. The Creek middle shifts attention from causes to effects (states or inchoatives). The Creek direct causative has the opposite function of shifting attention from effects to causes. The Creek impersonal plural serves to background the cause. Finally, the Creek indirect causative introduces primary causes:

(77) POSTVERBAL ELEMENTS CHANGING EXTERNAL (CLAUSE-LEVEL) ORIENTATION

UNMARKED   MARKED

Towards cause $\xrightarrow{\text{Cr. middle}}$ Towards effect

Towards effect or state $\xrightarrow{\text{Cr. dir. caus.}}$ Towards cause

Towards cause $\xrightarrow{\text{Cr. impers. pl.}}$ Away from cause

Towards cause $\xrightarrow{\text{Cr. indir. caus.}}$ Towards primary cause

This pattern contrasts sharply with English, where passive voice combines functions of the Creek middle and impersonal plural.

The voice-related prefixes in Creek can be described in terms of the changes they bring about in internal (predicate-level) orientation:

(78) PREVERBAL ELEMENTS CHANGING INTERNAL (PREDICATE-LEVEL) ORIENTATION

UNMARKED   MARKED

Towards effect $\xrightarrow{\text{Cr. dat. applic.}}$ Towards secondary effect

Towards effect $\xrightarrow{\text{Cr. inst. applic.}}$ Towards manner

Within a predicate, the unmarked orientation is towards the effect. The dative and instrumental applicatives function to reorient the predicate towards secondary effects (benefactives or malefactives) and/or towards manner (how the activity was performed), respectively.

Describing these two systems of external and internal orientation as a single phenomenon of 'voice' may be too broad, but, as we have seen, it offers certain advantages over descriptions involving valency. Describing the Creek middle as valency-reducing fails to explain why it fails to create S = A intransitives (e.g. *John cooks*). Describing causatives and applicatives as valency-increasing ignores the important functional differences between these patterns. Describing a causative as 'adding an agent' ignores the fact that aspect is often affected in direct causatives and that indirect causatives add an event in addition to an agent.

In describing the Creek phenomena in this chapter, I have begun to question whether valency or valency-changing have any real significance in language. It is clear that verbs can be classified based on the number of arguments they take, but it is not clear that this classification functions elsewhere in the grammar. The chemical metaphor has been useful in allowing linguists to categorize morphological processes and lends a certain scientific aura to our work, but it remains to be seen whether describing a particular process as adding or subtracting an argument adequately characterizes its function or whether humans engage in arithmetic processes as they speak.

This chapter has begun to suggest a way that valency can be reduced to event view. Valency can be seen as the ability of a predicate to incorporate entities into a particular event view, thus assigning those entities roles within the clause. Predicates that customarily involve an initiator and one or more affectees (*John painted the house, Mary gave John a book*) will develop grammars in which the inclusion of these entities is unmarked; clauses in which there is no initiator (*The snow is white*) or where the initiator is unknown and the endpoint is of interest (*The snow melted*) will develop unmarked forms with fewer arguments. Just as valency is the codification of these unmarked event views, valency-changing processes are perhaps better described as changes in event view from the unmarked to a marked perspective.

If this approach is right, then it may be time for a new metaphor in linguistics: perhaps the chemical metaphor has exceeded its half-life.

Texts cited

1936. Mary R. Haas, Creek Notebook I, University of California, Berkeley.
1939. Mary R. Haas, Creek Notebook XV, University of California, Berkeley.
1992a. Stories told by Linda Alexander, Norman, Oklahoma.
1992b. Stories told by Toney Hill, Norman, Oklahoma.
1992c. Stories told by Robert Washington, Norman, Oklahoma.

References

Baker, M.C. 1988. *Incorporation: a theory of grammatical function changing.* Chicago: University of Chicago Press.
Barber, E.J.A. 1975. 'Voice: beyond the passive', *Berkeley Linguistics Society* 1.16–23.
Booker, K.M. 1984. 'Directional prefixes in Creek', pp. 59–87 of *Proceedings of the 1983 Mid-America Linguistics Conference*, ed. D.S. Rood. Boulder: Department of Linguistics, University of Colorado.

Breen, J.G. 1981. 'Margany and Gunya', pp. 274–393 of *Handbook of Australian languages*, Vol. II, ed. R.M.W. Dixon and B.J. Blake. Canberra: Australian National University Press.

Comrie, B. 1989. *Language universals and linguistic typology: syntax and morphology*, 2nd edn. Chicago: University of Chicago Press.

Croft, W. 1994. 'Voice: beyond control and affectedness', pp. 89–117 of *Voice: form and function*, ed. B. Fox and P.J. Hopper. Typological studies in language 27. Amsterdam: John Benjamins.

Crystal, D. 1985. *A dictionary of linguistics and phonetics*, 2nd edn. Oxford: Basil Blackwell.

Grayson, G.W. 1885. 'Creek vocabulary and verb paradigms with occasional ethnographic notes', National Anthropological Archives #568-a. Smithsonian Institution, Washington, D.C.

Haas, M.R. 1940. 'Ablaut and its function in Muskogee', *Language* 16.141–50.

1977. 'From auxiliary verb phrase to inflectional suffix', pp. 525–37 of *Mechanisms of syntactic change*, ed. C.N. Li. Austin: University of Texas Press.

Hardy, D.E. 1988. 'The semantics of Creek morphosyntax'. Ph.D. thesis. Rice University, Houston.

1994. 'Middle voice in Creek', *International Journal of American Linguistics*, 60.39–68.

Jespersen, O. 1924. *The philosophy of grammar*. London: George Allen and Unwin.

Kemmer, S. 1993. *The middle voice*, Typological studies in language 23. Amsterdam and Philadelphia: John Benjamins.

Klaiman, M.H. 1988. 'Affectedness and control: a typology of voice systems', pp. 25–83 of *Passive and middle voice*, ed. M. Shibatani. Amsterdam, Philadelphia: John Benjamins.

Martin, J.B. 1991a. 'Lexical and syntactic aspects of Creek causatives', *International Journal of American Linguistics*, 57.194–229.

1991b. 'The determination of grammatical relations in syntax'. Ph.D. thesis. UCLA.

ms. 'External possession in Creek'. To appear in *External possession*, ed. Doris Payne and I. Barski. Amsterdam, Philadelphia: John Benjamins.

Martin, J.B. and Mauldin, M.M. ms. 'A dictionary of Creek (Muskogee) with notes on the Florida and Oklahoma Seminole dialects of Creek'. To appear. Lincoln/London: University of Nebraska Press.

Munro, P. 1996. 'Valence arithmetic in the Tolkapaya lexicon', pp. 113–29 of *Proceedings of the Hokan-Penutian Workshop*, ed. V. Golla. Survey of California and Other Languages Report 9. Berkeley: University of California.

Munro, P. and Gordon, L. 1982. 'Syntactic relations in Western Muskogean: a typological perspective', *Language* 58.81–115.

Nathan, M. 1977. 'Grammatical description of the Florida Seminole dialect of Creek'. Ph.D. thesis. Tulane University.

Index of authors

Index of languages and language families

Subject index